Dear Helen

As an intelligent and feisty woman we hope that you will enjoy this book about another intelligent feisty woman.

Love

Catherine & Les

*Hobnobbing with
a Countess*

Alice Barrett Parke just after her wedding in January 1893.
(Barrett Family Collection)

Edited by Jo Fraser Jones

Hobnobbing with a Countess and Other Okanagan Adventures

THE DIARIES OF ALICE BARRETT PARKE,
1891-1900

For Helen Reeve Dawson,
With Best Wishes
from
Jo Jones

UBC Press · Vancouver · Toronto

With the exception of the photographic insert, this book is printed on acid-free paper that is 100% ancient forest free (100% post-consumer recycled), processed chlorine free, and printed with vegetable based, low VOC inks.
ISBN 0-7748-0852-7

National Library of Canada Cataloguing in Publication Data

Parke, Alice Barrett, 1861-1952.
  Hobnobbing with a countess and other Okanagan adventures

  (The pioneers of British Columbia, ISSN 0841-0847; 14)
  ISBN 0-7748-0852-7

  1. Parke, Alice Barrett, 1861-1952 – Diaries. 2. Pioneers – British Columbia – Okanagan Valley – Diaries. 3. Frontier and pioneer life – British Columbia – Okanagan Valley – Biography. 4. Okanagan Valley (B.C.) – Biography. I. Jones, Jo Fraser, 1935- II. Title. III. Series: Pioneers of British Columbia; 14.
FC3845.04Z49 2001   971.1′503′092   C2001-910995-4
F1089.05P37 2001

This book has been published with the help of a grant from the Humanities and Social Sciences Federation of Canada, using funds provided by the Social Sciences and Humanities Research Council of Canada.

UBC Press acknowledges the financial support of the Government of Canada through the Book Publishing Industry Development Program (BPIDP) for our publishing activities.
Canadä

As well, UBC Press acknowledges the financial support of contributors to the publishing fund of the Greater Vernon Museum and Archives.

We also gratefully acknowledge the support of the Canada Council for the Arts for our publishing program, as well as the support of the British Columbia Arts Council.

Set in Adobe Caslon by Brenda and Neil West, BN Typographics West
Printed and bound in Canada by Friesens
Copy editor: Joanne Richardson
Proofreader: Andrea Kwan

UBC Press
The University of British Columbia
2029 West Mall, Vancouver, BC V6T 1Z2
(604) 822-5959
Fax: (604) 822-6083
E-mail: info@ubcpress.ca
www.ubcpress.ca

For David

For more than four years he displayed his customary grace and good humour as he lived with two women – Alice Barrett Parke and me. His rigorous intellect, probing questions, and emotional support during the darkest hours were of inestimable value.

Contents

Acknowledgments

This book would not have been produced without the help of the following people:

In Ontario

Harry Bemister Barrett (Barrett family historian) and his wife Joan; Mary Beerfoot; Emily Molewyck; Bill Yeager (curator of the Eva Brook Donly Museum in Simcoe) and Bill Terry, Cathy Thompson, Bill Jackson, Mary Murray and Donna Gable (Simcoe volunteers); The Printed Word in Port Dover (Lorin MacDonald and Marie); Terry Esselment; Paul Shrimpton (archives assistant, University of Toronto Archives); Marian Spence (archivist, Upper Canada College); Georgia Painter (researcher in Port Dover); Mike Baker (curator of regional history, London Regional Art and Historical Museum); and Glen Curnoe and Arthur McClelland (London Room, London Library).

In Vernon, British Columbia

Ron Candy (curator, Greater Vernon Museum and Archives); Linda Wills (archivist and friend); Barbara Bell (education coordinator); volunteer researchers Paddy Mackie, John Shephard, Patricia O'Byrne, and Ken Ellison; Pat Bayliss; Art Sovereign, MD, and William Sanders, MD (for their help with paleo-diagnosis); Mike de Tourdonnet; Joan Sasges; Daphne Thuillier; Ken Mather (manager/curator, O'Keefe Ranch); Richard "Duff" Pratt; John Baumbrough; Carol Stratton (reference librarian, Vernon Branch, Okanagan Regional Library, and fellow staff members); Pauline Legg.

In British Columbia

Shannah Twiss (Hedley Arts and Crafts Museum); Jessie-Ann Gamble (Armstrong Museum); Susan Cross (Kamloops Museum); Brenda Hamm and Anne Cossentine (library, Kelowna Campus, Okanagan University College); Norman Worsley and Mary Mara of Victoria; Jean Barman (University of British Columbia); Kirsten Walsh (head librarian, Music Library, University of British Columbia); David Mattison (reference librarian, BC Archives); "Tiger" McKinnon (Vancouver Archives); Duane Thomson (head, History Department, Okanagan University College); Dr. John Cassidy (Pacific Geo-Science Centre); Lyn Gough; Dr. Anita Bonson.

IN THE UNITED STATES

Lorna G. Kaiser (Parke family historian); John R. Gonzales (senior librarian, California Section, California State Library, Sacramento); Carolyn Marr (Museum of History and Industry, Seattle).

AT UBC PRESS

Jean Wilson; Darcy Cullen; Joanne Richardson; Holly Keller-Brohman; Eric Leinberger.

My sons, Adam and Craig, both published authors, gave their unfailing support and practical help during the production of this manuscript.

ABB   Alice Butler Barrett
ABP   Alice Barrett Parke
EB   Emily Barrett (Alice's mother)
HB   Henry Barrett (Alice's uncle)
NCW   National Council of Women
OHSR   *Okanagan Historical Society Reports*
TBB   Theobald Butler Barrett (Alice's father)
WB   Emily Louisa "Wese" Barrett (Alice's brother)

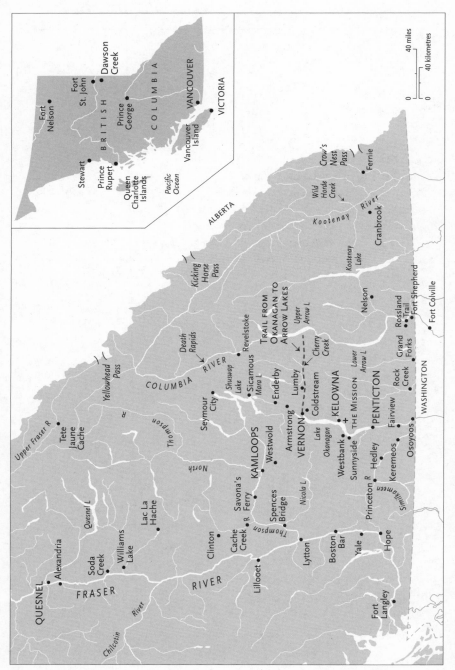

The southern interior of British Columbia

Introduction

One can read a poem or a novel without coming to know its author,
look at a painting and fail to get a sense of its painter; but one cannot
read a diary and feel unacquainted with its writer. No form of expres-
sion more emphatically embodies the expresser: diaries are the flesh
made word.

— THOMAS MALLON, *A Book of One's Own:*
People and Their Diaries

A young Anglo-Ontarian woman born more than a century ago was removed from her loving family and comfortable home in Port Dover, transported across Canada to British Columbia, housed in a tiny log cabin in an isolated southern interior valley, put to work on domestic chores, given a pen, ink, and an empty scribbler, and encouraged to keep a diary. This woman was twenty-nine-year-old Alice Butler Barrett, and this was the situation in which she found herself early in 1891.

Diary writing is a cheerfully unregulated undertaking compared to essay and letter writing. Alice Barrett Parke's work is of such vast scale that only selections are offered here. Her diaries offer a series of entries that follow each other like snapshots in an album, without the transforming benefit of hindsight and the sense of personal identity that such a perspective creates. Despite her protestations about the "chore" of diary writing, Alice worked on them for ten years, showing both ambivalence about creating them and reluctance to stop. It was just as satisfying for her to observe and record the life of the world around her as it was to confide her own life to the diaries, and it was not long before her musings and reflections began to make their appearance. And these were close to the psychological bone. She displayed a childlike avidity for any new piece of information, but disease and death form a grim wreath around the themes about which she wrote – family, home life, her husband, ranching, friends, religion, children, entertainment, prospecting and mining, feminism, racism, and travel. A parade of the ordinary, the great, and the near great passed through her diary as, with an alert eye and attentive ear, she chronicled the daily, the "here and now," in all its humanity.

The diaries of Alice Barrett Parke were written during an eventful decade in the life of the westernmost province in the still new nation of Canada. Between 1891 and 1900 she filled many scribblers with her reactions to life among British Columbia's pioneers, and, upon completion, each volume was mailed home to Port Dover, Ontario, read by the Barrett family, and then stored away. Had it not been for the foresight and generosity of her great-nephew, Harry Bemister Barrett, the diaries might still be lying in an old rawhide box in the attic (where they languished for 100 years), and a Canadian writer of unquestionable talent might still be unknown.

The Barretts were descendants of a long line of warriors and aristocrats who had settled in Ireland in 1170. Alice's branch of the Barrett family (whose motto is *Omnia virtute non vi* – All by virtue, not by force) lived originally in Normandy, and its members are believed to have been among those Crusaders who accompanied Richard the Lionheart to the Holy Land.[1] That these Barretts were influential is evidenced by the fact that the Barony of Barrett in County Cork still bears their name. Alice's forebear, Phineas Barrett, lived in County Down and, during the 1750s, purchased land, known as Castle Blake, near Clonmel. In 1790 his grandson Quintin (Alice's great-grandfather) married the Honourable Emma Massey, daughter of the first Baron Massey. In January 1811 their son, Hugh Massey Barrett, married Caroline Butler; Alice's father, Theobald Butler Barrett, was the fourth of sixteen children eventually born to this couple. Nicknamed "T.B.," "Toby," or later "Fa," he was born in 1817 in Banagher, Ireland, and he was thirteen years old when his family sailed to Canada on the *Bolivar* and settled in Sorel, Quebec.

It was T.B.'s generation that migrated to southwest Ontario. Missionaries were the first Europeans to reach the confluence of the River Lynn and Black Creek (site of the future Port Dover), and they arrived in 1669. They wintered there and returned to Montreal the following year. After the end of the American War of Independence, thousands of people still loyal to the British Crown headed north into Canada, and many made their way west to the shores of the Great Lakes. Port Dover became the largest village in the township of Woodhouse in Norfolk County. Situated on the north shore of Lake Erie, about 100 miles southwest of Toronto, the present site of the village was laid out in 1834 on land owned by Israel Wood Powell Sr. and Moses Nickerson. By 1840 a market was established and the export of lumber and timber became an important industry; a commercial freshwater fishery also developed. The village's harbour was in part a natural reef of rocks extending out from the shore about three-quarters of a mile and forming a breakwater. The pier was an important link for lake steamers, which were large and numerous. Port Dover also became the terminus of the Port Dover and Lake Huron Railway. By the 1870s, the village was already becoming a summer holiday destination for visitors who built cottages along the lakeshore. Port Dover was surrounded by some of the best farmland in Ontario, and its relatively mild climate accommodated a large swath of Carolinian (temperate) forest.

After T.B.'s marriage in 1850 to Emily Langs, he obtained a position in Her Majesty's Customs Service and moved with his new wife to this growing community. He built a substantial home, Riverbank Cottage (which still stands today), on five lots – three fronted on Bridge Street and the other two on St. Patrick Street to the south. The property boasted a barn and other outbuildings, and it overlooked the River Lynn, which flowed by at the bottom of a steep embankment north of the house and then curved its way to Lake Erie, half a mile further south.

Between 1851 and 1869 T.B. and Emily Barrett had eight children. The eldest, Phoebe Caroline (Carrie), was born in 1851 and died tragically at the age of thirty-three after giving birth to her fourth child. Hugh Jacob Francis (Frank) was born in 1854, and Emily Louisa (Alice's beloved Wese) was born in 1857; a third daughter, Clare Georgiana, was born two years later but survived only to the age of twelve. Next came Alice Butler, the fourth and final daughter, born on 5 November 1861.[2] Over the following eight years, Emily Barrett gave birth to three more sons – William Henry (Harry), born in 1864; Hubert Baldwin, born in 1867; and Arthur Clarence, born in 1869. Alice had a very strong sense of tradition and showed a passionate loyalty to her family. All of these family members, except the long-dead Georgiana, figure prominently in the diaries.

Alice received an education that included a solid grounding in Latin, provided by a retired army officer's widow who tutored several of Port Dover's girls in the classics. Her father spoke enough French to pass that language on to his children and insisted that they all read widely and diligently. As a result, Alice became a voracious reader of all kinds of literature – classics by writers such as Dickens, Scott, and Schiller, modern novels, magazines, newspapers, and books on history, biography, and religion. She was never without something to read during her leisure hours. Religious instruction was extremely important; since Mr. Barrett was a founding member of St. Paul's Anglican Church and a lay reader there, the whole family was required to attend church twice on Sundays. Alice was thus raised in a large, loving, devout, intellectually lively, and close-knit family, with many siblings, uncles, aunts, cousins, and friends making up her circle. As the only two remaining unmarried daughters in their family, Alice and Wese were often called upon to spend weeks and sometimes months with other members of the family, nursing or otherwise caring for them. We know that Alice spent time in Chatham helping her elder sister, Carrie Scott, with her children. She also stayed with her Aunt Louisa and Uncle Frederick Wyld in Toronto as well as with other aunts and uncles in various parts of southern Ontario. After Carrie's death in 1884, her two boys, Walter and Roy Scott, moved to Port Dover and were raised by the Barrett family, with most of their care devolving upon Aunts Alice and Wese, who both adored children.

Alice and her sister were typical of the Victorian ideal that confined women to the home, where they exercised no power but had great responsibilities and, through their own example, demonstrated high ethical standards to the men around them. The sisters were encouraged to think of themselves as powerful arbiters of moral goodness but were discouraged from expecting to exercise any power outside the home (e.g., in the worlds of business or government). This middle-class ethos was underpinned by the sexual division of labour that existed within most families. Maintaining one's middle-class status required that women not be gainfully employed outside the home (other than in strictly defined professions such as those of governess, nurse, or teacher) unless they were in reduced financial circumstances. The true woman was not allowed to follow such a course; instead, she was expected to demonstrate purity, piety, domesticity, and submissiveness – virtues that could be achieved only by curbing her feelings and desires. Hers was a domestic mission; women were urged to make family and home their sphere and to stay within it. Anonymity was the norm for her. Under common law, a husband assumed control not only of his wife's property and earnings, but also of her person. Outwardly Alice conformed; inwardly she struggled.

Alice knew little or nothing of the British Columbia to which she headed at the age of twenty-nine. Aboriginal peoples had inhabited the land for thousands of years before the southern interior was explored by Whites for the first time during the summer of 1811. American David Stuart, an employee of the North West Company, became the first recorded white man to enter the Okanagan Valley. In search of a route for the fur trade, he made his way overland to the interior of British Columbia and followed a trail north along the west side of Okanagan Lake. With the coming of the Hudson's Bay Company, this route became known as the Brigade Trail. Compared to the United States, Canada's approach to the settlement of the west had been a conservative one; development took place within a framework of civic control rather than frontier laissez-faire. Until 1858 the land between Vancouver Island and the Rocky Mountains had been known as New Caledonia, but with the creation of the new colony Queen Victoria herself had decided it should be called British Columbia. The colony entered Confederation in 1871, encouraged by a Canadian government determined to check the expansion of the United States and the possible annexation of the Pacific coast region.

The early fur trappers had been succeeded in the 1850s by miners who came streaming in from the south looking for gold. Then came the first white settlers in the Okanagan Valley, most of them travelling in search of better conditions for themselves and their families, who brought their sense of adventure and their vision to a new land and pre-empted acreages from Sicamous in the north to Osoyoos in the south. Throughout the final decade of the nineteenth century, the Okanagan accounted for 25 percent to 50 percent of all the pre-emption records in the province; the government issued more certificates of improvement for the Osoyoos division of Yale District, which encompassed the whole Okanagan Valley, than for any other area in British Columbia. Pre-emptions were not to exceed 160 acres and could be obtained for one dollar per acre. After two years of personal occupation, and after making improvements valued at $2.50 per acre, the pre-emptor received his Crown grant.

Since 1862 people had come to a place where several fertile valleys met and which became known successively as Priest's Valley, Centreville, Forge Valley, and, finally, Vernon. The population of the little settlement was a lively mix of all kinds of people – young men from England and other parts of Canada, retired East Indian civil servants, professional men, shopkeepers, women looking for husbands, men looking for wives, gamblers, loggers, builders, prostitutes, and farmers. By the end of the 1880s the town already had two hotels fronted by wooden sidewalks. There was, however, no proper delivery system for water, which flowed in an open irrigation ditch running through the middle of the town; later on this would be boxed in, with wooden tanks every 300 feet providing citizens with access to the water. By 1892, the City of Vernon, with an area of 3.12 square miles, was legally incorporated, and the men of the town elected their first council the following year.

During the 1880s, two Barretts had moved to western Canada to seek a better future for themselves in the Okanagan Valley – Alice's elderly, irascible, and misogynist uncle Henry Barrett, and her much-loved younger brother Harry. After many years as a miner in California, "Uncle" (as he was called throughout the diaries), had purchased 320 acres in the Spallumcheen Valley and subsequently asked Harry to come out to help work the land at Mountain Meadow Ranch while he (Uncle) followed his trade as a finishing carpenter.

The British Columbia to which Alice headed in 1891 was undergoing a profound transformation wrought by the completion in 1886 of the transcontinental railroad. The province was already preoccupied with the questions of race and white supremacy. Indigenous peoples and Asians were disenfranchised, certain occupations were barred to them, and they faced legalized discrimination and acts of verbal and physical violence. By the 1890s the assumption of racial superiority came as second nature to most Canadians, and Alice was no exception. She could be snobbish and occasionally mean-spirited in her dealings with people of a different culture. By the time she arrived in the Spallumcheen, Europeans and aboriginal people interacted very little. Settler communities had evolved to the point where white families no longer relied on aboriginal people for help; two distinct societies with fixed boundaries had already been established, and the settlers continued to agitate for expansion of their own land to the detriment of aboriginal peoples. In 1892, aboriginal people in the Okanagan numbered 852, divided into thirteen bands. Assimilation was the aim of the federal government, and aboriginal peoples had already undergone massive cultural disruption.[3] The Indian Act, 1876, had removed all traces of aboriginal self-reliance, dignity, and independence; traditional forms of aboriginal justice were banished, and the federal government treated aboriginal people as though they were children.

Settlement had brought to the region many kinds of Europeans who felt no need to understand the traditional aboriginal way of life and no qualms about disrupting it. Alice's racism was a product of the theory of social Darwinism that pervaded the period. Its insistence that physical distinctions were outward manifestations of innate moral differences found a ready believer in Alice. To her it was absolutely natural to accept the superiority of the white race, especially in the face of Western society's demonstrable technological achievements, colonization, and the growth of capitalism. Since the pioneer community was already established when she arrived, Alice had no need to enter aboriginal society at any level, and her attitude to the local indigenous community was akin to that of an anthropologist observing, with humour and curiosity but little sense of human connection, the antics of some exotic creature. Alice believed that she belonged indisputably at the top of the social hierarchy, and it would take much experience of other races, and considerable soul-searching, before she was willing to have these assumptions challenged and to change her attitudes. She differed greatly from another respected resident of the southern interior – Susan Moir Allison[4] – who was deeply concerned about the degradation of aboriginal peoples and who welcomed the presence of the local aboriginal population; indeed, Susan had depended on aboriginal help during her many confinements.

When, in March 1891, the twenty-nine-year-old Alice Butler Barrett made the journey by train and ship from her home in Port Dover to the interior of British Columbia, she had no idea what to expect. She had come to the Okanagan Valley in response to a plea from her beloved Harry; he and their uncle needed Alice to take care of domestic duties so that Harry could concentrate on the ranch operation and Uncle could focus on his carpentry, and she made a commitment to try the arrangement for a year. After an uncomfortable five-day trans-Canada crossing, during which Alice found herself confined in a railway car with many "very common" people, she finally emerged at Sicamous to a rapturous welcome from the brother she had not seen for many months. She found herself in a wildly mixed population that was making major strides towards developing more than a subsistence living in the wilderness. However, her thoughts on reaching the primitive living quarters of the ranch – a three-roomed cabin known variously as "the cabin" or "the house" – can easily be imagined; her introduction to life among the pioneering settlers would prove both daunting and rewarding. Nevertheless she sought to civilize her surroundings and to replicate as quickly as possible the life she had left behind. In comparison with those in eastern Canada, societal structures in the Spallumcheen were flexible, and the accumulation of land and the wealth it generated bestowed ready acceptance on those fortunate enough to succeed.

There is no evidence that Alice Butler Barrett ever maintained a diary while she lived at home in Ontario. Indeed, she is different from most other diarists in that her writings did not emerge from an innate need to communicate (she was already the writer of copious letters home). After her arrival she acquiesced to the pleas of her younger brother Harry, who thought that the "home ones" in Port Dover would be interested in a record of their doings, and she settled down to writing a diary. (Harry himself was not exactly without an ulterior motive in his suggestion, for if Alice began a diary, there would no longer be any need for him to continue writing his own.) Once persuaded, Alice applied herself to the task with a deep sense of duty, diligence, and seriousness, shaping her writings carefully during moments of leisure. In her pages she created the Alice that she wished others to know – the correct and morally upright sister/wife, and the God-fearing young woman who was hard working, hospitable, sympathetic and outwardly submissive to others while retaining great independence of mind. Indeed, these two qualities –

submissiveness and independence – were constantly at war. Her diaries were like others written by nineteenth-century Canadian women in that they show that, once committed to the task, Alice demonstrated a desire to describe in them accurately and in detail her experience in the new land; she was intrigued by the unanticipated personal changes that pioneer society wrought upon her.

When Alice arrived, she learned that her brother Harry was courting the young Minnie Shickluna, grandchild of well known Ontario ship-builder Louis Shickluna. However, there were problems with the relationship because Minnie was Roman Catholic and her aunt/chaperone looked askance at the possibility of her marrying outside that faith. During this period there was one adult non-aboriginal woman for every three men, and the average age of white women at marriage was twenty-two years. Alice, at twenty-nine, considered herself a confirmed spinster, though her future husband, Harold Parke, first saw her within a month of her arrival and began a persistent courtship a few weeks later. (Within four months she would receive from him the first of several proposals of marriage.) While not conventionally beautiful, Alice was tall and slender, with strongly defined features, large dark eyes, and cascades of curly black hair that was always pinned up tightly in a bun.

What kind of woman emerges from the authorial persona? Alice displayed an immense appetite for the life of her times, together with a high degree of self-confidence and resilience; she also possessed a genius for friendship. She had a lively mind and disposition and was psychologically complex – a woman of incisive intellect who suffered cruelly from the childish fear of being alone at night; a seemingly mature woman who relied a great deal upon the emotional support of others; and a woman who could be selfish, stubborn, and possessive. Although often sentimental she was never self-pitying, and she attracted others to her through sheer personal magnetism. By turns prim, flirtatious, independent, pious, and inquisitive, she was always ready to offer wise help, and she showed an unfailing love and friendship for those in her immediate circle. If any of her friends were in real trouble or difficulty, then their first reaction was often to talk things over with Alice. She was guided by a strong sense of purpose and, most of the time, her quiet optimism, practical intelligence, and massive common sense remained untroubled. Alice was lively, vivacious, and energetic; people recognized her as a dignified, sociable woman of charm, affability, and total competence.

Her religious inclination had always been profound, and she displayed a strong humanitarian ethic. She considered herself to be as morally upright as anyone, and Christian conviction was central to her actions throughout her life. Alice viewed hardship, suffering, and tragedy as an opportunity to test her faith, believing that reversals occurred only so that she might build something better upon them. She also showed great compassion and generosity of spirit to those less fortunate than herself. She was a pragmatist who discovered her own strengths as she confronted and overcame adversity. At all times she was hospitable, well-mannered, cheerful, and generous. I learned from her great-nephew, who is still living in Ontario, that she was also a marvellous cook, a fastidious housekeeper, and a consistent observer of the niceties of social interaction. She had been taught to "keep up standards." On many occasions she was called upon to display both physical and moral courage, and she did not fail. A strong will, emphatic opinions, and self-assuredness were always apparent, and Alice's personality reverberates throughout her work. Her strong sense of self is also evident in the recollections of those who knew her later in life. Her influence has not dimmed, for she has maintained a large presence in the memory of family members.

The faith of her childhood remained strong, and she continued to attend religious services twice on Sundays, all the while exhibiting a deep dislike for all aspects of the Roman Catholic faith. She was not what one would call an early feminist – indeed, she prided herself on *not* being a "New Woman." By the 1890s this unconventional concept, preached by women like Agnes Machar,[5] was already attracting much attention and gaining adherents among Canadian women. The New Woman espoused non-traditional attitudes towards religion, work, and marriage, sought entry into higher education, and did not look to a man to furnish her with her destiny. However, this non-traditional creature did not appeal to Alice. Not for her an independent lifestyle; instead, she depended on the kindness and actions of others to provide for her physical and emotional needs. In order to feel emotionally fulfilled, she desperately needed to know that she was loved. But she also demonstrated tremendous independence of mind. Despite these contradictory aspects of her personality, and perhaps because of her very human foibles, her diaries are witness to the honourable, steadfast, loyal, and endearing quality of her nature. She was, in short, a woman of immense character.

Once Alice began writing her diary, vignettes of the early residents and activities of the Okanagan Valley spilled from her pen, and they are a delight – the work of an accurate and astute observer who possessed a deliciously ironic eye and ear for details of appearance, accent, and character. She loved gossip, and her pages contain detailed portraits of the people she met and befriended. She was both politically aware and interested, although, as a woman, she was denied suffrage. She offered cogent and pointed comments on the Liberal government of Sir Wilfrid Laurier and on many provincial and local politicians. Some of her best friends in Vernon were the wives of local aldermen, and her observations on their menfolk were often scathing. Year after year during the final decade of the nineteenth century, with deft strokes of her pen, Alice brought such individuals vividly to life.

Besides her interest in people, Alice detailed many of the events that occurred during her years in the Okanagan. The stagecoach service between centres at the northern end of the valley came to an end. The Shuswap and Okanagan Railway Company had pushed through a spur line from Sicamous to Okanagan Landing, which meant that residents of Vernon, Lansdowne, Armstrong, and Enderby could travel by train all the way, via Sicamous, to Vancouver or to points east. Kelowna and Penticton to the south were serviced from the Landing by luxuriously appointed Canadian Pacific Railway (CPR) sternwheelers. In Alice's pages, too, we read of periods of severe drought, devastating floods, earthquakes, deadly winters, and widespread epidemics of such diseases as typhoid, scarlet fever, and diphtheria, which, in her day were often fatal to children and adults alike.

Meanwhile, Harry Barrett helped to ease his sister's way through the rigours and disorientation of pioneer life. During the first fifteen months of her diaries the daily grind of life as a ranchwoman in the Spallumcheen was faithfully recorded. Her days were spent cleaning, baking, preparing meals, doing the laundry, hanging clothes to dry (either outdoors or, if the weather proved inclement, on ropes strung throughout the tiny cabin), ironing, shopping, writing numerous letters to the home ones and to friends and acquaintances in the area, and paying and receiving visits. The formality of the visiting ritual and the importance attached to it are astounding to the contemporary reader, but the practice was an essential means of communication in the days before the telephone. On countless occasions, Alice was forced to stop what she was doing, or put her personal plans for the day on hold, because of unexpected visitors. Food and drink were always offered, which required a steady supply of home-made bread and butter, cakes, muffins, pies, cookies, and so on. She kept her old educated self alive by teaching literature and history to Nonah Pelly and Lucy Crozier (her neighbours' daughters), and she soon became deeply attached to the young Pelly girl, who had a quiet, gentle, and accommodating disposition. Alice tended a large vegetable garden, churned butter, and gathered eggs from the henhouse (both for family consumption and for sale in Lansdowne or Vernon). In the evening, when not writing letters or completing an entry in her diary, she could be found sewing, mending, working on handicrafts, or setting bread to rise. One job that Alice described in detail showed her and Uncle spending hours each day in the cellar, "rubbing shoots from potatoes"; this was necessary in the spring in order to keep the remaining supply of tubers edible until the next crop could be harvested.

The outdoor labour of the ranchers she depicted as unremittingly heavy: they felled trees, built homes, stables, privies, smokehouses, and animal pens, split rails, and constructed fences. They cleared fields and ploughed them, sowing and harvesting the subsequent crops. They tended livestock, butchered animals, and preserved their meat. It was a never-ending round of activity undertaken in the knowledge that lives depended on everyone's conscientiousness, cooperation, and care. Many of the men at that time helped their wives and neighbours with "womanly" chores. Brother Harry helped her wash floors and paint and sweep out rooms; Price Ellison was proud of his coffee-making skills – the Victorian equivalent of today's "man in charge of the barbecue" – even Uncle Henry made biscuits.

Despite the intensity of their labours on the ranch, these men and women still found time to enjoy simple pleasures. Alice and her brother went for long rides and walks in the country and gathered flowers to beautify the cabin. Alice was a voracious and eclectic reader and enjoyed reading aloud from the classics by lamplight during the long winter evenings. She played the piano and organ and sang, and she and her brother both enjoyed attending dances and concerts. Harry was in great demand as a singer of comic songs and always brought the house down; he had a strong, clear voice and a winning delivery. Alice had become entranced by a landscape in which she found herself surrounded by hills filled with game of every kind, echoing with the call of flocks of ducks and geese flying overhead, coyotes howling to the moon, timber falling, hawks shrilling, and plough teams tramping. Her eyes gazed across meadows carpeted with wild flowers and fields of golden oats, and she caught sight of an occasional black bear on the fringe between forest and field.

We learn a great deal about the preparation and content of pioneer meals. A hearty breakfast was served early in the morning, and it included a selection of meats, eggs, fruits and vegetables in season, bread and butter, muffins, biscuits, and coffee or tea. Dinner was eaten in the middle of the day and consisted of a generous spread of meats, potatoes, other vegetables, pickles, salads in season, bread, and pies. The final meal of the day was tea – an impressive spread high in carbohydrates, frequently with meat and pickles, but always with cake, cookies, pies, jams, jellies, scones, and, of course, cups of tea or coffee. (And always, since Sunday was a "day of rest," Saturday was given over to the preparation of meals for both days.) Wild fruits were there for the picking just outside the door: olallies (saskatoons), blackberries, and blueberries were favourite fillings for pies. Cultivated fruit was also becoming available in the Okanagan; the valley would soon develop a fine reputation for the apples, pears, cherries, peaches, apricots, and plums that its young orchards were beginning to produce. Much of this was put up for the winter, but exotic fruits such as oranges and lemons were also readily available, especially in time for Christmas. Caloric intake was obviously high, but then most people were on the move all day long, performing hard physical labour, and thought nothing of walking long distances every day.

Alice's suitor, Ontario native Harold Randolph Parke, was a man of many accomplishments who, throughout his life, turned his hand to whatever job presented itself. Born on 25 January 1846 in Port Colborne, Parke was the youngest son of a well-to-do and politically very well-connected family, most of whose members lived in London, Ontario. He was one of four lawyer sons of Irish-born the Honourable Thomas Parke (1793-1864). Parke Sr., a master builder by trade, with his brother Robert had constructed a gristmill near London that the brothers subsequently sold in December 1835. He then became the partner of Scottish-born architect John Ewart; the firm of Ewart and Parke built the Gothic-style courthouse and gaol in London, and the Ontario parliament buildings in Toronto. Parke Sr. later entered politics in Upper Canada and was appointed surveyor-general in the Baldwin-Lafontaine administration. A Wesleyan Methodist and a Reformer, in 1839 he co-founded the *Canada* (later *London*) *Inquirer* with George Heyworth Hackstaff; the newspaper gave special attention to the introduction of responsible government, municipal institutions, public schools, free grants of land to settlers, and the secularization of clergy reserves. In his later years, Parke Sr. was commissioned a magistrate and, by 1845, had assumed the offices of collector of customs and of canal tolls at Port Colborne. In 1860 he was given the same two positions for the community of St. Catharines, and he held them until his death in 1864.

Harold was the youngest child of Thomas Parke and his second wife, Harriet Rose Wilkes. He was educated at Upper Canada College, from which he ran away as a teenager to join the Confederate forces during the American Civil War; he was wounded in action and eventually rescued through the efforts of an irate father who managed to bring him home. Young Harold tried to settle down into respectability and, after completing his training in law, worked for a time at his brother Ephraim's London law firm. He married at the age of twenty-two; his bride was the twenty-year-old Edith Barrett (no relation to the Port Dover Barretts) of

Durham, Ontario, who died not long afterwards. Perhaps because of her death, Parke decided to leave his eastern establishment family and strike out on his own. He longed for greater adventure in his life, and in 1878 enlisted in the North-West Mounted Police; he remained a member of the Force for two years and, while stationed at Wood Mountain Fort, took part in a memorable encounter with Sitting Bull. When he met Alice, the forty-five-year-old widower was living in Vernon and operating a business hauling freight between that town and Enderby. He was also co-owner, with Robert McDougall, of a Vernon sawmill and brick kiln, and agent for several insurance companies.

Alice was very much a product of the Victorian era in that matters of the heart and passions were not exposed to the world. Pregnancies were never mentioned; in a patriarchal society such as hers, the topics of labour and childbirth were not considered fit subjects for public discourse, and her education had taught her not to express emotions that centred on this female activity. Indeed, emotions were generally held under a tight rein. She sometimes made her diary the confidant of her deepest feelings, but rare were the occasions when she erupted with the intense anger that her culture prohibited women from expressing in public.[6] Although Harold Parke proposed to her several times during the summer months of 1891, we learn nothing of the details as they were happening. The reader watches as Mr. Parke progresses from being "the teamster," to "Mr. Parke," to "Harold," and finally to "Hal." He was clearly devoted to Alice and pursued her diligently until the day – finally – she wrote of her anguish at feeling obliged to choose between commitment to him or to her parents and family in Ontario. In the beginning, the family won out over Mr. Parke and she rejected his proposals several times; obviously, though, she changed her mind, since she married him in Port Dover in January 1893. The marriage constituted a step up the social ladder, and she became a member of an illustrious, well-connected, and highly respected Ontario family.

The couple returned to Vernon, where Hal assumed the position of assessment officer for Vernon city council. He never again attempted to go into business for himself but, instead, sought the relative security of regularly paid government positions. Subsequently he found work as assistant postmaster, constable for the city, jailer, manager of the BX Ranch, provincial superintendent of roads, and, finally, postmaster in his own right. Their marriage developed into a comfortable, mutually respectful, and deeply loving, if not overtly passionate, one. The quality of their relationship had much to do with Alice's sense of well-being and comfort. Short, chubby, balding, and bearded, Parke was a well educated

man and proved to be an easy-going, practical, even-tempered, and sup-
portive husband; he was always willing to help with meal preparation if
Alice requested it, and he produced delicious pancakes and macaroni and
cheese. Although his wife was too modest to write about their physical
relationship, we do know that he and Alice settled down to become loving
companions, and their partnership was the envy of many of their friends,
one of whom described them as "the happiest couple in Vernon." They
enjoyed deep mutual trust and were intellectual equals and soulmates who
thoroughly enjoyed each other's company, spending contented hours in
the evening talking, reading aloud to each other, playing cards or cribbage,
or receiving visitor after visitor. Hal displayed a wry, gently tweaking sense
of humour and willingly ceded domestic authority to "the Boss," as he
called his wife. At that time Vernon boasted a population of only 400 people, and during the thirteen years Alice lived there she touched the lives
of scores of them, the influential as well as the lowly. With new loves,
friends, and duties emerging, her diaries helped her to integrate the old
life with the new.

Harry's romance with Minnie Shickluna had failed in 1892 when the
young woman left the valley, never to return; by 1894 he was courting
neighbour Nonah Pelly, who had by that time grown into a beautiful and
dignified young woman. The couple was married in Vernon in October
1894 and made their home at Mountain Meadow. Nonah gave birth to two
boys in the following three years, and the couple developed a deep contentment with, and love for, each other.

That same year Hal Parke left local government to become a provincial
constable, and, when his duties took him away from Vernon, Alice either
stayed at Mountain Meadow Ranch with Harry and his growing family
or accompanied Hal on his travels. During the early years in Vernon,
Alice made a host of new friends, most of whom were women, several the
wives of government officials, landowners, and local merchants. Having
grown up with four spirited brothers, Alice was not at all shy around men;
indeed, within weeks of her arrival in the city she had attracted a group of
four young "cavaliers" who remained prominent in the diaries until the
end. Three were Ontarians and the fourth was from New Brunswick.
Government agent Leonard Norris, *Vernon News* editor Jack McKelvie,
surveyor and Royal Military College graduate Forbes Kerby, and McGill
graduate and new physician in town Osborne Morris became her devoted
admirers. The men were attracted by her lively intellect, her sense of
humour, the warm welcome she offered, and the tasty meals she prepared.
They danced attendance upon her and frequently presented her with
small gifts, tokens of their esteem and respect.

In 1895, while in residence at the Coldstream Ranch, Ishbel, Countess of Aberdeen, wife of Canada's governor general, coopted Alice into the vice-regal circle, with the result that neither she nor the town were ever quite the same again. Alice had never encountered the whirlwind of feminism and determined social activism that characterized Lady Aberdeen, and despite initial reluctance to join any committees she soon found herself agreeing to become the first corresponding secretary of the Vernon chapter of the National Council of Women. Alice was both admiring and apprehensive of such a formidable mover and shaker, but she quite firmly rejected the countess's feminist convictions.

By 1896 Hal had grown disenchanted with his roving life as a provincial constable and readily accepted the job of manager of Francis S. Barnard's BX Ranch when it was offered. The extensive ranch holdings were located on the outskirts of town, about a mile and half from the Parke home. Hal and Alice moved there in October of that year and remained for nineteen months. It was there that Alice's racist attitudes faced their stiffest challenge, undergoing a sea change thanks to her daily contact with the ranch's Chinese cook, Goo-Ee, whom she quickly recognized as a kindred spirit. To her surprise she found him to be fastidiously clean both in his person and surroundings, and there is no doubt that they connected on a deep personal level. Alice undertook to help the admiring man improve his English, and Goo-Ee reciprocated by plying her with little dainties to savour. Her two winters at the ranch were long and gloomy and, increasingly, Alice missed her friends in town. It was at her urging that Hal resigned from the BX Ranch in May 1898 when the position of provincial superintendent of roads for Upper Yale became available, and the couple happily returned to Vernon. Alice subsequently went on several lengthy inspection trips with her husband, and the current volume of her diary went with her. Hal himself took a great interest in the contents of her scribblers, and he chided her gently if she fell behind with her writing. Indeed, he even wrote several entries himself, when Alice was away at the ranch, to ensure that each volume was kept up to date.

In October 1898 tragedy struck the Barrett family. Harry's twenty-two-year-old wife, Nonah Pelly Barrett, died a few days after giving birth to her third son, and her distraught husband, already disheartened by his inability to make a decent living from the ranch, made the immediate decision to leave the Okanagan Valley and return to his family in Ontario. He, Alice, and his two older boys, Toby and Dick, departed soon after the funeral, leaving baby Frank with his grieving grandmother. In Port Dover Wese took charge of the two toddlers while Harry eked out a living farming locally. Alice returned to the Okanagan after a stay of two months.

Meanwhile, after the provincial election of 1898, Hal was dismissed from his job and spent several uncertain months looking for work before being appointed as Vernon's postmaster in May 1899. Despite her exposure to several early feminists, Alice herself never sought official positions or outside employment; however, after Hal's appointment as postmaster, she found herself with a job – albeit an unpaid one. The couple divided the office work so that Alice took care of the wicket for several hours a day, receiving and distributing mail and selling stamps, postal orders, and sundry other items, while Hal oversaw the heavier tasks and administration. They worked efficiently together, although Alice, while thoroughly enjoying her experience in the world of work, nonetheless experienced pangs of guilt because her duties in the post office interfered with her diary writing and her household duties. Many of the comments she made about her diaries were prompted by her neglect of them; more and more frequently they fell to a lower priority as other matters intervened. All the while she remained an assiduous letter writer.

As the months went on the diary entries became more and more desultory, and they came to an abrupt end in May 1900; the final entry stopped suddenly in the middle of a sentence in the middle of a page, with no further explanation. The end of the diaries coincided with the totally unexpected conception of Alice's only child; after eight years of marriage a daughter was born on 14 February 1901. Alice was thirty-nine at the time of the delivery and, tragically, little Emily Louisa Parke survived only nine months.[7] The residents of Vernon, who held the Parkes in the highest respect, poured out their sympathy to the couple, and Jack McKelvie wrote in the *Vernon News* a week later that Emily's "was the largest child's funeral ever held in Vernon."

The Parkes remained in Vernon until Hal's retirement from his job as postmaster in 1905; by that time he was suffering eye problems that required the attention of a specialist. They consulted doctors in Ontario, came back to Vernon for a short visit the following spring to sell their property, and then left for good.

EDITORIAL COMMENTS

The diaries were written with a definite audience in mind – Alice's family in Port Dover – and all that her parents and siblings were required to bring to the reading of them was an interest in human beings and the things that they did.

Until now, the papers of Susan Moir Allison have offered the only record of the life of a pioneer woman in the southern interior of British Columbia. The writings of the two women differ significantly in style and content; Susan's eighty pages or so of text bear little comparison with the half-million words of her successor. She did not keep a diary, and her memoir was published as a thirteen-part series in the *Vancouver Province*, beginning on 22 February 1931, when the writer was eighty-six years old. It comprises a retrospective account of her early days as a pioneer and is written through the filter of her sunny disposition and faltering memory. It conveys a sense of nostalgia for a way of life that has since disappeared, and this stands in stark contrast to the raw immediacy of Alice's diaries. Susan's style is smooth and displays the polish of reworking; Alice's prose, written in the moment, was never edited and, of course, never published during her lifetime. (Although Susan did not appear in Alice's work, it is intriguing to speculate that the two women might well have met each other during one of Alice's jaunts down the lake after 1900; they had several friends in common and the CPR sternwheeler stopped at Sunnyside [later Westbank], where Susan lived for several years.)

The Parke diaries can be divided into five distinct sections. The first, from March 1891 to June 1892, covers Alice's arrival in the Spallumcheen, a visit to Vancouver and Victoria, and her return to Port Dover at the end of her promised year. The second, from 27 January to 6 February 1893, offers a brief account of the harrowing, blizzard-plagued trans-Canada journey she and her husband undertook after their marriage in Port Dover, and it is written on the blank pages of a CPR railway timetable. There is a pause of nine months, and then the diary continues from November 1893 to October 1896, recording her life in Vernon. The fourth section deals with the sudden move to the BX Ranch and her residence there from October 1896 to May 1898. The final section, from June 1898 to May 1900, shows her resettled in Vernon. There are several gaps in the text, which coincide with lengthy visits to Port Dover; while with the home ones, she felt no need to record events.

It was during the late summer of 1996 that I was asked to begin transcribing the contents of thirty-one exercise books and scribblers that Harry Bemister Barrett had recently donated to the Vernon Archives. All I was told at the time was that they were written by "a Vernon postmaster's wife" (I didn't even know her name) and that they covered the years from 1891 to 1900. I expected the task to be lengthy and not a little tedious, but by the end of the second volume I found myself captivated by the life and personality of this exceptional woman whose words spilled from the sometimes crumbling pages. I could hardly wait to finish one volume and move on to the next, for to read the diaries was to watch a woman engaged in finding her place in Canadian life. I learned before long that my chair in the archives office was about 100 yards from where many of the originals were written, for Alice had lived a little way along the street. During the following fourteen months, as I accompanied Alice on her journey through the Okanagan Valley, I came to realize that here was a writer of uncommon power and depth who deserved a wider audience than the one she would receive if her words, once transcribed, were returned to the obscurity in which they had lain hidden for so long.

Writing and literacy performed an important function in Alice's life, and her diaries have literary as well as historical importance. During the years that she faithfully recorded her activities, she displayed a prose style that is poised, even, smooth, and has a surprisingly contemporary flavour. Her vocabulary was that of a well educated woman, and there is a crisp confidence in her work that we associate with a more experienced author. The firm, confident, dense, and steeply slanted Victorian handwriting covered hundreds of pages. The paper in the thirty-one books she used varied widely in quality from one volume to another: some entries were written on paper that has withstood the passage of more than 100 years in almost pristine condition, others were on pages that threaten to crumble at the slightest hint of rough handling. Some display minor blots and scratchings as Alice adjusted her ink supply and reworked her text, but she never went over the diaries to erase or rewrite complete entries or tear out pages. Alice recognized that she was no artist and so refrained from any attempt to illustrate her text with drawings. Although several religious tracts were found among the pages, there were no photographs.

Alice believed herself qualified to offer an opinion on any subject, and in editing her diaries I confronted the task of reducing her expansive writings to a manageable size for publication while retaining the flow and vigour of the originals. My solution has been to step outside convention and offer a combined chronological/thematic framework. The reasons for this approach are twofold. First, the vast text lends itself readily to such treatment and, second, there are many continuous strands throughout the work. Lengthy sections of two volumes are therefore interspersed with chapters collated along thematic lines so that the reader gains an overview of the candid style and intimate quality of the original. Less than one-quarter of Alice's text is presented here. For this manuscript I have inserted notes where they are necessary for the reader's understanding of the major people and events portrayed. To avoid confusion I have used mostly forenames to identify the numerous Barretts and two Parkes.

Although well educated by the standards of the day, Alice's spelling, apostrophes, capitalization, and punctuation proved frequently capricious and inconsistent; in transcribing the volumes I have retained these idiosyncrasies, since they add such a distinctive character to the work as a whole. Her underlinings of words, used for emphasis, appear as italics. The spelling of names often changed from page to page – sometimes from line to line. Mr. McCall, for instance, entered as "Mr. McCaul," then became "Mr. McColl," before finally being established under his correct surname; Mr. Kirby was by turns "Mr. Kirby," "Mr. Kerby," and then "Mr. Kirby" again (entries written by Hal always referred to him as "Kerby"). There were very few paragraph divisions in the original, and I have retained the flow of the writer's thoughts and words without breaking up the text into arbitrary sections. I have also retained the use of the dash, since this conveys the speed of her writing.

The size and mobility of the extended families entering the valley at the time proved both daunting and problematic for an editor; frequently there were four generations sharing a home. Many people arrived, looked around a community, stayed a while, and then moved on to what they believed would be greener pastures. Could I be certain that the Mr. Smith of Enderby in Volume 1 would prove to be the same person in Vernon in Volume 7? By dint of repeated reading of the text, and investigation of a wide selection of local historical sources, I slowly discovered a host of small clues that enabled me to resolve difficulties such as these. Nonetheless, it proved impossible to identify every one of the people Alice mentioned.

I chose to be as unobtrusive as possible when working on the transcription and to avoid indulging in "silent" editing. That said, I saw no point in including her occasional scratchings-out, since they add nothing to our understanding and are a distraction; nor did I wish to insert a myriad "[sic]" notations to highlight her individualistic spelling and punctuation. I have left untouched all the parentheses ( ) that Alice herself used and have inserted my own square brackets [ ] only where I felt a need for greater clarity. Also, I chose to retain Imperial measurements in both my text and footnotes.

There are two major transcripts of the complete diaries. Both unpublished, they are (1) the complete non-footnoted transcript with a detailed index and (2) the fully footnoted version. These transcripts, together with the original diaries, numerous family letters, photographs, and other documents, now form part of the collection of the Greater Vernon Museum and Archives.

By the summer of 1998 it had become clear that I would have to make the journey to Port Dover in order to complete accurate footnoting regarding Alice's family and friends in Ontario. To my great joy, I was invited by Harry B. Barrett to stay at Riverbank Cottage while doing my research. I remained for over two weeks, exploring Port Dover, enjoying long drives through southwestern Ontario along the shore of Lake Erie, meeting many of Alice's family members, listening to anecdotes about "Aunty Alice," doing research every day at the Eva Brook Donly Museum in Simcoe, and asking countless questions of my host.

I walked under T.B. Barrett's huge pear tree in the back garden and beneath the maples he planted just around the corner on St. Patrick Street to celebrate his eightieth birthday in 1897 (and which had become almost mature trees by the time he died in 1910). I inspected the old rawhide box in which the diaries had been stored out of sight for almost 100 years. I held in my hands Alice's monogrammed silver tea service and the inkwell she used to write the diaries. I saw the ancient cactus plant started by T.B. Barrett almost 150 years ago and still lovingly tended by his great-granddaughter. I walked along Main Street and inspected the impressive old brick city hall, designed by Alice's brother Clarence and built in 1904; a few steps further west was the office of the *Maple Leaf* newspaper, still at its original location. As I strolled along I saw many of the homes where Alice was a regular and welcome visitor – homes that have been carefully maintained through the years. I visited St. Paul's Church and sat in the pews where Alice worshipped. Finally, I drove out to the Port Dover cemetery and paid silent homage at her grave, where she lies below a small, simple headstone beside Hal Parke and surrounded by members of her family.

Without a written record there is very little history, and although they were prolific letter writers, the women of that time left behind very few major documents. Alice Barrett Parke has bequeathed a primary source document to us that offers a superb panoramic overview of her place and time – the southern interior of British Columbia during the final decade of the nineteenth century. There is no other record of the Okanagan Valley at that period that takes us under the pioneer skin with so much immediacy. In a world where historians most often examine the lives of extraordinary men, her diaries cast a shining beam on the lives of the pioneering women of her era. Their resolute spirit sustained them as they struggled with physically punishing tasks in order to create homes, nurture children, work with their neighbours, and contribute to community affairs. As a human being Alice proves to be a lively companion, and as a chronicler of her time she has a fascinating tale to tell. The Alice of 1900 is not the same Alice who arrived in British Columbia nine years earlier; through observation and experience she learned and grew and changed. It is the immediacy and "dailiness" of the diaries that endow them with their exceptional power.

During the preparation of this book, Harry B. wrote from Ontario: "I keep wondering what Aunty Alice would think of the stir she has created. I expect she would be amazed and a bit shocked, but secretly pleased."[8] If I have been able to do justice to the memory of this remarkable woman, I am content.

JO FRASER JONES
VERNON, BRITISH COLUMBIA

*Hobnobbing with
a Countess*

hardly wait. It was all good news.
Father is much better – & Mother well.
This bright Spring weather will be so
good for her – It worried me a little
that Bese had been sick with a
bad cold but she said she was quite
better – This morning, very soon
after breakfast old Mrs Schubert came
Mr Jus goes every day, to the
"Gun-boot" to feed cattle – & brought
his mother down. He called for her
tonight about six o'clock – and so
we had a long day together, and I
thoroughly enjoyed it. She was
telling me the story of her married
life, and the dangers and the
hardships she underwent were
enough to kill any ordinary
woman – She was married in
Massachusetts (having come out
from Ireland sometime before) and
then went to St. Paul – where they
lived until three little children
were born; – when the youngest was

5 March 1892 (The beginning of Catherine Schubert's account of the
Overlanders' trek in 1862.)

CHAPTER I

Quite away from all my people

Arriving in the Spallumcheen Valley

Alice Butler Barrett had set off for British Columbia full of excitement and anticipation. She was leaving the comfort of the Lake Erie community of Port Dover for the raw and newly settled interior of British Columbia. More importantly, she was leaving the safety of a large extended family and an agreeable home life for the isolation and loneliness of the Okanagan Valley. The Empire Loyalist country in which she had been raised had long enjoyed a settled way of life. There she had followed a regular routine of work at home, visits to friends and relatives, and regular church-going. Her parents were aging, and while her father still enjoyed robust health, Alice was devoted to helping her frail mother meet the demands of a family that included four adult children (Wese, Alice, Hubert, and Clarence) and the two adolescent Scott boys, Walter and Roy (the children of her dead sister Carrie). Alice had never lived alone and was, therefore, eager to undertake the journey west on her own; however, her parents would not hear of it, and she travelled in the company of former Port Dover residents Harry and Lizzie Harding, who were returning to the west.

The Spallumcheen Valley was first settled in the 1860s and was a magnificent stretch of flat land north of Vernon in the southern interior of British Columbia. A small and tight-knit community of farmers, ranchers, and merchants already existed there, and Alice entered into the life of the settlers with great enthusiasm. Uncle Henry Barrett owned 320 acres at the Mountain Meadow Ranch, north of Otter Lake, and twenty-five-year-old Harry Barrett[1] had arrived over a year earlier to help work his land. Harry had fallen in love with the young Minnie Shickluna and was courting her fervently. Alice arrived at Sicamous to a rapturous welcome from her beloved younger brother, followed by the novelty of a sleigh ride to her final destination, Uncle's cabin. She was determined to fulfill her promised year of domestic work, to maintain the high standards to which she was accustomed, to make whatever contribution she could to the life of the community, and then to return home. But within four weeks of her arrival, teamster Harold Parke caught sight of her and was much taken by what he saw. His dogged pursuit and her eventual acceptance of his hand in marriage caused her final return to Port Dover to be postponed by fourteen years.

Volume I is reproduced almost in its entirety.

SPALLUMCHEEN MARCH 1891

March 22 – Palm Sunday
Ever since I came a week ago Thursday, Harry has been trying to persuade me to keep a diary, so though I think it very doubtful that I'll have anything to say worth remembering, I'll make a beginning at least. It all seems very new and strange as yet. I had a tiresome rather unpleasant journey of five days and nights. After many grand determinations to come out quite alone and have an experience of looking after myself, I was forced to come with Harry[2] and Lizzie[3] Harding. Mother[4] was so distressed at the thought of my coming alone, that I gave in very reluctantly to the safety and convenience (?) of having an escort, the more reluctantly because the Hardings were coming on a colonist excursion and I had to pay for the privilege of their society by coming in that way too. It was an experience which I may – in time – look back upon with indifference but at the time and even yet I confess there was nothing but discomfort and even misery in it. The car was crowded. The people were – no doubt – respectable, but very common, and we were all so close together. Then the weather was bitterly cold and stormy most of the time. All through that dreary, desolate North West (I couldn't live contentedly in that country) we had clouds and heavy snow storms, so much so that the train was delayed, and we were 9 hours late in reaching Sicamous,[5] my R.R. termination. How glad I was to leave the train and step out on the platform to find Harry there to meet me, with Dick Taylor.[6] We spent the rest of that night at Colonel Forrester's hotel[7] – such a pretty picturesque little place, perched on the side of a mountain with barely room for a waggon road between it and the railway track, which runs immediately along the edge of a lovely little lake, on the other side of which rises another mountain.

We got up early Thursday morning, and after a breakfast served by a dirty-looking Chinaman in a room thick with smoke of burning fat, we set out on our 32 miles drive. Harry and I in front, Dick and Harry Harding on the back seat. Oh! and such a lovely drive, perfect sleighing, splendid horses, sunshine and pure air, the change from a close, stuffy car, with uncongenial people about, was enough to enjoy, even without the beautiful scenery, thrown in such profusion around. Every sense was pleased. Nature has been so lavish of the beauties she has showered, in both quantity and quality on "all outdoors" that one readily puts up with a little economy in the interiors. That is what strikes me most forcibly. Everything outside is so large and the houses and all their contents on such a small scale, except our appetites. I am hungry all the time, and see no cause of complaint in the amount the others eat. We reached the cabin[8] at about six in the evening, and found Uncle[9] here to welcome us. It is a tiny place, just three rooms – kitchen first, facing the road, then the sitting room, then my bed-room – but I have already made it more homelike with carpet, curtains, pictures, etc. I never thought I had any taste for house decorations, leaving all that to Wese's[10] artist eye and deft fingers, but any woman's presence makes a difference in a house. I never realized before the wisdom of the words "It is not good for man to be alone"; it would be amusing, were it not too strongly pathetic, to see the little makeshifts of bachelor housekeeping. There is no doubt in my mind that woman's sphere is, as a rule, in the house. Of course, genius may force her out of it, or dire necessity drive her forth to soar – or to struggle in higher flights or harder paths, but the quality of a house maker is essentially woman's, and perhaps if she did her work better in this line, men might be stronger and nobler. One can see that, at the very first, her presence is almost an impossibility in a new country. It needs a hardier stock of womankind – both physically and mentally – than is often produced by our eastern civilization to stand the loneliness and hardships of this western life, but oh! how the country needs women strong in character, gentle in words and ways, to soften while they strengthen the rougher manners of the men.

I have been much struck with the kindliness and real politeness of the men here to a woman. Men who talk atrociously ungrammatically, who have dirty hands, and dirtier clothes, seem to take quite a courtly air, and more real chivalry of manner than many so-called polished gentlemen, when they address a woman, and there seems to be no limit to their kindness of heart.

I was at the little church[11] last Sunday, but was disappointed not to get there today. The roads are so shockingly muddy, and there was no way of getting down. Mr. Joyce read the service. He is a very nice man – an English gentleman. He and Mr. Wood[12] are the only two I have met that I think I'd enjoy as companions – the others are kind, interesting, amusing – almost anything but congenial. I am alone most of the day but have already begun to look on the mountains[13] as companions. When I begin to feel lonely I just go and gaze at them. Like the face of one dearly loved, there they are – always, and yet never, the same. The same in general outline, but with ever varying beauties of expression. I have persuaded Harry to go over to Fred Heathcote's to a bachelor dinner. I was invited, but declined, so Uncle and I will be alone for awhile.

Tuesday
It may be waste of time and paper to write when one has no thoughts to put down – but I'm afraid my diary would grow by very slow degrees if I waited for ideas to fill it. I remember an old diary of Clarence's[14] where all through one summer his daily record was chiefly "Got up, curled sweet potato vines, went to bed" – and a record of the facts in most lives might not sound much more interesting – one cannot put in the sunshine and the rain that made the boy and the vines grow – one cannot write the sound of the wind that kissed his cheek – and the bird songs that filled the air – & yet it all went on with the curling of the sweet potato vines!

I had a long morning visit from Miss Lucy Crosier[15] yesterday. She came before eight o'clock & stayed until twelve – a quiet gentle kind of girl – who has never seen a railway train – and has never been out of this valley. She does not aim to soar however – would not like to live in a town, it would be so lonely!

Mr. Grant was here all Sunday afternoon.

Wednesday
It is pouring rain – Gulliver[16] and I are all alone. Harry went to Swanson's[17] early this morning for the cow – and is not back yet, though we expected him before dinner. I have been doing more mending – but it is something like drawing water in a seive, getting all the holes patched up, but one can easily see that any but very strong – if ugly – clothing is out of place here.

Monday, March 30th
I have spent a very idle afternoon walking up to the shop twice with Harry, and reading most of the rest of the time. I rode nine miles yesterday and am paying for the pleasure in good deal of stiffness & soreness today. We rode to church in the morning – I got on very well – had Harry

Harding's pony – it trotted, cantered, & once broke into a run but I managed to keep my seat – & enjoyed it. Mr. Joyce read the service, & I played and am afraid I led the responses. On Saturday I had a lovely drive behind four horses – two of them Harry's colts which are just being broken. We went up to Joe John's. Harry drove up, Tommy Glendenning was with us – and when we got there we found Miles Macdonald,[18] Gus Schubert[19] & Mr. Swanson there. While the men were busy branding cattle, I was left to the tender care of Bridget West, Joe's housekeeper. For Joe is quite a swell in style, if not in stature, he having a frame house & a housekeeper. He is a funny little man, looks something like a monkey – but he has a beautiful ranch. His house is just at the foot of a mountain, called Joe John's mountain. Bridget – a fat old Irish dame – and I climbed part way up and gathered a few wild flowers – on the 28th March – I would have liked to go farther up the view was so lovely – but I pitied the fatness & fears of the poor old body – she was all out of breath and assured me there were bears farther up, so we came back carrying as many very pretty white stones as we could manage. I brought them home to put round a flower bed. Mr. Swanson drove coming home – and in that great high waggon with four horses, down the mountain road – it was almost as nice as tobogganing. Mr. Swanson is a picture – in brilliant colouring. He is our nearest neighbour, a Scotchman and a widower. He is a small man with tawny hair and a huge red beard. He had an abscess on one side of his chin, & the lancing of this has left one bare spot, giving a unique air to his beard.

Wednesday April 1st

I have had another ride this afternoon. Harry has bought Harry Harding's horse (Pinto) for me, so now am quite independent having a poney of my own. He ran away with me today, & gave Harry a fright – but I did not feel frightened, & had time in the midst of the excitement to hope I would not meet anyone for my hat was on the side & my hair coming down. We have had a loss – our little calf is dead. We think the mother must have lain down on it, for it seemed quite well at noon, & at night when Harry went in the stable it was lying there quite dead. Harry rode down for the mail last night, & brought [a] lovely long letter from home & Carrie Mac-Donald[20] & Frank.[21]

Thursday April 2nd

Just three weeks today since I arrived here – four tomorrow since I left home! It seems a great deal longer than that – and yet I think I am enjoying everything that comes along. Tommy Glendenning has been here, &

Harry has ridden down to town with him. I baked bread and pies this morning. This afternoon have been sitting on some logs talking to Harry while I peeled posts.

Saturday April 4th
I could not write yesterday, as I had a ride in the morning, and visitors all the afternoon. Harry was making fence and saddled Pinto for me, charging me just to ride up and down in his sight – I came off once and gave him quite a scare. I was not really thrown, but felt myself going and jumped. Lucy Crosier came quite early after dinner, and brought her cousin, a young lad from Oakville named Carpenter. Before they left Mrs. Emkie came in & they all went away together. This morning I did some cooking, & picked two grouse which young Carpenter shot for me yesterday. This afternoon Harry & I spent clearing up the place ... We cleared away all the rubbish & made two little border beds for flowers in the front, along by the house – convenience is consulted here, much more than appearances, for instance the woodshed is in front of the house a little at the side – of course as the front door (the only outside door) opens into the kitchen, it would be a little awkward to have to go to the back for wood. We have made it nice and tidy looking, & I hope it will be pretty when the flowers come up. We got done about half past three, and I was just dressed when Miss Schubert[22] (a regular Amazon in appearance, being six feet tall, with a strong frame, and nice face) and Miss Norris, a little bit of a school-teacher, rode up. They made a pretty long call, and then suggested that I should go for a ride with them, so Harry saddled my horse & we were out an hour. I enjoyed it very much. I get a little more confidence each time. We had early tea & Harry has just ridden to town leaving me alone in the evening for the first time. He did not half want to go until Uncle got back, but it is not dark yet, & I did not want him to wait any later to start. It is a strange thing, but I believe being much alone makes me more courageous. I have been wondering if it [is] simply from force of habit – or if the spirit really grows stronger in solitude.

Monday April 6th
It is exactly a month today since I left home. How long it seems. On Saturday Harry and I began clearing up the place a little – but there is much to do yet. Uncle got home before dark Saturday night & Harry came about nine bringing Mr. Taylor with him & letters for me from Wese & Clarence. We both long for home letters. Mr. Taylor drove up from Enderby in the funniest two wheeled concern, so he drove me to church[23] Sunday morning & Harry rode. It rained pretty hard, but we were prepared. Service had begun however when we got there, but I played two

hymns & Mrs. Waters,[24] Harry, Mr. Heathcote, Mr. Joyce & myself stayed after church to practise next Sunday's hymns. Mr. Joyce lent me his book to bring home. As soon as we got back I prepared dinner and they did enjoy it – especially Mother's mustard pickles, & lemon pie. We had roast grouse & prairie chicken. After dinner Mr. Taylor helped me wash the dishes and then we sang until about six. When he left, Harry & I took a little walk & came in, intending to spend a good long evening writing letters, but had just got in when two more visitors Mr. Wright[25] and Arthur Young came and stayed till nine o'clock. Harry went to Enderby[26] this morning – when he got back, at about 2 o'clock, we went together over to Miles Macdonald's for a chain. I rode Pinto & Harry walked. Mr. Macdonald has a nice ranch, but his house is in a much more lonely spot than ours, being a mile in from the road just at the foot of a mountain. He was in his shirt sleeves ploughing. I did not get inside the house, so cannot report on it.

Wednesday April 8th
I am disappointed that we have not yet been able to get last night's mail, for I feel sure there are some letters for me. However Harry and I are thinking of going into town in the morning & then I'll know. Yesterday was rather a dreary rainy day – Lucy did not come, so I had the afternoon all to myself & finished reading Schiller's Wallenstein – what a beautiful character Max Piccolomini had! This afternoon Gulliver & I have been off with Harry building fences. I took a book, but did not read – I never can out of doors. All the fences here are shake fences – no civilized greed of customizing every foot of ground has as yet crept in – there are lovely uncultivated "fence corners" full of wild roses and other graceful growths. I do believe Nature is more graceful, if not so profitable, where left to herself – all wild things grow more peacefully – no, not quite all wild things. I must except our cow, Nancy, she is wild enough and decidedly graceless. All my life I have feared cows, but now the tables are turned for poor Nancy is terrified if I come any where near. I have felt pretty homesick today. Harry is very diligent about his music, practises nearly an hour every night.

Monday April 13th
It is always hard when one gets in arrears in anything, & especially I think in a diary. I have almost a week's report to make, and it is so warm & bright out of doors that I am sorely tempted to desert pen & ink & go off. I am going presently to sow some peas. Harry is harrowing the field near the house so I am going to get at my garden soon. I have been having a lot of holidays lately. On Thursday morning, quite early, Harry & I took

the colts with a "go devil"[27] such a name and walked over to Mr. Swanson's. There we got a truck & hitching them to it started for town. The machine had no springs and only a board put across the box for a seat – as the roads were pretty rough I soon deserted that for a seat "on the floor of the house" or rather of the box on some straw, & found that much easier. The colts went splendidly. We found such a budget of letters at the Post Office. I read most of them to Harry on the way home. Such a lovely long one from Wese and very amusing ones from the children[28] & one too from Nellie Workman, she has been ill at the Scott's. We got home about two had a little dinner, & then drove back to Mr. Swanson's with the truck again walking home with our "go devil." We took Gulliver that time – he drove there, but his poor little short legs got so tired coming home that I had to carry him a good part of the way. Harry & I intended riding down to Enderby Friday Evening to a calico ball which Miss Shickluna[29] asked us to – she asked me to stay on with them but when Friday morning broke in the pouring rain I thought we'd have to forego the ball – however Harry made me go down in the stage[30] in the morning & he came after tea. All the ladies at the R.R. house were very kind to me. Mr. & Mrs. Riley,[31] Mr. & Mrs. Patterson[32] (Mrs. P. is Mr. Riley's daughter) Mr. & Mrs. Smith[33] & Miss Shickluna, Mr. Riley's niece, live there together just while their new road is being built – they are the contractors – Mr. Riley & Mr. Patterson. It is a large house. They have two Chinamen[34] servants, & everything very comfortable – late dinners – and no early rising. They were so good to me, wanted me to stay longer, but I was quite glad to come back to the cabin & Harry. Enderby is very prettily situated, in a little valley almost surrounded by mountains with the Spallumcheen River & Sicamous stage road winding through the town. I could fancy one getting a rather shut-in feeling if compelled to stay there long. The town proper does not amount to much – about 30 wooden and log houses, a Presbyterian Church and a school house. It poured rain all the way down, when I got there we had lunch & then Miss Shickluna & I went up to the S. [Station] house where the dance was to be to help arrange the room – Mrs. Taylor, Mrs. Lambley,[35] Mrs. Knight & a few others were there – we had some fun – and then went back to dinner. Harry came down about eight, & we all went up to the S. house. Each lady had a rosette like her dress, these were put in a bag & drawn by the men – whoever got yr. rosette was yr. partner for the first dance. I pleaded very hard that I did not intend to dance & therefore need not be represented in the bag but they insisted & I was unfortunate enough to fall to the lot of Dr. Edo Offerhause[36] a great tall awkward German. He insisted on my dancing, & as it was a country dance which I had never even seen I made a pretty mess of it, but he didn't know any better. There were some very nice people there, & altogether I enjoyed it only they kept it up too late – half past two. The next morning we went up again to clear up, & in the afternoon Miss Shickluna, Miss Lawes[37] & I climbed one of the mountains. Oh! it was lovely, but we got even a prettier view Sunday morning, for we went for a longer & higher ramble with Mr. Taylor and could see far up & down the valley. It was my first experience of mountain climbing & I did enjoy it, only we were so disappointed on getting back at one o'clock to find that Harry had arrived in town shortly after we set out. We did not expect him until dinner time or we would have waited. In the afternoon we idled away more time and started for home a little after five. We had a lovely drive home – Mr. Wood offered to go down to Enderby for me & bring me up to Lansdowne[38] in time for church, but I knew Harry was counting on coming down to dinner and would be disappointed. I was sorry to miss church. They only have it in the evening in Enderby, and we could not wait for that. Our old Gulliver was nearly crazy with delight when he saw me back & I was glad to see him.

Tuesday 14th

Harry has gone to town for the mail. Uncle & I at the table he reading and I writing. I have not very much to say tonight. I was busy this morning, washing.[39] I am reading a book of Hawthorne's & was struck by the little sentence "It is odd enough that the kind of labour which falls to the lot of woman is just that which chiefly distinguishes artificial life – the life of degenerate mortals – from the life of Paradise. Eve had no dinner pot, no clothes to mend & no washing day" and it does seem as if these common household duties take one pretty far from Paradise. It is a question if the men are, after all, so cruel in those countries where they make their women work in the fields. I had a trial of both today, for after dinner and Miss Lucy had gone (she came by very early) I went with Harry back to the field near the mountain and tried to help him pick up roots. I didn't really do any work, but enjoyed the afternoon out in the sunshine – Gulliver went too. Yesterday Harry sowed the field near the house with wheat. The grain will come up to within a few yards of the cabin on one side, & on the other we are going to have potatoes – at the back there is a little grass & farther back a clump of birch trees, where we have the clothes-line.

Wednesday April 15th

Harry has been off all day harrowing the back field, just coming up for dinner. He was pretty tired tonight, but is drawing a birthday card for Mrs. Riley, & is going to send her a loaf of bread. Uncle has been working at the garden, he sowed a lot of onions, & I put in a row of peas, but the nights are so cold as yet that there is not much use trying to put much in the garden. Harry forgot to take the P.O. keys & as Mr. Bright [the post master] was not there he could not get the mail – we had no chance to get it today, so are still without our letters. I took a sleep this afternoon, & felt quite refreshed.

Thursday April 16th

I wrote to Mr. & Mrs. Lawson today – I don't seem to be in my best writing trim. I was raking up in the garden and got pretty tired – so came in and rested awhile, and then walked along the trail to the field where Harry was working. Gulliver went along, he is getting to be quite a walker now, but wants to follow Harry and the horses, which isn't quite safe when they are harrowing. I lit a fire to burn roots round two stumps, and felt quite like an old Pilgrim father, clearing up land. I have not accomplished very much today, but it was not so hot as yesterday. Mr. Grant was over this morning for some eggs, Mr. Lamley[40] has just been here to ask me down to Enderby again tomorrow. He says he will call for me in the morning and take me down, & guarantee that I'll get home on Saturday, but I am very doubtful about going.

Tuesday, April 21st

Of course I went to Enderby![41] I am getting to be a tremendous gadabout. Mr. Lambly called at about half past nine . . . I enjoyed the drive so much. We stopped at Lansdowne and got my mail, letters from home, Frank, Maude[42] & a card from Nellie saying she was going to sail on the 2nd of May.[43] At Lansdowne we picked up a Mr. Ireland[44] and took him on down to Enderby – such a nice man – an Australian. I went to Mrs. Lambly's to dinner and then over to Miss Shickluna's, where I stayed the rest of the time I was in the town. I had a very happy little visit. We went up to the S. House in the afternoon to prepare for the dance. Mr. Taylor called for us, but when we got opposite the hotel Mr. Gardener came out and said that Mr. Macintyre, the man who owned the violin, had unfortunately never been invited, and it was rather a delicate matter to ask for the loan of his violin when he was not going to the dance, so Miss Shickluna and I went over to visit him, but he was on his dignity, and sent word he was in bed – polite fiction! – so we did not see him, but he lent the violin. Mrs. Bales[45] & Mrs. Morkill were giving the dance & were greatly distressed to find they had neglected to ask Mr. Macintyre, for they hardly knew what to say, it wasn't exactly flattering to tell him the truth, that they had forgotten all about him. I enjoyed the dance, I was just in the humour for talking, strange to say!, and had some very nice companions. Miss

Shickluna & I talked until three o'clock, & then did not get up till nearly nine. We went up again to the ball-room to dismantle it. Mr. Rashdale[46] broke the stove, and we discovered nail holes in the black-board – where the flags & greens had been tacked up, but no one seemed to care. Mrs. Lambly drove me down to Lansdowne and I stayed and had tea with Mrs. Waters at the store. Mr. Wood was away and Mr. Rabbit[47] went while I was there with his two sisters[48] up to the O'Keefes.[49] One of his sisters is quite old, and very stiff & stern, the other is about thirty, & rather bright. After tea we called on Miss Sneider the blacksmith's[50] sister – "All things to all men" is a good motto here. Harry came down for me with Pinto, & I rode home, finding Gulliver all right & glad to see me. On Sunday morning, Harry & I walked over to Pleasant Valley[51] to hear Mr. Wright. There were just ten in the congregation. We tried to sing, but Mr. Wright was slower than Mrs. Waters, & Harry would start in too soon. Mrs. J. Crozier asked us there to dinner, but we wanted to hurry home, however we did not get here very soon for on the way we saw a poor cow stuck in a ditch, and Harry, with two other men, tried to get it out, but did not succeed. When we got here we found Mr. Grant and Ned Thorne[52] here – they stayed to dinner, and after dinner we went down to Lansdowne to church. I was sorry to meet Mr. Joyce, & hear that he was not to take the service. He went to Enderby and Mr. Ford preached. We went up to Mrs. Waters, & had a piece of pie, then home. I finished my letter home and we went to bed early. Monday morning we all got up early. Uncle went off up the lake. I did a washing, while Harry did some work around here,[53] then about half past ten I went with him up to the shop, & held the horses heads while Harry loaded the wheat on the "Go devil." I trembled a little, but managed to do it – we went over to Mr. Swansons and stayed there to dinner. Mr. Swanson gave me a nice little calf, but I don't know whether to bring it home or not. I am afraid Nancy would not adopt it. I came home and Harry stayed in the back field working. I baked pies and cleaned the kitchen floor. Mr. Heathcote & Mr. Burke Taylor[54] were here to tea & stayed all night. Mr. Swanson came in the evening & stayed until ten o'clock – he went to sleep in his chair. I wish I could draw his picture – it would be a treasure to grip. This morning Harry Harding came to breakfast, so I had five in family. After breakfast when they all got off, I did a little gardening, then set at my ironing, and had only got a little done, when I had a very pleasant interruption in the shape of Miss Shickluna. Mr. Riley was going up to O'Keefe's & dropped her here, intending to take her home tonight, but we would not let her go, are going to try and keep her until Friday, when we hope to all go down again to a dance the bachelors are giving. Harry went over directly after dinner to Harry

Harding's (having finished his own piece of seeding) to help him put in his crop. He really ought to be at home, there is so much to do, but Harry Harding could not get any one else to help him. We got a package of trees from home, & I have been busy putting them out. This afternoon Lucy came for her lesson, and I had Minnie, of course all day, which was a great pleasure. It is so nice to have her but I'm afraid I'll feel awfully lonely when she goes. Harry did not get home until nearly eight – we may go over to Harry's with him tomorrow.

Saturday Evening 25th
I am really too sleepy to write properly. I never went to bed atall last night, & have only had 2 hours sleep today, so I am rather heavy & stupid. I have caught a cold too, which does not make me any more brilliant. We did not go to Harry Harding's on Wednesday. It looked so much like rain that Harry went off alone, & we did not get up very early to our breakfast, however it cleared off so nice and fine that about half past nine we decided to walk to town for the mail. We walked down in an hour and five minutes, & intended walking home, but going into the store for some things, Mr. Rabbit offered to drive us home if we would stay until after dinner. This, of course, was too good an offer to be refused so we waited. Mr. Ireland & Mr. Paton[55] had dinner with us at the store. I got a lot of letters, and Mr. Wright gave me some tomato plants and currant cuttings. When we got home, we found that Uncle had come back and Harry had been home. The wind was so strong they could not go on sowing the wheat, so he had left Harry Harding's and come home. Finding we were not there he had gone up to Miles Macdonald's. We hurried up there after him taking Gulliver with us. Miss Shickluna is a splendid walker. We found Harry & Miles sitting on a heap of straw in the stable. After a little rest we came home, and gardened until driven in by a heavy shower. We got our currant bushes in good time – I hope they may live. We planted them up on the knoll. Thursday morning we got up at five, had breakfast, & set off with Harry for Pleasant Valley. We had only one horse for the three of us, so Minnie & I took turns. I am afraid I had the lion's share of the riding though, & enjoyed it. When we got to Harry Harding's cabin, Mrs. Alloway (the woman living there) made us very welcome. Her daughter "a giggling young thing" made taffy for us. We all went out & tried to sow wheat, bothering poor H. Harding sorely I'm afraid, though he is too polite to show any vexation. After dinner we went to see Mrs. Megaw and Mrs. Mulraney.[56] H. Harding has several neighbours in sight, but I'd much rather live here than over there, though one does get a good view of a very lovely country. I liked Mr. Megaw. He took me out and showed me

an old beaver dam and had a great deal to tell me of the mountains and various natural features. He is an observant, intelligent man. I thought of Hubert[57] and his reasonings about an unlettered man taking in so much more of the ways of nature. Of course, Mr. Megaw is not what anyone could call an ignorant man – Harry says he reads a good deal – but he has evidently spared time from books to observe closely out of door objects. He has promised to take me up the mountain over there. Harry could not go with us to old Mrs. Mulraney's. We were sorry & so was she. She made us stay to tea, & went to a lot of trouble to get it for us. I enjoyed it so much – the table linen, china & silver were so nice – & the cookery delicious – Mrs. Mulraney asked Miss Shickluna and me to come together & spend a few days with her. It would be nice if Harry could go too, but I don't like leaving him. We went back to H. Harding's & started home from there, had to pass through the camp where the railway men are stationed.[58] We had a lovely ride home in the moonlight, I again having the best of it, as Minnie preferred to walk. Friday we did some gardening & in the afternoon drove down to Enderby, getting there just in time to get ready for the dance. Miss Sneider lent us her cart & horse, so Minnie & I drove & Harry rode Pinto. The ball was a great success. The bachelors had gone to a lot of trouble decorating the warehouse with wreaths, flags & bunting. They had hung all the walls with coloured blankets and had good music & lovely refreshments – but I did not enjoy it so much as either of the other dances. The night turned very cold, the place was draughty, and I was quite uncomfortable. At last I went over to Mr. Harvey's[59] rooms, Mrs. Gibbs[60] went too, & Mr. Perry[61] & Mr. Costerton.[62] They put up a fire & I enjoyed a cosy little time. Four of the bachelors live there,[63] & keep a Chinaman. We started home at about 3 o'clock & got here at nearly five. Uncle hurried up & got us a fire & a strong cup of coffee, both of which we enjoyed. I did not go to bed as I wasn't sleepy then. I took a little nap later on in the morning and this afternoon I slept 2 hours, but have still enough arrears to make up to be ready to go to bed now at eight o'clock ...

Monday Morning April 27th
... I did not go to church yesterday morning, it looked like rain & I had quite a bad cold so Harry rode down alone, & got home at about one bringing letters from home, Maude & Phil Walker, & a lovely parcel of seeds from James,[64] & a package of geranium slips from Wese. I spent the day quietly writing & reading ... This morning I have been busy putting my geranium slips in cans – I hope they may grow, but I feel very ignorant about any kind of gardening & it seems to me it takes more patience

than any other occupation. Other work one can hurry up by extra effort, but one just has to wait until the seeds are ready to sprout and grow. I have a few sweet peas & garden peas up.

Tuesday Night 28th

Harry & I have just come in from a lovely ride. We went up to Mrs. Pelley's,[65] he on Ethel, I on Pinto. Ethel went well – it will be so nice if Harry can break her for a saddle horse, we'll be able to fly round in fine style. I liked Mrs. Pelley exceedingly, she is an Irish lady, quite pretty, though very delicate looking. Their house is very prettily situated on a hill just at the head of Otter Lake. I enjoyed our call there, but the visit I did enjoy was one we had last night. I wished for Hubert. A traveller came along at tea time, & asked if he might stay all night. He had left his home in Minnesota ten months ago to look for land for himself & seven other men, his brother and brothers-in-law with their families. He said he had been all through Idaho, Montana, Wisconsin & part of British Columbia, & had several times seen enough land for himself & his children, but when he wrote that home to his "Missus" she wrote back that he'd "better keep 'a skiting" till he could get enough for them all. He gave a comical grin and said "I'm 'a skitin' yet." He was en route for the Chilcotin district, about three hundred miles away & then only an uncertainty before him. He has a sister in the Sandwich Islands[66] who wanted him to go & see her on this trip! offered to pay all his expenses, but he thought he couldn't manage it – it would be a little out of his way! She is very well off, her husband is an "architecture." He sang for us somewhat a la Davy Low style and we had quite an evening. He had had nothing to eat since noon the day before, said he wasn't any too neat himself, but he couldn't stand eating with Siwashes,[67] & as he had struck no white people just went hungry. He far exceeded Sara Jeanette Duncan[68] in his graphic power of description. I laughed until I felt almost sick. We had to let him sleep in the stable. Harry hospitably lighted him to bed with a lantern, & he was here for breakfast, starting off cheerfully on his little poney at about seven. He is getting pretty anxious to see his "Missus & the kids." This morning I washed & made a cake after dinner I went over to the back field with Harry to help him by picking up roots, out of the way of the plough. I had to hurry back on account of expecting the fair Lucy. She was here when I came. I gave her her lesson, & some flower seeds, then got tea, & immediately after we went to Mrs. Pelley's. I am having my own time with the garden – what with Gulliver, the chickens & the cats I am afraid I will have a good many things spoiled. I sowed my moon flower seeds today, hope they'll grow.

Wednesday April 29th

Lulie's[69] wedding day! I have thought of her very often, I do hope she had a brighter day than we have had, it had been cloudy since morning & has now begun to pour. Harry & I were going to ride over to the Schuberts, but it is out of the question now. Harry went up to Mr. Grant's early this morning & did not get home till late in the afternoon. I ironed, & then worked in the garden, sowed radish & summer savory seeds. I was so tired this afternoon that I did not do anything but rest & read silly novels.

Thursday

A busy day, I feel rather tired. Harry has gone to town, & as I hope he may possibly bring back some letters I don't want to go to bed. I did some gardening this morning, or rather clearing up. I had two big bon-fires, they were not like those old bon-fires at home, which we always saved until night to burn, because the flames showed off better. I can see now the eager faces peering over the Warren's fence, and the ducky little figures hopping round the big blaze. How we used to enjoy them! I had mine to myself, Harry wasn't here, he was rolling the wheat in the back field, but I nevertheless felt some satisfaction in knowing that I had made one corner of this western wild a little cleaner & tidier ... About 3 I went back to where Harry was & together we went over to the Schuberts to ask for the waggon ... Gus said we might have the waggon on Saturday – we went on however and called on his sister, also his wife.[70] He has one quite pretty sister, Mrs. Le Duc.[71] She, poor woman, is at home with four boys, having had to leave her husband on account of ill treatment. His younger sister, Nora, has been ill with La Grippe ... Harry rode to town immediately after tea, & is not back yet. He has to go out tomorrow with a petition, something about the R.R. station. They are all anxious about here to have it on the "Island."[72]

Friday May 1st

... This has been a rather doleful day – first of all I was so disappointed in not getting my letters off – we missed the stage. I don't see how it got by without our noticing it. Then Harry was digging a flower bed for me when Gulliver came out from under the house, whining & shivering, sick at his stomach & evidently in pain. We poured castor oil down him & did all we could, but I was so afraid he would die. Jim Wright came for Harry to go round with the petition. Uncle was away so I was all alone, & I felt pretty unhappy & discouraged. I never knew I could get so fond of a dog. While he was sick a little bird flew in the kitchen, & I caught it on the window sill ... Uncle & I had just finished dinner when Harry & Jim Wright came for theirs, but Gulliver was getting better – I think he is himself again tonight. I did a little gardening this afternoon & went to sleep. Lucy didn't come for her lesson. Harry went & got the waggon so we will (D.V.)[73] go to town in the morning.

Monday May 4th
... I have not had any time to write since Friday night. We started for town immediately after breakfast Saturday morning, taking eggs & potatoes to the store, & getting quite a lot of provisions to bring back with us ... I had set bread[74] the night before so had to attend to it after dinner,[75] & as we expected Mr. Taylor & Miss Shickluna up I wanted to do some baking. I had left the house all unswept & undusted and was in the midst of my baking when Mrs. Davis, Miss Schnyder and Mr. Dave Wright came. I had to get my hands out of the flour, & entertain them for nearly an hour, then I went back to my work again. I hardly got through before tea time. We had just finished tea when Minnie & Mr. Taylor drove up, so I had to get tea for them, & then we had a nice evening. We had breakfast in good time Sunday morning. Harry got up at half past four & went to town for the mail. He brought me letters from home, Nellie & Carrie Macdonald. Right after breakfast we set out on our trip up to the head of the lake,[76] Harry & Minnie on the front seat, Mr. Taylor & I behind. We had a lovely drive, but I cannot say as much for the service, after we arrived at our destination. It was a Roman Catholic church – we had two priests, one a jolly red-whiskered Belgian, the other a dark, black haired Frenchman who kept his hands (very white ones too) crossed over his breast most of the time. The little church was filled, quite a contrast to any other church I have been in since I came, as the congregations number generally ten or 15 people. Oh! I hardly knew whether to be sad or angry to think of the religious food offered to these poor people – most of them Siwashes.[77] The altar was covered with tinsel flowers, sham gilt candlesticks, & cheap lace, the two were decorated with parti-coloured vestments. It seemed all a type of the religion – so much outside show. I feel so sorry that Minnie belongs to them. It gave me a little frightened feeling. Mrs. O'Keefe asked us to come to her house for dinner, & we went. There are just two houses,[78] Mrs. Greenhow's[79] and the O'Keefes – then there is a post office[80] & a lot of barns & stables. You have to cross a bridge to get to their houses, which are built on a low bit of land, very near the head of the lake, with mountains at the back. They are all R.C.'s. The two priests dined with us at the O'Keefes – were staying there in fact. I rather liked the Belgian (Father Carion they called him) but I did not like the other [at] all. We started home early in the afternoon, drove a little way on to get a glimpse at Lake Okanagan,[81] & a beautiful place it is. When

we got home about half past four we went off to the woods for a walk, and after tea we tried some mind reading, & then some hymns. I don't seem to have had a real Sunday since I came here. Even when I get to my own church, it seems a little like an excursion, there is so much going & coming. This morning Harry & I went to the back field & put in a little garden. We did not get nearly finished – came up home at noon & after dinner drove home with the Schubert waggon – of course we had to walk back, & a good heavy shower came up wetting us a little, we were only too glad however to see the rain.

Wednesday May 6th
Just two months today since I left home, & such a pouring wet day that we have all been driven in. I have written some letters, Harry, Uncle & Gulliver took a sleep after dinner, until awakened by two teamsters taking refuge from the downpour. Yesterday we did a little more gardening and after dinner Harry & I went to the back of the ranch for earth, saw Mr. Swanson looking quite dressed up, actually with a coat on.

Friday May 8th
Clarence's birthday yesterday & I have been thinking of him so often today. I had another visitor today, just as we were half through dinner again. He was a cross eyed man, named Brown, who turned out to be a nephew of Mr. Matthew Martin's – in Dover. He wasn't very interresting. Mr. Rashdale was here to dinner on Tuesday – we were finished when he arrived, but it was a regular downpour when he came in. We have been busy all day yesterday & today gardening – it makes me so tired – but I like it. I do believe a farmer's life is the best after all. I often think of David's wish "let me fall into the hands of God, rather than men" – and it does seem with tillers of the soil that their prosperity depends more directly upon what God sends in the way of weather than that of any other class. I don't like the predictions of summer frosts that we hear so much about – & hope this may be an exceptional season. Lucy came this after-noon for her lesson. I did not get any letters atall this week.

Monday May 11th
Harry & I are alone tonight – Uncle went yesterday up to Mrs. Green-how's while we were in Spallumcheen[82] at church. On Saturday I did some cooking in the morning & had intended going with Harry to the back field, but I felt so tired that I thought I'd lie down with a book instead. Harry came home about five so we had an early tea & went up to Mrs. Pelley's on horseback. We had a lovely ride and I enjoyed our call there. I asked Miss Nona[83] to come down & read with me on Tuesday

afternoon when Lucy is here – so I expect she will be here tomorrow. On Sunday morning Harry & I rode down to church & we met Mrs. Davis going home, so I had to play again – we stayed after church for a little practice, & then I went home with Mrs. Waters for dinner. The Rabbits had gone to Enderby to church & Mr. Wood had not got back from the mines, so we thought we'd be alone, & Fred Heathcote, Burke Taylor and another man all came upstairs intending to stay to dinner, but I presently looked out, & announced that the Rabbits were coming. It was amusing to see the stampede. None of the young men seem to like Mr. Rabbit's sisters, & wouldn't stay. Of course I stayed, & Harry came in as soon as he got the horses attended to – they were all very cordial to us. Miss Rabbit, the elder, was especially kind. She is going to stay & keep house for her brother, so Mrs. Waters will have to leave. She was quite tearful about it, poor old thing ... While in Lansdowne we called at the Pringles, & they told us we might have their cow for the summer if we could feed her & pasture her. We saw her on the way home, & tried to drive her – I flew about quite fast on Pinto heading her off, but Harry was carrying ... eggs so could not do much, so we left the cow, rode home and he went back for her on Pinto bringing her home in a little while. We have quite a family of stock in the field now – 3 horses & 2 cows, but Harry is worrying that there isn't pasture enough for them all. I don't quite know what he will do about it. This morning Harry Harding & Mr. Grant were here, & I washed flannels – after dinner I went to the back field with Harry where we put in beans & a little corn. While we were gone, someone must have been here, for I found a package of sunflower seeds on the window, & something had also been here, & killed one of our Ontario chickens, the only hen Harry fears of the three. We were going for a ride tonight, but I felt too tired, so we have had a little music & are going to bed early.

Thursday May 14th
I have been too busy to write much this week. Nona Pelley came quite early in the afternoon on Tuesday & we had a nice little reading, beginning Motley's History of the rise of the Dutch Republic. Nona has some funny ways of pronouncing big words. After an early tea Harry & I rode home with her, but she had such a slow old horse. We enjoyed the ride home better. Yesterday Harry worked around the place in the morning, & we were having an early lunch at half past eleven when up drove Mrs. Laws, her two daughters & Mr. Hall.[84] I gave them just what we had – they did not stay long, being on their way to Vernon.[85] We set off about one, stopped a while in Lansdowne, & got to Enderby by four. We could not go fast for it was so hot. I went right to the Railway House, & after a

little Minnie & I went up to the store where we found Harry. We had a talk there with Mr. Gardener & Mr. Taylor & then had a walk over the new bridge. We started for home soon after tea, & had a lovely ride, mostly in the moonlight. Today we have just had a lovely half idle day – I have not felt tired atall after the long ride. I expected to be half sick.

Saturday Night May 16th

Mr. Taylor & Miss Shickluna have not come up. I suppose the Reillys wouldn't let her. Uncle came home this morning & is going back again tomorrow to be gone all the week. Harry is going to let a man, Mr. Parke,[86] a teamster, put up his horses here four nights in the week, & get his tea and breakfast with us. Of course, if it doesn't work well we need not keep it up. Yesterday I washed in the morning, & Lucy came in the afternoon, & stayed to tea. After tea Harry & I went home with her, I walking, she on Pinto & Harry on Ethel. After we left her, I mounted Pinto & we went on to the Thompsons.[87] Mrs. Thompson is quite nice – she was a school teacher, but is evidently a little rusty in her grammar. She has a lovely garden. This afternoon I have been framing [pictures of] the house, tannery, & the group of children. Have hung them all up, & made quite a homelike little corner. My right hand is quite sore in the palm – I think I hurt it wringing clothes. I so often think of that sentence "The hand of little use hath the daintier touch." It is true enough – use & beauty may be combined in some things but not very often in a hand. I suppose it is the same all through the heart too that has done hard work passed through rough & weary work may be stronger, but it isn't often sweeter & softer. I think though the world needs strong hearts more than soft ones.

Monday May 18th

It is nearly tea time. I see our teamster[88] has arrived, & is putting out his horses. I have not done very much today, neither has Harry. He went up to the Pelleys this morning to borrow their waggon, & as he had to go on to Eaton's he did not get home until noon. This afternoon he has been working at the stable, but it rained every little while and drove him in. While he was gone this morning I first washed some flannels & then tried to churn – again in the milk pail with the egg beater – but after struggling for nearly an hour & a half I finally had to get Harry to help me with it. We were away all day yesterday. We started for Lansdowne quite early in the morning, riding. Harry had had tooth-ache, & went to see the doctor, but of course he had gone to see his lady love, so we borrowed Mr. Wood's buggy & drove on to Enderby. Mr. Lambly pulled out Harry's tooth. We did not stay there very long, but took Miss Shickluna out to the Fortune's[89] & all stayed there to dinner. Harry then drove Miss Shickluna home, & called for me on his way back. I had a nice talk with Mrs. Fortune, found she had gone to school to Mrs. Renaud for three years in Montreal, & Mrs. Baldwin[90] was one of her fellow students. I ran in for a few minutes to see the Rabbits, & we rode home, getting here about six … We were very disappointed that we got no mail. There was a wreck on the CPR & our mail is either delayed or possibly burned – I hope not the latter.

Sunday May 24th
This has been a horribly hot day – even now at five o'clock it is too warm to be comfortable. I have a whole week to record, & don't feel very much like writing either. I am too wilted. Mr. Parke got here quite early Monday, & came in before tea to get warm & dry. I did not much care for his appearance – a short, fair man, partly bald & evidently over forty. I was half sorry Harry had let him come, but at tea time I knew he was a gentleman. One can always judge pretty well of a man's place in the social scale by the way he eats, & in the evening I found by his conversation that he was an educated man as well … We had a small cyclone in the afternoon & some rain. It only blew down a few panels of our fence, but it blew down a lot of fence of Mr. Macdonald's, & took the top storey off his stable. Mr. Parke was late in getting here, & I began to feel uneasy fearing he might have been hurt by falling trees, but he arrived a little after six. Wednesday morning early Mr. Macdonald was here after Harry to go up & help him with his stable … in the evening Harry & I rode over to the Davis'. Mrs. Davis was not at home. Mr. Joyce & Mr. Parry were just finishing their tea. It looked so funny to see Mr. Joyce washing dishes with a dirty little blue checked jacket on. After a while Mrs. Davis came in, & Mr. Joyce took Harry out, & poured grievances into his ear – Mrs. Davis goes off & leaves them to cook their own meals, or when she does cook for them bakes beef, pork & potatoes all in the same pan without ever washing it in between times. Her house & garden are certainly very dirty and she has lived there since last November. On Thursday Harry was again away all day but I had a call from the Misses Snider, & afterwards the Rev. Wright. Mr. Parke came at six & we had some soup in the evening. Friday morning I got up before five, had a very early breakfast. Harry & Mr. Macdonald were going to town again for lumber, so I rode down with Mr. Parke on his waggon, the seat of which is very nearly as high as our house top. We had a nice, though a very slow, drive – four horses. I found out he is an uncle of Mr. Tom Steven, who used to be Manager of the Federal Bank in Simcoe,[91] and knows some of the Toronto[92] & London[93] people who I do. He ran away from Upper Canada

College when he was fifteen to enlist in the American War, on the Southern side – was taken prisoner, but through his father's influence was
released & brought home – a month afterwards his father died, and he
went into a law office in Toronto, was there two years, passed his exami-
nations and went to practise law in a little country town, but couldn't
stand it, was offered a position as a purser on a Mississippi steam boat &
went off there – stayed three years then went home used up with fever and
ague. After a short stay came out to the W.W. [Wild West] & has never
been back to Ontario since – twenty years ago – he is a rover evidently.
When we got to Lansdowne Mr. Wood had to bring out a step ladder to
get me down from my lofty perch. Mr. Parke left me there & went on to
Enderby & I came home with Harry on the load of lumber. I was counting on a quiet rest, but saw two white figures just turning away from the
gate – of course they came back, proving to be Mrs. Alloway & her daughter – they stayed to dinner & until about four o'clock. Jim Wright was here
too, for about an hour. Harry got back just as the Alloways were leaving,
& soon Harry Harding & Mr. Parke arrived. Harry stayed all night, so I
had them all for tea & breakfast, & Friday night Mr. Dave Wright & Miss
Snider drove out. Saturday Harry was again away & I had no visitors. We
had early tea & Harry rode to town for the mail, I was so anxious to hear
from home. He brought letters from Wese & Maude, with a letter &
package of geranium slips from Emma Inman ... This morning Harry &
I drove down to church but had no service. Mr. Joyce had been ill, came
down at about half past eleven looking very pale & worn. The congregation had scattered, so we decided not to have service, & came right home.
Jim Grinton[94] was here this afternoon, another runaway boy, he left home
when he was eleven & has never been back since.

Tuesday May 27th
I am alone this afternoon – it is so unbearably hot that I don't suppose
Lucy & Miss Nona will come. I think it must be going to rain, the air is
so sultry. We had not had tea Sunday night when Miss Norris & her
brother[95] came – they did not stay very long however. We sat up rather late
– Uncle asked me to write to Aunt Hettie,[96] so I did ... Harry made me
get ready quite early in the morning to go to Enderby if a good chance
offered itself, so I dressed in my light print, but I was truly glad that no-
one passed who he cared to send me with, for the day was so hot. He
worked at the cellar in the morning & in the afternoon we just had a quiet
time together, resting, reading & sleeping. I am sure we enjoyed it far
more than broiling at Enderby. Mr. Parke came at tea time, & we were
just going to have a nice cosy evening when up drove an old man & three

children, who asked if they might come & eat their lunch in the house. This proved to be Dr. Chip, Mrs. Dewdney's father,[97] & the three Dewdney children from Vernon. They had been at Enderby for the celebrations. I thought it rather a cool proceeding myself, but could not refuse very well. They came in – the old Dr. spread out his cakes & sandwiches & producing two bottles asked me to put them in water to cool them – cider & porter – then leisurely proceeded to enjoy first a meal, then a smoke, talking all the time. I liked the children but did not fancy the old fellow much. Mr. Parke went off to the stable when they came. I was quite glad when they got off & we went to bed. Harry & I got up early & I washed, baked, roasted coffee, scrubbed the kitchen & entertained eight new visitors, so I have not done so badly. Mr. Rabbit came in about noon and had some milk & blancmange. Mr. Smith and Mr. Rounding came in for a drink of milk, & after dinner Miles Macdonald & Harry Harding were here … It is beginning to rain. I am glad to see the rain – everything was so dry.

Wednesday
The rain did not amount to very much after all, but it has been cool and cloudy all day today. Harry has been up at Miles Macdonald's helping him with the stable – Harry Harding is there too. When Harry got back from Mr. Swanson's yesterday we had our tea, & he went to town for the mail. I gave Mr. Parke his tea when he came, and then Harry got home so we all talked till bed time. I do believe all the men out here get cynical – poor lonesome things, I don't much wonder! …

Thursday May 28th
I have been alone again today. Harry went up to Miles Macdonald's immediately after breakfast, just coming home for dinner, & going off again. Mr. Smith was here this morning – he says the Rileys won't let Miss Shickluna come up. Mr. & Mrs. Davis & Mr. Joyce were here to tea last night. Mr. Joyce told Harry this was the neatest place in the country, & I believe he wasn't far wrong. He is very miserable – may go home next month instead of early in the Autumn. I liked Mr. Davis – he is very like Mr. Denton in appearance and manner. We had some singing after tea – they did not go until nearly eleven o'clock, & Harry & I got up at five o'clock this morning, so I didn't get my little nap this afternoon …

Friday 29th
I did not write much yesterday, for a restless spirit took possession of me – & I went out to wander in the garden. Mr. Parke came along about four & just got his horses put in when a heavy rain began to fall. He came in,

bringing me a bunch of flowers, & we sat in the kitchen and talked until time to get tea, when he lighted the fire for me, & presently Harry came. He had had tea, so Mr. Parke & I had ours together, and afterwards we had a little music – it was very hard to get up. Harry went over to Mr. Swanson's. Mr. Pelley came bringing me nice radishes, lettuce and cress. It was very kind. This afternoon Harry has gone up to Miles – if Lucy doesn't come I think I'll go & meet him.

Saturday Night

Uncle has just come home – we hardly expected him, as it had got so late, but it takes a good deal to keep him away from home on Sundays[98] . . . We went over to the Schuberts yesterday, taking Lucy & Gulliver with us, the latter very noisy, the former very silent. We got home about six. Mr. Parke did not come until nearly eight o'clock, so when he had had his tea, the evening was nearly over. This afternoon I drove up to the Pelleys with him and walked back. I had to do some cooking & was in the midst of it when Mr. Wood came for "a little visit" – then I had Harry Harding & Mr. Macdonald to dinner, & was tired enough afterwards to rest and sleep for nearly two hours.

Tuesday June 2nd

I am alone again this morning. Miss Shickluna came up with us on Sunday from Enderby, & she and Harry have gone to the back field for earth to put out our moon-flowers. We went down to Enderby Sunday morning, leaving here about half past eight. We went to Lansdowne in the Pelley's lumber waggon, & got Mr. Williamson's buggy there. We got to Enderby in good time and went right up to the Laws. I did not enjoy the service – there is too much attempt at ritual, & more & more that seems so unreal to me. Mr. Sheldrick[99] gave a very good sermon – I liked it. We went up to the Laws for dinner, & afterwards Miss Effie[100] & I went down to the Railway House, & got Miss Shickluna. We went back to the Laws & started from there. Mr. Taylor had intended coming up on Sunday if we had not gone down. We did not get home until nearly seven, & when tea was over & the work done, we were all pretty well ready for bed. We were late getting up Monday morning, & everything seemed to go wrong all day. I fell down twice, upset a pail of water, all over the kitchen floor. Harry was late to dinner (he was working up at Miles) & as we had roast heart I especially wanted to have dinner on time. We left our two Ontario chickens shut up in their barrel all day instead of letting them out in the morning, went out to gather wild strawberries & could only get two or three doz., & last, but not least, one of our little pigs crawled under the curb, into the well & was drowned! I made hot biscuits for tea, & thought they were particularly nice ones, but Uncle said they tasted raw – that made me feel cross – though I managed not to say anything. Mr. Parke was late, not getting here until we had finished our tea. He had a heated axle, & had to come slowly, and altogether it was a dismal kind of a day … We walked up to Miles with Harry after dinner & came home & had a sleep. I am thinking I'll be pretty tired tonight, for we all talked until nearly eleven last night, & I was up before five this morning. I expect Lucy & Nona will be here this afternoon, & then Harry wants to go over to the Graham's[101] tonight, so I won't have any time to rest atall.

Friday June 5th/91

The girls came as I expected on Tuesday and we had quite a nice reading lesson, but I had to almost suggest to them to leave as Harry was in a fever to have an early tea that we might go over to the Grahams to borrow their democrat.[102] We had tea at five, & then drove over in the lumber waggon – we had a little visit at both the Grahams & Mrs. Cummings.[103] I don't care for Mrs. Graham atall. When we got home we found Uncle & Mr. Parke having their tea. I had left it laid out for them on the table. After tea we had music and conversation, & got up quite early Wednesday morning hoping to make an early start for Vernon. We were very much disappointed to find it pouring rain – however after breakfast it looked a little like clearing off, so we concluded that we would start. Uncle preferred driving up on the freight waggon with Mr. Parke, so we called in at the Pelley's and asked either Mr. Pelley or Nonah to go with us – however Mr. Pelley wanted to go, so he got in the back seat with me and we had a very beautiful drive – it was cloudy & breezy but did not actually rain – just a perfect day for a drive, and I fell quite in love with Vernon. As we entered the town we passed a lovely old orchard of fruit trees, & there are a good many cotton wood trees all through the town, such a relief after these stiff spikey pines, which I am getting so tired of. We had dinner at the hotel, meeting Mr. Smith there – then Harry took us up to call on Mrs. Ellison.[104] Her house looks more like a home than any I have seen. We went at once into a long low room – with some pretty pictures on the wall – & a nice piano – little evidences of taste & refinement were there, & when Mrs. Ellison appeared I liked her too. She is a tiny little thing, very merry & bright. She has asked me to go up for a couple of weeks. After we left there Minnie & I went to call at Mrs. Dewdney's. Mr. Dewdney[105] (a brother of the Dewdney of Riel Rebellion fame[106]) is Registrar & manager of the County Court business. They have quite a nice place. Mrs. Dewdney was very kind, insisted on our coming back & having a cup of tea with her before we left. We went back to the hotel however to find Harry and went with him to inspect Mr. Parke's quarters – "The Saint's Rest." Mr. Parke did the honours & introduced us to his partner, Mr. Macdougal.[107] We had a walk on the board side-walk which was quite a treat. We started for home at about half past four – we came the back way – a road through the woods the greatest part of the way ... We had got just about to the Thompsons when a tremendous storm came up – rain, hail & wind – we were drenched right through to the skin. Little Gulliver was pretty glad to see us – the poor little soul had been shut up all day. Yesterday we did some gardening. Uncle came home at night. I don't know when he is going away again. Today it has been cold & cloudy – I daresay it will freeze again tonight.

Saturday June 6th
Exactly three months today since I left home! It is quite cold tonight – we are glad to have a warm fire in the kitchen. Harry & Uncle are sitting beside it now, while I write. Mr. Smith has just come for Minnie & taken her away. I was very sorry to have her go – I have enjoyed having her here so much – last night we had quite a little concert – we all sang. Minnie has not much of a voice, sweet but weak – mine of course isn't any good. Mr. Parke & Uncle were both hoarse, so Harry was really the only one who sang well – but we didn't mind – we did our best & laughed at each other. This morning ... we did some gardening, & this afternoon Minnie & I picked enough wild strawberries for tea. So we had hot biscuit, pressed beef, strawberries & cream, cocoa & cookies – not bad for a western wild! We were beginning to hope that Mr. Smith wouldn't come tonight but he did. I think Minnie enjoyed herself. She is a dear loveable little thing. I wish she could have stayed a month ...

Wednesday June 10th
It is after nine o'clock & quite light outside. Harry hasn't quite finished his night work – he has just brought me home from the Pelleys – I went up to spend the afternoon – walked up – as Harry was afraid to let me ride Pinto. He has not been ridden for some time, & is very lively. We went to Lansdowne on Sunday – walked down for the mail – we intended to come straight back, but went into the Williamsons, & a great rain came on so they persuaded us to stay to dinner, & after dinner Mr. Williamson drove us home. He also drove his wife & friends up, & they came in and stayed to tea – Mr. Grant, too, was here, and Mr. Ireland & Mr. Barclay called in the afternoon, so it wasn't a very quiet Sunday. I don't like Sunday here. On Monday I did a lot of work, & Mr. Parke came quite early, so we had tea in good time and argued all the evening. Tuesday Lucy & Nonah came quite early, & we had a nice long reading. It isn't much like our old

reading class, when I was a co-learner – with these girls I feel more like a teacher. I gave them a glass of milk & they went off about half past five. Harry had gone to town for the mail – he & Mr. Parke got here about half past seven & we all had tea together – then another talk until nearly eleven o'clock. I am afraid I argue too much – there are so few things we all agree on – & sometimes I believe they just talk to set me going. Nonah asked me to go up there & spend the day – I went early after dinner & had such a nice talk with Mrs. Pelley. I really enjoyed it very much – I like her better each time I see her.

Saturday June 13th
I am alone. It is a lovely damp day, not too hot. I have been taking a little rest after setting out some celery plants. On Thursday I churned & did some gardening in the morning, & after dinner Harry & I picked wild strawberries for tea. Mr. Parke came early. I like his Vernon days best. Friday morning I went down to town with him, & again the step ladder was brought into requisition. I stayed a couple of hours – did a little shopping, & drove home with Mr. Rabbit and his sister. It wasn't very comfortable, for they had the new organ for the church on, & a lot of stores for the mines. I liked the drive down far better, but didn't want to wait until Mr. Parke came back. I did some more gardening – we had tea – Mr. Parke was late. He said Mr. Gibbs told him that I was the only Canadian lady he had met who he did not feel called upon to talk nonsense to. Mr. Parke said his patriotism compelled him to retort that maybe Mr. Gibbs experience of the better class of Canadians had been limited ... It rained all this morning, so Mr. Parke stayed until after dinner. He & Uncle sat in the kitchen all the morning – & I had to churn, make bread & pies & get dinner. I suggested their coming in here as I wanted to sweep, so they moved with apparent reluctance, & I thought I got rid of them for the rest of the morning, but the dust was no sooner gone than they posted back, & settled themselves down again. Harry was out cutting grass in most of the rain ...

Sunday, 14th June 1891
Mr. Taylor & Mr. Reeks came up this morning, & were here all day – they have only gone a little while ago. Mr. Rabbit came along with his sisters & Miss Shickluna – the latter got out & went on home with Mr. Taylor. I am afraid they are getting wet, as it is raining quite heavily. I cannot write any more until I can get a new book – they have none in Lansdowne, but I'll be able to get one in Enderby if I go on Tuesday ...

CHAPTER 2

The real, the useful, the necessary — these occupy one here

Life in the Spallumcheen Valley

Volumes 2 to 5 of the diaries were written during the remainder of 1891 and the spring of the following year. The grind of daily life was unavoidable, but for the most part Alice undertook her household tasks with good grace. Harold Parke continued his dogged pursuit, but the sparkling eyes of stagecoach driver Bob Hall also impressed her. The change of seasons and the beauty it brought to the landscape moved her deeply, and she wrote feelingly of the valley landscape. Receiving and paying visits played an ever-increasing role in her life as she developed friendships with the settlers, and she filled her pages with vignettes, by turns serious and amusing, of many of them. Alice and Harry spent hours in the evening reading the classics aloud; during 1891 and 1892 they made their way steadily through several Dickens novels. Alice also acted as nurse to both Harry and Uncle while they were sick and cared for them with great compassion.

The railway station was taking shape on the swampy island that later became the centre of the town of Armstrong, and Alice followed its construction closely. She continued to welcome Nonah Pelly and Lucy Crozier to the ranch for "readings" to improve their minds, and the girls attended faithfully. Despite the disparity in their ages, a close friendship began to develop between Alice and the oldest Pelly child. The settlers relaxed with a series of concerts and socials, at which Harry Barrett was often the star turn. Alice continued to write letters to family and friends every day.

She began to come into contact with local aboriginal people, and her reactions to them were a combination of curiosity, fear, revulsion, and superiority — a blend that was typical of the settler society of the time and that was never challenged. Her attitudes were set, and she did not question her assumptions. She did not speak Chinook and never had intimate enough contact with the local aboriginal bands to be able to reconsider her attitudes.

The remainder of her promised year in the Okanagan flew by, and she recorded events and people diligently. Harold Parke pursued Alice in his usual calm, methodical, and gently romantic way.

Mr. Parke churned and washed the dishes for me. It looks so funny to see a man doing work of that kind. He is very nice to me. [22 June 1891]

Yesterday I got up rather late & had to fly to get breakfast – I made pancakes and Mr. Parke fried them. [1 July 1891]

I was writing when Mr. Parke came and as usual he sat down and talked until tea time. We never do much in the evening – by the time our work is finished we are ready to chat until bed time. Last night we had a little supper of strawberries & cream *and* cake. [3 July 1891]

Mr. Parke was late last night – we waited until nearly seven & then had tea without him. He came just as we were finished. He brought me some oranges. [4 July 1891]

Mr. Parke came along while I was there, & when I got back he & Harry came in the house, & talked nearly all the rest of the afternoon. We had tea early, & Harry went over to Mr. Swanson's for a tongue. Mr. Parke & I went up the road and gathered a lovely bunch of flowers. [8 July 1891]

Mr. Parke came early too, & I came in again to give him a glass of milk, & then stayed reading that ridiculous book to him and talking. [14 July 1891]

Saturday morning when we awoke it was pouring rain ... so Mr. Parke thought he would not go until afternoon. We made good use of him all the morning, for the night before a mink had come and killed twenty of our young chickens. Of course they were perfectly good as it had bled them – so Harry and Mr. Parke picked twelve and I cleaned them & cooked them in all sorts of ways ... we had quite a grand dinner – spring chickens, new potatoes, green peas. [19 July 1891]

Mr. Parke came along – when we were coming home quite a heavy shower came up, & I made rather a laughable picture rolled up in Mr. Parke's light rubber coat & the waggon sheet ... When I got home I got tea ready – I fried some of the beef, and we had peaches & cream ... Mr. Parke helped me water the cucumbers and tomatoes ... [25 July 1891]

Mr. Parke came back from Enderby with a headache, but he helped me water the garden after tea. He brought my raspberries – 14lbs. – lovely ones too. [30 July 1891]

Mr. Parke came early & he helped me get tea – we were very late, not finishing until about eight o'clock. [1 August 1891]

Mr. Parke was late getting here this afternoon, and I had visions of an upset on the Pelley's hill, and all sorts of direful accidents – but he arrived safely at about four o'clock. [6 August 1891]

It was very cold – froze a thick ice, and touched my geraniums, so Monday afternoon I set to work to pot them. Mr. Parke came early and helped me get earth for them. [24 September 1891]

I quite forgot the most important item of the week – Mr. Parke brought me a dear little dog on Monday, a brown spaniel pup – such a pretty little fellow, but he made night hideous with his howlings the first two nights he was here, and poor Gulliver was consumed with jealousy. They are both in a happier frame of mind now. We have named the little fellow Jeremiah, with Jerry for an everyday name. It seems queer for me to have a pet dog. I always professed a dislike for pets of all kinds – and dogs in particular. I have changed a good many of my lines of action out here. [24 September 1891]

Mr. Parke never came at all yesterday – I felt a little uneasy at this. I thought probably something unimportant might have detained him – it turned out to be a broken axle. He came this morning, had dinner here, and went on to Enderby – will be here on his way back tomorrow, and after this week I think he will have only one more week of freighting. I am sorry, but he says he will come quite often.
[29 September 1891]

Mr. Parke left this morning, and does not expect to be here any more, except that he will be coming often to visit us, we hope. He will be in the office in Vernon most of the time. [10 October 1891]

[Harry] brought letters from home – and here I have a confession to make to my poor old book. I thought I had quite outgrown the age of inspiring or feeling love – I mean falling in love – but! even I in this out of the way place have been indulging in a little romance. Mr. Parke asked me quite a long time ago to marry him and I said no – a good many times – because I could not bear the thought of ever coming so far from home. But at last I have written home about it, and this mail brought an answer from Mother and Wese[1] – I am afraid it has made them unhappy, and that grieves me terribly. I don't love him well enough to marry him unless they are perfectly willing at home. I cannot imagine any woman loving one man so well that it dulls her love for those who have been near & dear to her all her life. [21 October 1891]

… dear Mother and Wese! I know they are worrying over the fear of my deciding to come out here, and when I think of home I almost feel that I *cannot* give it all up – but I think I do feel more as if I fitted here than any- where I have been.[2] A very homely illustration came to my mind today. I was thinking of Mother's old-fashioned fruit bottles, that she sealed up with corks and resin. I remember she used to get corks and bottles ready, & place them carefully so that she would fit the proper cork in its own bottle – sometimes it needed much squeezing and pressing, but when it was in there it stayed, and kept the fruit perfectly until we were ready to use it. But trying to force in a cork too large or too small always proved disastrous. I feel as if I were a cork being squeezed into the right bottle – here. [25 October 1891]

Parke continued the courtship by letter:

I ought to be happy – I had such lovely, loving letters from home friends and *Vernon*.[3] I do think everyone loves me too well. We also got splendid photographs of Clarence & Hubert, & Walter sent me a new exercise book for a diary – I will soon be needing it. Each one at home wrote me for my birthday, which will be on Thursday. I will be thirty years old – heigho! I ought to know that I am too old to be thinking of making a new home. It has always seemed to me that that needs youth, and the energy and hopefulness of youth, rather than the superior experience of older years. [3 November 1891]

They are so kind at home about my little affair – thinking first of my hap- piness – I dare not be altogether selfish when everyone is so thoroughly unselfish towards me. I wish I could please them all but, in this case, that seems impossible. [3 November 1891]

I got a lovely present today – Harold sent me a Russia leather portfolio. He intended it for my birthday, but did not get it in time. He is coming down tomorrow or next day. He sent a little note in the portfolio. It is very nice, but I don't like to think of discarding my old one – it has been my companion for so long. I will never like any other as well. I remember as well as any thing the day I got it. All at home gave it to me just before I went to Toronto – fifteen years ago. If it could write a story, what a lot of nonsense it would bring to light. All the letters I have written on it. My new one has some paper & envelopes in it. I will have to begin a new volume tomorrow. [16 November 1891]

When the stage came along Mr. Hall gave me a newspaper, from Harold, and it had a lovely pair of buckskin gloves in it. They fit beautifully and will be very useful, especially if I ride at all ... [1 December 1891]

Mr. Hall brought me a letter from Harold. He is sick. I am quite worried. [7 December 1891]

I told Uncle about [Harold] this morning – he seemed rather surprised – said he had suspected long ago that he was smitten, but could not tell about me. He said "Well, my dear, I think you have made a wise choice[4] – as far as I know the man." [4 January 1892]

Harold & I had a long talk together. He showed me a plan of a house which he may build next summer. It is small, but would be cosy I think. He wanted to start for Vernon about five, but wouldn't leave me alone ... [11 January 1892]

Mr. Parke had come down the night before. I was dreadfully disappointed to hear that I had missed him, for I don't know when he will get down again. Monday will be his birthday. I wish I could see him then. [23 January 1892]

... Harold come down for the day and wanted to start back as early as possible. He was going to have a very busy day tomorrow, and indeed a very busy week. He was rather low spirited as he has not had much good news from his mother. I am afraid she won't get better. I do wish he could go home. We stayed quietly at home all day ... Harold and Mr. Macdougal are going in partnership with Smith,[5] who has the saw mill. I hope it may turn out well, the prospects look good. [28 February 1892]

When Harry got here he had a box of fruit for me – Harold had sent it down from Vernon by Mr. Rabbit – and a letter was in it, telling me his Mother is dead. I am so sorry. I can't think of anything else much. Her improvement only lasted a little time. I feel so very sorry he did not go at once – there are always so many regrets – when it is too late! Is it ever too late though – this world does not end all. Ah! if it did – how could we bear the imperfections, the miserable beginnings that only show what might have been done had we started soon. Yes, but thank God! they show too what *may* be done on a higher plane in another life. [12 March 1892]

Only fancy having wild flowers in March. Harold brought me some yesterday. He came down in the morning – it was a delightful day. We went for a walk in the afternoon and the rest of the day just talked quietly in the house. Harry and Uncle were here too. Harold had the plan of a house which he brought for my inspection. It was very nice. He thinks he will soon begin to build. He is to have the office at the Mill in Vernon, so thinks he will get a lot near the mill. It is a little way out of town, but will be all the nicer for that. He was very hopeful over the business. We had a long talk about his Mother – & he was telling us more about his family. He stayed until this morning. I drove with him a couple of miles & walked back. [21 March 1892]

[Harold] has bought a lot up on the hill, & says nice people have already bought near him. [8 April 1892]

Sometimes I wonder if I ought to have promised to come back – I get so homesick. [14 April 1892]

... Harold drove up. He stayed until this morning, so we did not do much but talk ... [16 May 1892]

I told Mrs. Pelley that I may come back here to live, & she, of course, was pleased. [22 May 1892]

Yesterday morning Harold came down quite early. I had made two pies in the morning and was just changing my dress when I heard his voice. We only had a cold dinner, and stayed quietly here all day, for it was very hot ... Harold drove down from Vernon with Mr. Cochrane[6] and wanted to go back by train. [25 May 1892]

Robert Storey Hall, the handsome English-born stagecoach driver, had met Alice soon after her arrival and stopped regularly at Mountain Meadow to pick up the mail. He was very taken with her:

Mr. Hall was alone, & wanted me to go for a drive, but, of course, I could not go. [21 December 1891]

Mr. Hall said he would come to dinner on Xmas, but I don't know if this delay will make any difference. He usually goes up to Vernon on Tuesday, or to the Mission[7] on Wednesday, back to Vernon Thursday, & then down past here to Sicamous on Friday. He seemed to want to drive with us. I hope he'll be able to. [22 December 1891]

I went to Enderby Monday morning with Mr. Hall. We had a cold but very pleasant drive. He drove me up to the Lawes house and would not let me pay him. He was so kind and nice ... [30 December 1891]

I got up to find Mr. Hall had run in to say this is his last trip.[8] I am so sorry – all our letters will have to be posted in the post office now. [16 January 1892]

... Mr. Hall came along. I got him some lunch and he began to beg me to go to Vernon with him, to the Ellisons. When Harry came in he added his persuasions, so I went, Mr. Hall promising to bring me back next day if I wanted to come. [23 February 1892]

After dinner Mr. Hall did not stay long. I sewed some buttons on his overcoat for him, and asked him to try & come down to spend a Sunday with us. [23 February 1892]

Alice's brother Harry continued his courtship of the young Ontarian Minnie Shickluna, who had visited relatives in the Okanagan for a few months:

I have still another romance to confide to my old diary, but I think I am too sleepy tonight – it must wait until tomorrow. [4 November 1891]

... now for the romance – Harry's this time. He is in love with Minnie Shickluna, and she with him. It has been going on more or less all summer, and sometimes I have felt very troubled. I seem to have had so many perplexities and responsibilities thrust on me this summer. Minnie is a dear, sweet little thing, but she is a Roman Catholic! And though I think she is by no means a bigot, one never can tell what these priests will do. I dread them – & fear them. Harry says a priest shall never have any power in his house, and I really believe that Minnie may turn before long. She will be away from her own people and to tell the truth I am glad she will be away from the Rileys, for though they have been kind enough to me, Mrs. Riley had not been nice to Harry since this came out. I cannot understand why, except that he is a rancher, and not a very rich one, & a Protestant. But Mrs. Riley herself is not an R.C. and Mrs. Paterson is married to a Presbyterian, so they cannot consider a difference in creed of such vital importance. Minnie says Mr. Gallagher wants to marry her, and Mrs. Riley favours his suit – but he is a horrible man. If only I knew what they will say at home! I feel oh! so glad to think of Harry having a home. He needs some incentive to work. He gets terribly low-spirited sometimes, but has seemed so happy since Minnie's letter came on Tuesday, saying her Father & Mother did not object.[9] What a summer this has been for love making! I was reading in a paper that it is the suicidal mania sometimes strikes the earth as an epidemic, and citing Boulanger and Balmecida,[10] drew grave predictions for the coming year. I don't know about suicides, but I do believe falling in love is catching. [5 November 1891]

[Harry] got nice long letters from all at home about his engagement – and one from Minnie. She is a good, sweet girl – I hope & think they will be happy if they marry. [25 November 1891]

[Harry] said last night "There is no use talking – I'll never get a wife who will do as much for me as you do" – but I hope he may. Oh! I would like to see him in a happy home of his own. [28 November 1891]

The romance faded. Minnie did not return to the Okanagan after her journey east. Her parents were living in Chicago and she died there in 1902 at the age of 28, from complications arising from diabetes.

Meanwhile, household chores continued to occupy much of Alice's time:

Yesterday morning I ironed two print dresses, churned, washed my hair, made lemon pies and a cake, & got dinner – so I was pretty tired by noon, but only had a little rest before Lucy came. [5 July 1891]

Tuesday morning I washed, baked bread, boiled meat, stewed peaches, & was a very busy creature generally. [14 July 1891]

This morning I was very busy – washing, churning, cooking – as Harry says it is a "grind" or would be if one's thoughts had to be on one's work. [27 July 1891]

Mr. Hays was here this morning, so I had the men to dinner. I had intended ironing this morning, but I had to churn, attend to the bread, cook beets, carrots & potatoes, boil a shank & cut the meat[11] up for hash – & just as I thought I'd have a minute's breathing space Mr. Hays ran over a hen in the meadow, cutting its legs half off, so Harry cut its head off & brought it in – & I had that to pick & clean. I roasted it for tea. I was glad when dinner was over & now the bread is all baked too, so I think I'll take a little rest, although I really want to write some letters. [28 July 1891]

I have everything to make me conceited out here – I do really feel of great use. I have been so busy since I came back [from Vancouver] that I have not had time to write. Everything in the way of clothing was soiled, so I have had great washings – & they were pretty hungry for dainty cooking, so I have been busy enough. [17 September 1891]

Harry says I have earned a man's wages today, and I am sure I have earned more than a man's weariness. I am awfully tired. We have picked over all the potatoes into sacks, & Harry carried them to the cellar. We have about two tons of big ones (they count everything by weight here) and half a dozen sacks of smaller ones – and of course we have been using potatoes for the house since August, & have been feeding small ones to the cow for about a month, so I don't think it was a bad yield for half an acre of ground. We got the cabbage in too, and none too soon. We pulled them last night and put them in a heap covered with blankets and an old coat. [11 November 1891]

I am sure a good housekeeper would pronounce me sadly shiftless, for at half past six I have a pan of bread still unbaked. I set the bread last night, but when this morning broke fine & frosty and Harry suggested a walk to the Hardings, I could not resist, so I left the poor bread to rise in a cold house, with very poor results. I have been trying to coax it up ever since we got home at half past two, but it is very sulky. [9 December 1891]

On Thursday Harry & I did a great housecleaning. We took up the carpet, turned everything but the book-case out of the room. Harry mopped the floor and then we whitewashed and oh! such a mess we made of everything. We spattered the floor, & ourselves and the stove – fortunately I had dressed the book-case up in a sheet so it escaped. We did not get done until dark, & then the floor had to be washed again. We sat down to tea ... quite satisfied with the result of our work. [12 December 1891]

Alice was willing to help with outdoor chores as well:

I have been helping Harry clear up around the hen house. This is a very grand one – much better looking than the cabin. Uncle is spending a lot of work on it, & Harry is "mudding up" the sides – such a funny performance. He stands about two yards off, and throws a mixture of hay and mud between the cracks of the logs, then plasters it in tight with a wooden paddle – this makes it very warm inside. [19 September 1891]

The last day of September. Fall seems here in earnest now. Harry & I have had a great clearing up in the woodshed, and had a bonfire of rubbish. [30 September 1891]

I saw an interesting enough sight this morning – a steam thrashing machine at work. I went over to the back of the ranch directly after breakfast and inspected the whole performance, and was especially interested in one Indian who was pulling away the straw. He rode on a rail up to the top of the stack, & I would have like to have one trip on it, but did not dare to ask. [9 October 1891]

[Harry ploughed] the piece [of land] up here where we had potatoes last year, and as he turned out a lot of nice potatoes which he had missed in the Fall I had an excuse to stay out doors & pick them up. I like working outside, but it makes me very tired ... I went out this afternoon & picked up the rest. [25 March 1892]

After dinner Harry & I went up to the old cabin, & were most of the afternoon working at the carrot bed. I sowed the seeds but Harry did all the rest. [3 May 1892]

Alice felt a great need to include in the diaries her thoughts and reflections on all kinds of subjects:

I am often quite glad to be left alone a little – of course I don't mind if Harry is around the house all the time, but anyone else gets tiresome, for it is such a small house that you have to be near together in it. I believe that is why people need to love each other a great deal better to be happy if poor than if they are rich. In a big house they have room to live farther away from each other in spirit as well as in body. [28 June 1891]

We got into a great discussion of the merits & demerits of constancy and fickleness. I am afraid I shocked Mrs. Lawes by some of the views I advanced. Sometimes I really believe that at the bottom of my heart I am both frivolous and fickle – but I have lived so long with good & noble people that a kind of superstructure of their opinions and beliefs has reared itself on the native soil. Only when any unusually deep or strong emotion gets stirring up the old natural soil, the upheaval shows the true nature of the place. [28 June 1891]

This is a terribly dull life for youth & energy – it is well enough for those who have lived their most intense days. I think older people often forget the craving – the real *need* – of youth for pleasure & excitement. A repressed nature is very apt to break bounds some day, perhaps in a dangerous, damaging way. [1 July 1891]

I think there is something in the air out here which makes one less industrious – men & women all seem ready to waste so much time. I wouldn't think it wasted if the conversation were atall edifying, but it isn't very often. [7 August 1891]

Soon I'll have been here 7 months, & I feel like quite a different person from the girl who left home that morning. I was thinking of those winters I used to spend in Toronto, & could hardly believe this is the same Alice Barrett. I suppose it takes a very adamantine character not to be influenced by circumstances & companions. The real, the useful, the necessary – these occupy one here, rather than the amusing and pleasant. Not that the latter elements are quite lacking here, but they are accidental, not the business of life. Sometimes I think I like this best – and then sometimes a very strong longing for a really giddy exciting time seizes me. I don't suppose it would be very good for me though. I have excitement too, and interest, but not of the frivolous kind – it is all so intense. I suppose all rather lonely lives are – it needs the stirring of a crowd to make froth. [4 October 1891]

I do love to see a place freshly cleared up. I always vow I don't like system, but in some things I can appreciate the fact that "order is heaven's first law." [24 October 1891]

I am thirty years old today! Quite an old maid. Just eight months ago tonight, the last night I spent at home – I remember I felt so unhappy, and it seemed as if a year would never go by. Now two thirds of it have passed. I never spent a birthday so far from home. I wonder where I will be on my next birthday – perhaps not here at all. I may never see another one on this earth, or I may live to be very old. Oh! I do hope I'll be able to do something useful and good – my time seems so filled with trifles. [5 November 1891]

I do love every word of my home letters. They are so good to me – I feel bowed down with humility for having so much love showered on me. [14 November 1891]

I wonder where the end of this year will see us – God grant it may find us better and nearer to Himself. [2 January 1892]

For that new wild life a man needs a peculiarly strong and yet flexible character. If he be of a nature that too readily can suit himself to circumstances he is apt to sink to fit his surroundings. On the other hand, if he cannot put up with the absence of luxury & refinement his life must be a kind of purgatory. Very few are able to raise their surroundings to meet them, though, thank God, there are both men and women who live noble, loving, true lives in [the] Wild West as in the older East – in backwoods as in cultured drawing rooms – & they are a boon and a blessing wherever they are. I think, though, that even the strongest feel a longing sometimes for the ease and rest that wealth and luxury (in its ideal sense) bring. [26 January 1892]

It matters very much to me what – & *who* – my surroundings are. I know in theory & in one way of looking at the truth

  "Stone walls do not a prison make" etc.

but it needs a strong and noble mind to live above circumstances, or else a hard unfeeling heart. The latter, I hope, is not mine, and the former, alas! I know I have no pretensions to. [10 February 1892]

How scattered [we Barretts] are, and yet how near we are in spirit. I think more & more the Heavenly Home grows dear to me – for there we need never again be apart from those we love. I suppose when our spirit is freed from its earthly part space will be nothing. We can in reality travel as far and as fast as our mind does now. [23 April 1892]

I suppose there is no genius [in me], & very little originality, for I do like well-beaten paths – and established conventionalities. Of course I would not like to be slave to them, & never be able to get over the fence of custom, but one feels safer in the main on a thoroughfare than in a lonely way. It takes so much courage & self-reliance to choose out a new path, & sometimes one finds after all the hard struggling that it doesn't lead to anything so good as old beaten way reached. [25 April 1892]

Alice was not immune to the accidents that plagued many of the population:

We were coming along in great style – I was getting a little too proud & reckless & in turning a corner (the horses running) I lost my balance & was thrown off – fortunately striking my head first, it being my tough spot. Harry was very frightened and no wonder – it is a wonder & a mercy that I wasn't killed or at least some bones broken – but I have escaped with a very sore side, & bruises all over my body – I think I struck on every side & every bone, knees, back, shoulder & sides being bruised. I have not felt up to much today. [14 July 1891]

I was disappointed at not getting to church today, but my side began to hurt again last night when we were riding home, so Harry wouldn't let me go today. I put my hand up to my head, which startled Pinto, & she jumped, giving me a fresh wrench – I wonder if I have cracked that rib again. I nearly fell off the horse, & it hurt me so I cried. I frightened Harry, & made pretty much of a goose of myself. [19 July 1891]

... when we were on our way home, we had quite a little excitement. Some silly person has thrown a lot of empty barrels just at the turn of the road on the top of Deep Creek Hill. We noticed them going to town & Ethel, the silly horse, noticed them too, and was disposed to be frightened, but got by all right. Coming home, Harry said "It will be a bad thing if Ethel starts to run at the top of the hill." Sure enough she was frightened and began plunging & shaking – but he had her well in hand & under control when just as we turned the corner there were two squaws. They began to scream and run for the bank at the highest side of the road – which scared Ethel more than ever, & worst of all one of the squaws fell right under Ethel's feet. Harry, to escape running over the woman, had to pull out on the very brink, & I don't think either of us would have been much surprised if we had gone over. We were very thankful, though, that no-one was hurt & Harry got the horses stopped about half way down the hill. We waited until the squaws came up laughing and chattering. Harry asked them if they would ride and they scrambled in, and kept up a jabbering & laughing all the way. They evidently thought it a joke, but it came very near being something else. One of them (not the one who fell) was young and quite good-looking. They had handkerchiefs tied on their heads, bare hands and only thin thaws about their shoulders, but seemed quite warm & content. [29 January 1892]

Entertainments were welcome diversions from the daily struggle for existence:

The concert has come and gone & Harry was undoubtedly the star of the evening ... Mrs. Marwood sang very nicely – and Mr. Hicks, the new Methodist man, had a sweet plaintive voice. He sang "'Tis but a little faded flower" and Dr. Offerhaus thundered out "Rocked in the cradle of the deep" – he has a good voice, but his German pronunciation makes it sound queer, & he hasn't very much idea of how to manage his voice. We had raspberries & ice cream and cake during an intermission. Harry had sung at the first of the evening, and then his name was on for the last song. He sang the "Slave Chase" first, with "Paddy's Dream" for an encore. I accompanied him, but for his last song he sang, without any accompaniment, "Time enough for that, said I" – and literally brought down the house. I think Mr. Wright had got anxious to have the thing finished, & he said "When Mr. Barrett's song is ended we will all rise & sing God

Save the Queen," but even he laughed & encored with the rest until Harry had to go back & sing "The Exciseman." [24 July 1891]

[We] dressed and went over to the dance. We had great fun – I quite enjoyed it, though I would think myself crazy if I were to go to one like it at home. Mrs. Graham & Mrs. Meighan had their babies there, tucked up in shawls & bundled away on old school benches, which were moved back against the wall. The music was execrable, and they "called off" the square dances, the figures of which were wonderful to behold. Lizzie & Harry Harding were there & Lizzie did her duty bravely, dancing with everyone who asked her. [16 January 1892]

The only major trip Alice undertook during her stay at Mountain Meadow was a visit to the coast. In July 1891, Alice was invited by Lizzie Harding to go to Vancouver, so she began to plan the first long journey ever undertaken on her own. While there, Alice went sight-seeing and entered into lively and spirited conversations with the Harding girls and their friends:

Vancouver.[12] I have at last had an experience of travelling alone, and it was not anything extraordinarily exciting after all ... Monday morning ... at half past two, I started – on the Jenny Lind – for Sicamous. It is a little steam car – open – holding eight passengers and the engineer. It was quite full – indeed we had to leave three passengers behind in Enderby. We spun along at a good rate and reached Sicamous before six ... We found the train was to be an hour & a half late, so decided to get our dinner at the Colonels. Mr. Hall, (the stage driver) had come with us, also Effie Lawes, & we saw Mr. Bannerman at Sicamous – he had come by boat. We four had dinner together – both Mr. Bannerman & Mr. Hall wanted to pay for my dinner, but I would not let them. Mr. Hall was awfully kind – he stayed with me, saw after my luggage, took me on the car & put me in the porter's charge – & at last I was off on a journey looking after myself. I got my berth made up & very soon went to bed. I was so tired, but it was a long time before I slept, and then only a troubled, broken sleep – I am a poor traveller, I think. There was a very nice lady in the berth opposite me – we talked a good deal – and a funny old man, who grew very confidential, asked me if I was married, and then if I thought him too old to be married a second time! He is a widower. He knew the line pretty well, & pointed out the spots of interest. I stayed in the observation car a good deal – all along the grand scenery by the Frazer.[13] It is very beautiful. I enjoyed it better than the Rockies – I suppose because I was not so tired.

We reached here about one and there was no-one to meet me. After looking around for a little, I decided to take a cab, & come up. Fortunately I had the house address, so found it without any difficulty – & Lizzie [Harding] at home. She had never got my letter – I don't see what can have become of it. The other girls are at school.[14] They have such a nice large house in a very pretty situation – a little ravine and bridge at the back, a creek called False Creek[15] running up quite close. It is in a new part of the town. [18 August 1891]

... It is a very queer change into this household of spinsters – from the ranch with its old bachelors. Mary[16] & Maggie[17] seemed very pleased to see me – they have another teacher living with them, a Miss McDougal, a big, fat, red-faced girl, but nice & refined in her conversation and her ways ... This is a queer place. There are some very nice large buildings, good shops & pretty residences, but right in the midst of them rize old blackened tree stumps, and all the streets except the principal business ones are a tangle of ferns – they grow like weeds – a tall coarse variety, looking so strange in city streets. This part of the town[18] is a good way from the shops and is full of ravines, which have pretty, picturesque little bridges built over them, adding greatly to the beauty of the place. We do not see the Gulf[19] from here – only the Inlet[20] – but it and False Creek are affected by the tide – the water almost all leaving the latter for part of the day, and then slowly coming back, until there is a wide sweep of water before us – between us and the city proper though this is, I believe, within the limits. It is delightfully cool & pleasant, but I don't like the air so well as our valley air – it is very enervating, and there is a horrid electric light factory[21] not far away which sends out so much soft coal smoke & gas, that I feel half the time as if a dozen matches were being lighted under my nose ... [20 August 1891]

Last night we went for a boat ride, and I am afraid I am getting spoiled in that upper country. I am so accustomed to the protecting care of two or three men at a time that I actually felt quite nervous going out without even one. It was lovely on the water though – we rowed about half way across the Inlet, almost to a little peninsula they call Stanley Park.[22] It is laid out in pleasure grounds. We did not land however, as it was beginning to get dark. We rowed back as the moon was rising – a great red ball of fire – some boys were singing that horrid Annie Rooney & two men in another boat were murdering another song, so we did not try to sing but only looked at the beautiful view. The mountains just across the Inlet have two peaks that look like reclining lions – so much so that Vancouver has gained the name of The Lion's Gate. [21 August 1891]

We went to a little church nearby yesterday morning, and listened to a smooth-faced little man talk – not preach. Oh! I wish I could hear someone who would stir me up. [24 August 1891]

We were all talking about marriage the other night, & Mary said so many people wondered why she had never married – how she had managed to withstand the opportunities and importunities of a new country, where so many men are walking about unattached. It seemed to me they are something like the little pigs in our old nursery rhyme who used to run about with knives & forks sticking in them, crying "Who'll take a piece of me" – only these self-sacrificing creatures are pleading to be allowed to give the whole of themselves. However, to return to our subject, Mary said she had so long earned her own money, and spent it as she pleased, not having to give account to any one, that she could not bear the idea of having someone else give it to her, & she added "To tell the truth I don't care to give up a sixty dollar school for a forty dollar man." It sounded so funny that I had to laugh. I felt half ashamed to confess that I had none of this independent spirit, being quite willing to have my father or brother earn the money for me to spend. Of course, I don't think I'd be satisfied to be a helpless encumbrance – I'd like, as the catechism enjoins, to "earn my living in that state of life to which it has pleased God to call me," but one can often do that quite as usefully in one's home, without being paid any money, as if one went out into the world & struggled with other money getters – and ah! how much more pleasantly! I do feel thankful that I never had to be independent as these girls have. I honour and admire their cheerful energetic spirit and the wisdom and management which they have shown in getting this nice home – but I don't envy them one bit. Indeed I think I pity them because they have had to leave their old home. [24 August 1891]

We heard Mr. Hobson preach. He has charge of Christ Church here, but I believe the people are trying to get rid of him. He looks unhappy, poor man ... I used to hear him every Sunday in the Cathedral in Toronto. [24 August 1891]

I have been trying to be on the sick list, & feel anything but energetic yet. Monday night I had quite a heavy chill and a fever which lasted all night & part of the next day. I was awake all night, & felt very miserable. It is not my fancy that the air of the place is most offensive, for the papers are full of the subject of bad drains & malaria. There are eleven cases of typhoid in the hospital and others in the town. I never thought I was susceptible to malaria, but I suppose the sudden change from that pure, bracing mountain air to this poison is enough to make anyone ill. The mental atmosphere is very different too – from talks about crops, cattle, garden & animals to nothing but school and school teachers – intellect & improvement makes my poor spirit faint sometimes as well as my body. I like it though. I like all the girls here so much. I was too sick to sit up yesterday or to eat a mouthful. Lizzie went & got me some quinine, & I have been taking it very steadily. I do hope I'll be able to go over to Victoria on Friday. I feel that I must get out of this place. I am a little better today. [6 August 1891]

Alice made her way across to Victoria to meet with old Ontario friends and had a hilarious encounter on the ferry to that city:

At last the charms of British Columbia are beginning to make themselves felt. I am already in love with Victoria, and I only came last night. I feel quite well already – the air is so keen and fresh, with just that delightful watery smell. The day was perfect yesterday, and I enjoyed the sail over. I did not talk to anyone for some time, but finally fell in with a very funny old American lady, & enjoyed a conversation with her so much that I was quite sorry when we reached port. She looked absurdly like the portraits of the Queen – indeed she told me that she had often been taken for "Victoria," "passed for her a whole year once." She had some young lady with her, I fancy her daughter. She was very enthusiastic over what she called "her mission" – a scheme to reform the world in connection with the Methodist Church. She has been making an extended tour through the eastern states and Canada, & is now going down to California "collecting girls" to help in this scheme. Whenever she sees a suitable one she tells her to hold herself in readiness to be called on. She was pleased to say I was a likely subject, & enquired my whereabouts very particularly. Where the headquarters of this mission are to be located, or exactly upon what lines it is to be run, she has not yet decided. She says she has lots of money, and various "Messengers of Satan" have tried to get hold of it for their own purposes, but she has circumvented them. Mr. Kains[23] asked me laughingly if my purse was all safe after the conversation, but I don't think she was so much a fraud as a crank. Mr. Kains and little Marion[24] met me at the boat, which got in a little after six, and we drove up here in time for dinner ... This house is in a very pretty situation, facing the sea – only the road between it and the beach – we are going on the shore this afternoon. My window looks out over the sea and the first sound I head this morning was the waves breaking on the shore. It made me feel more at home. I just shut my eyes and tried to fancy they were the waves of dear old Lake

Erie, and that I was lying on the beach at home. I feel quite well again. [29 August 1891]

I have not seen the Powells[25] yet. Mrs. Kains is quite distressed about my appearance – she thinks I look so ill. She says she knows if my mother could see me she would not let me stay in this country one month longer – much less a year – but I think I look much thinner & paler after that little illness in Vancouver. [31 August 1891]

... I am getting into very lazy ways – not even waking until nearly eight o'clock. Monday afternoon we went to Beacon Hill Park,[26] & had such a nice walk and a beautiful view ... Yesterday we were down town in the morning, and in the afternoon Mr. Kains took us out to Esquimault – it is about four miles away & it is the harbour for the navy. A large flag ship, The Marsprite, is [in] the dry dock for repairs, & we went all over it. I enjoyed seeing it so much ... I do like this old place, but it is awfully far from home. [2 September 1891]

In some ways it seems so foreign – such a lot of Chinese and Japanese with shops filled with the wares of their own lands. They call one part of the city China Town[27] and a nasty dirty part it is. [2 September 1891]

After dinner Mr. Kains took us to China Town – we went through a lot of shops and bought a lot of trinkets, I enjoyed it very much. It was so odd. The Chinamen here are fat & happy looking for the most part – very different from the specimens we see up the country. [5 September 1891]

I went to the Powells – did not see Mrs. Powell, she is ill. I saw Dr. & Miss Powell – I don't know if I will go there at all to stay. I'd much rather remain here. They have a nice place. [4 September 1891]

I set out for the east again – (D.V.) tomorrow night. I expect to spend a few days in Vancouver, and the North Arm,[28] then on to the cabin ... I have enjoyed my little visit here. Monday afternoon Miss Powell came and took me for a drive – we went to the top of Mount Tolmie,[29] and had a beautiful view. Tuesday I went over to the Powells in the morning, took luncheon there ... then back to the Powells to dinner, and to a concert in the evening. Last night we went to hear Emma Thursby[30] and were a good deal disappointed in her singing. [9 September 1891]

On Sunday morning we went to church and heard an old Scotch clergyman who told us that Indian mothers threw their children into the Nile! I rather wished I could have seen the acrobatic feat – it was a good long throw. [17 September 1891]

After the return trip to Vancouver:

Mrs. Jaffary was waiting on the verandah for us – and I don't wonder at all at Harry's affection for her. I quite fell in love with her. They have such a happy, lovely home – not rich or luxurious at all – no servants, and everything very plain – but there is such a pervading air of love and goodness that one must enjoy being there. They have two little children, and bring them up so nicely. The baby, of course, isn't brought up very far yet – only six months – but one can already see the result of love in her teaching. I do believe that love counts for more than anything else in the training of children, because it is love that underlies all the Heavenly Father's teaching of his children ... [17 September 1891]

While protesting that she really did not like animals at all, Alice wrote delightful passages describing their antics:

It is after nine o'clock. Gulliver is barking at some weary wayfarer, & having a gay time of it. Harry is often quoting a speech of Mr. Meighan's[31] "I wish I were a rich man's dog" – but I doubt if Gulliver could be any happier if his master were worth a million. He romps and plays all day long. When he gets too much discouraged in his merriment by all the humans he goes over to the stable yard and has a high time with the six little pigs & Sandy the colt. Sandy won't allow much nonsense though – she is of a grave & sedate turn of mind and only unbends her dignity enough to give a very decided kick if Gulliver gets too funny. [2 August 1891]

I am sadly afraid little Jerry is going to be more mischievous than Gulliver ever was. His snatching and tearing stage has begun already. It seems so queer that I should have had the care of two little pups – it is only a type, I expect, of the many old prejudices which have had to be laid aside, or fought down, out here. [26 September 1891]

I don't know which had the worst start today – Jerry or myself. I had gone over to feed the chickens, and Jerry, of course, had to follow. Gulliver took to chasing a pig and the two came suddenly upon Jerry around a corner of the stable. I never saw consternation more plainly expressed in a dog's looks & action. He ran for the house as fast as his poor little legs would carry him. That was his fright – mine came as I was standing near the chicken house throwing wheat to the chickens. My thoughts were wandering a long way off, when all at once they were pulled up short by a sense of some presence near, and a breath on my face. I looked quickly around, and there stood our old cow ready to eat out of the dish. My feeling towards cows is too well known for me to need to say how I felt. I did not run for the house quite so fast as Jerry did, but I did not linger in the barnyard, & when I got over here I felt so ashamed of being afraid of that meek old cow that I went back & fed her three carrots – only I stayed on this side of the fence. [27 November 1891]

[We laughed at] poor Jerry's fright when he saw little Nellie [Meighan] – the only little child he had ever seen. He ran into my room to be safe – & there lay the baby, kicking & crowing on the bed – so his only refuge was outdoors. He and Gulliver evidently talked [about] the matter outside, and agreed that this new specimen of an animal wasn't to be trifled with – for when they came in, they very meekly lay down by the stove. [2 March 1892]

Once back at the ranch, the family in Ontario was again at the centre of her thoughts; she thirsted for news from home and enjoyed visits from Ontario acquaintances:

This is Clare's[32] birthday. How I wish I could see the dear girl – I miss her very often. I have been thinking today of that little old fairy story of the boy who was so fond of candy that at last he gladly went off with an old woman who promised to take him to a town where everything was candy – and how soon he was cured of his sweet taste. Mine is not exactly a case in point, for although I never was a man-hater I always fully appreciated the fact that I liked my own sex best – but here I don't see one companionable woman once a week. I had a little glimpse of Mrs. Pelley yesterday on her way to and from town, and I just hated to see her drive away. I think I could get very fond of her, and she is so nice to me. [5 August 1891]

We had some blackcurrant jam that I brought from home, & it made me homesick. But everything makes me homesick these days. Wese said in one of her letters last night that Mother was not well. It does worry me, & yet I am glad that they tell me quite truly how they all are. [20 December 1891]

We had a call this morning from Jake Laur. He was in a very talkative mood, & wanted to bet me a big bunch of blue ribbons that I would not be home two weeks before I'd be wishing myself back here. [20 December 1891]

I was very homesick this morning, and had a hard cry. I am not one who feels better after crying – it upsets me for all day … [14 January 1892]

I am afraid I'll always feel like an exile here. [24 March 1892]

At last a letter has come from home, posted on April 1st, so evidently the last week's letter was lost. I am afraid I am very greedy, for long and lovely as this one is, I long for "the letter that never came." I am greedy over every word that comes from home. [8 April 1892]

[Harry] brought a long letter from Wese, telling us about the Dover Xmas, and saying that it is rumoured there that Father is superannuated, & the office given to a man named Davis. However, as he had had no official report, we are hoping there wasn't any truth in it. I know even the report will bother Papa though. [11 January 1892]

The home letter gave the unpleasant news that Father really is superannuated.[33] It will make a difference in our circumstances at home, & may make a difference in my plans – for, of course, if they need my help at home I won't think of getting married and leaving them. [23 January 1892]

Uncle brought us a long letter from home – two indeed – & they rather frightened us. Poor Father has broken two ribs – fell off a chair which he was standing on. It made us both wish to go right home, but they tell us he is doing very well … it is a very painful hurt, I am afraid. [15 February 1892]

… a nice long letter [arrived] from Wese telling us that Father was much better, the shock to his ribs seeming to have cured the rheumatism. [23 February 1892]

Mr. Matheson and Mr. Crawford … came in & had dinner … We discovered in course of conversation that Mr. Matheson sailed our lakes for five years, and the other man was born in Dover! He – the Doverite – was very solemn and still, but after dinner he warmed up, and told a great tale of the Red River flood, when he had his house chained to a tree to keep it from floating away, & various other experiences. Mr. Matheson was a burly, talkative Scotchman … [18 January 1892]

A ubiquitous theme in the diaries was Alice's deep love of nature and the seasons:

On Friday morning we set out for our long talked-of mountain climb. Mr. Harvey, Mr. Ponsford, Miss Shickluna and I. We went about two miles up the river in Mr. Harvey's canoe, and then began the ascent. It was pretty hard climbing in some places, and once I felt like turning back –

but we persevered and at three o'clock reached the summit of the big cliff[34] – the Giant's Head the Indians call it. The view from the top repaid us for all the trouble of climbing – we could see the whole valley from Lake Okanagan to the C.P.R. track at Sicamous. We had taken a lunch with us and enjoyed it thoroughly. The coming down was very easy – we got home at about eight, drenched by a heavy shower which overtook us before we reached the canoe. We found that our feat had caused quite a stir in town, as they had all seen the fire. We are the first ladies who ever made the ascent. We were not very tired – Mr. Reilly seemed quite elated by our efforts. [22 June 1891]

We had a very rattly, noisy drive – but everything looked so beautiful we could put up with a little discomfort. I think I never saw the mountains look so lovely – a faint blue haze hung over them, heightening, not hiding their beauty, & the clouds were constantly throwing different shades on rocks & trees. Then the prairie fields at their base are looking their best – acre after acre of golden grain, fields of hay in cock, with men and waggons looking like specks in the landscape. [4 August 1891]

... we all set off for Pleasant Valley church. It was a nice morning, and the woods were lovely – great snow drifts on the evergreens, & where our road went through the woods many of the trees were bent down over the road, making a regular arch. It looked beautiful, but did not feel quite so charming when a big branch would hit us, sending a shower of snow down our necks. [27 December 1891]

During her stay at Mountain Meadow Alice always welcomed visitors courteously, with food and conversation. Despite the distances to be travelled, visits were frequent and often lengthy:

I have so much to tell that I hardly know where to begin. That rainy Friday proved to be quite a reception day. First Mr. Parke stayed all day, then about five o'clock his man came along, and as it was pouring rain Mr. Parke asked if it would be very much trouble to me to have him here to tea and breakfast – of course I said no, so he stayed. I was bustling about getting tea, when a rap came on the door and there stood Alec Scott.[35] We were so pleased and surprised to see him, although we knew that he was in Vancouver – we hardly thought he would come up here from Sicamous, but he did, and stayed until this morning. He seemed to enjoy every hour of his visit. Had two or three rides. On Sunday we drove to Vernon, and had such a nice day. We took the two Pelley girls, and I never saw two children enjoy themselves more. We went in to the Methodist Church, though we were very late for service, and from there to Mrs. Ellison's, where we spent the day. They were all so kind. We came home towards evening, and picked Uncle up at the Head of the Lake, where he had gone in the morning with Mr. Parke. We were all pretty hungry, and enjoyed our repast immensely. On Monday, Alec went for a ride in the morning, and early after dinner we drove down to Enderby. We had a nice canoe ride in Mr. Taylor's canoe, and I stayed to dinner at the R.R. house, and Harry & Alec dined with Mr. Harvey. We did not get home until about eleven, and were very cold. Alec was telling me little confidences, which ought to have kept him warm, but he frequently regretted having left his overcoat at home. This morning Harry & Minnie took the democrat home to the Ehmcke's, & I stayed at home to bake. This afternoon I was just about to take a nice rest when who should come along but Lucy Crozier. I was really not glad to see her – she stayed three hours and it was hard work to make talk to entertain her. Harry & Minnie went for a ride after tea. Mr. Parke & I were watering the garden when I heard Mr. Berry's voice down here, & he is just the extreme of Lucy Crozier – he talks all the time. I did not feel like talking to him, so I stayed up on the hill a good while, but at last, in common politeness, I had to come down, and Mr. Grant soon came along bringing us a quarter of venison. [5 August 1891]

I have been visiting all day long, and am pretty well tired out, as a good many of the visits were duty ones. I went down to Lansdowne early this morning, and called on nearly everyone in the place. As they all asked me to dinner there was no occasion for my "flesh" to come home hungry, but my spirit did. It gets very little food that is palatable in the way of companionship. [14 August 1891]

The worst of our visitors is, that they always come just as we have finished our meals. [16 November 1891]

I don't like Sunday visitors, & sometimes find it hard to "exercise hospitality without grudging" towards them. [30 November 1891]

She also enjoyed outings to Vernon to meet Harold Parke's friends:

We had a lovely drive up [to Vernon], reaching Mrs. Ellison's about three o'clock. Harry left me there, and took the horses back down town to Harold's stable. I had a nice visit with Mrs. Ellison[36] in the afternoon. She has three dear little children[37] – the baby especially is a darling. Harry & Harold came up in the evening, and Mr. Hall was there, so we had quite a pleasant evening. Harry sang, we had candies and nuts & Mr. Ellison made a splendid cup of coffee. They were so kind and good to me. Sunday morning Harry came to take me to church before we were done breakfast. He, Mr. Hall & I went to hear Mr. Outerbridge. Harold was there – there was a very good congregation. Harry said he would come up in the afternoon to take me for a walk if it stopped snowing (it had been quite stormy all the morning) but Mrs. Ellison asked me to go with her to S. School so I thought I would forego the walk. I enjoyed the S.S. very much. I was in the Bible class. We then went up to the Ellison's where we found Harry waiting, so after dinner he, Mr. Hall and I walked down to post my letter. We inspected the new Post Office.[38] It is really a very nice building. I hope they will keep it clean. Nearly all the buildings out here are allowed to get so shabby and dirty. Vernon has grown even since we were up there at Fair time. Harold went up to the Ellisons with us, and walked with us to church. Harry helped them in the choir. He sang the verses of "What shall the harvest be" & the choir the chorus, while the collection was being taken up, and Harry had a splendid voice, there is no doubt about that. I enjoyed the day very much. They were bound that we should stay until morning, but Harry wanted to come home, & so did I, so we resisted all coaxings. [15 February 1892]

... Harold went with us for a walk around the town. It is growing and some nice houses have gone up. I went up then to enquire for Mrs. Ellison[39] and Harry called for me there. As we were coming out of town Harold was at old Mr. Girouard's and brought him out to introduce him to me – a big old fellow with a solitary front tooth left in his upper jaw which has the appearance of a fang. [3 May 1892]

Once undertaken, her writing became important to her:

I am afraid I am losing any little facility I ever had with a pen. I don't seem to have anything to say ... [9 October 1891]

What a farce keeping a diary is after all! I don't tell every thing that happens. Tonight I am almost too sleepy to tell any thing. This has been a long and busy week. I feel the need of & wish for a day of rest. [17 October 1891]

I actually sat down and busied myself for about an hour writing an Essay! The Spallumcheen Agricultural Society are offering three prizes for an Essay on the benefit this Society is to be to the community, so I thought I'd make a try. The first prize is ten dollars, second five, third Vernon

News[40] for a year. I am not very sanguine, but it is worth the attempt. [21 October 1891]

That first Christmas in the Okanagan Alice did her best to replicate the food and celebrations of the home ones:

My Xmas party is rather uncertain, no-one but the Hardings & Mr. Parke having accepted positively. It is a little provoking – I'd like to know, but it can't be helped. [22 December 1891]

Dear old Harry! he has been so good to me today, baked a splendid lot of bread today – twelve loaves! – and picked the chickens, for our turkey has proved a vain illusion – fancy a Xmas without a turkey! We are going to try & have a jolly one though. [23 December 1891]

Christmas has come and gone. I think we all had a happy one. I must go back to Wednesday night, when I made my last entry. I sat up until half past ten, to keep a fire going as I was afraid the house would be cold when Harry got here. I was asleep when he came, at twelve o'clock, but awoke to hear there were letters and parcels from home. We did not undo them though, or even read our letters. I opened them the next morning as soon as we had finished breakfast, and read the home ones aloud to Harry. We had not got up very early, and all this made us late in getting the work done. Uncle did not come down on time for dinner (he was working on the sleigh at the shop). Harry and I waited until half past twelve, and then thought we'd have our dinner, so Harry could get at his scrubbing directly after dinner. We had finished when Uncle came and while he was still eating who should walk in but Harold. We were surprised, as we had not expected him before the afternoon. However he had some lunch, and after the work was done he drove me up to Mrs. Pelley's. I took the pork from Harry, and a little handkerchief to Nonah, but did not stay long, as Harold could not go in & leave the horses. We came right home, as it was very cold, and found Harry had finished his work & put up some greens as decorations. We had a nice cosy homelike evening, and Xmas morning. All woke up pretty early calling Merry Xmas to each other. Uncle actually kissed me, and said he hoped I'd have a happy day. We had our presents on the breakfast table. I think Harry & I fared the best. I got a pair of mocassins from Harry, a book from Mother, a lovely little pair of pins from Wese with some frills. Harold brought me a pair of embroidered buckskin gloves, and a Chinese handkerchief, & Lizzie brought me a nice pair of black kid gloves. She brought Uncle a lovely tea cup & saucer, and Harry a silk handkerchief. Harry got the Scott I gave him. Wese sent him

Lucille – Mother a splendid pair of gloves, and Harold brought him a very
nice Meerschaum pipe. Oh! and Mother sent me two pairs of stockings,
then Uncle got the necktie I gave him, a book & book marker from Wese,
and a pair of gloves from Mother. Harold only got a "Longfellow" from
me, a necktie from Harry, and a card from Wese. After breakfast we did
not do much of anything. I put a little postscript in my letter home, got
the vegetables ready for dinner and sat here talking until about half past
eleven, when active preparations for dinner had to begin. We got in the
table which has not been used since last Xmas – we had our ordinary dining table over near the wall, as a side table. I laid the table for eight,
expecting Mr. Grant. Mr. Macdonald told me the day before he would not
be here. About twelve the Hardings came, & soon after Mr. Hall. He
brought me a big string of popcorn from Mr. Ellison.[41] We had dinner at
one, & I think I can safely say it was a success – everything passed off very
nicely, & the cooking was a success, but Mr. Grant did not come so we
were only seven at the table. We had quite a jolly dinner though, and
afterwards all sat around and talked until four o'clock, when Mr. Hall had
to go. Harry Harding left about nine in the evening, but Lizzie stayed –
she will be with me until tomorrow, as Harry was going to Vernon today,
and did not want to leave her alone. We had quite a gay time in the
evening playing games & acting as if we were young & jolly. Uncle actually joined in, though he pretended he would rather read. Well, I was so
sleepy I wanted to go to bed, but Harry was in the humour to sit up, so I
stood it until nearly eleven and then had to go to bed. [26 December 1891]

    One of the greatest "treasures" to be found in the diaries is a descrip-
tion, from the lips of Catherine Schubert herself,[42] of the travails of the
Overlanders' trek in 1862:

It is strange that when we have been thinking so much of going over to
the Schuberts', Mrs. Schubert[43] should have come today to spend the day
with me ... This morning very soon after breakfast old Mrs. Schubert
came. Mr. Gus goes every day to the "gum-boot" to feed cattle, & brought
his mother down. He called for her tonight about six o'clock, so we had a
long day together, and I thoroughly enjoyed it. She was telling me the
story of her married life, and the dangers and hardships she underwent
were enough to kill any ordinary woman. She was married in Massachusetts (having come out from Ireland some time before) and then
went to St. Paul, where they lived until three little children were born.
When the youngest was four months old they decided to move to Winnipeg, or Fort Garry as it was then called. This Journey had, of course, to

be taken in wagons. She said an old black cow they had followed all the way, like a dog. They lived in Winnipeg two years, and then, in the winter of '62 the Indian Rebellion broke out. Mrs. Schubert said she was so terrified, & the children got so frightened, for bands of Indians were constantly in & about the place, fighting, drinking & threatening, that she begged Mr. Schubert to leave and declared that the first party which left the place for east or west – she would go. At last an expedition was to start for Oregon – a hundred & fifty men, but no woman. However, her fears of the Indians outweighed every other consideration and she started. At first they travelled in waggons – for seven weeks – but when they came to Edmonton, they were told they could not possibly go farther except on horseback – for I forgot to say that here all the party changed their minds about heading for Oregon, & decided to keep on over the Rockies – the gold fever having just broken out in Cariboo. Of course the Schuberts could not keep on alone for Oregon, so had to travel with the majority. They sold their wagon to a priest for three horses, & perching the children on in front, started on. The old black cow was again following, being milked always by someone in the train, & petted by all. Mrs. Schubert says all the men were so kind to her & the children, giving them the best of everything – and indeed, towards the end of the journey there was little enough to eat. They had only the Hudson Bay posts along their route to replenish their stores, & through the Rockies and west of them these were few and many long miles apart. They had dreary climbs, & many rivers to ford or get across, in canoes made on the spot. Only once, she says, her courage failed – when she saw one river they had to cross, wide and swift – the canoes could not live in it – a man tried if his horse would go over, & when she saw man & horse in the water with only their heads above, she sat on the bank and cried. However, over she had to go – the transit was made safely, the children crying with fright the whole way over. In all their four months journeying only one man was lost – he was drowned. When they were eighty miles from Kamloops they came to another river. They had no canoes, their provisions were gone and they were living on blackberries. The men decided that she was to be sent over on a raft, with enough men to man it, & the others would follow when they had their canoes made. They pushed on & at last reached Kamloops. The Hudson Bay trading post was on a point of land across another river. They had hoped to find quite a town here, but there was not a woman in the place, or a house to shelter them. They pitched their tent on the river bank, & there, the next morning, a little daughter was born[44] – the first white child ever born in Kamloops. This was in October, and a winter of great hardship followed. The only work Mr. Schubert could get was to cook for the Hudson Bay man at $15.00 a month, & as flour was a dollar a pound, & everything else in proportion, this barely kept them from starving. In the Spring they moved to Lilloit,[45] & "There," as the poor old woman said, "our luck changed." She got the job of milking ten cows – taking care of the milk and making butter – while her husband went off, like so many others, to seek his fortune in the mines, and again like many others, found only hard work & no gold. It gave me a keen feeling of reproach for any grumbling that I may have done over hardships – that she should have thought this "good luck" – hard and constant work from morning till night, her little eight year old boy helping her to "raise the others." Poor woman – one would think she had had her hard days and ought to be comforted – but though they are no longer poor, her troubles are not over. Mrs. LeDuc, the little girl born at Kamloops, married at fifteen a schoolteacher. As the old Mother said sadly "I thought a man with learning would make her happy," but alas! he has proved to be more a brute than a man. After about thirteen years of hard treatment she has had to leave him, & is living at home with her five children – & Mr. Gus – the good little boy who helped his mother and is still her pride & her treasure, grieves her by being "too fond of liquor." I thoroughly enjoyed her visit, and I think she did too. We have promised to go over there some evening next week. I want to write to Wese now. Harry has taken to reading David Copperfield to himself now. I forgot to say that one of Mrs. Schubert's many trials on this dreary journey of about fifteen hundred miles was that they had to kill the faithful black cow – at a spot where they could not possibly get her over a river – they left many mules behind there too. They called the place Slaughter Camp in memory of the poor old cow. Every man in the train was sorry to kill the poor faithful, gentle creature. As they say in the west, she must have been a woman with "good stuff in her." She comes out with funny little expressions in such a grave, quiet way. "By gollies" – "Confounded" and "that's what it is." [5 March 1892]

CHAPTER 3

A very cosy, happy home

At Home in Vernon

At the end of May 1892, Alice prepared to leave for the east. She had made a commitment to Harold Parke to return, and she went home to prepare for her marriage to him. The journey back to Ontario was uneventful, and she received a joyful greeting from her family in Port Dover. The intervening months passed swiftly, and Harold Parke left Vernon on 16 December that year to travel east. The "Town and Country" column in the *Vernon News* reported that, "after an absence of twenty-three years, Mr. H.R. Parke left on Thursday last to visit friends in the east. His objective point was London, Ont., where his sister is dangerously ill."[1] He evidently wished to conceal the true reason for his departure because he would be looking for employment in Ontario and might not return to the Okanagan. His engagement to Alice was confirmed, and he obviously charmed her family and won her parents' approval. Their marriage took place at St. Paul's Church in Port Dover on 4 January 1893; the Reverend J.R. Newell conducted the ceremony, and the witnesses were Harry and Wese Barrett. Alice was thirty-one years old and Hal was forty-seven.

To the couple's chagrin, Hal failed to find a position in London, and the Parkes made their way back to the Okanagan Valley by train through the brutal storm still known as the blizzard of '93. After being delayed for more than two days, Alice wrote: "In Vernon at last! Left Sicamous about nine. Saw some friends in Enderby. Uncle met us at Armstrong; came on the train for a little while – seemed really glad to see us – Harry left us there" (6 February 1893).

Alice considered this return to the west but a temporary obstacle to the realization of her dearest ambition – to go home and stay there. However, that return would be delayed by twelve years. There was a lengthy gap in the diaries – this time nine months. Alice, of course, was in the throes of setting up a new home with a new husband, in a new town, and with, for the most part, new friends and acquaintances. On arriving in Vernon, she and Hal settled into a small rented cottage while planning and building their first home. The City of Vernon had just been incorporated, and the first city council appointed Hal as its assessor, which also required him to act as jailer and constable, duties for which he was eminently suited. By the time Alice took up her pen once more, the couple had moved in to their own two-storey house on Schubert Street, two blocks north of the main street in the middle of town.

During the week Alice organized her days so that she spent mornings working in her home and afternoons visiting neighbours, friends, and the needy. Friends were almost always within her own peer group – white and middle class; she seldom explored outside this set. She demonstrated great compassion and empathy with the plight of those poorer and less fortunate than she, preparing and delivering nourishing food, sitting up with them overnight when they were sick, and taking care of their children. Saturdays were reserved for the home, preparing food for Sunday, taking part in social gatherings in town, or enjoying quiet evenings alone with Hal. Sunday was devoted to church going, Sunday school teaching, and other devotional activities. She developed a wide circle of women friends, most of whom remain shadowy, undeveloped figures in her pages; she saved her critical and humorous comments for those who were not close to her emotionally. She also showed a commendable affinity for the elderly in the community and enjoyed the many hours she spent in their company.

At Mountain Meadow Ranch, Harry continued his life as a rancher. He missed his sister and was depressed after the collapse of his romance with Minnie Shickluna; he was also having problems with ranch operations. Alice felt duty-bound to visit Spallumcheen from time to time to do some of the household chores that she had performed there before her marriage and to prepare tasty dainties for the two bachelors. She also took the opportunity to meet again with old friends she had made there two years earlier. Ties with the home ones in Port Dover were nurtured, as always, with frequent letters.

Once again, at the urging of her brother, she took up her pen with a sense of duty rather than wholehearted enthusiasm. Volume 7 (the first of the Vernon diaries) contained a dizzying array of new names, most of which would continue to appear throughout the diaries to come. It is reproduced here almost in its entirety.

VERNON – NOV. 3RD/93

Friday Evening

Harry is constantly urging me to begin another diary, thinking the home ones would be interested in it, so – although I think my letters give all the news – I will make another effort. Clare[2] is sitting at the other side of the table reading – I have got quite used to seeing her here now, & will miss her dreadfully if she decides to go back to Seattle. I should not wonder if she would stay all winter with Harry. She felt so dreadfully sorry for his loneliness. If he had a different nature he would not feel it so much, but he has a keen appetite for companionship, & when it has to go hungry there must be a pain. I had a nice little visit down at the ranch last week – with Harry and Clare – Uncle was away. The new rooms down there are very pleasant – we made an attempt at settling them up, but didn't get on very far. I came back on Saturday, Clare not until Wednesday. Last night I had my first little party. I asked the Spinks[3] but Mrs. Spinks was ill – then I asked the Cochranes,[4] Beckingsales,[5] a Mr. & Mrs. Gilroy from the hotel, and Dr. Morris.[6] We played whist until half past ten, & then had coffee, thin bread & butter and two kinds of cake. Altogether it was twelve before we got to bed, & that was terrible dissipation for such early people as we are. Today I had some straightening up to do and after dinner I had promised to go over & read to Mrs. Macintyre,[7] Mrs. Martin's[8] grandmother. I really felt very tired, & didn't half want to go, but I had said I would, so about three o'clock I left Clare to keep house & started. The Martins live quite near. It has been a miserable day, half snow half rain falling all the time. First – I had quite a long talk with Mrs. Martin – the old lady was dressing; not having been well all the morning, she did not get up until afternoon ... The old lady [told] me some interesting stories of her early life & of her family. Her forefathers were ardent Jacobites. Her grandfather, a Colonel Robertson, fought for Prince Charlie at Cullodin, & was wounded. Some faithful follower managed to drag him off, & hide him in an outhouse, under straw, for some days. The wound in his arm had no attention, & he even had to pick worms out of it (so Mrs. Macintyre says) with the straw in which he lay hidden. A woman used to smuggle food to him through a chink in the wall, until his father & brother were able to manage his escape, which they did, hiding him in a cart, under sheep skins & barrels. They got him to a cave by the sea side, where he waited for a ship to take him to France. But before he would leave, great as was the peril, he would see his lady love. She lived with an Uncle, & one night leaving the parlour to get some cream for her Uncle's tea, she was confronted in the hall by her lover, the chaplain, & a friend, and then and there, in quietness and haste, they were married. Two days later the welcome ship came & together they fled to France. When they came back, the[y] built a house with the 1st paper money that was used – given Colonel Robertson by Prince Charlie. Of course his property was forfeited before that. In this house Mrs. Macintyre's childhood was spent – she showed me a picture of it. I got my birthday letters from home today – such nice ones from all the dear ones ... Clare had some funny experiences at the ranch too – she said one morning at four o'clock a drunken Siwash came to the door, & when Harry got up to answer his rapping, said he wanted a drink of water. When his own thirst was satisfied he asked if he might take one out to his mother! There is a big black bear prowling about in the woods near Ned Thorne's – it killed one of Gus Schubert's pigs and tore one of Ned Thorne's. The Schuberts don't allow their children to go to school, on account of it.

Saturday, 4th November 1893
It is ten months today since we were married. It is a miserable wet day, raining & half snowing, but Clare & I are going out.

Sunday Nov. 5th
My 32nd birthday! Clare & Hal both gave me pretty presents – Clare such a nice Japanese brush & crumb tray, and Hal a beautiful volume of Scott. They had them on my plate at breakfast, & I was pleased, but it made me a little homesick too. Yesterday afternoon Clare & I went first to Mrs. Ellison's – she has a bad cold – then in to Mrs. Woods.[9] Her sister-in-law was there knitting, so we found out some points about knitting socks, for we want to knit some for Harry if possible ... Then we went into all the shops pricing wool – and when we came home I came in to get Hal's clothes out, & get ready to go ... We made ourselves very pretty for our dinner party at Mrs. Coryell's[10] – Clare wore her black silk, & I my petunia silk. We made Hal, too, don his black clothes, and altogether we were very fine. Mr. & Mrs. Costerton[11] were there, & of course Mr. & Mrs. Macdonald,[12] so with Mrs. Coryell, her son & Mr. Kirby[13] we were quite a party. I am very glad Mrs. Coryell & the Macdonalds seem to get on well, for I suggested to her to have them there – she is left alone so much. We had a pleasant evening. Mrs. Costerton & I took our music – she plays very well – Mr. Clement Costerton[14] came in after dinner, & towards the end of the evening someone suggested table turning. We used to do it at home so much just for fun, that I didn't mind entering into it – but really the Costerton men believe in it. They think spirits really communicate with human beings through the medium of a table – it seems pitiful. We didn't continue long at it – it was too serious once we saw they thought

there was more in it than simple fun ... Hal got dinner – a very fine venison pot-pie. Since then I have been studying my Bible lesson – he & Clare
are fast asleep.

Monday Nov. 6th
Hal asked Mr. Norris (our new Government Agent)[15] and Mr. Megraw[16]
(our departing editor) to come to tea last night – & they arrived before
five, so we got tea ready, & afterwards they stayed and talked until after
ten. They got me started telling stories of my first impressions of the
ranch – & the people – & I am afraid I talked a good deal. That first year
was an interesting one – everything was so new, & I seemed to come
across more odd people at the ranch than I do here. There is more observance of the conventionalities here – and far less originality ... this afternoon before we went out Hal brought up the mail. A splendid long letter
from Harry, a letter from Walter, another from Nellie Parke[17] and a lovely
long one from Wese ... oh! I got sleepy before they went away – and this
morning I hated to get up ... Mr. Megraw is going to Wiarton to live –
Clare & I tried to give him a description of Henrietta Low, & to arouse
his curiosity about her.

Tuesday Night Nov. 7
I have a great deal to say tonight – and it is sad too ... I must not forget
to say that last night I did *not* go to bed early for the very good reason that
I couldn't. We were all terribly sleepy, & Hal didn't feel well, so we had
concluded to go to bed before nine o'clock, & had lighted our bedroom
lamps, when Billie Holliday[18] came. I was nearly desperate, I was so
sleepy, & Hal's head ached so, that about half past nine he went to bed,
but Billie stayed on. I was really ashamed of myself – twice I actually went
to sleep talking, and Clare says I talked simple nonsense. About ten I
began to wake up a little, & by the time he left I was getting really chirpy.
Well! I got up early this morning, as I had a little ironing to do, and had
got at it, when Clare got down to breakfast ... Clare & I went down to
Cameron's.[19] It was a beautiful morning, & I thought we'd go for a longer
walk, but as we got nearly to Cameron's we saw Harry riding in on Tiny.
It struck me as strange then that he was riding Tiny – we told him we had
to go to the shop, & then would go straight home – however I thought he
would likely be still at the stable, so we went over there and walked up
with him. I knew at once that something was wrong, & I said to him
"What is the news?" "Bad news," he said. My first thought was home, &
I asked if it was anything there; but he said "Bad news from the ranch. I
buried Ethel yesterday." Of course, then he told the story, and grieved as
I am for the poor mare my strongest feeling is one of keen thankfulness

that Harry himself was not seriously hurt. He said at one time he quite expected to be killed, but did not even get a scratch. Tiny was frightened by a breaking bar, & ran away when the horses were hitched to the plough. Harry's gloves were wet and slippery, & he could not stop her at once – & before he knew anything he, the two horses & the plough were so tangled together that he quite expected they would none of them get free alive. Poor Ethel's hind legs were cut all the cords & sinews, so that she could never have got well, and Harry said he ought to have shot her at once, but he couldn't do it. He went for Gus Schubert, who wasn't at home, then over for Miles who came, & shot her where she fell, & there they buried her. Poor Harry feels dreadfully – she was his pet – more a friend & companion than an animal. He said she put up her head & whinnowed for him as he went away to get Gus – as much as to say "Don't leave me." The plough was all smashed, but neither Harry nor Tiny got a scratch. I am very glad Harry came up – I think it comforted him to tell us, and to have us sorry with him. I cried hard – I couldn't help it. It grieves him so that he was to blame, he says – but I don't think he was to blame, it was just a sad accident ... Mrs. Beckingsale came first, and she offered me to have her piano over here for the winter, if I cared to have it. She says it gets used more in the hotel than she cares to have it used, & also she has to pay $20.00 a year for the insurance, while in a private house she would only have to pay $2.60 – and she knew I would take care of it and enjoy it. Of course I am delighted, but it seems almost too much of a favour – however she put it very nicely, and as if she would be the one obliged. She wants me to let Minna (her little girl) come sometimes and practise and I will whenever I can help her, though Mrs. Beckingsale did not ask me to. She wants us to bring it over this week, and I am so glad we may hope to have it here on Saturday, for we expect Harry up again ... He will be tremendously surprised to see a piano here ...

I cannot help thinking of Mrs. Beckingsale's kindness. It seems strange she should have chosen me, for there are so many other people she has known longer. She has always been nice to me, & I'll try to repay her by helping Minna.

Wednesday Night [Nov. 8th]
Uncle is reading at the table beside me – he came up this morning, and may go back tomorrow – or may stay until Saturday ... He seems to like our house, and to be comfortable. I will have to turn Hal out of his bed tonight, & give him the sofa in the dining room. Clare & I will have our room, & Uncle the spare room ... Clare ... has decided to go back to Seattle on Tuesday. I just hate to have her go – I can't bear to think of it,

& Harry hates so to say goodbye to her ... It was a lovely day, & Clare & I thought we would go out for a walk early ... [but] we only had time to run up to Mrs. Martin's for a few minutes. Poor old Mrs. Macintyre has been suffering from rheumatism. Mrs. Martin, too, looked very miserable, I don't believe she is getting well very fast ...

Friday Night Nov. 10th
I did not get anything written last night, as Clare & I spent the evening at Mrs. Spinks ... Yesterday morning we went for a little walk and in the afternoon we meant to go out early, but I was so sleepy that I went & had a little nap, & it was nearly four when we started. We went to Mrs. Martin's door to ask after her, & then up towards the station for a walk ... When we got home I thought we'd have maccaroni and cheese for tea. Hal came with us, so I got him to light the fire, but we found we hadn't enough cheese, so he went off down town to get some, & was preparing the maccaroni when Mrs. Beckingsale came, to say we could have the piano today, if we would send for it. Hal didn't want to go to the Spinks last night, on account of not getting on very well with Judge Spinks, so we let him stay at home. He walked over with us, & Dr. Morris brought us home. Not very many were there – Mrs. Dowding,[20] one of the old time settlers of Osoyoos,[21] was one of the party. Her first husband, Judge Haines,[22] brought her up here 20 years ago. Hal says she was only 13 years old when she married, & she certainly doesn't look a day more than 43 now. I would like to have a long talk with her, for I'm sure she could tell many an interesting tale. Judge Spinks talked spiritualism to Mr. Macdonald most of the evening – I think he is trying to make a convert. Today I made two pumpkin pies. Uncle had to have an early dinner, as he wanted to start at one ... Soon after they brought over the piano – it makes quite a difference in the look of the room – I know Harry will be pleased, & I must try to practise regularly now ...

Saturday Night [Nov. 11th]
I had a very busy morning, and nothing seemed to go just right. Trying a pen – I felt rather tired, & not much inclined to work, but it had to be done – and Hal came in with some beef, wanting us to make some beef tea for Mr. Girouard.[23] The old man is quite sick, in bed. Clare made the beef tea, & Hal took up some blackcurrant jam to make him a drink, while the beef was cooking. I made a ginger cake, some cookies, a pudding for tomorrow, a little red cabbage pickle, & a hundred and one little jobs. Clare swept upstairs, & did all the dusting, & went out twice. After dinner I took a sleep, & just got dressed in time to take the Vernon paper down to the post office. I send it to Hubert every week. Hal came home

with me, and just as we got near the door, we saw Harry – he had just got here. He was greatly surprised to see the piano – but it is so out of tune that our pleasure in it is much tempered. Harry & Clare went for a walk to see Mr. Taylor,[24] while Hal & I got tea. We had sausages, fried potatoes, stewed apples, mustard pickles, baker's bread & ginger cake, which, as it had fallen in the centre, was a great favourite of both Harry's & Hal's. After tea *the boys* had to go out for a while, & Clare & I dressed up in two of her uniforms, & when they came in we showed them off for a while. However, as it was rather a cool dress I soon changed back to my own garments – since, we have been singing & playing. I stop every few minutes to go and play an accompaniment or to listen.

Tuesday Night [Nov. 14th]
I must not get too much in arrears. The last three days have been very much occupied, and I couldn't bear to use up the last of Clare's visit writing all the time. Soon after I stopped writing Saturday night Mr. Taylor came in, and he stayed pretty late, so it meant bed time when he left. He & Harry sang, & Hal sang, so we had lots of music. In the morning (Sunday) we were all up late ... When we got up, we found Jerry here, but he seemed most unhappy & uncertain, not to find Harry, & after eating some breakfast, & searching all over the house, disappeared. When Harry came over he said Jerry had slept in Mr. Taylor's room, but when he was let out in the morning must have come over here. Mr. Taylor said he came back there about eleven, looking for Harry, who had left there, & that is the last we have seen or heard of Master Jerry. We think he must have started back for the ranch – I am quite anxious to hear if he turned up there all right ... [In] the afternoon Harry went back. He took Nancy, one of Hal's horses, & as she was a little hard to lead, Hal walked out with him more than a mile ... Yesterday morning I set some buns, and Clare did a little washing for herself – some things she didn't wánt me to give the Chinaman. We weren't very long working in the kitchen, then we sat down & worked. There were a few little odd jobs of mending she wanted me to do for her – sewing is so hard on her eyes. Just after dinner, the Ellison children came down with a note, asking us up there to dinner at six. We almost hated to go our last evening, & yet I didn't want to refuse to go to Mrs. Ellison's – so we accepted, but said we must come away early. Mr. Mackelvie was there, & we had a very pleasant time. We left before nine. Hal went up with us, & stayed all the time we did. I began to think in the afternoon that we were never going to get there – we had to go & see Mrs. Coryell & Mrs. Martin, & when we got home had Mrs. Dewdney and Ethel Lawes for a long time – afterwards Mrs. Lander my next door

neighbour. I was rather uneasy as I had Clare's buns in the oven and didn't want them to get too much done – however, all the troubles were over at last, & the buns were not spoiled, though a little crusty. This morning we didn't do very much. Clare finished knitting one of Hal's socks – we have a pair done now and I have begun on another, but this pair won't go so fast I'm sure, for I'll have to do it alone and I am only a beginner – besides, now that we have the piano here, Hal likes a little music in the evenings. I have been playing for him tonight, & I tried to sing, but I haven't any voice ... Hal got Tom[25] to come for the luggage. He went up to the station, and got [Clare's] ticket & cheques, & brought them home – then when Clare went we both went to the station of course – Harry meant to see her at Armstrong. I suppose she is safely on the main line now. I hope so I'm sure – I'll be most anxious to hear of her safe arrival. I do miss her. Mr. Girouard is better. Hal coaxed him to see Dr. Morris. I have made something for him every day so far & Hal takes it up – today I made a blanc mange. I think everyone is pretty good to him.

Wednesday Night [Nov. 15th]
I have been writing to Harry, Wese & Clare – and my hand actually aches – but I must not neglect my daily record. We began a new plan this morning. Hal thinks seven o'clock breakfast is too early for me, now that the mornings are dark & cold, so he is going to get up, light the fires, go down to the post office[26] & send off the early mail, then about nine come back to breakfast. So when the house is well warmed I can get up to get breakfast. It seems very lazy of me, but we are going to try it ... When I got home it was after eleven but as the train was late, I knew dinner would be too, so I had time to make an apple pie and roast the ducks Jack[27] sent me ... A little black cat came today and insisted on coming in, scratching at the kitchen door, until for the sake of the paint I had to open it. The cat is a pretty little thing and makes itself quite at home on my cosy corner, but spits at me when I come near it. I don't like to turn my luck away, so suppose we'll have to let it stay, especially as Tom seems quite pleased. He was afraid of the little kittens Harry sent up from the ranch. The Vernon News has changed hands – Mr. McKelvie[28] is our new editor – if he proves as good an editor as he is a man it would be all right.

Thursday Evening [Nov. 16th]
We had Mr. Angus Stewart[29] here to tea – he & Hal have just gone out. He is a very nice looking fellow, and pleasant too – I quite enjoyed his visit. He came along as Hal was working at the back door, and came in through the kitchen. Fortunately I had a nice tea – I was getting ready to make biscuit (which were delicious) & I had a cold roast duck, celery, and

plum preserves, with pickles & coffee, so we all enjoyed it ... I was out for quite a time this afternoon. Hal has had a man here today, leveling the earth around the house. This morning I made cookies, and wrote a little more in the home letters, besides doing some sweeping and a little reading. Mrs. Costerton came in for me to go for a walk – it was such a beautiful morning – but I was too busy. Then after dinner I took a good long rest before dressing. I went up to Mrs. Martin's intending to read to Mrs. Macintyre, but I couldn't make them hear my rap – so went down town, & then in to see Mrs. Godwin[30] & Mrs. Birnie.[31] The Godwins are having quite an addition put to their house. It will be so much nicer, & more comfortable for them ... I have not heard any interesting news for quite a long time, think I must try to hunt up some of the old timers & hear some of the adventures, or this will be rather a tame volume of diary. I am going to read now in Scott's poems – until Hal comes in – & then will knit while we talk.

Nov. 19th

This is Sunday afternoon and Hal & I are having a very cosy, happy home afternoon. I wish so much that Harry were here too. It really looks as if winter had set in in earnest. It has been snowing steadily all day. It will be a bad thing for the cattle men if they have another long severe winter – as there is not an ounce of old hay left in the country, and this was not a particularly good year for any crop. I did not write either Friday night, or last night. Last night I got so interested in my knitting that I didn't want to stop. I was trying to knit the heel, and as I had never done one before, but had only watched Clare, I was a little uncertain how I would get on. However, I got past the difficult part all right, & felt duly proud of myself. Friday night I really felt too bad to write. Mr. Horan had been down at the ranch and he brought me up a letter from Harry, saying that the old white cow was dead – choked on a piece of root, & he had had to kill Harriet, his pig that he had meant to keep always. It seems as if Harry were having more than his share of ill fortune this fall. I am so sorry for him – more for him than for many another, not only because of my love for him, but because he takes all these losses so keenly to heart. I have thought of him so much lately, and wished I could do something to help him ... I really felt too badly to do anything. It isn't the financial loss which grieves me so much, as the discouragement it all is to Harry. He would not find it so hard to be cheerful, if he had more of his own people with him. One thing Uncle is always nice & kind when anything goes wrong, and tries to do all he can to make matters happier. When Hal came in he comforted me as well as he could. He is so sorry for Harry, but we cannot do anything for him ... We have breakfast quite late now – not 'till after nine – & consequently have little appetite at noon, so I think, for the winter, we'll take to having dinner at night ... Before he went away little Rose Weddell[32] (Mrs. Coryell's grand-daughter) came over with her doll to pay me a visit ... Yesterday evening, while Hal went down to see Mr. Girouard, I ran over to Mrs. Smith's just for a few minutes to see how she was – then, as I said before, I got engrossed in my knitting, & when Hal came in, we read "The Old Curiosity Shop." This morning I went to church, & we meant to go up to the Presbyterian church[33] tonight, but it is so very stormy I think we'll stay at home. I have been playing & singing for Hal – he has just now gone up to see Mr. Girouard, and I have been in to see Mrs. Lander. She is quite sick with a bad cold ... I want to study my Bible lesson, & write a little more in my home letter, so must stop scribbling. Mrs. Lander has three such pretty children and they seem nicely brought up. I do feel sorry for her – I think they must be quite poor, their house is so barely furnished – but she is always cheerful, even now when she can hardly speak, having such a bad cold. She has evidently been used to better circumstances though she does not say so – which is one good mark for her. Jack Martin[34] sent us some prairie chickens yesterday, & I sent her in a pair – she seemed quite pleased.

Tuesday Afternoon [Nov. 21st]
I did not write last night in this, as I had such a lot to say to Mother & Wese, and before I was finished my letter Harold came in – he had a little assessment writing to do, & then we read The Old Curiosity Shop until quite late – we have just been introduced to Mrs. Jarley. It is a relief to come to the comical parts – little Nell's troubles are so real that it makes one quite sad – & yet I do like Dickens best in his pathetic vein. The funny parts so often verge upon the vulgar. He had a wonderful sympathy for the joys & sorrows of childhood ... Minna didn't come to her practise before school, so I had a good long morning, & did quite a lot of knitting. I think I'd grow very fond of knitting, & soon be able to do it fast. I finished one sock last night, & set up another. In the morning I hired the two Lander children & Clem Smith[35] to clean off the sidewalk: I had to go out every few minutes to superintend, & they did not get nearly all the snow off – however they thought they worked, & when they began to get tired, I gave them the promised five cents, & they went off very gleefully to buy their candy, assuring me that they would like to work for me again. Hal was very late coming to dinner. It was after two; however, I only had cold things so it didn't matter so much. I had just got the dishes done when Mrs. Coryell came over, & before she left Mrs. Smith

came to get me to go again to the dentist's with her. I had meant to go &
read to Mrs. Macintyre but, of course, I couldn't refuse to go to the dentist, so we went there & afterwards in to see Mrs. McDougal ... [Hal and
I] did not try to have tea early, but read for quite a while before hand. I
am actually not looking at the end of this book, but am often sorely
tempted to do so.

Thursday Afternoon [Nov. 23rd]
This is Thanksgiving Day,[36] but as we had no service, & it has been snowing fast since early morning, I have not gone out atall. Hal has been home
most of the morning, but has gone out just now. He had to go down town
to see about some assessment work. They are dividing the city into wards,
& need Hal to give them the valuations. I am sorry he had to go, as he
doesn't feel very well today & it is so nasty & wet. I was making more
preparations for my mince meat this morning. I made one pie, though I
haven't quite all the ingredients ready. It was very nice too – I think my
mince meat is going to be a great success. I expect Mrs. Smith over this
afternoon (her husband was going out shooting, so I asked her to come
and spend the day with me) and I think I'll stone the raisins while I talk
to her ... Yesterday I went down town in the morning to get spices, fruit
etc. and after dinner Gertie came to ask me to go for a walk. I had wanted
to go to see Mrs. Ellison, so we walked up there – we found her looking
miserable, & the baby quite sick – we did not stay long, as she seemed to
be busy and the baby was very fretful. We went in to Mrs. Wood's, but as
a new son had that morning arrived there, we cut that visit short too. I
came home, while Gertie went to do some shopping ... After I got home
I began the cloth scrap books I want to make. I'm afraid I haven't nearly
enough pictures. Hal pinked the edges of the leaves for me, & read to me
in the evening while I pasted in.

Saturday Night [Nov. 25th]
Mrs. Smith came on Thursday as I expected. I got most of my raisins
stoned for mince meat. We had quite a pleasant afternoon. Mrs. Smith is
young & bright. I think she gets pretty homesick & lonesome sometimes,
& she is farther from home even than I am – her people live in Moncton,
N.B. Evidently she has had a very nice home, and plenty of friends – her
school friends all about her, & here she seems to know very few people.
She told me she did not know anyone else so well as she knows me, & I
could easily count all the times I have seen her. She is too young to be
thrown so much in upon herself. I am sure she must miss young bright
companionship. She seems very fond of her husband.[37] He is a nice looking young man and very nice in the shop (a book store) but Hal says he is

the most miserly young fellow he ever saw; & Mrs. Smith was talking to
me of how she was learning to economize – it plainly was a new lesson to
her. She said ever so many times how much she had enjoyed her afternoon. I think it was a delight to her to find a sympathetic listener while
she talked of home, & I always am sympathetic on that subject. On Friday I finished stoning the raisins, swept and did lots of odd jobs – dinner
was late again, on account of the train. Afterwards I went over to Mrs.
Martin's with a book & my knitting. I read to Mrs. Macintyre for awhile,
& then we talked while I knitted. The old lady seems to enjoy having me
come & I do like to have a talk with her – she is a woman of character, &
has seen some great men & women of Scottish history – I am hoping to
make some notes of her different stories. Hal was home when I got here
and had made the kitchen fire – so I got tea ready, and afterwards got out
my writing things, expecting to have a long, solitary evening – as it was
[Hal's] lodge[38] night. I wrote the home letters first, meaning to write in
this afterwards, but about half past eight Harold came in so we read until
bed-time ... We got some eggs – 3 doz. for a dollar seems pretty dear, but
Harry's haven't begun to lay yet and it won't do to be without eggs for my
Xmas cooking. It is very mild tonight & sounds as if a Chinook were
blowing. That is what they call a warm wind which sometimes comes and
in a couple of hours will take off a foot of snow. Hal says he has seen it in
Calgary, that it almost seems a miracle the way the snow disappears. I
went to see Mrs. Lander yesterday after I got back from the Martins ...
Mrs. Martin knew her in Calgary, says they are very nice people. I knew
that, but they do seem terribly poor. Just one month more to Xmas.

Nov. 26th Sunday Evening
It is almost time for evening church. We have spent a quiet, restful Sunday. We had no service in our church this morning; at first we meant to go
to the Methodist Church.[39] They had a woman temperance preacher but
we were up late, & it was snowing, so we stayed at home & read together,
& I played some sacred music. After dinner we read again, & Hal took a
little sleep – then we went out for a walk. It has been a beautiful bright
winter's day, but mild. A little more snow fell last night & this morning;
so – although it has been thawing, we seem to have just as much on
the ground. We went up to see Mr. Girouard. He says he doesn't look
quite all right yet – has some difficulty in breathing. His house looked so
cheerless – poor old man! though he is rich in money and money's worth,
and probably may be pitying me for my way of life – still I say again poor
old man! I often think of that sentence in Drummond's little book, "No
worse fate can befall a man in this world than to live and grow old alone,

unloving & unloved." I don't suppose there is one person in the whole world who really loves this old man, though many like him. I have all my life been so rich in the best wealth – love – that my heart runs over with pity for those who are in poverty (lacking it).

Monday Night [Nov. 27th]

It is very cold tonight. I am so sorry if it turns very cold now – I am afraid my poor plants will suffer while I am away, though I'm sure Hal will do all he can to keep the house warm. This morning I washed some flannels, made bread and apple pie & a lot of little mince pies to leave for Hal ... After dinner I dressed, & went up to Mrs. Ellison's. I sat and talked a good while with her; when I got home it was almost dark. Harold had been home, & had made a good fire in the hall. I didn't light the kitchen one atall, but boiled the water for some tea on the hall stove. It is very cold. I have lifted most of my plants out of the windows. I hope Hal won't be very late, as I feel quite lonesome tonight – but there is a council meeting, & they are settling the wards, so Hal has to be there. I think I will begin a home letter. As I was coming back from Mrs. Ellison's past the Kale-malka[40] yard, I saw a cow (which had been tied to a log, by the leg) fast strangling. The poor thing had fallen over the log – and her head was dou-bled right under her body. I ran to the hotel, but saw two men on the way. I hailed them, & told them the trouble. They ran over to the cow, & one of them cut the rope, so the poor animal got up, but she soon would have died if we had not seen her.

Tuesday Night – The Ranch – Nov. 28th

It is another very cold night – I hope my plants won't freeze. I came down on the train this afternoon – Harry met me at Armstrong.[41] I was very busy all the morning. I wanted to cook a few things for Hal and had a lit-tle ironing to do. Then after dinner I was sweeping & dusting, and before I got my dress changed Mrs. Megaw[42] came. While she was still there Mrs. Watson came, & I began to be in despair of ever getting ready in time for the train. Mr. Wood, too, came in, & I had my plants to attend to, & sweeping and dusting to do. I just put all my plants in the corner of the dining room, away from the windows, & warned Hal to try & keep the fires as much as he can, but I daresay some of them will be touched, if this weather keeps on. I am sure it must be ever so much below zero. Harry's fine heifer is sick now; he is afraid it will die. I do hope not – he seems to have had his share of trouble this fall. Hal came home, & carried my things up to the train for me. The station was quite gay – a wedding party were coming off. Dr. Reinhardt,[43] too, was on board – he had been telegraphed for to Armstrong. At Larkin[44] Mr. O'Keefe and his two little girls got on the train. He is taking them back to Ottawa to school – & very homesick they looked, poor children – they wanted so much to stay at home until after Xmas. Mr. O'Keefe still bears the mark of his cut in his face.[45] It looks very crooked & swelled, but he seemed in his usual spirits and laughed as much as ever. We walked up – it was a beautiful night for a walk, bright but very cold. I was so well muffled up however that I didn't get a bit cold; & when we got here had a good tea of roast chicken, cold pork, & head cheese.[46] Since tea we have sat & talked, until just now Harry has gone out to the stable.

Wednesday [Nov. 29th]
It is after nine o'clock, & I am tired and sleepy, but don't want to fail to record today's events, for tomorrow will no doubt bring its own duties. Harry & I have just come in from the Pelleys' where we spent a very pleasant evening, but I mustn't begin at the wrong end of the day, so will start at half past five, when I awoke, hearing Harry & Uncle get up & light the fires. I waited until the rooms were warm and when I came out found breakfast all ready. Uncle had made biscuit. I missed the lovely thick cream we have had all along here for coffee – they have had to go back to condensed milk since the old cow's death. Right after breakfast I made the beds, & swept up, & then made two apple pies & some turnovers – then cookies for Uncle. Mr. Evans came in almost as soon as we had had breakfast, & Jack Lawrie and Harry Harding came about nine. They got their bloody deed over pretty soon, & were all done the disagreeable part by half past eleven. I had a nice dinner for them – cold meat, potatoes & boiled cabbage, & two apple pies which they nearly finished. After dinner we washed up all the dishes, & the dirty tin pans & pots were innumerable – then I swept again and tidied – then we dressed ... and when Mr. Evans came by, on his way back home, we got in with him, & drove up to the Pelleys & stayed to tea. I asked Nonah to go up with us on Saturday – she will probably stay a week with me. We had to walk back from there, so started soon after eight. It isn't nearly so cold tonight; & as the walking was a little slippery, we took an hour to come home. We had such a nice tea, & I did enjoy it. Nonah got it all while Mrs. Pelley sat down and talked to me. Nonah is such a useful girl and so quiet and thoughtful for her Mother.

Thursday Night [Nov. 30th]
I don't feel much like writing, for my fingers are tired & tender, they have been in water so much this morning – & indeed nearly all day – I have washed them fully a dozen times. After breakfast I had quite a lot of flannels to wash, & it was such a stormy, snowy day I didn't want to hang them

out doors, so Harry put up two lines for me across the sitting room, & I hung the things on them, making a passage from door to door. Harry called it his "avenue of chestnuts." After they were done, Harry killed, & we two plucked and dressed ready for market, twenty fine big chickens – as we did not begin them until ten, & were all done before the clock struck three, we thought we were rather smart. We have since tea been singing together and reading …

Vernon – Monday Evening Dec. 4th
Four days since I have written anything. I will have a lot to enter tonight. Friday was another busy day at the ranch, and in the afternoon Harry drove me down to Armstrong. I had hunted up a dollar & a quarter's worth of flour sacks, & took them down. I got some nice turkish towelling in place of them, enough to make four big towels, which they were in need of … Harry had been over at Harry Harding's for Pat (the horse) and just got back in time for dinner … We had tender loin & roast heart … Uncle got a letter from California which has decided him to go down there for the winter. He will start next week I expect. It will be very lonely for Harry, still I can't help being glad that Uncle is going to have the pleasure. He hasn't had much pleasure in his life, poor old man, & he will be glad to see all of them. In the evening (Friday) I had some socks to darn & flannels to mend & didn't like to write anyway, as the boys seemed to feel like talking. We sat up quite late, & yet were all up early Saturday morning, and had our breakfast by lamplight. We got quite an early start for Vernon. Harry had loaded me down with presents – a fine pair of chickens, a roast of pork, some head cheese & lard. I am going to make him a cake and Xmas pudding, as three of the young fellows from here are going down for him the Sunday before Xmas, & will have dinner with him. We called for Nonah and had to wait a little while for her but got here soon after twelve. I was greatly relieved to find my plants all right – Hal sat up very late the cold nights to keep the fires going – indeed he had taken splendid care of every thing. The fires were both laid, ready to start, & we got them burning, & all the things brought in from the sleigh. In the afternoon I made a couple of mince pies, rearranged the plants, & with Nonah's help tidied up the house for Sunday. Harry was out in the afternoon, selling his chickens and getting his hair cut. He came back to tea, of course, and afterwards we had music until bed time. Sunday morning Nonah and I went to church, & we had a great service … When we got home, Hal had dinner nearly ready … We had roast venison, carrots, potatoes, mince pie, cheese, celery. Harry left about half past three … This

morning after the work was done we went down town to do some shopping, then home & got dinner. Hal was very late in coming. He brought me a splendid letter from Wese ... All are well at home − it always comforts me to hear that. This afternoon Nonah & I went up to see Mrs. Ellison − also to see Mrs. Lander. I had been telling Mrs. Pelley about the latter, & she gave me two bottles of fruit for her − I was so pleased to take it to her − only really I felt quite overcome by her pleasure. She said I had been her "good angel" here, coming to see her when no one else did. We went on to Mrs. Ellison's and she gave me a little basket of apples. Before we went out Mrs. Spinks & Maisie[47] called, and while we were gone Mrs. Dewdney and Rosie. Mrs. Spinks asked us there to spend Wednesday Evening. I accepted for Nonah, but declined for myself, as I knew Hal wouldn't go. Since tea Nonah & I have been sitting here, I writing, she reading. Hal has gone to a Council meeting.

Tuesday Evening [Dec. 5th]
After I had written last night, Mr. Walter Cochrane[48] came in, & stayed until after ten. I think Nonah must have been the attraction, as the young man never called before, & we don't care much for him. Of course we couldn't do anything but talk. This morning Nonah helped me. We made a splendid Xmas cake, with a small one for Harry, and I finished up the mince meat, besides doing the regular work ... Only Mrs. Beckingsale came to Bible Class, so we didn't have any, as it seemed a pity to begin a new epistle without the others ... I have just been reading aloud the closing scenes of Little Nell's history and it is so sad, my voice got very shaky, & my eyes rather dim. I don't think the child's death is so sad as the old man's despair. We are having a decided thaw − it almost looks as if the snow were going.

Wednesday Night Nov. [Dec.] 6th
Ten months today since we reached Vernon. How many people I have got to know! Almost everyone, I think.[49] I don't dislike the place quite so much as I did at first, though it never will be really dear to me, I fear. Mrs. Ellison wants me to teach in the Presbyterian Sunday School, & I believe I will. This morning I baked bread, made an apple pie, & a blanc mange for Tom Godwin, which I took over to him. He is sick in bed with grippe. I ran in to Mrs. Coryell's for a minute, & when I came home made a hat for Nonah. It is very pretty if I do say it "as shouldn't." She looks so nice & pretty this time, her dresses are pretty, and she has such nice manners. I am not getting on very fast with the little things I wanted to do for Xmas ...

Friday Evening [Dec. 8th]

Harold has gone to Lodge, & Nonah is reading, so I am going to take time to write a little – we had tea later than usual. We were out calling all the afternoon & got in late. I did not write in this last night, as I was busy trying to write a little story for Walter & Roy – one out of Hal's own life. I often wish I had the power to write the adventures he has told me of. They would make a splendid story if I had the pen to do them justice.[50] Nonah went to Mrs. Spinks Wednesday night. I began some home letters, and then knitted while Hal told me old reminiscences. Thursday morning I had things to do in the kitchen. Nonah helped me. It has been very nice to have her with me this week – & a great help. In the afternoon I took my home letter down to the post, then when I got back Rosie Dewdney came, & we three went up to call at the Cochranes. From there I came home while Nonah went to Mrs. Dewdney's to tea. When I got here Hal was home, & while he lighted the fires I ran over to Mrs. Martin's, & had a chat with her & Mrs. Macintyre ... Today we made Harry's pudding, & made doughnuts besides ever so many other things which don't count enough to put on paper, but which take up the time as much as more important actions. After dinner we dressed early as we had a good many calls to pay ... so we soon went out, & made a regular tour. Wese sent the little photograph frames & court plaster cases which I asked her to paint for sale and they arrived safely today. They are very dainty and lovely. I hope they'll all sell – I sold two on the way to Mr. Taylor's shop – 75 cents apiece – & Mr. Taylor said he'd do his best to sell the others ... When we got home from our calls I went in to see Tom Godwin – he is much better. Coming home I met Mrs. Weir hurrying along. She is a poor woman who lives back of us. I had heard her baby was sick, & stopped to ask her about it. She was crying and said she feared he was going to die. The Doctor had been there three times today, & was going to bring in another doctor. Poor woman! I felt very sorry for her. When we came home Hal was here, & then began preparations for eating. What a lot of time we have to spend in that! I give it grudgingly sometimes.

Saturday Night [Dec. 9th]

Nonah & I are sitting, one each side of the table, she reading. We won't have long alone I expect, as Mrs. Smith was in, and said her daughter Nina[51] was coming over to see Nonah tonight ... This morning we had a great tidying up – to look nice and trim for Harry and Mrs. Pelley. Hal was very late in coming to breakfast – indeed Nonah and I got so hungry that we began ours. Soon after breakfast Minna came, & I gave her a good long lesson, & then showed her how to pop corn. She had never seen any

popped before, & was most interested. We got our work all done by dinner time, & immediately afterwards started out for Mrs. Ellison's. We
went in to Mrs. Costerton's first. She did not go to her sister's today as she
had had neuralgia ... Mrs. Ellison was very nice about the Sunday School.
I explained that I wouldn't be able to go tomorrow if Mrs. Pelley came,
and she said it was all right, to come if I could. I think I will quite enjoy
teaching again – I only don't quite like leaving Hal on our one whole day
at home together ...

Sunday [Dec. 10th]
... Nina Smith came over last evening, so we played cards to amuse her &
Nonah – she stayed until half past ten. It was raining when Hal took her
home, & we were afraid that maybe it would prevent Harry's coming
today: but sure enough he appeared with Mrs. Pelley and May before we
had really got our work done – soon after eleven ... Harry had Mr. Rabbitt's big two seated sleigh and they set off very gaily, with Mrs. Pelley &
May in the back seat and Harry & Nonah in front. Nonah seems to have
got older so suddenly – she has quite a grave manner, except when she is
amused. She & Harry are getting to be great friends. I hardly had any
time to talk to Mrs. Pelley, as I was busy getting dinner about half of the
time. We sang a few hymns, and after dinner, we just cleared away the
things, & left them on the kitchen table. Hal & I had a great washing up
after they left – & a quiet tea. Harry said Uncle would be up tomorrow to
stay overnight, & leave for California on Tuesday. Harry says he is so
happy over the prospect, & can talk of nothing else. He is going by Seattle, so will probably see Clare – she will be surprised. I haven't heard again
from her. The Weirs' baby is better.

Tuesday Night [Dec. 12th]
I did not write last night, as Hal & I went to the concert. It was for the
benefit of the Odd fellows Lodge. They had a "star" elocutionist – she did
very well. I quite enjoyed it, still it hardly seemed worth a dollar & a half:
they charge so enormously for tickets here – 75 cents apiece – still, Hal is
an odd fellow, & felt he ought to go. I had letters from home yesterday
and Uncle came up on the morning train. I did not go out in the afternoon 'till towards evening – I just ran over to Mr. Taylor's with the other
things Wese sent. I only wish I could afford to buy them all myself for presents – they are so ... We left Uncle with a hot fire & some small mince
pies to comfort himself with – he had gone to bed when we got home. Mr.
Martin told Harold last night that Mrs. Macintyre is very ill, so I ran over
this morning to ask for her. Poor Mrs. Martin was in great distress; the
poor old lady has rheumatism round her heart, and one lung is slightly

congested, so they feel extremely anxious. I am going to sit up [with her] tonight, & do hope I'll be able to keep awake; but I have had a busy day, and am a poor one to keep awake even when I'm not tired. Hal is half afraid it will make me sick; but there seem so few people to offer – and Mrs. Macintyre likes me. I am glad to be able to do it for Mrs. Martin. I'll never forget she was my first caller in my loneliness that first week in the cottage – lonely – lacking friends – for fond as I am of my husband, & much as I loved & do love my old home, I think I need outside love as well here as I did there.

Uncle went off this afternoon as pleased & excited as a child. He left here at about half past three: nearly an hour before train time, he was so afraid of being late. He said Harry was going in to Armstrong to see him off. Jack Lawrie was with Harry, & likely will stay a good deal with him through the winter. The funniest thing I heard at the concert last night wasn't on the programme. They had a printed programme and of course the opening line was "Overture – piano solo – Mr. Cann."[52] Mr. McKelvie had brought Miss Wright,[53] & she was sitting just behind us – she bent over and asked me if I knew many of the "pieces" that were to be rendered. I said "No." "Oh," she said, "I know that first piece – overture – piano solo – I've heard it often – it is lovely." I can tell you I did want to laugh ...

Wednesday Evening [Dec. 13th]

I am very sorry I am so sleepy tonight as this must be the finishing up of my diary. I wouldn't like it to be late in getting home. I went over to Mrs. Martin's at nine – Hal took me, of course. I found Miss Kape there. I coaxed Mrs. Martin to go to bed very soon – & then began my watch. Miss Kape left but about half past ten Mrs. Smith came, & she stayed until after twelve – then Dr. Morris came – so we made Mrs. Smith go home. Mrs. Martin had a nice little supper ready for us in the dining room, but I wasn't hungry. However, the Dr. was – & then, while the old lady slept, I had quite a little romance told to me. I would like to re-tell it here, but the characters are too much in real life for me to do that. Story books don't monopolize all the heart-burnings, and disappointments, and misunderstandings. How little we know what is going on in our smiling companion's heart, until a chance touch pulls aside a curtain, and the scene revealed is often a surprise – last night's story has the materials for a first class tragedy, & already to the poor young Dr. it is anything but a comedy. I felt sorry for him. Harold declares I have a way of worming everyone's secret from them – but I'm sure it was the silence & loneliness last night, rather than curiosity on my part, which prompted confidence.

Thursday Afternoon

I hate to send any blank pages in this, but have not time to finish it if I send it off this afternoon. I was out in the morning trying to sell some of my little paintings & was successful in a measure. I want to go to Mrs. Macintyre this afternoon – I hear she is not so well today. I'll offer to stay again tomorrow night. I got home about half past six yesterday – undressed and went to bed, but I only slept until nine, & not again all day, so I was really too sleepy at night to write or do anything. I went to bed at half past eight, & slept until eight today.

Thus ends the diary! I wonder how it will find all in the dear old home. I know it carried loads of love from me in every page and every line.

CHAPTER 4

How many people I have got to know!

Vernon Friends and Acquaintances

Alice interacted most frequently with women of her own social stand-ing, and a friend once made was a friend for life. She wrote relatively lit-tle about her most intimate friends – Mesdames Costerton, Martin, Dewdney/Cameron, Smith, Cochrane, Ellison, Jacques, and Billings; they were such frequent visitors to her pages that they required no expan-sive portrait. She enjoyed frequent visits and sessions of gossip, and the workings of society in Vernon enlivened page after page. Her curiosity about the human psyche, including her own, was profound, and her under-standing of the quirks of human and animal nature was seldom inaccurate:

The ladies all seemed to have a pleasant time, and stayed quite late. It wasn't a gossip party atall. We talked about flowers, fancy work, the recent lecture – indeed anything but our neighbour's affairs. [6 January 1895]

William Fraser Cameron:
Yesterday morning Mr. Cameron came about nine and drove me down to the lake ... Mr. Cameron has a boat down there, & he took me for a lovely row. I did enjoy it, though it made me homesick to see the dear old waves, & hear the water swish against the boat. Mr. Cameron proved to be a very entertaining companion. I would have felt quite flattered at his giving a whole morning up to amuse me (for he is a busy man – & not atall a lady's man) only that I know he did it on Hal's account not my own ... When we were down at the Lake we rowed over to inspect a boat which Captain Shorts is building. One cannot but admire his pluck, though one can scarcely commend his wisdom. He is building a small boat – I should

think not more than 40 feet long, to run in opposition to the large C.P.R. steamer, on Lake Okanagan – & is quite confident & hopeful that his small craft can run successfully in competition with the biggest monopoly in the world. [16 June 1894]

Clara Dewdney/Cameron:
I have had two confidences reposed in me this week. Last night Mrs. Dewdney[1] told me that she is going to marry Mr. Cameron. It wasn't quite such a surprise to me as it will be to most people I imagine, for Hal had a suspicion for some time about it – but I confess I thought Mr. Norris a more likely man for her to choose. She thinks of going to England for a couple of months to see all her own people, and on her return Mr. Cameron will meet her & bring her back as his wife. I am glad for her – she has had so many worries & cares, and now she will have a pair of broad shoulders to bear them for her – & (unless we are much mistaken in Mr. Cameron) a very warm big heart to think of her comfort & happiness. Still they are, on the surface, an apparently ill-matched pair. She is bright, fond of society, almost giddy in manner sometimes – while he is almost a recluse. He is not old, but seems to have no liking for society – & I don't think he could talk "small talk." They are both really good & upright under all this, though I don't think Mr. Cameron is, in the least, a religious man – & Mrs. Dewdney is a thorough Christian. [22 June 1894]

We spent Thursday evening at Mrs. Dewdney's. I had the pleasure of playing whist all the evening in what should have been distinguished company – my partner was our worthy Mayor, Mr. Martin – and Mr. Mair[2] (the author of "Tecumseh"; one of our Canadian poets) with Miss Macintyre were our opponents. Mr. Mair, however, is by no means a brilliant conversationalist. He is short, stout, "bumptious," altogether impractical in appearance and behaviour, & I might add occupation, for he keeps a general store in Kelowna. He is not a bad whist player – but thinks he is even better than he is. [28 April 1894]

The Cochranes:
I always like a talk with Mr. Cochrane. He seems to take such a kindly, homely interest in even small things – and yet he is a very shrewd business man. [12 April 1898]

My talk with [Mrs. Cochrane] has been quite a rest, for we just talked about flowers and pickles & jam – and not people atall. I have heard more gossip today than would go for a month, & it was a rest to get plain household talk. [24 August 1895]

Nonah Pelly:
There is quite a fashionable ball at the Kalemalka tonight. We were favoured with invitation – indeed Mrs. Beckingsale & Mrs. Robbins came yesterday morning, and begged me to go, & take Nonah. Indeed Mrs. Beckingsale begged so hard to have Nonah go (even if we wouldn't) & offered to chaperone her, that I half consented. However when Hal came in & I spoke to him about it, he said he would rather not – he said if she were his daughter she certainly shouldn't go. I believe the last ball at the Kalemalka was really not nice atall – though it is supposed to be very select, & of the elite – some of the men were by no means well behaved, &, of course, I wouldn't run any risks of unpleasantness for Nonah. She is pretty, & fond of dancing, & all the young fellows would want to know her. She is so sweet about it, not showing a bit of disappointment, though I suppose she would have liked to go. I thought I'd try and make up a little to her, so I bought her a pretty sun hat today & trimmed it. She was so pleased, & looks very nice in it. I am going to get one like it myself. It is brown straw, & I had some flowers to trim it. [25 April 1894]

The Charlie Costertons:
We went in to see Mrs. Costerton. She doesn't seem to get much stronger – is not able to walk from her bed to the sofa yet. She had quite a throng of visitors – I think she sees far too many people, & if I were her nurse I would manage both her & the baby very differently. [4 April 1894]

... [there] was a special meeting at the Oddfellows' Lodge to haul Mr. Costerton over the coals. He is secretary and had given no account to the treasurer of monies paid in to him. He isn't fit to have an office, I think. He has not been steady again lately & apart from that he is such a flighty silly sort of man. [4 November 1894]

The Clement Costertons:
Another piece of news is that Effie Gibbs is engaged to Mr. Clem Coster-ton. I'm afraid there will be some heartaches over that. I don't quite under-stand it, & confess that I am sorry. When I first came out to B.C. Effie – then a very young girl – was in love with the head miller at Enderby – Mr. Macintyre[3] – and he with her. Mr. Gibbs was then manager of the mill and would not listen to the match, thinking Mr. Macintyre quite their inferior. Indeed, they sent Effie away for a year, hoping to break it off. However, all was of no avail, and last Spring when Mr. Gibbs lost his position, & was so disgraced, I believe Mr. Macintyre was very gladly received by the family as Effie's accepted lover – and I know he was very

nice to Mr. Gibbs, & I believe lent him a good deal of money. Well, ever
since Mrs. Gibbs has lived in Vernon Mr. Costerton has boarded with
them, & Effie's wedding, which was to have taken place last summer, has
been put off month by month – until now she is engaged to Mr. Costerton. I am sure she can't care for him. I know at Easter she was still engaged
to Mr. Macintyre. I don't like Mr. Costerton. He is a man I never would
trust. He was always very attentive to Mrs. Bales, a grass widow – in
Enderby – so much so that people said he was only waiting for her to get
a devorce to marry her. But this winter death stepped in, & set the widow
free. Poor Mr. Bales hanged himself, & then Mr. Costerton's devotion
showed for what it was worth. After having danced attendance on the
widow for years, while he was quite safe, and the only harm was to get her
talked about, he now turns the cold shoulder on her. [5 May 1894]

Today I went with Gertie to call on the bride – Mrs. Clement Costerton.
She has a parlour & bed-room in her Mother's house. It looked very
pretty and she was showing us her presents, she actually made a joke about
the one she had received when she was going to marry Mr. MacIntyre. I
don't see how she can. I think – I really do think – even if I could act as
she has done, I'd have the grace to be ashamed of myself, & be quiet over
past behaviour. [13 June 1894]

Rose Dewdney:
Mrs. Cameron had heard from poor Rosie & her Uncle (Lieut. Gov.
Dewdney) wanted her to stay on with them in Victoria until the Spring –
the poor girl is so homesick. Everyone says Mrs. Edgar Dewdney[4] is very
strict, & treats Rosie as if she were quite a young child – & in Vernon Mrs.
Cameron allowed her so much liberty, & was always so good to her – so
she feels the difference sadly. She is nearly eighteen – a very handsome girl
– tall & large – and it must be mortifying to be sent back to a childhood
which she has been well out of for two years … some of us wouldn't mind
taking some of the restrictions of childhood if we could again feel its
freshness & fearlessness – but I think I never feel regrets for the losses age
has brought, without remembering that poem of Holmes about the man
who would be a boy again, & it reminds one of the compensating gains of
added years. [2 January 1897]

[I] was more than surprised when Mrs. Jacques told me that Rosie Dewdney and Mr. Keating were married[5] that morning and had gone right
away. I felt very sorry that they had been married so quietly & hurriedly.
Mrs. Cameron had told no one, not even their most intimate friends.

Maisie Spinks & Mrs. Clark and Mrs. Burnyeat were at the church, and
no one else. I have not seen Mrs. Cameron since – I don't like to go soon,
it would seem like being inquisitive. [3 May 1898]

The Ellisons:
[Mr. Ellison] came in & had a long gossip. We were talking about Mr.
Crowell's possible fortune, & he said – well he did wish sometimes he was
not so hard up, & was talking about the delights and advantages of having plenty of money, & I said yes, I knew it was nice & one couldn't help
wishing sometimes for more, but, would we really be happier? "Well" he
said "I don't know any one who is happier & more contented than you two
are right here and you are not exactly wealthy." It is true too, we have a
very comfortable cozy home, & I don't honestly believe I desire any better circumstances if (there is always some little fox spoiling the vines of
content) my own dear loved ones were nearer to us – I would like to see
them often. [12 January 1897]

I went to see Mrs. Ellison and the new baby[6] – he is a very fine little child
– looks something like the other boy, but is, I think, larger. Of course he
is the king & pet of all. In spite of the frequency of their coming, the
newest baby is always a marvel and a source of worship to all the Ellison
household. Poor little Price had a very bruised eye – he fell when out driving, & hit his eye on the dashboard. [6 October 1897]

Lizzie Harding:
Lizzie was over this afternoon ... and was busy making out a new time
table – perhaps she will come in tonight. She says she thinks she can manage the school all right – she only had to whip three children today! – and
keep *six* in after school! [4 February 1896]

Lizzie is not very wise in some ways. She will not be cordial to any one
who she considers a little out of the "upper ten" class – and as nearly all
the parents of her pupils come under that heading, I am afraid she isn't
popular. We have said all we can – but she goes her own way. It is too bad.
She is a very loveable girl – we are really fond of her – but she is very headstrong. I hope she won't lose her school. [23 March 1898]

The Martins:
... Mrs. Schubert has been saying very unkind things about the Martin
men, and Mrs. Martin is angry over it, and she has much of the sturdy
Scotch uprightness which won't let honesty bow to policy. If she doesn't
like any one she won't pretend to. Sometimes I wish I were a little more

like that – but I believe I'd have asked Mrs. Schubert in her place. It seems so decidedly throwing the gauntlet down – and Mrs. Schubert has a bitter tongue, & of course, now she will be more bitter than ever. I am sorry on her husband's account. I think he is a nice man, though Hal says he, too, is vindictive in a quieter way. [13 February 1895]

I walked down the sidewalk with Mrs. Schubert, and was sorry when she opened the subject of the dance tonight. I don't want to be a partizan in the matter, as I wish to be friendly with both sides. I felt sorry for Mrs. Schubert. I think she feels pretty badly over it – more so than she will confess, although she said to me she was sorry she spoke so hastily at election time. I know I, myself, so often regret a speech as soon as I have made it, that I can feel for her. [14 February 1895]

[I went] up to the station so see Mrs. Martin off [to Rossland]. I was more sorry than I can express to see her go – she has been a good, good friend to me, and I'll miss her sorely. [27 July 1898]

A miscellany of friends and acquaintances:
I had just finished the work and settled down to write when the Postills drove up. Poor Mrs. Postill had caught cold in her eye, & was feeling very miserable. The children were very good. The little boy, of five years, was particularly bright & interesting – the little girl was young. They were not atall pretty children, but are obedient & full of life. I enjoyed having them & liked Mrs. Postill. I found Mr. Postill the least interesting of the party. He is very talkative & very prosy ... After tea Mr. Postill went to a meeting & I thought I'd get Mrs. Postill to go to bed early (her eye was very much inflamed and she looked miserable), but first Mr. Norris came in and then Mrs. Ellison, who said Mr. Ellison would come with Postill after the meeting. They were late getting in, & then all stayed until twelve o'clock. I was sorry on Mrs. Postill's account, but her eye was better today. They did not get off until after dinner, though they spoke of going in the morning. Mr. Postill is so unpunctual. He would send me "distracted mad" as Hal's old song says. He told Mrs. Postill to be ready at half past ten to start. She went out after breakfast to do some shopping and left the children with me. They were very good, entertaining me nicely with stories & songs (which had no tune). When their Mother got back she got them partly ready & herself too – but not a sign of Mr. Postill did we see till a few minutes to twelve. Fortunately Hal had warned me that he was likely not to start till afternoon if he said morning – or even tomorrow when he had fixed on today – so I prepared dinner enough for all & they got started between two or three. [3 March 1896]

Mrs. Buchanan was telling me she wants to call her baby "Alonzo." Mr. Buchanan ... would like to call it Calvin, but she does not like such an old fashioned name for her wonderful baby! She is an untidy, very ugly young woman, & her parlour is decorated with paper roses, etc. Just the kind of person one would expect to christen a baby Alonzo. [4 November 1895]

... Mrs. Poulin[7] was very lonesome. So after I had rested about an hour I got up and dressed, & went over to see her ... I found the poor little woman very lonely, & rather tearful. I feel sorry for her & yet I think she is a little pettish & childish – still she is very young &, I am sure, often very homesick and it isn't possible to be very philosophical when one is homesick, & I don't believe any of us would love the young as well if they were always wise and reasonable – their varying moods form their great charm. I suppose, too, one must make allowances for the French nature, which is so volatile – either up or down ... Mr. Poulin did not get home until twelve o'clock at night, & his wife was so frightened and nervous, she cried and would not be comforted ... [22 July 1895]

I am so sorry for Mrs. Smith. She has such a lot of work to do & rather an unruly lot of children[8] to manage. [29 October 1895]

We didn't either of us want to go to the Smiths but we want Annie to have as much pleasure as she can, and besides I didn't want to offend Mrs. Smith, or hurt her feelings, & she cares so much if people don't accept her invitations. [9 March 1899]

Mrs. Smith had some delicious coffee, & equally delicious cake, & it was after five, so I was hungry, & they insisted on my partaking so freely that the natural consequence was I couldn't eat any tea. The Smiths expect to build a very fine new house[9] – they are excavating for the foundation now, & will not build until next Spring. [3 October 1899]

Mrs. Martin said it is beginning to be whispered that there is something queer about [Mrs. Spinks's] illness – that she has contracted a habit of taking morphine and is not quite right in her mind. I will be so sorry if that is true. One of her sisters (Maisie's Mother) died insane; but she, poor woman had trouble enough to derange her mind. Her husband (Judge Spinks brother) was untrue to her and openly acknowledged his preference for a very bad woman, whom he afterwards married, & that is why Maisie always lives here. [7 March 1894]

After the death of Nora Spinks:
Judge Spinks is going to resume his spiritualistic séances – they asked [Lizzie] to join, & she said she could go on Thursday night, but both Hal

& I have advised, & begged, her to have nothing to do with them. Mrs. Monteith is suppose to be an excellent medium. I believe she goes into a kind of trance & talks all sorts of nonsense. I think it doesn't show a very nice spirit in Judge Spinks to begin these meetings again. Mrs. Spinks was strongly opposed to them, indeed at one time it almost led to serious trouble between her & the Judge – & now, as soon as she is gone, he begins again. I think it is actually wicked, for he tries to (& hopes to succeed) hold communication with departed spirits ... I suppose I am prejudiced but I really do not like Mrs. Monteith. I think she is rather a dangerous companion for anyone, and I sincerely wish Lizzie had some nice place to board. [4 December 1897]

Oh – [the concert] was a poor one. I don't think I ever heard much worse – even in Vernon – & that is saying a good deal. After the first selection – a violin solo which was not encored – Mr. Graham the chairman arose and said that as the programme was a short one encores would be responded to! After this very palpable hint *everything* was encored good, bad & indifferent, and as there were only about three things on the programme worth listening to, every one was so tired that the whole audience rose in a mass before the programme was finished and had to be implored from the platform to remain for God Save the Queen. [2 October 1898]

When Hal came home he brought the long looked for Mr. [Arthur] Craven and long he is truly – well over six feet, thin, with a long brown beard. He is a most uncommon looking man I think – the more I looked at him the more I thought so. When we had gone up stairs I said to Hal I thought he looked very Jewish, indeed much like the pictures I have seen of St. John – & Hal told Mr. Craven this morning, thinking it rather a joke. He didn't look a bit surprised, but said he would tell us – if we wouldn't speak of it – what the miners in Colorado often called him. Of course it was wrong, or hardly seems reverent to write it – but he said many of them used to call him Jesus Christ – and indeed that thought was in my mind that he like the pictures we see of our Saviour – the same shaped head, the long beard, the beautiful eyes & forehead and straight, strong nose. His eyes are beautiful & very sad looking, indeed his whole face is sad. His conversation isn't saintly – just that of an ordinary well informed travelled gentleman, but I think there must be something uncommon in his character or he couldn't have such a face. I was a little disappointed in him just at first, but liked him better all the time. [16 August 1895]

[We] called on the bride next door. They evidently like bright colours. I am afraid Jack Lawrie wouldn't approve of their taste – he doesn't like my scarlet flowers, as he thinks they look "loud." I don't know what he'd say to a gay red & yellow carpet, vivid blue draperies – and some pink silk scarves on chair backs, besides little etceteras of most of the other colours. The bride is colourless enough except for her tightly curled black hair – well even black isn't a colour! but it is definite. [3 April 1895]

The poor old "Dasher"[10] – an old timer (though a comparatively young man) – was found frozen to death on Monday. He had set out from town with some provisions one cold night last week, to go to where he & another man are camping up on the mountains. When he failed to arrive there his partner came down to look for him. Quite a party went out to search & yesterday morning they found him – frozen. Poor man! He had lived a wild and rather worthless life, and now it has ended in this sad way. It makes one feel very solemn. [21 December 1897]

I went to call on my Irish neighbour, Mrs. Conn Finn[11] this afternoon – and only wish I could do the interview justice. I thoroughly enjoyed it. Mrs. Finn is *very* Irish and gave me a history of her knowledge of Conn and how she had always been fond of him since they were little children together – but after he was grown up she went to service and he came out here, and never wrote to her, so she thought he had forgotten about her, until one day this Spring, she was in a shop & a man she knew came in "and he says 'Well Mary, who do you think has come home from Ameriky?' and I thought maybe it was me godfather Denny Finn for he had come out to Ontario with his wife and children, but was writin' back that he didn't like the country atall, & would be goin' home to Ireland – so I says 'An' maybe it is Denny Finn' an' he says 'No it isn't Denny, but it's Conn Finn come back' – and I says 'It's a whale ye are – God knows – for it's never Conn Finn come home – but he says 'Yes it is & he's up at his Uncle's.' So up I goes – & Conn was up stairs washin' & dressin' after his journey, & I never make meself known – & sure enough down he comes, & when he sees me he says 'Well, Mary, old girl, how are ye?' – & I says 'Oh, he don't care much, when he never wrote to me all these years.'" However, Conn explained to her satisfaction that he had thought of her if he didn't write – and persuaded her to promise to marry him. She confessed with candour that she "didn't need much coaxin'" for she had never been fond of anyone else, but alas, the course of true love had its inevitable breaker. Their Parish priest would not marry them – he said Conn had been away so long that he didn't know whether he had a wife out here – & he would not marry him to her unless he waited to write to the priest here and find out. However Conn wanted to come back to America at

once, so she decided to come back with him, & they were married here –
& now she is "happy as the day is long." She has only one eye, and is a little deaf – but beauty is in the eye of the beholder and I suppose Conn is
satisfied. When I rose to go she put her hand on my arm & said "Now
won't you have a little drop of brandy?" However when I declined that she
brought out her wedding cake, and cut off a most generous piece, & sent
a piece to Harold. She said Conn had told her that he was a *nice steady
man*" – I wanted to laugh. It was very nice cake. When I came home I had
quite a long visit from Mrs. Woodhouse – but her conversation didn't
seem so interesting after Mrs. Finn's, which was really quite romantic. [30
July 1895]

Mr. Germaine[12] decamped yesterday – ran away from his lady love![13] It
seems his friends have known for about a week that he contemplated such
a move, but he never told the Cochranes, & did not take the train here,
but drove to Armstrong to catch it. The young men try to take his part, &
say he never wanted to be engaged to Norah, but he was so run after. I do
not think, however, that *anything* can excuse his behaviour. If he wasn't
man enough to know his own mind, & show what he wanted, at least he
need not have permitted a formal announcement of the engagement, and
then slip off in this cowardly way, making the poor girl a laughing stock
to the whole town. I don't know how they will carry it off. It will be very
hard for her to bear, I am sure. [12 December 1894]

I had fallen into a doze when I heard a strange voice – & sure enough
there was Billie Holliday come to pay a call. He does come at most unsea-
sonable hours, & of course poor Harry had to sleep on the uncomfortable
sofa in the sitting room. He had had such a hard day's work too – I was
really grieved over it. [11 August 1895]

Truly [Billie Holliday's] cheek is colossal. The last time he was here [at
the BX Ranch] Hal almost told him that we didn't care to have him come,
but evidently he couldn't or wouldn't understand and more still he left his
camera here, as he "didn't want to carry it into Vernon, but could come for
it tomorrow." I told him we would see that it was taken in to him. I really
feel guilty at having to say such uncourteous things to anyone in my own
house, but in self defence one cannot be hospitable to a little creature like
Billie. [9 January 1898]

[Mrs. Lawrence] is a peculiar woman – she hasn't taking manners – rather
free & loud – & she says perfectly shocking things sometimes – but she
has what always attracts me – originality of character – and I believe she
is a very kind-hearted woman as well. [4 March 1899]

Mr. Marjoribanks – Lady Aberdeen's brother – was riding in the yard with two other men, rounding up cattle. He rode up to the sleigh and took off his hat to us – but none of us knew him, so he went away again. He is a great heavy man & I have never wanted to know him, for he is not a particularly nice man. [31 January 1894]

I went to call on two nurses who have taken some rooms here. They are graduates of the Jubilee Hospital, in Victoria – Miss Moss and Miss Parnell[14] – the latter, a little dark girl, I liked very much, but I'm sure I shouldn't like to have Miss Moss take care of me were I ill. She is a big, fair, silly-looking girl who laughs a great deal & talks with a thick lisp – just the kind of person to try weak nerves exceedingly, I should think. I don't think they are getting much to do – I feel rather sorry for them. They have been here quite a long time & have each had only one case, I think. [2 May 1894]

Mr. [Arthur Gore] Pemberton[15] is here for his health. He has some heart trouble – has just recovered from a very serious illness, and is by no means strong yet. He is a good deal older than his wife, is very well off, & seems to be a really nice man. He is Sheriff for the district. They have a nice property near Kamloops. [9 December 1894]

It seems there is some talk of reducing the staff of teachers in the school here, & of course they each one feel a little insecure in their position. Great dissatisfaction is felt over Mr. Sparling,[16] & I don't think myself that he is a good man for the place. I don't think he is a man who influences the young wisely or well, though no one would call him a *bad* man – but he does little mean underhand actions, & he can't be a good leader of young impressionable minds. Of course, no one urges this against him – they say he is lazy & indifferent and too fond of meddling with outside matters, while what seems to me the gravest charge, his lack of honour, is passed over & never mentioned. [26 November 1899]

... we had a long discussion on various topics, notably on Mrs. Stevenson,[17] who has just lost her *fourth* husband. Some way one cannot feel so very sorry for her, as one feels that, with her, it cannot be considered an irreparable misfortune. [23 May 1895]

... I came home [and] rearranged the rooms a little, & got ready for my afternoon tea. I had asked Mrs. Leggatt, Miss Phipps, Mrs. Freer, Mrs. Perry, Mrs. Costerton, Mrs. Poulin, Mrs. Macdonald, Mrs. Billings, Mrs. Morris, Mrs. Cameron, Mrs. Burnyeat and Mrs. Johnson – all but the last three came. I don't know what prevented Mrs. Johnson, but Mrs.

Cameron was having a party for the Burnyeat children which kept them away. Mrs. Clerin happened in, and Louisa Middleton came for her doll, so I had plenty of visitors – from three until after five. [11 December 1895]

I had rather an unpleasant experience today. I went up the hill to see Mrs. Arthur Watson, and she told me in some particulars of the trouble there is between her husband & his brother.[18] Poor little woman she seemed to feel very badly. She cried, & it was hard to comfort her because I do think family quarrels must be just dreadful, I'm sure I'd worry very much. I am afraid the brother's wife[19] must be a good deal to blame – she doesn't seem to have been very truthful. I did what I could – which really was nothing – to comfort Mrs. Watson, & I had hardly got home when Mrs. Henry Watson came in to tell me her side of the story! I didn't listen very much to her – I told her at the outset that Mrs. Arthur was my friend so, of course, I couldn't listen to any thing against her. Mrs. Henry wanted me to read a letter which she said they had written to her, but I refused as gracefully as I could. I said I felt sure tomorrow she would be sorry she had showed it to me, that it was so much better to say as little as possible over any quarrel, particularly a family one. I am afraid she thought me unsympathetic, but I couldn't help feeling all the time, that perhaps she wasn't telling me the truth. She looked so pretty too, & seemed greatly distressed. I am sorry for them all, but I can't give any advice. [5 April 1900]

... one of our young men friends ... was in a very unpleasant situation, having just learned (from the girl's own lips) that one of his young lady friends had been misunderstanding his friendship, & taking it for love making. He was quite unhappy over it, poor fellow – and wanted me to advise him what to do. He didn't seem atall conceited over it – but truly distressed. He said he never had any idea he would be so misunderstood, & was sure his conscience is clear of even flirting, & I quite believe it, for I don't think he could flirt if he wanted to. [22 June 1894]

Despite her professed dislike of animals, Alice wrote feelingly about them:

Our little kitten is so sociable – it is curled up in my lap just now – and I don't atall enjoy nursing a cat, but it simply won't be repelled, and snuggles down so comfortably that I can't be hard enough hearted to throw it off always. [3 December 1894]

Hal had a pretty little pup given him this morning, & Snowball is so nasty about it – I have to keep her shut in the home. We have the little pup in the woodshed, & I caught her preparing to scratch his eyes out. Like Fred the Dutchman[20] I had to "put her aside mit force," & like Mrs. Fred she retaliated, & gave me a long scratch on my hand, which feels quite sore. [18 September 1895]

I was much distracted watching (from the window) the ways of a wild cow, which the butcher was trying to drive through town. There were four men on horseback, and a regular tribe of small boys who got in most dangerous places quite fearlessly. The cow was too much for the whole party – she finally broke into Mrs. Barnes' garden, and lay down there after doing a good deal of damage. [28 July 1896]

Sheep are … the most easily guided of all animals I believe. I am sure I don't see why a sheep should be thought stupid. I think it is uncommonly wise to recognize a wiser head, and be guided by it, instead of persisting in ones own wayward path that ends in trouble – however, I suppose the sheep are as easily driven to the slaughter house as to the fold, so maybe they are not very wise after all. [2 November 1897]

Alice was greatly amused by the antics of her friends' children, and descriptions of their behaviour formed an important strand in the diaries:

We were entertained by Mrs. Monck putting [her] dog through an exhibition of all his little tricks, and very funny they were. We all laughed & applauded – until finally little Helen Costerton evidently thought the dog had had admiration enough, & felt that it was her turn to show off – so she ran to her Mother's knee, knelt down & began to say her prayers! That is her latest accomplishment, & very proud of it she is. It was hard not to laugh. [15 February 1900]

I had noticed for some weeks what a shabby hat little Kate Costerton is wearing – & on Sunday at S. School she was sitting beside her little play mates who all had new hats and I felt sorry for her, so Monday morning I consulted with Hal, & then went over to the Miliner's & got her a very pretty hat & wreath of flowers & some chiffon, trimmed it and took it over. Kate was just delighted and so was Gertie – and certainly Kate looked very nice in the pretty new hat. [10 May 1900]

I think [the Jacqueses] all enjoyed themselves. The children are a comical pair – Hazel has a recitation which is not much as far as matter goes – but her manner is irresistibly amusing. The rhyme runs

"When we were very poor
And had no wood & fire
We used to tie our shoes up
With little bits of wire"

Short & to the point, and her opening & farewell bow are worth seeing. [9 January 1897]

Mrs. Lawrence was telling me today that she had great trouble in getting Sybil to begin to go to Sunday School. However I met her one day last Spring on the street & asked her to come, & the next Sunday, sure enough, she was willing to go. When she came home her Mother said she said "Oh – I like Mrs. Parke ever so much, she was awfully nice, and Mother, do you know, she didn't even ask me who made me." I thought perhaps it wasn't such a good recommendation as Sybil thought, that I made my scholars comfortable as to their mental acquirements. [19 December 1895]

Little Jim Monteith was in great fear that I would not come when he saw the snow. He said to Mrs. Cameron "Doesn't God know that Mrs. Parke was to come to dinner today?" "Why yes," Mrs. Cameron said. "Well," said Jim "what did he send the snow for?" When I knocked at the door I heard him scream out "Here she is, here she is" & he ran to open it. [28 January 1897]

I think [teaching] must be a dreadfully wearing life – not the teaching – that would be easy if the children wanted to learn – but so few of them seem to centre their thoughts on their lessons. I believe inattention would be the hardest thing to overcome in this school. The children did not seem naughty, or stupid, but so painfully indifferent. It was expressed in their faces, their posture – even their feet, sticking out under the desks, had a listless position. I couldn't help contrasting them with the children in the public school at home. There is so much more alertness manifested there, & even if it often takes the form of mischief, I think it is easier to bear. I do believe there is something in the climate here which tends to promote indolence of brain & body – a good land for the lotus eaters. [28 March 1898]

At Sunday school:
... we were talking of Adam & Eve & the devil tempting them in the garden, and Ellie Ellison surprised us all by gravely telling me that she had seen the devil. She finally explained that it was at a concert – I remember it was a man who had dressed for the carnival, & his dress was most conspicuous. [8 April 1894]

The [Christmas] tree [gift-giving] went off very well. Some tiny little children sang & recited. They did it nicely too, but someway I don't altogether enjoy hearing children perform before so many people. I daresay it is a silly feeling – they do it perhaps without much self consciousness – some of them I know do, but some of them look so overflowing with conceit. [25 December 1895]

I was quite amused this morning. I heard a rap at the door, and there found little Rose Weddell (Mrs. Coryell's granddaughter who is up on a visit from Kelowna).[21] She is a little child about six with a voice that would fit a big boy. She said "Who preaches today?" I thought her mother perhaps wanted to go to our church, so I explained to her that we would only have evening service. However, that plainly did not satisfy her, as she stood doubtfully eyeing me & then said "I want to go to the church on the hill – who preaches?" I said Mr. Langil and was going on to tell her about their services, when she said "Don't you preach up there?" I understood then that she wanted to go to S.S. – so told her to call for me, which she did, and I am forced to admit, behaved rather badly all through the school. [1 April 1894]

    Alice had an amazing affinity with the elderly. She loved to visit them and to listen to their stories:

How true it is that saying that "every death bed is the fifth act in a tragedy." I am sure poor old Mrs. Godwin looks common-place enough, & talks too in a hum-drum every day style ... 18 years ago her husband (who was an organist & music teacher) left her with four little children in London, Ont. while he came out west, to Oregon "to seek his fortune." For several years he wrote regularly, sending her money all the time, & then suddenly the letters ceased, and to this day she has never been able to hear a word about him. Think of the weary watching and waiting, the hope & disappointment that each day would bring through all those long years. Miss Godwin said her Mother wrote to the place his last letter was sent from, and made enquiries in every possible way, & hoped on, but after many years she has given up hope, and feels sure he must have died suddenly, or perhaps been killed. Portland, Oregon, where he was, was in those days a very rough place ... [25 December 1895]

Mrs. Godwin was here this afternoon for quite a long gossip – & she dearly loves a gossip, poor old lady. She is a constant surprise to me. How she learns so much of everybody's affairs when she never goes out is a mystery. [1 July 1899]

I was surprised in Mrs. Costerton's grandmother [Mrs. Perry]. She is not feeble a bit and does not look so very old. I daresay she will be a help instead of a care for Gertie. She is Irish − & a great talker. [8 November 1894]

... old Mrs. Perry came in. She has a great many troubles, & tells them very freely. I am sorry for her, & yet I can't quite like her − she talks too much. It does not make me like people any the better when they are extremely confidential on first acquaintance. [15 January 1895]

Mrs. Perry attached herself to me − and I did wish she wouldn't. I can't fancy her atall, & I am really sorry − she was telling me today how romantic she is − she is only 77! [30 January 1895]

Mrs. Perry confessed that she is easily made low spirited − indeed she says the daughter she lived with used to laugh at her in the mornings, & say "Well Mamma have your toast & tea any way − you may as well go to Heaven with a full stomach as an empty one." [16 April 1895]

Mrs. Perry ... was telling me how anxious she is about Gertie, though she will probably be up again tomorrow, doing her work ... She said "Gertie thinks so much of you − she often talks of it. I know there is no one to whom she would rather leave her child." I did not say any thing − but it made me very unhappy for her even to suggest such a thing. [17 March 1896]

... old Mrs. Pulcifer ... died last Thursday at Mara. Her husband came up here to make arrangements for the funeral. They were to bring her to O'Keefe's by train & Pulcifer[22] and the Finns were to drive from here to Larkin (the station at O'Keefe's) to meet the funeral. Well, early Friday morning, before we had had breakfast, Pulcifer came to the door to ask if I wouldn't go down with them. His eyes were full of tears, and his voice broke as he said "She was so awful fond of you." I did not feel that I could go, and made as kind excuses as I could, saying "I couldn't be ready in time − that long drives always tired me so" etc. & finally he went off, but all day long I felt guilty as if I had been selfish to refuse to go with them when they were in such grief ... Mrs. Barnes went (she is a French woman and rather queer) and she was telling us about it. "Oh," she said, "we had lots of fun − a regular picnic." It seems they turned the drive into a merry making jaunt − the old widower being the gayest of the party. He had taken candies along to treat them, and a bottle! Oh how glad I was I hadn't gone. I suppose as they had no wake, they had to have something in the way of a demonstration. [24 June 1896]

A love of nature was displayed in several descriptive passages:

I wish I were not so sleepy & tired, for I'd like to be most enthusiastic in my description of the beautiful drive we had to Kelowna. I cannot imagine a more beautiful road – wildly picturesque in some spots, dreary enough to make you shiver in others, and down near Kelowna well laid out farms and substantial looking buildings, speaking of prosperity & thrift. The land all has to be irrigated though, which, to my mind, is a great drawback – it makes farming so much more laborous and expensive, & for grain is not a success. Fruit, hops & roots thrive well if judiciously irrigated, but rain is needed for perfect grain crops. We left here about ten Friday morning. It was very hot, but as long as we were skirting the shores of the lake we had a breeze. We got our first view of Long Lake about six miles out of Vernon, and for fourteen miles the road is near the water – near, at least, in so far as one can see it beautifully but alarmingly high above it with great steep banks. The water is very deep, & so a dark green colour prevails, but near the shore one saw almost all the rainbow colours, for there is a pink gravelly bottom and it seemed to make the water quite red in some places. We took a lunch, & ate it at a place called Rattlesnake Point,[23] where Hal says they never see any rattlesnakes . . . oh! I was tired. The last ten miles of the drive had been very hot. We left Long Lake (really two lakes 20 miles long and hardly 2 across at the widest places) – fifteen miles before we reached Kelowna – then we passed a small lake called Duck or Postill Lake. The Postills are very large landowners and cattle raisers. They have two beautifully situated ranches, & vast stretches of cattle range. We could see the buildings on Lord Aberdeen's Mission Ranch – "Guisichan"[24] – but did not go very close to them. Kelowna is on Lake Okanagan – a flat spot in the midst of hills – opening towards the Lake. The opposite shore is not far away, & rises up in a high, thickly wooded mountain, with one beautiful point of land which is Indian Reserve – more than a thousand acres of good farm land which lies idle, as the Indians are not numerous enough to work it. [19 May 1895]

It was pretty warm in the afternoon, but everything is looking so lovely. The plentiful rains that we have had have kept every thing so bright & green and the wild syringa blossoms are a picture of beauty, & fill the air with perfume. Along the shores of Long Lake they grow in great profusion, and there are also many wild sumacs, the foliage of which is so pretty. [30 June 1898]

Since tea Mr. Knox[25] has been up here in the parlour – he is one of the wealthiest land owners in this section – a Scotchman about 35 or 41 I should think. He is a kind of Pariah, as a few years ago he was sent to jail, accused of burning hay stacks belonging to Mr. Ellis at Penticton. He always declared he was innocent, & many people believe that he wasn't guilty, but the Judge condemned him, & he served his term, & now has come back. He is not married. He invited us quite cordially to go & see him. [30 June 1898]

Mrs. Le Quinn [Lequime][26] is an American. Her husband[27] had been in this country nearly all his life – indeed I'm not sure whether he was born here. A shrewd quiet business man – they say he owns nearly all of Kelowna. She has been so kind to Mrs. Wilson that I was disposed to like her. [4 June 1898]

Mrs. Le Quinn ... had some very pretty paintings in her little parlour – a panel of chrysanthemums, & one picture, a sea scene, were very pretty – some others she had which seemed to me rather poor. She came in in a very swell heliotrope tea gown – she looked pretty too. We made rather a long call. She wanted to give us tea but we begged her not ... [9 June 1898]

We had a great old visitor today. Hal brought two men in to dinner – two Frenchmen – they had come on some business. One a young man named Léger,[28] was just an ordinary bright talkative young fellow, but the old one "Verdun"[29] – or *Greenish* as he calls himself in English – was a character. He speaks excellent English and wants to speak it all the time! He has been a wanderer in the west since '59 – in Montana, Alaska, B.C. & I don't know where else. He says he has several times been very sick – has had carpets in his house worth three dollars a yard – & now he lives all alone in a log cabin with a dirt floor. He says he was a millionaire once, but didn't know it. He sold a mineral claim once for $8000, & the man who bought it from him sold for $1,000,000. He has had many ups & downs & says sometimes he gets very discouraged. "Oh dear Madam" he said "If you knew all I have gone through, if you only knew, you would not blame me that I have one little fault. I sometimes take a drop too much – but never unless I can afford it. When I get any money I pay what I owe, & if there is anything left after I got the necessaries of life I buy my little bottle and I become inebriated." He has a small ranche up White Valley & gave me a most pressing invitation to come & see him – to get "Mr. Frank"[30] (as he called Hal) to bring me to see him & his companions "two little kitties." If I could only draw a picture of him, & then truly tell how quaintly he expressed himself sometimes, it would be worth reading. He was very garrulous, & very amusing, & the young man would occasionally break in in a brisk cheerful way – they were a great contrast to each other.

The old fellow was small & dark, with a long beard – when he got ready to go away he looked very funny – he had a very wide soft black hat, which was twisted up at one side, and his over-coat, instead of having buttons, was tied together with long strings of black velvet. He said he was robbed of $8,000 worth of gold dust once – in Montana. Highwaymen held him up & took his gold & his horses from him and though, by the help of the Mounted police, he recovered the horses, he never saw a pound of his gold dust again. He kept a large hotel in Colorado – has had a horse ranch in B.C. – has mined in ever so many parts. When he was telling of all the money he had made I said "Well, what did you do with it?" "Dear Madam," he said "I put it all in tunnels in Alaska. I was like the great Napoleon – I was not content with having plenty, I wanted more – & so, like him, I must now put up with less." I can't do justice to his peculiarities, so think I won't write any more. Poor old fellow – his story was very amusing, but the pathos of it followed close after the fun, & touched one keenly. His wife died before he went to Alaska and he never had any children. He says he has relations very well off near Montreal & they think he is dead. He meant to go back some day, very rich, & be good to them all – now that he is poor he does not want them to know where he is. I can't fancy how any one can voluntarily cut themselves loose from their own people. [9 March 1897]

[Mr. Stansfield] introduced us to his sister "Mrs. Thomas,"[31] & I was surprised – she looked, and was, nothing but a child. She told us she had been married three years, & is only seventeen now! Her home was about 13 miles farther on, she said, up in Cherry Creek, and she just *loved* to live up there. She stays all alone for days & days when her husband is away trapping in the winter, mining sometimes, or working on the road in the summer. I asked her if she didn't get dreadfully lonesome, but she said Oh! no – she had an old cat that was as good as a person to talk to and she had chickens. She said sometimes it was a little lonely after the hens went to bed, but she slept a great deal herself. She has a horse, & rides a great deal, & once she walked from Cherry Creek down to Lumby – 21 miles – without stopping any where to rest or eat any thing. She says she is never sick, & does not know what fear is – even when she is alone day after day & night after night. It is a marvel to me. She says in the last year she has been once to Lumby, & a few times down to her fathers, and her mother has been to see her – but no other woman has been near the place. Hal asked her what she did in the winter when her husband was away, & she said oh! I slide down hill & snow ball the cat, & read. She laughed a little & said "I guess I haven't quite got over being a kid yet – I think sliding down hill

lots of fun." I used to think it "lots of fun" myself – even after I was seventeen – but it was when I was one of a merry crowd ... To think of sliding down those desperately lonely hills with a cat for company and no
human being in sight or call is a terrible picture, I think. She seemed thoroughly to enjoy company too, chattered away at a great rate all the time
she was getting dinner ready. I had a starving appetite – I don't know
when I've been so hungry – & enjoyed the ham & eggs, good bread and
butter, cake & stewed rhubarb. We soon said good bye to our youthful
hostess, & came back past the workers – they were camped for their dinner and looked as if they were enjoying the rest. [23 June 1898]

CHAPTER 5

Oh! I do hope I'll be able to do something useful and good

A One-Woman Social Welfare Service

At a time when people in need relied on each other for help, Alice Barrett Parke responded immediately and in a very practical way to those in trouble. Prompted by a genuine Christian faith and a sincere empathy for people less fortunate than herself, she was more than once referred to as "an angel in the sickroom" as she hurried from patient to patient with food and good cheer.

... Mrs. Smith came in to tell me that Mrs. McCall next door is very ill – she asked me to go in & see her, so I did. She is not dangerously ill but was taken suddenly ill in the night. The Doctor says she must stay in bed a week or ten days. She has two small children, one not a year old, so it is rather hard on her. Her husband is staying home from his work to take care of her. I have been in as much as possible, & have been making things for her to eat. I went in and brushed her hair this morning – I can't help by taking care of the children because they are so shy they won't let me touch them. Poor Mr. McCaul looks worried to death – and I don't fancy he is a very good nurse ... I ran in to see Mrs. McCaul, before coming home to get tea. I did not stay there long as more visitors came in. I think she sees far too many people & talks too much. It would make me very ill if I were weak and in pain to have to talk so much. I have seen so many sick people today. I was just saying to Hal I feel I have so many blessings – none of those I have seen are so well off. I have such a nice home, and everything I need for comfort, & that one time I was ill since we were married Hal took such good care of me – no nurse could have been better – & then everyone was so kind. I had meant to set to work at some fancy work, but I really think, while there is so much sickness I'd better give my leisure time to helping them. [8 November 1894]

After tea Hal went out for a while, & I ran in to Mrs. McCaul's. I go three or four times each day, & generally take her some little thing – she gets a little low spirited if she is left much alone, and yet the Doctor does not like her to see very many people. She is so used to seeing me that I don't excite her, unless I act as I did last night. I went in to help Mrs. Fuller and was trying to support Mrs. McCaul in a sitting posture, in bed – when I began to feel faint, & before I could get out of the room I fell flat on the floor in a faint. I had been in a strained position for a long time and had resisted the faintness as long as I could, but it overcame me at last. I can't fancy why I did such a thing – I never did before. I only lost consciousness for a few seconds & picked myself up off the floor before anyone could help me – but it was a couple of hours before my legs stopped shaking. As soon as I was steady in my head Mr. McCaul brought me home, and then I felt all right so far as being looked after for Hal always knows exactly what to do. I was very much worried for fear I might have harmed Mrs. McCaul – she is so very weak & ill – but she has good nerves, & seemed more concerned about me than for herself – they were all so kind. [12 November 1894]

I was in at Mrs. McCaul's only twice yesterday, & only twice today. [14 November 1894]

I have not been out today except for a little while in at Mrs. McCall's this morning – I went to take her some chicken broth and coffee. I often make her a cup of coffee – she enjoys it. Poor woman – she has been sick two weeks tonight – she told me this morning she was much better & hoped to be up tomorrow for a while; but I heard this afternoon she is not so well again. [20 November 1894]

Both the Parkes were saddened by the decline of their good friend Luc Girouard:

Hal came in with some beef, wanting us to make some beef tea for Mr. Girouard … Clare made the beef tea, & Hal took up some blackcurrant jam to make him a drink, while the beef was cooking. [11 November 1893]

Mr. Girouard is better. Hal coaxed him to see Dr. Morris. I have made something for him every day so far & Hal takes it up – today I made a blanc mange. I think everyone is pretty good to him. [14 November 1893]

Old Mr. Girouard is sick again. He seems to be breaking up fast. The hard lives these pioneers live tell when old age comes on. [8 November 1894]

I made a watch pocket for old Mr. Girouard this afternoon. Hal thought he'd like to have one. [21 November 1894]

I sent Mr. Girouard a bowl of vegetable oyster soup last night, & am quite anxious to hear if he liked it – I think it is very nice. [13 December 1894]

It is after tea. Hal has gone up to Mr. Girouard's with some soup ... [24 December 1894]

Tom Godwin came up with some beef. Hal had sent it for me to make more beef tea for Mr. Girouard. He had had none since the jug full we sent him on Sunday. I got it on at once, & thought I'd send it up by Mr. Kirby, but then I thought the walk would do me good – so when it was ready, at eleven, I started out. I was glad I went – the poor old fellow seemed glad to get it. I was shocked at the change in his appearance. He was sitting up in front of his fireplace – but he looked so ill & weak. It looks so cheerless there for a sick man. He is, I suppose, far better off than any two people (put together) in Dover, and yet he does not seem to me to have common comforts – not from stinginess, I think, but just because he doesn't know how to make himself comfortable. [9 January 1895]

Hal & I have been up as far as Mr. Girouard's. I had not been out all day today, so thought I'd go up there with Hal to take the old man some beef tea. He was lying on his bed, in front of the great fire place. He looked better than when I saw him last, but was much disgusted with the Dr. because he forbids any other food than milk and beef tea. I think it was a shame for Hal to suggest – as he did – that pork & beans was just what would be good. The poor old man's eyes quite shone as he described how they should be cooked – in a dutch oven – by a roaring camp fire. "By tunder!" he exclaimed, "they taste good when one has had a twenty-five mile ride." We left him happy over the remembrance of past pork and beans – & longing for some now. I don't think Dr. Morris will thank Hal for his suggestion. [17 January 1895]

Dr. Morris says poor old Mr. Girouard is sinking fast.[1] He hardly expects him to last through tonight. Everyone will miss him. It will hardly seem like Vernon without "the old man," who was the first settler here. Hal feels badly over it – and I think it was hard for him to go away today, but he is something like a Stoic – I never saw anyone who can bear a grief as bravely as he does. [22 January 1895]

The old man passed away last Tuesday night. They did not have the funeral until today, as they waited for his brother's coming ... The masons had made all arrangements to bury the old man, but the brother is a Roman Catholic (though a mason too) and he objected to it. The priest would not, or could not, have a service because it was not consecrated ground – not one of the clergymen even went to the funeral – so Mr. Poulin – the Hudson's Bay Manager – read a few prayers at the grave. The affair has quite upset Hal – he says it seemed so full of prejudice on all sides. The old man, who has for many years lived a uniformly kind honourable generous life in this place, should have had all honour and respect shown him – as far as laymen went he had. From far & near they came to the funeral, and all through his last sickness he had constant kind care – but I cannot help feeling very sorry that the clergyman did not, at least, go to his grave. He was formerly a Roman Catholic – but for years had not had a priest near his house. He was a strong mason, & I believe said that was his religion. He was not a Godless man. I think he has never even been accused of wronging his neighbour by word or deed. [27 January 1895]

Alice had a deep affinity with elderly people. Elizabeth Macintyre was one of her favourites:

Mr. Martin told Harold last night that Mrs. Macintyre is very ill, so I ran over this morning to ask for her. Poor Mrs. Martin was in great distress; the poor old lady has rheumatism round her heart, and one lung is slightly congested, so they feel extremely anxious. I am going to sit up tonight, & do hope I'll be able to keep awake; but I have had a busy day, and am a poor one to keep awake even when I'm not tired. Hal is half afraid it will make me sick; but there seem so few people to offer – and Mrs. Macintyre likes me. I am glad to be able to do it for Mrs. Martin. [12 December 1893]

I want to go to Mrs. Macintyre this afternoon – I hear she is not so well today. I'll offer to stay again tomorrow night. I got home about half past six yesterday – undressed and went to bed, but I only slept until nine, & not again all day, so I was really too sleepy at night to write or do anything. [14 December 1893]

I did not go to see old Mrs. Macintyre yesterday, & it would never do to neglect her two days consecutively. [24 January 1894]

After dinner I took my photographs and went over to Mrs. Macintyre and showed them all to her. I took the calendar Clarence did for Harry too. She enjoyed looking at all ... [I] went in to wish Mrs. Macintyre a happy birthday – she was 90 today ... I went this morning in to Mrs. Stills with a bowl of mutton broth. I sat and talked to her for a little while and then went over to Mrs. Martin's. I have neglected my old lady lately & I think she misses me – I must try to go oftener. [10 February 1894]

Yesterday evening I went over to see Mrs. Macintyre – Mrs. Martin was going out to practise and Miss Macintyre was asked up to Mrs. Cochrane's. I sat for a while with the old lady – I think she gets pretty lonesome sometimes. She can't read or sew much and not so many people go to see her now that she is well again. I feel sorry that I have not more time to give to her, because I think she really cares to see me. [17 February 1894]

The old lady was alone, and wanted to keep me for a long visit, but I had to come home to get tea. [22 February 1894]

I am very sorry the Martins are going to move farther away up on the hill – I will miss them, for I can't run in as often as I do now. I think Mrs. Macintyre will miss me too. [7 March 1894]

[I] went on to sit awhile with Mrs. MacIntyre. I had taken my work so I stayed until nearly four ... They made me have coffee and cake – the old lady always seems so glad to have me that I feel guilty for not going oftener. [15 January 1895]

Today was old Mrs. MacIntyre's birthday, & I knew she would miss me if I did not go – so I went up right after dinner, & stayed most of the afternoon. [8 February 1895]

[I went] on to see how my old lady was after her dissipation, for she went to the dance! Mrs. Martin said they were surprised in the afternoon to have her say that *of course* she was going. They had it down on the new block, and everyone says it was a great success. Mrs. MacIntyre did not seem atall tired. I stayed there talking quite a long time ... [20 February 1895]

Alice was greatly concerned that each child in her church community receive something for Christmas:

I think my next job will be dressing some of the dolls, and that I don't enjoy atall. [16 November 1895]

Last night when I had finished my writing I got out the box of dolls I am to dress, & made a good start on their clothes. I got two quite dressed, except their petticoats – I found I had nothing to make those of – & one other dress partly made, so I did a good evening's work. Mr. Wilson & Mr. Ellison came in – Mr. Wilson to say that he found we would have to get six more dolls than we had counted on, & wanting to know if I could manage to get them dressed. Of course I said I'd try. [17 November 1895]

The dolls for the Xmas tree have not come yet. I am greatly concerned about it, as everyone is anxious to get at the dressing of them before the last hurry of work comes on. However I can't help it, there is nothing to be done but wait. [2 December 1895]

Mrs. Morris brought in her doll this morning. It is very pretty in yellow silk. Mrs. Lawrence brought over three lovely ones last night. She sews beautifully, & had taken so much pains with them. I have a sheet spread out on the spare bed, & the array of beauty up there. I have only had two brought in so far that are a disappointment, and I'll have to do something to make them prettier. Mrs. Smith brought hers today, & I am surprised it is really dirty. I didn't think she would have sent one like it. Its clothing is made of old white muslin, & it isn't even clean, & Mrs. Carswell sent a very shabby one. [14 December 1895]

Mrs. Jacques brought her children over to see the dolls. Their delight was very great, and it was hard for them to keep their fingers off. At half past two Teddy came for the dolls, & drove me up to the church too. [26 December 1895]

Visiting the sick continued meanwhile:

[I found Mrs. Lawrence] sick in bed. She got worse after she went home from here, and the Dr. put her to bed. He is afraid of the cold on her chest. I sat with her for a little while and told her to send her little servant girl in for me if she needed me, or [if there was] any thing I could do for her. She was so very kind when Hal was sick that I'd like to be good to her ... She is pretty sick. I think I'll go over again when Hal gets home. [4 March 1899]

Even while travelling on a train, Alice appointed herself caregiver to the sick:

"I gave a cup of beef tea to the sick woman next me – I am really quite concerned about her. She has to settle a new house, too, when she gets to Ashcroft. [25 September 1897]

After the death of Hal Parke's business partner, Robert Macdougall, Alice brought succour to his widow, Louise:

I went over to Mrs. Macdougal's to take a little orange marmalade & some oat cakes. [1 December 1894]

This morning I took some mutton broth & oat-cakes down to Mrs. Macdougal. [2 December 1894]

Alice offered the best post-natal care she could:

I went before Church to see how [Gertie Costerton's] baby was – she isn't much better yet. I went & stayed with them in the afternoon instead of going to S. School. It seems to comfort Gertie to have me there, though really one isn't much use, as the baby wants her Mother all the time and frets when anyone else has her. [16 April 1895]

Saturday morning Hal told me he had heard Mrs. Shatford was very ill, so after dinner I went up to ask for her. I saw Mr. Shatford,[2] and I did feel sorry for him. He looks ill himself – with anxiety. She had a little baby[3] on Friday, & all that night the doctors thought she could not live; but she is slowly improving now ... Mrs. McCall came to tell me she thought it would be a kindness if I would offer to help them at the Shatfords – so few people have offered any help – and Mrs. Fuller, the nurse, cannot manage alone. The doctor says she must have some one in the house to help her every minute, & Mr. Shatford is there too. Of course I went as soon as we had had dinner ... It was about one when I went to the Shatfords, & very grateful they seemed. Mrs. Pound was there, but wanted to go home, so I stayed until after seven in the evening. Dr. Morris was there twice in the afternoon – he said he was glad I came. I never saw anyone look so ill as Mrs. Shatford does – she cannot move, & only speaks in a faint whisper. The night the baby was born Dr Morris said he could not find any pulse for an hour & a half, & only revived her by injecting stimulants in her arms and legs. The husband was nearly crazed with grief – I feel very sorry for him. They are very young – neither of them twenty yet ... Dr. Morris has hopes of Mrs. Shatford's recovery now, but she is still in a very critical state. So few people have offered to help and such constant, watchful nursing soon wears the watchers out. As I said, I stayed until 7 last night, & promised to go over again this morning. Hal had washed the dishes, got his own tea, and made meat balls for breakfast ... I went over to Mrs. Shatford's right after breakfast, as soon as Hal had got started for the Mission. The baby was very fretful all the morning – I had to spend most of my time taking care of it, occasionally sitting beside Mrs. Shatford for a little while. The baby is a dear little thing – very small but nicely formed ... I did not get home until two today, & then I could not rest, as I knew I must do some cooking, for I have promised to go to the Shatford's again tomorrow morning. Not many people are as free from home cares as I am – so it is easiest for me to go in the morning. [22 January 1895]

I went over to the Shatfords for a short time [on Thursday] afternoon and then came home and rested ... Mrs. Shatford is much better – she is getting restless, and wanted a good deal of attention this morning. I wonder how Mrs. Fuller stands it night & day, for she has not had one really good night's rest in a week. She is uniformly bright and brisk – moving about with quiet energy. I never could be a nurse – I think I'd really rather be a washerwoman. The smell of drugs in a sick room makes me so miserable, & it wears me out to witness suffering – I think one reason is, I feel so ignorant of what should be done, that my mind is constantly strained lest I should make mistakes. [26 January 1895]

Friday afternoon I went out right after dinner, first over to see Mrs. Shatford. She had not been feeling quite so well again, and they wanted me to go over. I sat quite a time with her, until some other visitors came in ... [24 February 1895]

I went to the Shatfords on Monday afternoon for Mrs. Smith came over in the morning to tell me that their little baby was dead. Poor Mrs. Shatford was very sick. The little child died very suddenly. It has never been – & never would be, I think – a healthy child. Altogether it seems to me a blessing that it was taken away. No one seemed to love it much – even its Mother is so very delicate that she didn't have much pleasure in its existence. [19 June 1895]

Laura Poulin presented a greater challenge:

Our poor little French neighbour – Mrs. Poulin – is very ill. It seems she has been in bed a week, but we did not hear it until this morning. I went over at once – to find that she is dangerously ill. Miss Parnell is nursing her. Mr. Poulin insisted on my going in to see his wife. I did not stay long, as she was so very weak. I thought it could not be good for her to talk to a stranger, especially when she is both shy, & talks English very imperfectly. Poor little thing – I felt so sorry for her, she looked very wan & pale – it must be hard to be sick among strangers who don't even speak one's own tongue. I went over again since tea to ask how she was and Mr. Poulin asked me if I would come in for an hour or two this evening to let Miss Parnell get a short sleep. I think he feels pretty anxious. I said of course I'd gladly go if they thought I was competent. I don't ever feel very sure of myself as a nurse. It is some sort of inflamation & I know enough to know that that needs prompt and wise treatment. However, I can explain to Miss Parnell that I am not experienced, & can surely not go far wrong in a few hours – besides I can call them if necessary. [25 May 1895]

I went to Mrs. Poulin's a little after nine Saturday night, & stayed until four the next morning … Mrs. Poulin had had a great fright the night before – a mouse got on her pillow, & of course in her nervous & weak state it alarmed her terribly. Mrs. Cameron was staying there for the night – she had run for the doctor, while Mr. Poulin & the nurse attempted to sooth their patient – but it was a long time before they got her quieted, & the rest of the night she could not sleep. She is very weak, but has not much pain now. The doctors had to have an operation on Saturday, & had her under the influence of chloroform for two hours, so she is weak both from the effects of that and from pain. She is very young – only 20 – and so far from all her own people, & among those who do not even speak her own language. She speaks English very well though – she never would try until she was ill, but could read & write it well. I think it is wonderful how well she gets on. She talked a good deal to me this afternoon (I stayed with her until half past four) more indeed than I thought she should. I said to her, she should not talk so much, and she said with such a pitiful expression "Oh, but I am so lonesome." I have lent them Snowball for tonight, to see if she will frighten the mice away. I would have gone over tonight, but Miss Parnell thought she could manage by lying on the bed beside Mrs. Poulin. [27 May 1895]

Saturday Evening we walked up to Mrs. Ellison's and I went in to see Mrs. Poulin for a few minutes … After tea I ran in to see Mrs. Poulin for a few minutes, & to old Mrs. Godwin's, & then we went for a walk. [3 June 1895]

On Wednesday I baked bread & took a little fresh loaf & a glass of raspberry jam over to Mrs. Poulin in the morning … Last night Mrs. Poulin came over and brought me a large bowl of lovely ripe strawberries. She was very weak when she got here, but I saw her today & she said she was none the worse for her walk. She & Uncle talked French a little. [13 June 1895]

One of Alice's favourite families was the Martin clan:

This morning directly after breakfast I made two pies, & some more soup for Mr. Martin. I took it down to him ... [3 June 1895]

Lizzie brought me sad news from Vernon – that Mrs. Martin was dangerously ill with inflamation of the lungs. She said they had telegraphed to Victoria for a nurse, & to Rossland for Mr. Martin. If Hal had been home, I'd have got him to take me in last night to stay if they needed me, but the Harries were here & I did not know how late they'd stay, & I didn't know whether I ought to go, so I waited until this morning. Marshall drove me in right after breakfast & I was so glad I went – Miss MacIntyre looks really worn out, and said she would be so glad to have me stay with her tonight. They have Mrs. Carey there doing the work, & Mrs. Morris goes every day, but Miss MacIntyre has sat up every night since Thursday and is very tired. The nurse had not arrived, but they were expecting Mr. Martin this morning. [22 February 1898]

I am very tired and sleepy tonight. Angus drove me in to Mrs. Martin's last night at half past seven, & I stayed until nine this morning. Of course I did not sleep atall, & had so much running up & down stairs, but I was very glad to do it for Mrs. Martin. She is very ill – not yet out of danger, but she had a pretty good night – slept nicely towards morning though she was restless until three o'clock. Mrs. Morris stayed until twelve – then Miss MacIntyre & I managed together until three, & then I made her go to bed, she was just worn out & slept so soundly ... Mr. Martin got home yesterday, and wasn't he nervous and excitable! Marion, too, is just a bundle of nerves – rather a hard child to look after because of her nervousness – not that she is atall naughty. I had to cover her up ever so many times in the night, then I had to go in to Mrs. MacIntyre's room several times, & coax her back into bed – she would sit on the edge of the bed – she is getting very childish, poor old body. In one way it was much easier to sit up when there was plenty to do. There was no fear of getting sleepy and I was so glad I had gone. The nurse came in on this morning's train. [23 February 1898]

Miss MacIntyre said Mrs. Martin was really better – they hoped to be able to leave off the poultices tonight. Miss MacIntyre said to me "Do you know you are an angel?" I was rather surprised and said no. She said "Well, after you were gone this morning, Kate asked for you, & she said 'Oh she is an angel in a sick room – I began to get better when she began to take care of me.'" I was so pleased that she liked to have me with her. She likes the nurse now too, though at first she didn't care for her. [24 February 1898]

I stayed a long time at Mrs. Martin's – she is able to sit up for a short time each day, now, but looks very white & thin yet. [13 March 1898]

Gertie Costerton and her grandmother Perry also commanded Alice's attention:

I went up to the Costerton's this morning with some blanc mange and jelly, & saw Gertie, but didn't go into her room. She was out of bed, but looks so ill & weak and is dreadfully distressed about her grandmother. Their Chinaman left last night, & Mr. Costerton was doing all the work, nursing Gertie & taking care of the children. Mrs. Macdonald told me this afternoon that *he* has measles now, but Mrs. Pratt has gone to take care of them for which I am truly thankful. [5 February 1899]

Gertie Costerton came in this morning to tell me her grandmother is quite sick, so I went in to see the old lady after dinner. She is in bed, & the Dr. says she has pneumonia. If she has of course it is very serious, but I did not think she looked so very ill, & she was very cheerful. [25 January 1899]

I went in to see old Mrs. Perry yesterday – poor old lady, she is in a tangle of troubles, & they are real troubles too. I feel very sorry for her, and there doesn't seem to be much I can do for her. She is really sick – a heavy cold, I believe Grippe, which is serious for one of her age … and she has no one of *her own* to care for her. I know she is trying and hard to get on with and she has offended Mrs. Milne with whom she is boarding, and who now refuses to keep her any longer. She cannot find any one who is willing to take her. Gertie Costerton, who would love to have her & care for her, is ill with measles – besides, their house is very small. They actually haven't a bed room to put the old lady in, & Mr. Costerton doesn't want to have her. He says taking care of her before nearly killed Gertie & he isn't going to have a repetition of it. Still, she is Gertie's own grandmother, & is like her Mother, as she brought her up, & it is terribly hard for Gertie to know that she is ill, and not even be able to go to her. I have been quite unhappy over their troubles ever since I found out yesterday. I made some gruel for Mrs. Perry yesterday & Lizzie took it in at tea time. I went over this morning, instead of going to church, & sat with Mrs. Perry for awhile. She had a lot of woes to pour in my ear. I must say I sympathize with Mrs. Milne too, but my heart aches for that poor old woman – no home – helpless, dependant on paid care which is given very grudgingly. I wish she could go back to Gertie. I know it is out of the question for me to ask her over here – even if Hal were well he wouldn't be willing, for he knows how exacting she is – but with him still half sick and Uncle still here I couldn't possibly have her – and yet those words have been ringing in my ears "Inasmuch as ye did it *not* unto one of the least of these ye did it not unto me." [5 February 1899]

Lizzie Harding was glad to have Alice there when she was ill:

On Tuesday morning Hal awoke about five & heard Lizzie coughing so badly that he went up to see if he could get any thing for her – he found her suffering from quite a bad attack of croup, so I went up, and we dosed her until she got relief – she fell asleep then, & I went back to bed until seven. Hal was thoroughly awakened and I don't think he slept again. We kept Lizzie in bed all day, and Hal went in in the afternoon, and told Mr. Sparling & Mrs. Cochrane that she was ill. She stayed in bed until noon on Monday, and I did not want her to get up then, but she thought she'd be able to teach today . . . [26 April 1898]

While living at the BX Ranch Alice oversaw the diet of sick ranch hands, and they loved her for it:

I have looked after [Johnson's] nourishment, and have been kept busy making him beef tea, gruel, chicken broth, egg nogs etc. He is very patient & uncomplaining and does not look very sick, but I think what the Dr. fears most is some permanent lung trouble unless great care is taken. We don't have to sit up with him, & I am thankful to say he is really better today. [1 January 1898]

The Dr. doesn't seem quite satisfied with Johnson's progress – he says it will be some time before he'll be able to go to work – we are to try to feed him up as much as we can to get his strength increased. [9 January 1898]

CHAPTER 6

A great many people have ailments here

Health and Social Issues in the 1890s

Within a few weeks of her arrival in the Okanagan, Alice became aware of the sometimes severe social problems that existed among all levels of society. Having left the sheltered atmosphere of her family home in Port Dover, she was thrust into a world where alcoholism, domestic violence, disease, and poverty were common. Buoyed by her religious faith, and with her usual energetic interventionist approach, she set out to help in any way she could.

Euphemisms encoded her description of the behaviour of many of her male acquaintances – "unsteady" was preferred for those who overimbibed.

... we went over to the Schuberts to ask for the waggon. We had to pass through Mr. Swanson's barn-yard, & found Gus Schubert there. I am sorry to say they were both in the cabin, enjoying, or perhaps having enjoyed, a little Hudson Bay[1] – even Mr. Swanson showed a very little that he had been imbibing. [30 April 1891]

I would hate to go and live with that horrid old LeDuc. He drinks, & was so bad to his wife she had to leave him, & is – with five children – living at her father's, old Mr. Schubert's. She was married to him when she was only fifteen, & he fifty! – and she is now a young, pretty *woman* while he is a nasty old wretch. [7 December 1891]

Mr. Gus Schubert came in. Harry tried to keep him out as the poor man wasn't exactly in a visiting condition, but he would come in & I thought we'd never get rid of him. [4 January 1892]

The Hon. Mr. Majoribanks[2] is the nominal manager [of the Guisachan Ranch], but he isn't much good and has practical men under him. The family of Majoribanks come from the banks of the Tweed, where they have lived ever since an estate there was given them by Robert Bruce. I am afraid this man at the Mission isn't worthy of such long held honours – rumour says he was sent out here because he was no credit to his family at home. I have not seen him, but I hear he drinks too much. [7 January 1892]

Mr. Tom Lambley also came in for a few minutes, & although I asked him to stay to tea, I was rather relieved that he did not, for he was not in a fit condition to stay. [8 April 1892]

Jack Macnamara[3] ... had hurt his horse, & wanted Harry's help to dress the wound. He had only too evidently been, as he said, "having a time with the boys." It would have been amusing to listen to him – if it were not sad to think of the way he, & so many others, just waste the best of their lives in this idle carousing. It isn't only wild, untitled *land* that abounds here. The human specimens are too often as uncultivated and running to waste. [28 April 1892]

I have been so distressed all day. I noticed last week in the Mail that Addie Elliot[4] (Mrs. Lobb) had died suddenly in Nanaimo, but today, in the Coast papers I see that her husband is being tried for her murder. It is very dreadful, & I long to hear more. The paper said he had been drinking heavily, & has no recollection of what had happened. It is not quite three years since she was married and there are two little children. [27 June 1894]

I wish I were near enough to Nanaimo to care for those poor little children – their Mother dead, their Father in jail. The papers say Mr. Lobb has just recovered from a terrible drinking bout, and is overwhelmed with horror and sorrow, having no recollection atall of what happened. His counsel are trying to prove it was suicide but no one seems to believe it. That poor man! If he is freed what a life of remorse and anguish is before him. The Elliots never wanted her to marry him, simply because of his dissipation, otherwise he was a very nice fellow and had a good position. [29 June 1894]

I can hardly think of anything but the news we heard there – Poor Dick Taylor[5] is dead. He died a week ago at Greenwood, from an overdose of prussic acid – taken by mistake. Poor fellow, he has been inclined to be unsteady for some time, but had been keeping straighter since he went down to Greenwood, until just lately again. He was accustomed to take bromide to clear & steady his head – this time he came in late at night –

his room-mate was in bed & saw him go to the shelf for a dose – the two bottles bromide & prussic acid stood side by side – he took the wrong dose & died in a very short time, without saying a word. It is indeed awful – I know Harry will feel it terribly. He was so fond of Mr. Taylor. [5 January 1897]

… the Sheriff siezed all of Mrs. Leggatt's furniture yesterday except the kitchen stove & two chairs. Jack Bond had lent them a stretcher for Lizzie to sleep on – the Havertys (their neighbours) lent them some chairs, & Mrs. Costerton sent up a table. Hal asked Lizzie to come out here, but she said no, she wouldn't leave them now – that she thinks Mrs. Leggatt will go to her husband in Rossland, & she & Miss Phipps will manage some-way to live in the house until the summer holidays. She said she would have come out here today, but Mrs. Leggatt was having a tea party! – I suppose just one or two in to afternoon tea – I suppose it is Campbell who siezed the furniture – it had never been paid for. [8 May 1897]

Poor Lizzie is having a great experience at Mrs. Leggatt's. She says they all joke, & try to make fun out of the situation – but I am sure it was often a tearful laugh for poor Mrs. Leggatt. She is expecting her brother any day now, & hoping that he may arrange something to make it possible for her to stay on in Vernon. She does not seem to want to go to her husband – I fear he is very intemperate and very probably not doing well financially. [9 May 1897]

Mrs. Tunstall is going to sell all her furniture, break up house, & go to the coast for an indefinite visit. Mr. Tunstall has been very dissipated ever since his little boy's death, and I suppose the home is very desolate for poor Mrs. Tunstall – still, I don't think it is right for her to go & leave her husband – it will be all the harder for him to make an effort to overcome his temptation, & the grief for their little child is his as well as hers. [18 February 1898]

Nora Cayley seems delighted to be home again, and I don't wonder. I am afraid, from all we hear, that Mr. Cayley isn't a bit steadier since he was married than before – but of course she doesn't make any complaint. [9 June 1898]

Last night [at the Ram's Horn Hotel] we had quite an excitement – there was a drunken man making a great disturbance down stairs. The children were dreadfully frightened – they ran up here to the parlour crying & so excited I could hardly quiet them. Their Mother was out and they were afraid the man would kill her. [22 June 1898]

I went to Mrs. Armstrong. The poor woman is breaking up her home – to go to Midway. Such a nice home they had! – and a few years ago Mr. Armstrong was doing a good business here – but he failed last winter, & indeed I'm afraid there isn't much prospect of happiness ahead for them. He is very dissipated. [31 August 1898]

[Mr. Monteith] had to leave the office yesterday morning – the Doctor came in for him – & he is now at home very ill. I feel sorry for his wife and for him too, poor man. He is thoroughly diseased, & too weak mentally & physically to make an effort to resist his temptation. This is an unusually bad attack. [7 June 1895]

While we were coming down through Pleasant Valley on the train, it stopped, & there was evidently something wrong outside; so when the brakeman came in I asked him what was the matter and he said, "Oh, we've been trying to run over a man." I asked if he was hurt, but he said "no." Presently one of the passengers came in, and sat down laughing beside another man, & began telling of the mishap. He said the brakeman was very angry at the man for not trying to get off the track. It seems the cow catcher hit him, & turned him over in the snow, so they stopped as soon as possible and went back to see if he was hurt, & the brakeman said, "Why didn't you get off, haven't you any sense?" The man, who had just picked himself up exclaimed ruefully, "Not much just now." I wasn't surprised to learn that it was no less an individual than our old friend Patsey Mulraney. [9 January 1894]

Drug abuse and gambling were problems:

A young girl of seventeen was married here this summer to young Hann[6] who has the orchard & nursery at the B.X. ranch.[7] Two weeks ago he went away on the train telling her he was going to Sicamous for fruit trees, & would be back in two or three days. She has heard nothing from him since, & is nearly distracted with anxiety. She wired to Sicamous, & found he had never been there, but she learned that he got off in Armstrong. He is not there now however, and she can't find where he is. People say he had been acting queerly lately, & it is hinted that he must have gone queer in the head. [15 November 1895]

Mrs. Macdougal was in this morning and was telling me that they say young Hann, who left so mysteriously, is an opium eater, that he and his wife have never lived happily together. They are so young, it seems terrible to think that they have made so grave a mistake as to marry unhappily. [26 November 1895]

It seems instead of [Mr. Poulin] being given the management of the Klondike stores in Vancouver, he has quietly made off to San Francisco. When Mr. Graham came up to instal the new man the books were found in a most unsatisfactory state – & Mr. Poulin thought it safest to "skip out." Mr. Billings says he knows of one instance where Poulin sat down to play poker at the Victoria Hotel, in the evening, & stayed there playing until 12 the next day – losing $150.00 – so if he often indulged in that kind of sport, it is no wonder he couldn't live on his salery. [12 December 1897]

Episodes of domestic violence aroused the deepest sympathy in Alice:

Harry was telling us the life story of a young fellow out here which I think I must put in my diary – though Harry says I mustn't put in the real name, so I'll call him Billie Jones. He told it all to Harry himself – he has a ranch not so very far from Harry's, over at Salmon River. I should think he is about Harry's age, or a little younger. He was born in Muskoka. He had one sister older than himself & a brother younger. The father was a very passionate cruel man & on poor Billie the brunt of his ill-treatment fell. The Mother, a delicate gentle woman, did all she could to screen him, and the loving little sister comforted him when she could. When he was only seven years old his father used to make him go to the woods to help split rails – & would sometimes send him to town with a yoke of oxen! – and whenever he failed in any given task his punishments were terrible. He owned to Harry that all love of truth was beaten out of him & he would tell falsehoods as soon as anything else. One day, while his father was with him in the yard he had some work to do, & child-like stopped to have a play with his sister. His father saw, & cutting a long supple switch ordered him to take off his trousers (his only other garment being a shirt) & following him home to the house lashed his little bare legs until the blood streamed from them. Bloody & bruised he ran to his Mother, who was then ill with her last sickness. He says he remembers yet her face & voice as she said "Oh my poor little boy, what will you do when I am gone." She gave him the name of a dear friend of hers in Cooksville, and to this friend she also wrote, begging her, if possible, to be a friend to her boy – & before long she died. Poor little Billie only seven years old! felt the burden of his life then greater than he could bear, & one day gathering up courage started off bare-footed – with nothing on but the shirt & trousers – to go he knew not where, but *anywhere* that wasn't home. Fancy the desolation in that! He was sorry to leave his sister. On & on he ran – at first in the woods – afterwards by road until he came to a tavern many miles from home, & here, it being potato digging time, the man agreed to give him some work. I daresay they knew him & his pitiful story – Harry didn't say. Anyway, he stayed with them all winter, doing chores – until one unlucky day in the early Spring one of his uncles came to the place, saw, knew him & spoke to him. He tried to pretend that he was not Billie Jones – gave another name – but it was of no avail. The Uncle went home & told his father, who at once came after him. They were outside when his father drove up – in the sugar bush – the father sternly ordered him to go to the house, & if he had any "duds" make ready to come home. He made no answer, but turned as if to go – however he made for the deeper woods. There was still some snow on the ground, & although he tried to keep on the bare ground, he had to sometimes leave tracks on the snow, and by these he was followed, caught & carried home. For two years then again he lived a miserable, beaten, loveless life – except for the love he got from his sister. He did not say much of the little brother. When he was nine years old his father gave him five dollars & sent him to town to buy some things. On the way an aunt called him in & gave him 90 cents to get a couple of school books. With this money he resolved to make his way to Cooksville to his Mother's friend. This was on a Thursday and he knew the boat would not leave the town until the next Tuesday – so he went and hid himself in a mow full of baled hay. The next morning he was nearly famished, & crept out to a baker's and bought some cakes. Saturday morning he was afraid to go out, as he saw so many people in town & was afraid some of them might know him. So Sunday he was dreadfully hungry, & when he heard the owner of the barn downstairs, went down & told him he had lost his way the night before, giving his home as one in quite a contrary direction from the real one. The man asked if he was hungry. He told the truth for once when he said yes, & was told to go up to the house & get some breakfast, when the man directed him as he thought for home. Billie pretended to set out, but soon turned back and again took refuge in his loft. He ventured out again on Monday to the baker's and on Tuesday made ready for his next bold stroke. The boats then running down to (Cooksville) would not take children passengers unless they were accompanied by older people, and he knew this – but desperation is a mighty teacher of cunning, so he waited until the gangway was taken up & made a sudden run & jump on the ship. Of course they were then started, and while the Captain questioned him they were getting farther from the land. He had a story already composed "His father had written for him & sent him money." As he had the money for his fare the Captain finally let him stay on. He said he supposed he was a forlorn enough looking creature, as he wandered round & finally settled down near the engineer. The man asked him if he was hungry and went away & got him a plate of food – such food – meat, potatoes, pie etc. The famished child devoured it all and still had such evident craving in his face that the kind-hearted engineer asked if he wanted more. "Yes, yes." "Well," said the man, "you take that plate & go to the cook & tell him I sent you, & come back here." He did as he was told & began devouring the second supply, until the engineer took it from him, fearing he would hurt himself. The boat journey safely ended, he had no more adventures but took the train to Cooksville, where with his Mother's friend he found a safe & happy haven – for they took the poor little waif in, and gave him a home indeed. They lived on a farm, & I fancy were not very well off, for he told Harry he was not sent to school except for a few months & has no education except what he has picked up. Even here his whippings were not over, for the habit of lying which fear and pain had taught him had to be cured by pain – but he said he only got punished when he deserved it, & after a while learned that it was better to tell the truth. His father did not discover his whereabouts for 2 years, & then he would not go home. He stayed in Cooksville until he was 17 – then came west. He says twice since he came out here he has helped his father with money. The little sister is dead – the brother a commercial traveller in Chicago ... The father is now at the coast worth $10.00. This year Billie had a letter from his old Cooksville friend saying her husband was dead & begged him to come back & manage the farm ... [4 February 1894]

Poor Stewart Martin was in sore disgrace. He had played truant the day before, so his Mother was keeping him in bed all day. It seemed to me a tremendous punishment but perhaps everyone is not constituted as I am ... I suppose it is a weakness to be so impatient over restraints – for, after all, strength comes from proper control – steam confined becomes a mighty power, the ship with its helm broken drifts to danger & destruction – freedom does not always lead to satisfaction or even to safety. All of which is suggested by poor Stewart spending his day in bed. [23 February 1896]

... poor Nellie Schultz was here in great grief, crying & wanting Hal to go over & talk to her husband,[8] as he was beating her. Hal went and said when he got there he saw a quarter of beef, several broken dishes etc. out in front of the house, and Nellie (who had gone on before him) was leaning out of an upstairs window wildly gesticulating to him to go away, so he supposed they were making it up, and was not sorry to come home without interfering. [10 April 1896]

Apart from the occasional cold and toothache, Alice remained remarkably healthy. But in the valley, a wide variety of diseases struck down young and old alike. In Vernon:

Mrs. Billings was here this afternoon with her baby. He is a pretty boy, but Mrs. Billings says he never shows the slightest affection for anyone. He does not like even her or his father to kiss him, and will scream with anger if she tries to cuddle him up to her, & to love him.[9] I think I'd be very much distressed if I had a child like that – but I hope she exaggerates the matter a little. [21 October 1895]

Poor Base,[10] the public librarian, died very suddenly Thursday night – of heart disease. He had only been ill a few days. I did not know him much, but always felt sorry for him. He was dreadfully deformed, and had such a sensitive pain-stricken face – though it was a very good-looking face too. I fancied he had always been a cripple, but it seems he was all right until a few years ago. He came out from England to the North West, & there some young fellows "for fun" put him on a bucking horse, though he was no horseman, & he was thrown, with the terrible results of making him deformed & a nervous wreck. Mrs. Godwin said he was saving up his money to go back to England. [31 October 1896]

Robert MacDougall, Hal Parke's former partner, died an agonizing death from tetanus:

... there is another sad case which comes closer to our sympathies, & has made Hal especially feel very low-spirited. Poor Mr. Macdougal has quite lost his mind. They think it is a paralysis of the brain. He is gentle, but like a little child, does not know what he is doing. He is worse in bodily health too. He got as far as Sicamous on his way to Winnipeg & got so much worse there that the Colonel telegraphed to Mrs. Macdougal – & Tom Godwin went down for him, and brought him home in this unhappy state. [24 November 1894]

I went in to ask after Mr. Macdougal ... I am afraid there is not much hope of improvement – the doctor thinks Mr. Macdougal has softening of the brain, & that is always hopeless, I fear. [26 November 1894]

Mr. Macdougal is not so well today. He is in bed and has a severe pain in his chest. [1 December 1894]

Poor Mr. Macdougal had a bad night. He has a great deal of pain now. His wife & Tom were up most of the night with him putting on hot poultices. If they need him Hal will sit up at night. [2 December 1894]

Hal came back home to tell me that poor Mr. Macdougal was gone. He died about eight in the morning, after a night of terrible suffering. Tom Godwin told me he never saw such suffering. Lockjaw set in, & though he tried hard to speak he could not say a word. Of course as soon as Hal told me I left everything and went down ... [9 December 1894]

A contaminated water supply and low standards of personal and community hygiene led to the sickness and death from typhoid of several of Alice's friends and acquaintances:

Mr. Lawrence is ill in bed with either Mountain Fever or Typhoid. [3 May 1892]

I met Mrs. Macdonald at the gate – she says Mrs. Shatford has typhoid fever[11] now. I feel very sorry for them. I think there must surely be something very unhealthy about the house they occupy, three inmates having had fever one after another, & last year Miss Kape, living next door, had it. [23 September 1895]

Since tea I went over to ask how Nina Smith is. They are afraid she has typhoid fever. I am so sorry for Mrs. Smith. She has such a lot of work to do & rather an unruly lot of children to manage. [29 October 1895]

Young Tom Godwin, a good friend and former freighter with the firm of Parke and Macdougall, developed typhoid. The disease followed its usual up and down course:

[Mr. McKelvie] said Tom Godwin was sick with fever. [24 August 1896]

Tom is just the same – the fever isn't broken. [28 August 1896]

I had heard in the morning that Louisa Middleton was dead[12] ... Louisa was such a bright, happy, healthy looking young girl – she had only been ill three weeks – typhoid fever. It is hard for her father and Mother, but Mrs. Ellison says they take it in such a beautiful Christian spirit. I must go out & ask after some sick people this afternoon. Tom Godwin is better. [3 September 1896]

... I went over to ask for Tom Godwin. He isn't quite so well today – had a bad night and has been delirious all day. [5 September 1896]

Tom seems to be improving, but of course he is very weak. [13 September 1896]

[I] went over to Mrs. Godwin's to ask after Tom – he has not been so well the last few days. [17 September 1896]

Yesterday morning Hal came in and told me that poor Tom had died[13] the night before. I went over in the morning & then on down town. [19 September 1896]

Mr. Meighan was in [the bank] – I held out my hand to him. He shook it, and then backed away with a hasty, frightened manner and said "You'd better not come too near me." I said "Why! what's the matter – whooping cough?" "Oh no" he said "typhoid fever. I have just been to the doctor & he says go home and go to bed and live on milk." I could hardly believe that a man walking around & making ready to drive 14 or 15 miles could be actually ill with typhoid fever. He said "It is on me pretty hard, I don't like the thought of being made a calf of, but the Dr. says nothing but milk I must take." [19 February 1897]

The infant mortality rate was high:

I have heard such a sad thing, I cannot forget it. Hal came in yesterday and told me that Dr. Morris was just starting for Armstrong – a telegram had come for him to go down – the Hugh Woods little baby was dead, & they wanted a post-mortem, fearing it had been poisoned. I had not heard it was ill, but it seems Dr. Williams has been attending it for some days. I am anxious to hear more particulars. I feel so sorry for Mrs. Wood – she is so entirely among strangers – her husband is still away ... She was talking so much of her baby that day, saying he was growing so fast and was so well. It is very sad. [22 September 1895]

The [James] Schubert's little baby[14] was buried – it died Sunday night. I saw Mr. & Mrs. Gus Schubert there & asked them if they were going to stay in town to come here to sleep – but they were going right back. [8 September 1896]

... Mrs. Tunstall's baby[15] is dead. It died this morning at four – the poor little thing had convulsions all day yesterday, from teething. I was up there this afternoon with some flowers ... Poor Mrs. Tunstall was in bed. [26 September 1896]

A little child died in town this week – it had whooping cough which got so bad it turned to pneumonia. [28 January 1897]

On Wednesday I had been at Mrs. Crowell's to ask after her little baby – it has been very sick with inflamation of the lungs – the poor little thing died last night.[16] It had suffered very much. [2 July 1896]

Mothers, too, were at great risk in childbirth:

All other news seems put out of my mind by the sad piece of news that Mr. Kirby has just brought. Mrs. Weddell is dead – and my heart is sore for poor old Mrs. Coryell. She has had so much sorrow, & Mrs. Weddell was the apple of her eye, so young and pretty & loving[17] – I think she was barely twenty-five and has left four little children, the youngest a tiny baby about a week old. Mrs. Coryell will be so glad she was with Mrs. Weddell most of the winter – but it will almost kill her I am sure. [11 February 1895]

Mr. Kirby ... says Mrs. Coryell is bearing up wonderfully but that Mr. Weddell is acting like a man distracted – and the children think their Mother is only pretending to be asleep, she looks so natural. It seems she was, they thought, out of danger, and was sitting up in bed to have her breakfast, having been laughing & talking to her husband, when quite suddenly she fell back dead. Tom Riley told Hal today you would think every man in Kelowna had lost his wife – such universal sorrow is felt ... I have felt so sad since I heard it – and yet, how much happier for those who go while life is joyous and fair, than to linger on to face many sorrows perhaps. [13 February 1895]

Diphtheria was a dreaded and frequently incurable disease, which occasionally developed into an epidemic:

We heard tonight of Miss Edith Askew's death. I don't know what the Drs. call her affection but her throat gradually constricted inside, until it was agony for her even to attempt to swallow a fluid. Of course she had consumption as well, but this hastened the end. [9 December 1893]

There are two cases of diphtheria[18] in town. Some people who came up from Fairview[19] with it. They have been put in an isolated house and no one is allowed to go to them, except of course the doctors. It is a lady, Mrs. Thompson,[20] & her brother who are ill & Mr. Thompson has to nurse them, as they cannot get a nurse. The school has been closed for fear of infection. Hal has just come in & says Mr. Thompson has had two nurses sent up from Vancouver & a doctor from Kamloops, beside Dr. Morris & Dr. Williams.[21] [19 November 1894]

Everyone has something to say about the diphtheria. It seems to me a strangely careless thing for these people to do. They brought a little child up – dead – & they knew it had died of diphtheria, but the Mother could not bear to have it buried down there with no clergyman and no graveyard. She did not think how she might spread the disease I suppose – but

it seems hardly right to indulge one's own wishes at the risk of lives ...
The little child – six – was their only one. They say the Father is nearly
crazed with grief. [20 November 1894]

Hal came in and told us both the nurses have both developed diphtheria
today. The Council are getting alarmed, they have sent to the coast for
four more nurses. I feel a little anxious about Dr. Morris – he looks so
worn out. [24 November 1894]

Mr. Martin told Hal he had had a telegram from Vancouver – four extra
nurses start from there today to take the diphtheria patients here in
charge. I think they are brave women, for they undoubtedly risk their
lives and that – not in a moment of excitement, when enthusiasm would
help to make great deeds easier – but with cool deliberation, & patient
endurance ... I believe the two nurses here are not very ill with the disease, & I daresay they may not have it badly – as from the first they will
know how to fight it. [25 November 1894]

[Mr. Norris] was on his way to the station, having been sent for to go
down to Fairview & establish a quarantine over the diphtheria cases there.
He smelt strong of disinfectants[22] – everyone here, nearly, is using them.
I made Hal get something to wear about him. It is right to be careful. It
harms no one, and may avert trouble. I don't think there is any thing like
cowardice in taking every precaution against the spread of a disease. I hear
the two nurses are worse tonight – four others arrived on the train this
morning. Hal did not know whether they all went to the infected house
or not. [26 November 1894]

    Other epidemics recorded at the time included scarlet fever and
smallpox:

Mrs. Cochrane said that Mrs. Tunstall's two children are ill with scarlet
fever[23] in Kamloops – she had gone there for a visit. Scarlet fever is very
prevalent there. [19 October 1897]

Hal said that news came that the Tunstalls have lost their youngest boy.
He died of scarlet fever in Kamloops. I feel so sorry for them – a year ago
this summer their baby boy died and now little Cuthbert – such a fine
handsome healthy child he was – they have only one child now and he has
the fever. [20 October 1897]

Hal had seen in the paper that Miss Gertie Loewen[24] was ill with scarlet
fever & had been sent to the isolation hospital. Mr. Hodges said he had

had a paper from Miss Loewen saying that Mrs. Barnard had it too. Hal has not heard from Mr. Barnard for over a week – I suppose they are all quarantined. Hal heard in town today that Mrs. Spinks has scarlet fever in Kamloops & there are two cases of typhoid in Vernon. [2 November 1897]

They told me the sad news that Mrs. Spinks[25] is dead. She died in the Kamloops hospital. The Judge only got to her for a few minutes before the end – they had not apprehended any danger until the last day. Judge Spinks had taken his trip to Nicola, & was coming back to Vernon had reached Sicamous when they telegraphed to him to come at once to Kamloops. [12 November 1897]

They say the Judge is coming back to Vernon tomorrow. It seems strange that they will allow him to do so. I should think he would be quarantined for a time ... Lizzie tells us that little Marmaduke, Mrs. Tunstall's only remaining child, is left stone deaf by the scarlet fever. I am hoping this is an exaggerated report. [14 November 1897]

Mrs. Tunstall was on the train with her little boy. Poor Mrs. Tunstall – I did feel sorry for her. Marmaduke is very deaf – not entirely so & he looks so white & wretched. He was very sick on the train. She seemed hardly able to speak, she felt so badly ... [1 December 1897]

... Hal, Lizzie and I were vaccinated.[26] The Council is making it compulsory, as there is a smallpox scare down in the lower country. Dr. Morris said we ought to be done, on account of handling the mails, & I daresay the public would object if we said it wasn't necessary, so we thought the sooner the better. It isn't a very nice ordeal to go through ... [15 February 1900]

Many residents were prone to diseases of the chest:

Mr. Ellison says the children have whooping cough badly – especially Myra – & Mrs. Ellison herself has a very bad cough. It sounds like whooping cough. She has had such a hard summer & fall – some of the children sick nearly all the time – & now it seems she is going to have another siege of nursing. [12 January 1897]

[Mrs. Ellison] really looks and seems sick. She has a very heavy cold on her chest, & said she knew she ought to be in bed, but the two children Myra & the baby have whooping cough so badly that she can't think of taking care of herself. [28 January 1897]

Mrs. Fuller has a little baby a little over two months old, and the poor little fellow has whooping cough. He ... looks so wan & miserable. [16 February 1897]

... the [Ellison] children were all having croup, so Mrs. Ellison has her hands full, as Mr. Ellison is away. [21 February 1894]

Lizzie has another sore throat – said she felt a good deal like having croup ... [7 November 1896]

Lizzie was sick in bed with one of her croupy colds, so I went over to see her. She is looking miserable again. I think the truth of the matter is that teaching does not agree with her. She always gets sick if she has a school for awhile. It is a good thing the holidays are nearly here. [20 June 1896]

Mrs. Costerton's sister – Miss Perry – ... passed away late Saturday night – her life dying with the old year, and her spirit going home for its New Year's Day. It is a blessed release for the poor girl. She had been ill for just a year, & for many months now has lived a weary life – not suffering pain but great weakness and distress of breath. She was so bright & cheerful through it all, & yet was willing to die. [2 January 1894]

On Saturday morning I did some cooking for today, & went to take some blanc mange & jelly to a poor woman who has lately come to town & is dying of consumption. They have taken a small cottage up near Mrs. Ellison's, just a man & his wife – I think they are very poor. The woman's face has haunted me ever since I was there. She has great large beautiful grey eyes, & such poor white sunken cheeks. I thought she seemed rather fretful, & the man is a very talkative Englishman – not people that I was drawn to, still they are "strangers, and anhungered" and so deserving of our help and sympathy. Mrs. Cochrane had told me about them the night before, but did not know their name, so I asked the man what it was, & he said "William & Salome Hawksby,"[27] and lest I should forget he wrote it on a piece of paper which he insisted on my taking. The woman reproached him for telling her name, which she said she did not like atall. I said I thought it was a very pretty & an uncommon name. "Oh" said she "I know it's a Bible name – Salome was at the Sepulchre of Christ, but Salome danced before the king. I think people always personate their name more or less, & I never liked mine because of that Salome who danced before the king for John the Baptist's head." I couldn't help being amused at the incongruity of the idea of that poor muddled up bunch of bones dancing anywhere, & yet it was pitiful. [3 November 1895]

Mrs. Smith was telling me a long story she had heard about the Hawksbys to the effect that they are impostors and not poor atall – that the man is trying to starve his wife to death. I think it should be enquired into because if they really are poor it is only fair to themselves to have the report contradicted – & if they are not poor, the public should know it. [4 November 1895]

I ... took some flowers up to Mrs. Schubert. She is very miserable, and her little baby is sick. Poor little thing – it was lying on her knees, looking so frail & puny. The doctor says Mrs. Schubert has consumption. [3 September 1896]

Poor Mrs. Jimmy Schubert[28] was to be buried today. I had a few pretty Chinese lillies & took them in. [5 February 1897]

Ill health and depression caused some to take their own lives:

Mr. [Walter] Dewdney shot himself dead last night. He put a pistol to his mouth & fired it – poor man. We do not know any particulars, but suppose he must have been insane as we do not know of his being in any difficulties, and I think his domestic relations were happy. The present Mrs. Dewdney seems to be a nice kind wife & good stepmother to his three children – two boys and a girl – poor children! What an awful trouble this is. I do feel so terribly sorry for them all. We will hear more about it soon I suppose. Harry was saying tonight how wrong it is to worry over our little money troubles – being poor! When we hear of a sorrow like this it teaches us the smallness of other things. [26 January 1892]

[Harold] was telling us more about Mr. Dewdney. It seems the poor man has been in low spirits for some time, & this was a premeditated thing, for he left a note to Leonard Norris the constable, saying he was tired of life and was going to end it. Harold said it is disgraceful the way old Dr. Chip has been acting – intoxicated nearly all the time – and Mr. Monteith (Mr. Dewdney's assistant) is just as bad. The two men began wrangling over poor Mr. Dewdney's dead body about some trifles, until they were indignantly stopped by some mere outsiders. Dr. Chip would not allow the body to be moved until they sent to Kamloops for a coroner – two days and nights. It must have been, & now is, [terrible] for poor Mrs. Dewdney – this awful thing happening to her husband, and her father acting so shockingly. Mr. Dewdney's brother is expected so the funeral is not to take place until Monday. [28 January 1892]

Mr. Dewdney's funeral is to be tomorrow – a good many people already have passed going up to Vernon. It will be so hard for those poor children all their lives, that their father died in such a way. I was thinking yesterday that it is even harder to place our past (and the bygone days of those we love) trustingly in God's hands than it is to trust Him for our future. It seems as if the past is so beyond all undoing – its facts have left their indelible impress on our lives – at least that is what we are apt to think – but God must be able to undo even the past for He says "Though your sins be as scarlet they shall be white as snow." Yes – the pain & mistakes and the wrongdoing He can & will put "behind His back" – and we ought to be able to do the same. I think we are apt to grudge the past our dear ones have had apart from us – but how foolish when there is all eternity before us! [31 January 1892]

Mr. Simms came to the door to tell us of such a terrible thing that had happened. Poor Mrs. Poulin had taken carbolic acid in mistake the night before, & died very suddenly.[29] Poor little thing – she was just beginning to be happier here. She was very homesick at first. I have always felt sorry for her, though she was very fond of her husband & he of her. She was so young to come away from all her own people among those who did not even speak the same language, & she was shy too. All day Friday no one could think of any thing else. [22 July 1896]

Mental illness was no respecter of persons. The disease felled Hal's co-worker in the government office, young Walter Dewdney. The episode began with a fever:

Walter isn't so well today – the doctor is afraid he is going to have a fever of some kind … [Mrs. Cameron] says Walter is very nervous about himself, & apt to fancy himself worse than he is. [30 September 1895]

… [Lizzie] was greatly upset over poor Walter Dewdney. He has been quite demented, poor boy. I don't know whether he will recover, but they have had a sad time with him for the last week. Mrs. Cameron spent last Wednesday with me, & she said then he was acting so queerly, but we put it down to his being ill – however, on Friday he was quite crazy. I believe he is getting better. Mr. Norris brought him out here Sunday afternoon. It was very sad to see him. It was the first time I ever saw and talked to any one who was atall out of their mind. He acted very troubled – the poor boy knows his brain has gone wrong … [17 March 1897]

[Mrs. Cameron] was telling me about poor Walter. I am afraid he is no better, worse indeed. I think he ought to be sent away. It really isn't safe to have him going about with so much liberty. Poor boy. It is very very sad. [19 March 1897]

I thought [Walter] seemed a good deal better – he talked quite rationally all the time I was with him, & did not have that terribly agonized expression that he had at first. They heard that day from the Lieutenant Governor saying to take him down to Victoria – so Mr. Cameron and Mr. Norris went off with him Tuesday afternoon. [26 March 1897]

[Mrs. Cameron] is feeling better, but is very much worried about Walter. He came back a week ago. His Uncle did not think there was much the matter with him, & sent him back to resume his duties in the office, but he is getting as bad as ever again since he came home, & poor Mrs. Cameron is greatly distressed. She said all the time that he ought to be kept away from Vernon, and I am sure she was right. [7 May 1897]

While I was at Mrs. Vidler's Walter Dewdney was there – poor boy, he is much worse – they are going to take him to the Coast tomorrow, I suppose to an asylum. [13 May 1897]

I went in to Mrs. Cameron's too for a few minutes – Walter was just being taken away to the asylum – Dr. Morris was going with him. [15 May 1897]

[Mr. Norris] thinks he may go down to Vancouver for a week at Xmas time. He says poor Walter Dewdney is no better atall. [19 December 1897]

Against all odds, Dewdney did indeed recover sufficiently to be discharged from the provincial asylum after eighteen months, and he went on to a distinguished career as a government agent.

Dental hygiene was primitive and treatment at times fearsome:

... Mrs. Smith came & asked me to go with her to the dentist's. I could not refuse, though I had planned a very different morning ... however I went and really I never saw a braver spirited woman. She had five teeth & six roots extracted, without so much as a groan, and she did not take anything either. [15 November 1893]

... I went to the dentist's – I had made an appointment with him in the morning so I went over to his room at the Kalemalka at three. When I got there I found Mr. & Mrs. Ehmcke in his office. Mrs. Ehmcke had driven in from Spallumcheen to have twenty teeth taken out! I said I would give place to her and went up to the parlour to wait until Dr. Hall

Caroline Butler Barrett,
Alice's grandmother, c.1865.
(Barrett Family Collection)

Hugh Massey Barrett,
Alice's grandfather, c.1865.
(Barrett Family Collection)

Emily Langs Barrett,
Alice's mother, c.1897.
(Barrett Family Collection)

Theobald Butler Barrett,
Alice's father, c.1897.
(Barrett Family Collection)

Alice Butler Barrett,
aged about 16, c.1877.
(Barrett Family Collection)

Riverbank Cottage, Port Dover, c. 1885. (Barrett Family Collection)

Three Barrett siblings (left to right), Emily Louisa "Wese,"
Alice Butler, and Arthur Clarence, c.1891.
(Barrett Family Collection)

The Spallumcheen Valley, c.1891. (National Archives of Canada)

Harry and Alice Barrett outside the Spallumcheen cabin, 1891.
(Barrett Family Collection)

Henry Francis Barrett,
Alice's irascible uncle and owner of
Mountain Meadow Ranch, c.1875.
(Barrett Family Collection)

Four young Spallumcheen residents (left to right), Harry Barrett,
Richard Noble Taylor, William Pelly Horsley (standing), and William Rankin, c.1890.
(Barrett Family Collection)

Catherine Schubert, pioneer in the
Spallumcheen and the only woman to
cross Canada by land with the
Overlanders in 1862, c.1895.
(GVMA)

Alexander and Bathia Ross Fortune, pioneers in Enderby, 1908. He was a participant in the Overlanders' trek in 1862. (GVMA)

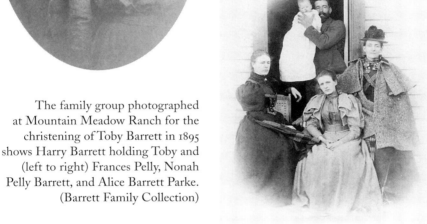

The family group photographed at Mountain Meadow Ranch for the christening of Toby Barrett in 1895 shows Harry Barrett holding Toby and (left to right) Frances Pelly, Nonah Pelly Barrett, and Alice Barrett Parke. (Barrett Family Collection)

The four Barrett brothers (left to right), Hubert, Clarence, Harry, and Frank, c.1898. (Barrett Family Collection)

The city of Vernon in 1892. (Provincial Archives of Alberta)

Harold Randolph Parke at Upper
Canada College, aged 15, 1861.
(Barrett Family Collection)

Harold Randolph Parke at the
time of his marriage in 1893.
(GVMA)

Clare Langs,
Alice's cousin, c.1885.
(Barrett Family Collection)

This photograph of the Okanagan Justices of the Peace in Vernon shows (seated, left to right) Edward J. Tronson, Bernard Lequime, Frederick Brent, Isadore Boucherie, Thomas Ellis, (standing, left to right) Cornelius O'Keefe, Moses Lumby, Luc Girouard, and James Crozier, 1890. (GVMA)

Price and Sophia Ellison with their daughters, (left to right) Elizabeth, Anna, Myra, and Ellen (on the floor), 1893. (GVMA)

William Fraser Cameron,
the Parkes' good friend.
(GVMA)

Alice's good friend,
Clara Cameron.
(GVMA)

Alice's good friend,
Adaline Cochrane, 1899.
(GVMA)

Her Excellency Ishbel,
Countess of Aberdeen, 1904.
(GVMA)

Harold and Alice Parke in a
Christmas portrait for the
home ones, 1895.
(GVMA)

Harry Barrett with his
wife Nonah and children
Dick (standing) and
Toby. On the right is
Henry Francis Barrett,
the "Uncle" of the
diaries, 1898. (Barrett
Family Collection)

Richard Pelly Barrett (left) and Theobald Butler Barrett II (right)
outside the Spallumcheen cabin, 1898.
(Barrett Family Collection)

Four of the Barrett cousins (left to right), Toby, Winifred, Quintin, and Dick
in Port Dover. (Barrett Family Collection)

The Parkes' only child,
Emily Louisa, died at the
age of nine months, 1901.
(Barrett Family Collection)

The Ng Family
(also known as Kwong
Hing Lung), c. 1900.
(GVMA)

Members of the Nez Percé tribe, Vernon, c. 1897.

A Chinese cook in Vernon, c. 1896. (GVMA)

Teachers and students at Vernon School, 1891. Boys standing at the back (left to right): Herbert McCluskey, Ernest McCluskey, Tomy Crowell, Fred Kerr, Fred Gartrell, Billy McNeil, Charles Fuller. Standing in front of them: Teddy Dewdney, George Gartrell and Eddie Duncan. Foreground (left to right): Elsie French, Rosie Dewdney, Alma Fuller, Annabelle Fuller, Edith Tronson, Mary Tronson, J. Sievwright (teacher), Mrs. Munro, Kenneth Burnyeat, Edna Christien, Delphine Christien, Walter Dewdney with Alex Munro on his lap, Annie Clark, Lavinia Christien, Mrs. Fuller, Mrs. Crowell, Mrs. Kerr, Mrs. Harber. Sitting on the ground: Percy French, George French, and Bruce Kerr. (GVMA)

The Vernon Pansy Club, c.1898. Members of the Young Conservative Association included (rear) Hugh Bell, Alec Birnie, (3rd row) Ed Birnie, Morley Davidson, Mabel McFarlane, (2nd row) Ida Birnie, Jack Holland, Flora Bell (front) Lou Haverty, Mike Holland, and Ada Gould. (GVMA)

Hal Parke in old age, c. 1910. (Barrett Family Collection)

Alice with her favourite
nephew Toby during the
Second World War.
(Barrett Family Collection)

Alice Barrett Parke,
aged 84, 1945.
(Barrett Family Collection)

was at liberty. He came for me in about a quarter of an hour and I did not have such a bad time as I had feared. [19 September 1896]

I feel too useless to get at any work this afternoon. I was at the dentist's both yesterday & today, and though the fillings were not very painful, it has made me very tired ... Hal made an appointment with the dentist for me to go the next day. I did dread it horribly but, like many other experiences, it was more in the anticipation than in reality. I was there all yesterday morning, & for a short time today ... Again this morning, soon after eight, we started for town. The dentist filled two today and three yesterday, and now he says my teeth are all right. It is a great comfort ... I did not feel much like visiting – my teeth felt queer, & I was tired, so we came home in time for dinner. [23 March 1898]

... I had been at Mrs. Billings for a few minutes earlier in the evening. She, poor thing, has been in the house with an ulcerated tooth, suffering a good deal, but she had the tooth out Tuesday night. [2 February 1899]

Dr. Morris & Dr. Corrigan came here on Saturday, administered chloroform & took [Annie Harding's teeth] out. Poor Annie she was so sick & weak after it. She was miserable all last week, & isn't a bit strong yet. [1 April 1900]

Diseases prevented today by infant inoculation hit hard:

Stuart [Martin] is sick in bed – they think he has measles. [27 March 1897]

[The schools] are to have another week's holiday, as the measles are still very bad in town. [4 April 1897]

... Baby Martin is pretty sick with measles. [8 April 1897]

Gertie Costerton ... is ill with measles ... Mr. Costerton was doing all the work, nursing Gertie & taking care of the children. Mrs. Macdonald told me this afternoon that *he* has measles now, but Mrs. Pratt has gone to take care of them for which I am truly thankful. [5 February 1899]

Circulatory diseases laid low many adults:

Mr. Cameron has gone to Victoria ... to consult a doctor. Hal has been worried a good deal about him. He has some kind of paralysis in his legs. He cannot go upstairs and is very stiff. Dr. Morris seems to think it very serious, & told Mr. Cameron he did not think it would ever be better. [26 March 1897]

I am afraid tonight that [Mrs. Cameron] is really a good deal troubled about Mr. Cameron, & I don't wonder. He seems to be threatened with paralysis in his legs, & the doctors he has consulted tell him plainly that he may never be better. [1 April 1897]

We heard this morning that Mrs. O'Keefe is very ill. She had a stroke of paralysis last night – they sent for the doctor in the night, & she is very ill today. Mrs. Cameron went out this morning and is still there, & Mr. O'Keefe came in for Miss Vickers. Dr. Morris is away & they had Dr. Williams. He is such an alarmist that one can't be sure if she is as ill as he says, but at any rate there is cause for alarm. [27 August 1898]

Poor Mrs. O'Keefe is not so well. It is very hard for those young girls. So much anxiety and responsibility thrown upon their shoulders, and I don't think their father is any help to them in the house. He takes no share of the responsibility in doors. It is likely to be a very tedeous recovery at the best of it. [10 September 1898]

This seems to have been a week of sad happenings. Early Monday morning Mrs. O'Keefe died.[30] Though she had been ill so long it was very sudden at the last – & oh! how hard it is for her husband & children. The eldest daughter, Nellie, is about eighteen – a pretty bright girl – so young for such sorrow & responsibility to come upon her. Mrs. O'Keefe was a good mother, & a good friend. She will be very much missed & mourned. [2 February 1899]

The diaries offer valuable insights into the methods of medical treatment in use at the time:

Harry [Hann] went to see the Dr. about his hand – Dr. Morris opened it a little and said to go on poulticing so I have been dressing it quite often since. [2 February 1897]

[Harry Hann] had rather a hard time. The doctor injected cocaine and lanced his hand. It was very painful, but Harry is pretty brave. The Dr. thinks it will soon get well now. It wasn't a felon, but a bruised cord, & all the little cords and muscles were inflamed. [5 February 1897]

... poor Mrs. Cameron, she is nearly a mate for Job – she has now cracked or broken some of her ribs. I found her suffering intensely – the doctor had bound her all up. [12 April 1897]

Hal's back was very painful. He went to see Dr. Morris about it in the afternoon, & the Dr. said to put a mustard poultice on so I got Hal to go to bed early and I sat up until it was time to take the poultice off. [25 June 1897]

I went to see Harry Hann yesterday – the poor boy is laid up with a sort of felon. I think he must have poisoned his finger handling meat – the Dr. was quite alarmed about him Sunday night, his fever was so high … the Dr. had just opened the finger and that, of course, relieved him … Hal heard in town today that poor Harry Hann had had to have one finger amputated. I thought he had got quite better. I feel so very sorry. [9 November 1897]

[Harry Hann] thinks his hand is getting on very well now, but says he won't try to go to work again this winter … Poor boy, he has had a hard time of it. He suffered very much for a good while. [14 November 1897]

The Dr. was to take the last wrapping off [Harry Hann's] hand yesterday, as it is quite healed. He is greatly delighted with Dr. Morris – being perfectly satisfied with his treatment and his bill! [11 December 1897]

Poor Mr. McKelvie has a kind of malarial fever. The doctor says he will have to be in bed a week or ten days. [23 February 1898]

I took a little bottle of marmalade to Gertie and stayed with her quite a little while. She looks very wretched, is back in bed again, & the Dr. has to inject morphine nearly every day, she suffers so from neuralgia. I hate that morphine, & it seems so hard to give up having it once the practise is begun. [29 March 1898]

[Mrs. Cameron] was very ill again last week, suffered so much pain in her side and leg – the Dr. has been treating her for a month, and she seemed to be no better, so she began to use Pond's Extract[31] – on her own responsibility – and, in the words of the patent medicine advertisements "the effect was wonderful," she soon felt relieved, & thinks now that she is decidedly better. [8 July 1898]

… [Dr. Morris] said Hal had a "little temperature" so must stay in bed for several days. He sent something for the cough, a lotion for the head, and told me to put mustard on Hal's chest last night. I did so, but I don't believe Hal feels quite so well today. He says his head isn't so bad, but his chest feels sorer, and he feels weak. He thinks it was bad for him to stay in bed, but he has tried to cure this cold for over a month, on the "fighting off" plan, & in vain – so I thought it was time to give in to it, & try nursing. [27 January 1899]

[Mrs. Meighan] has had to bring her little boy,[32] the youngest, up here to the hospital. He has a sore foot, & she had to bring him to have it treated. I saw her yesterday, & she was telling me about it and seemed to feel so badly. They are poor too, & the expense is hard to meet ... The little Meighan boy ... told [Lizzie] that the Doctor had to cut his foot right to the bone. Poor little chap – he seemed very brave over it, & only a baby really. The Dr. says he'll have to stay up here about ten days. His Mother would like to stay with him, but it is very hard for her to stay so long from home, besides the expense. [10 October 1899]

Hal feels so tired tonight – indeed he has for several days. I urged him to get some kind of a tonic, so tonight he got a bottle of Paine's Celery Component[33] – Muir said it was an excellent "pick me up." [19 July 1899]

[Hal] feels a little better lately I think. He is taking beef iron & wine. [20 August 1899]

Hal's rheumatism has been better for the last two days – still he doesn't feel quite himself yet. He got some medicine from the doctor & is going to try electricity. [1 January 1898]

Accidents and injuries also took their toll:

On Tuesday night half a dozen men came up from Armstrong on a hand car to go to a ball at Okanagan Landing. They were coming very fast, & the night was very dark, and just as they neared Vernon there was a car loaded with flour standing on the track – this they ran into with a tremendous crash. One of the men – Keys, the Armstrong Hotel keeper – was thrown off, his nose broken & his face badly cut & bruised ... Dr. Morris said yesterday that he is getting on all right, only he will be badly disfigured. News came yesterday of a terrible accident on the main line. [2 February 1899]

Such a sad thing happened on Sunday. Poor young McClusky[34] was out shooting – his gun went off accidentally, & shot his arm very badly. The wound in itself had not been fatal but he was six miles from home, & before the young lads with him could get him home & get the doctor, he had bled so much that Tuesday morning he died from exhaustion. He was only 18 – a great strong healthy looking boy. He was not a very industrious boy – so many of the young lads around here seem worthless – they want to idle about with a horse or a gun the greater part of their time, & it does seem too bad that no one can lead them to better things. [16 November 1899]

Many people arrived with high hopes of finding work or good farming land, only to be disappointed. Poverty was widespread:

... Mr. Butler, the clergyman from Enderby, called. He brought with him a Mrs. Wood and her little girl ... I don't know when I have felt as sorry for any one as for Mrs. Wood. She has been living for ten years on a bush ranch ever so many miles from the main waggon road, and with no near neighbours. I am sure too, from the way she spoke, that they are very poor. She said she was so thoroughly enjoying her little visit in Enderby – with the exception of going once to Kamloops, this is the only time she has been off the ranch since she went there ten years ago. [31 May 1896]

Hal had an old man come on Friday morning to cut wood & clear up the garden, and do a little digging. He has been working here for three days. He is old & slow, but a good worker. Hal said he wasn't able to do the work like a young man & consequently does not get much to do – so it was like Hal to engage him, paying him full wages ($2.00 a day) and giving him besides a good coat & waistcoat. [6 October 1895]

I am afraid we will have many calls upon our purses & our kindliness this winter – another poor creature is ill back of us, a poor little Salvation Army man. Dr. Williams says he has this fever. He & his wife live in a shack with one room & they have a sick baby – some people do have very few material blessings, & we[35] have so much. [3 November 1895]

... a man came to ask Hal for work – he was a gentlemanly looking & speaking man. He told Hal he had been 15 yrs. in a bank in London Ont. Then on a small farm of his own near Windsor. He came out to Rossland a few months ago & has not been able to get anything to do, so now he is looking for a job as a farm labourer. Hal said he would be able to give him work as soon as haying commences, & in the meantime he may come & do odd jobs about for the sake of getting his board. It seems pretty [hard] on him, & yet one very often sees just such turns of fortune's wheel out here. [23 June 1897]

Hal has had a man here splitting wood all day ... Hal would have done it by degrees himself but he knew this man needed work pretty badly, so thought it right to give it to him. I gave him a couple of partly worn flannel shirts yesterday, & he seemed most grateful, & some turnips & apples today. He is a very decent man, with a wife & three children. They came to Vernon last summer from the North West, where they own a ranch – but the man who rented it has had a total failure of crops & cannot pay the rent – consequently these people have only Mr. MacMillan's (that's their name) daily labour to depend on, and he has not been able to get steady work. I think they are pretty poor. I am glad Hal was able to give him a little work – that is the kindest charity I think. [3 December 1894]

Right after breakfast I had a visit from a tramp who asked for some breakfast, & undoubtedly the man was hungry. He ate six great slices of bread & butter, three cups of coffee, cold meat & jam. I was half frightened all the time he was here, but he went off quite peacefully & gratefully as soon as he had had plenty to eat. He didn't ask for money. [12 June 1896]

I got out at Mrs. Perkins[36] and went in to see her. I told Hal I'd walk the rest of the way home. Poor old Mrs. Perkins – she hasn't a very comfortable place to live. It is a low log shanty, just one room, & no floor! They have boards laid down to cover most of it and in this room she has to have two beds, one for herself & one for her son, a cooking stove, and indeed all that she has. It looked more clean & tidy than one would have believed possible, & indeed it looked picturesque, for all the rafters of the low flat roof were decorated with strings of bright red & yellow peppers. Mr. Topp (her adopted son) is a splendid gardener – he had just lovely flowers even yet, and his vegetables are a great success. I think they are pretty poor, but very proud. [19 October 1897]

[Mrs. Milne] is left with two little children, and very little money – and I think she is one of those helpless shiftless sort of women, that one pities, & yet feels provoked with. I suppose some one will take care of her – those who will lean generally find a support while those with a stiff back of their own generally have to hold up straight, no matter how heavy the load, or how aching the back – the law of compensation prevails. [12 April 1898]

CHAPTER 7

How I love them all

Some Members of the Barrett Family

F amily was a prominent theme throughout the diaries. After Alice married, her brother and Uncle were once again left to their own resources. She continued to make frequent visits to Mountain Meadow Ranch, during which she shopped for food, cleaned house, cooked, mended and washed clothes, and brought a woman's touch to the lives of the two bachelors. Harry was already courting Nonah Pelly, and she was a frequent visitor to the ranch when Alice stayed there.

Harry said this morning when we were getting breakfast "Why, it's quite lonesome without Nonah, isn't it?" He finished drawing his rails yesterday at noon, so today we have just had a good old visit. He has only done the necessary stable work, and was in the house most of the morning helping me, & reading or talking. I made an apricot pie & a raspberry pie & quite a lot of turnovers – it was from a bottle of home raspberries. I only used half, so I heated the rest over & sealed them down until my next visit. Harry likes pies so much better than the fruit with bread & butter, & he never makes a pie for himself. I also made a big fruit cake which I have put away in a jar. It was cool – I know Mother will think of that – & wonder if I put it up too warm. I also ironed all the starched things, & since noon Harry & I peeled & chopped up a lot of onions, which I am making into pickles after an original receipt. They were sprouting and spoiling & would, I knew, be wasted if I did not use them in some way. Harry wrote to Uncle & to Frank so I put a letter in each envelope. We are going to have roast duck for tea and I am roasting a fine big piece of venison to leave for Harry, so his larder will be pretty well supplied for two or three days.[1 March 1894]

Harry Barrett never became wealthy from ranching, and he suffered more than his share of bad luck. Apart from being engaged in such a weather-dependent activity, he also suffered from a sore back much of the time and, at one point, developed an abdominal rupture that made ranch work extremely painful until he purchased a truss.

It is nice to have [Harry] for this little visit – & I know he is enjoying it too. He has been working very hard this Spring and lately has had a touch of sciatica – he looks very thin and is just taking a thorough rest – reading, sleeping, talking most of the day. [24 June 1894]

I had a letter from Harry this morning. He is in rather low spirits over the weather as he has a lot of hay out yet and all his oats. If it would only clear now – I don't suppose much harm is done, but another week of rain would mean serious loss. Harry says most of the ranchers between him & Enderby have about half their crop out – Harry Harding has a lot out. [16 September 1895]

On Friday we housecleaned the sitting room and got the stove up. Harry did all the hard part of the work. [20 October 1895]

One of the life-long hobbies that Harry enjoyed was singing:

[The concert] went off very well, but even though I am Harry's sister I must say he was the star of the evening. It happened quite luckily that a Mrs. Macdonald sang "Call me back again." Harry has been wishing someone would, so he could sing the parody "Haul me back again." When he found out what she was going to sing he asked Mr. Wright to put him after her, & the applause was almost deafening. He is very popular. [16 December 1891]

Harry sang "Time enough for that," and forgot the words of the last verse. He retired from the stage amid great laughter & claps. [30 December 1891]

After tea we had to dress, & go down to the concert. It wasn't much of a concert – no body, except Harry, sang very well, & he wouldn't sing an encore. [16 November 1894]

We had a great evening last night. Jack came up from Armstrong about eight. He had been very successful at the shooting; so was in great good spirits. He & Harry played – Jack on the flute, Harry on the violin – then we sang and finally ate cake & apple pie. Harry & Nonah translated a little French song, & Harry wrote it out on the opposite page [of the diary]. We did not go to bed until after eleven, so were rather late in getting up this morning. [22 April 1894]

In April 1894 the engagement of Harry Barrett and Nonah Pelly was announced:

Harry met me at Armstrong & we walked up to the ranch. It was about six when we got here. After tea Harry had quite a lot of work to do, & afterwards we walked up to Mrs. Pelly's. I stayed all night, & Nonah came down with me this morning. We got here about ten, and have been pretty busy all day. It is pouring rain tonight – it has been very warm the last two days. Nonah is going to stay until I go, & then go up to Vernon with me for a few days. I suppose I may now tell the diary that she and Harry[1] are engaged. He has written home about it. I wonder what they will say. [30 April 1894]

I heard from home yesterday – they have heard of Harry's engagement & seem really pleased. I am very glad. [28 April 1894]

Harry ... seems very happy, and more contented than I have seen him for a long time. [12 May 1894]

Alice journeyed to Port Dover during the summer of 1894 and returned laden with gifts for her brother and his fiancée:

I had such a lot of nice presents for Harry & Nonah, & when I unpacked the trunks found everything had come in good order. I did not have much time to rest, as I had a good many visitors, & then I had to get ready for the wedding. First I went down to the ranch for a couple of days, & we worked away there getting it settled up for Nonah's advent, with new carpets & curtains and various little additions to furniture etc. – we made quite a difference in the look of the place. Uncle has put a veranda across the front, & has built a picket fence – so altogether it looks very well indeed. The wedding came off last Wednesday,[2] and now Harry is really a married man.[3] Nonah & Mrs. Pelly came up on Tuesday morning, & all was bustle & confusion then, until the great event was over. Nonah looked so pretty, in white silk with an exquisite old lace veil, which was her grandmother's wedding veil. She was a bonny young bride, & one any

man might be proud of – so sweet & gentle she looked, and yet so calm
& collected. I don't think she was nearly so excited as either her Mother
or myself. Harry looked very handsome. Oh! how I wished the other
home ones could have seen him, & Uncle looked splendid. There is no use
talking – dress makes a difference, & Uncle was carefully & well dressed
– he is often rather careless. Mrs. Pelly had a black silk, I a green. May,
the bridesmaid, had a very pretty dress of pale blue. They (with the few
guests) came over here afterwards for refreshments and stayed until after
three. Then we said goodbye to the bride & groom and soon after the others all drove off. Uncle stayed until today, so tonight Hal & I are having
our first Darby & Joan[4] evening since before the wedding. I can hardly
realize that it is only a week yesterday that they were married. It seems so
much longer. I was very tired when all the strain was over, and the excitement quieted down, and have been indulging in a little cough, & leading
a lazy time generally. I feel a certain energy beginning to stir in me again,
& yesterday began to pay some of the many calls I owe. [1 November 1894]

After her wedding, Nonah Barrett proved to be as hard a worker as
Alice. A quiet, gentle, amiable eighteen-year-old, she became pregnant
almost immediately (although her sister-in-law made no direct reference
to her condition in the diaries). After the birth of Theobald Butler Barrett
the Second, Alice became a doting aunt and wrote glowing entries describing his demeanour and progress. (Throughout her life, Toby remained her
favourite nephew, and he returned her affection in full measure.)

[The cabin at Mountain Meadow] looked so nice and home like – I think
I grow fonder of Nonah all the time. She has a lovely disposition – Harry
is very much to be congratulated. [12 January 1895]

News came from Harry yesterday that Nonah has a little son[5] & of course
I am very anxious to go down & see it. Hal has to go to Enderby tomorrow, & will take me as far as the Ranch ... [25 July 1895]

I can't tell yet what the baby will look like – I think he will be fair, and he
is a dear plump healthy looking little fellow – but he didn't open his eyes,
or make a sound while I was there. He weighs 7½ pounds, & Mrs. Pelly
says is good so far. Nonah thinks he is going to be exactly like Harry,
because he has such big hands & feet! – but I don't think he looks like
Harry now – still he is too young to tell I know. [26 July 1895]

The baby is a dear good little fellow, but – like all babies – demands a good
deal of attention. I could almost see him grow. He slept the greater part

of the time, & is very bright & knowing looking for so small a baby. Nonah is very fond & proud of him. I don't know how she is going to do the work & take care of him for he took up all our time, when he was awake. [3 September 1895]

On Wednesday morning Nonah churned and I took care of the boy. He is as good and sweet as a baby can be. He knows both his Father & Mother well, & took very kindly to me. He is just three months old today. I don't know which – Harry or Nonah – is the proudest of him. He certainly has the best blessing – love – in great abundance – dear little soul. [24 November 1895]

... even Hal, who isn't very fond of wee babies, was constrained to admire both his looks and his actions. [1 January 1896]

Nonah & the baby were at the door to welcome us. Baby has grown, but is just as good as ever. He has the happiest little face one can fancy on a baby. He was not exactly shy with me, but he knew I was a stranger, and regarded me very inquisitively all that evening. However we were great friends next morning & all the rest of my stay. Harry says I spoil him, but I don't think he would like it if I didn't take notice of the dear little fellow – & indeed he isn't easily spoiled, he is so good & happy. [12 February 1896]

The Pellys all came before dinner and last of all Mr. Butler arrived. We had dinner – roast chicken, cold corned beef, turnips, potatoes, lemon pie, corn starch & jelly, and christening cake. Then we had the christening. The baby was as good as gold. When Mr. Butler put the water on his face he looked up & laughed. [12 February 1896]

I brought [baby] on home & left them to pay their call. He woke as soon as I took off his jacket, but was quite good – sat in Hal's big chair surrounded with cushions while I got tea ready ... [9 March 1896]

Miss Johnson was praising up our baby, and greatly astonished me by saying she thought he looked like me! [14 March 1896]

We put the baby in the wheelbarrow, and gave him a ride. He does love to be out of doors & he is getting to be quite a load to carry. [31 May 1896]

Baby was sitting in his high chair out on the veranda, & Nonah was at the door. She too exclaimed "I had a feeling you would come tonight." The baby knows me I'm sure, he gets more lovable and winning every time I go down ... He looks so well. I think he will walk very soon – he stood quite alone one day while I was there. He does not try to talk, except that he calls Harry "Da-da," & begins clamouring for him the minute he appears – & he has a funny little sound (I can't say a word) which he makes whenever he sees the cat or kittens – but he is so good. I don't think Nonah looks well atall[6] – I wish she was not so thin. [3 July 1896]

He is quite a weight – my arms began to ache before I got back to the house – the dear little soul does so love to be out, it is a pleasure to look at his face. He runs all about now, in a most unsteady manner, and has five teeth. He had quite a cold but was not cross. [24 September 1896]

Harry said Nonah & baby were well – the baby[7] is getting to be a great mischief. [26 October 1896]

... Harry Harding said he was in Armstrong lately at Mrs. Weir's and she had occasion to reprimand her children for quarreling – she said to Harry "They are always spatting & wrangling – but I never was so ashamed of them in my life as I was the other day when little Toby Barrett was here – *he licked all three of them.*" As two of them are older than "Toby," & one just his age, Harry expressed surprise at his being able to "do them up," but she said the way he did was to run at them suddenly and knock them over. I can't fancy our gentle little baby up to such pranks – but I suppose the old Tipperary and Pennsylvania Dutch spirit must be hidden away in him some where and perhaps Jimmy and Petie Weir awakened it. I confess I'd have liked to see the encounter. [3 January 1897]

Toby was eighteen months old when a brother arrived, and the two siblings quickly became fast friends:

... Johnson brought out a letter from Harry telling us that Nonah has another little son.[8] Mrs. Pelly was with her – they want me to go down soon, and I'm sure I hope to go before long. [9 January 1897]

I had a letter from Harry today – he wants me to go down ... I am afraid poor Harry is having a hard time of it, trying to get his outside work done & take care of little Theobald too. I may go down tomorrow – I feel that I'd like to go & help them for two or three days. [13 January 1897]

... of course I had to get my clothes warmed before I could go near Nonah or the new baby. He is a little beauty – as pretty a little baby as I ever saw. He is to be named Richard Pelly, after Nonah's father. I think he will likely look like Harry. Little Theobald considers him a great joke & giggles unrestrainedly whenever he sees him. He wants to be most affectionate too, & as his kisses are not always wisely bestowed he has to be watched.

I think it will be very nice for the two little chaps – if they are spared to grow older – to be so nearly the same age. Harry & Nonah seem very proud of their boys. [19 January 1897]

The little baby, Dick, grows apace. He is as pretty as ever and is getting quite fat, but his eyes are not turning brown yet, though his hair & skin are dark . . . Poor wee Toby! I was so glad to think when I was down before that he was not jealous of the new baby, but now he is jealous if Harry goes to nurse Dick – he seems to take it for granted that the little one must have his Mother's care, but he considers Harry his own special property & does not like to share him. Harry is such a help in the house, & indeed anyone would be glad to help take care of those two dear little children. [14 February 1897]

I was busy making a little apron for Theobald – I did it mostly by hand as I did not want to go off up stairs to the machine. [21 February 1897]

Little Theobald seemed thoroughly to enjoy the strange faces. He sat up in his high chair beside his father (during dinner) smiling first at one & then at another occasionally wanting to shake hands with somebody. [2 March 1897]

Mrs. Ellison's baby is much quicker than little Theobald about talking – he is only six weeks older, and he says nearly every thing – even begins to put sentences together – while our baby only says three words Pussy, Jam & bow-wow. It looks as if he would be very fond of animals when he talks first about them. [27 March 1897]

I heard from Harry yesterday – he has cut Toby's hair & says he looks very roguish. [20 May 1897]

Toby was ready to welcome me. He talks a great deal now, and is most anxious to learn new words. They say he often talks of me, & says he is coming up to see me. [1 December 1897]

Dick began to get a little cross before [his mother] came home. He set up a very lively cry, & was refusing to be comforted, when Uncle came in and took him, & Dick quieted down immediately & became quite happy. Uncle gave him a cookie & declared I was "starving the child." Dick seems quite fond of Uncle, often tries to attract his attention, & isn't one bit afraid of his gruff tones, but Toby is more shy with him. [1 December 1897]

. . . in the afternoon [we] went over to see Mrs. O'Keefe. Dick had a lovely day. Mrs. Greenhow has two little nieces, & they played with him so nicely. He is not shy & is so pretty that he wins every one's heart. It was amusing to see him at the O'Keefe's – Nellie began to play on the piano. Dick was running around the room, & when he heard the first notes, he stopped as if he had been shot, looked all around in bewilderment – he couldn't tell where the sound came from. He wasn't exactly frightened – only astonished however – to Uncle's great delight & amusement he ran to him & held out his arms to be taken up, then sat quite contentedly listening. [13 March 1898]

[Nonah] doesn't seem very anxious to go to her Mother's to visit. It is so strange to me that she doesn't go there to stay oftener, & that May never comes here for a day or two to give her a helping hand. Mrs. Evans was saying to me that she & Mr. Evans had often talked it over and wondered how I found time to do so much for Nonah, while her own sister, & even her Mother, never seemed to do anything. Of course Mrs. Pelly is very good & kind, and she does sometimes come. She stayed for a month when Dick was born, & several times she stayed with the children to let Nonah go to dances – still I know very well if Mother and Wese lived no further from me than the Pellys[9] do from Nonah we'd spend more time together. [27 May 1898]

Toby is just at the age when all that he says is so interesting & original. I got quite a fright Monday night. He had been playing outside, when I looked out & saw that the gate was open & he had disappeared. I ran all round the house calling him, then up & down the road, & Nonah was just coming out to look when we heard a little voice "I'se comin,'" and here he was hurrying down from the field. He had thought Harry had gone into the field, & he had gone through the bars after him. He picks up every new word with great quickness. Harry called the turkeys "little beggars" one day, & I heard Toby saying it over & over to himself – "beggars," "little beggars" – with a very strong emphasis, just as Harry had said it. [2 June 1898]

[Toby] & Dick are very fond of each other, & play well together. The first thing Dick says when he awakes is generally "To – bee..." They dearly love a play – Dick goes into it with such whole hearted merriment. I wish I could describe Toby's look & attitude. He laughs very happily, but he always looks as if he were playing quite as much to amuse the rest of the people as himself. He is getting much prettier as he gets older. I think he is a very determined child and though much quieter and gentler than Dick will really be harder to train & subdue. I don't think he is a bit like any of us in disposition except in his love for home and relations. I am very fond of him & of dear little Dick too. I often wish they could know Quintin[10] – he is different again, I think – all three are bright, lovable little fellows, & all so different in character. I think Quintin will be the most musical – I am afraid Toby won't be musical – he loves a story far better than a song, & doesn't he remember it well. I told him a fresh one this time, about Androcles & the lion, & he was greatly taken with it, but best of all he loves me to tell him about old Jack, the dog that "Grandpa" brought from Dunville, & how he begged, & how George Walker put his eye out, & all the other details that I can remember or invent. [15 July 1898]

As soon as Toby saw me he began to ask if I'd take him down on the meadow, so I said I would "after a while." Hal left to go on to Enderby right after dinner and Harry & the others went down on the meadow to the hay field. It really was very hot and I was trying to persuade Toby to wait awhile, so I put him off as well as I could ... It was really comical. Whenever Dick expressed dissatisfaction with any thing Toby would say "Never mind, Dick, we are going down to the meadow." He was very good all the time – not fretting – but so constantly alluding in a most confident, cheerful way to this trip in store that at last I couldn't bear to keep him waiting any longer – so, although it was very hot Nonah, Dick, Toby & I set out, & went down the hill and across where the boys were working. They were stacking just near a little clump of bushes – a pile of rails was there in the shade, so they put a lot of hay on the rails & made us a lovely soft seat, & there we stayed with the children until nearly five o'clock. How they did enjoy it – & so did we! They noticed every little thing within their range of vision, & chattered & questioned and talked. Mr. Horsley went back with us to the gate, & carried the children over the stubble & up the hill – when we got to the house they were in great spirits & ready for a romp. They wanted to play, but Nonah & I were hot & tired. I said "Oh Toby, poor Mamma and Auntie have been for such a long walk they can't romp." He said "But I've been down on the meadow too, & I'm not tired" – & I said "Yes dear, but you know cousin Willie carried you all the way over the hay field, & we had to walk, so our poor legs are very tired." He looked then as if he quite understood and said in a very patronizing way "Oh well – never mind Auntie, wait until you get little, and somebody will carry you – bye 'm bye." Dick waiting nearby always is ready to echo Toby, & he nodded his head very sagely, & said "by 'm bye." It sounded such a comical turning of the tables – no doubt often Toby has to sigh for the unattainable, & is told to wait until he "gets big" – and I thought it was really clever of him to appreciate the disadvantages of grown-up-ness. Alas! – though – we have no hopes of getting back again the joys that belong to the time of being "little" – at least not the physical joys – but we might all learn more child-likeness of mind and heart – the trustfulness and delight in small things. [23 July 1898]

I went into [Nonah's] room & lay on the bed, but both the children clambered in after me so there wasn't any chance to sleep. I got up & showed them pictures until Dick got sleepy. I put him to sleep & talked to Toby a while longer … [11 August 1898]

Yesterday morning Uncle walked in while we were at breakfast. I suppose he will stay some time, as there is a little new son[11] down at the ranche. It arrived yesterday morning. I had a short note from Harry today. I am anxious to get down to see it … Today Annie came, & Harry's letter telling me about the little baby. I wonder what Toby and Dick think of him. Boys are very plentiful in our family. [19 October 1898]

Tragically, Nonah Barrett died one week after giving birth to her third child and was buried in the tiny Pelly cemetery on the banks of Otter Lake. Harry suddenly found himself with a ranch and three small children to care for. Distraught and bereft, he judged the situation hopeless and quickly decided to pack up and move back to Ontario with his two older sons, leaving the new-born Frank with his grandmother Pelly. He asked his sister to help him take care of the children on the journey home, and Alice did so willingly. By the end of November 1898, she, Harry, Toby, and Dick were on the train to Port Dover and she was away for six weeks. The care of Toby and Dick now devolved upon Wese Barrett. William Horsley took over the operation of Mountain Meadow Ranch:

It is three months since I have written any diary, so my hand will have lost whatever cunning it once had. I will not try to tell what has happened in the interval – none of us will forget, either the sorrow or the gladness of the weeks that have passed. My visit home seems already far away, though it is only a little over two weeks since I left there. The news still is good of dear Mother's increasing strength. Hal was really ill with Grippe when I got back, and I felt too sick the first week I was home to write any more than the home letters. Uncle is still here – Hal asked him to come and stay here while I was away, & he doesn't appear to think of going. He said, all along, that he was going to California, but now he speaks as if he had given up the notion. He is very miserable – has a bad cold & cough, & a *very* bad temper. Poor old man! he won't be happy himself, & tries his best to prevent any one else being so. I do feel very sorry for him – but oftener,

I'm afraid, I feel sorry for myself that I have to try to be patient. I wonder at Hal – he never says cross or nasty things to Uncle no matter what provocation he has.

I have not been able to get down to see the little baby at Mrs. Pelly's – at first when I came home I was too sick, & now the roads are too bad. It is such a pity there is no sleighing, for Hal could take me any day. [21 January 1899]

I miss Harry – & Nonah. It is hard to think that there is no one for me to love or care for at the old ranche. I used to look forward to my little visits down there, & plan about them constantly. Wese has been so good to write often & tell me about the children – I left them so well & happy. [21 January 1899]

Alice always showed concern for the well-being of her little nephews and continued to sew for them and send them gifts. Wese kept her up to date on their progress:

I had a nice letter from Wese yesterday. She says Toby & Dick are both learning their letters and Dick is well again. Such a nice letter too I had from Mrs. Pelly. She thinks the baby looks very much like his Mother – I am anxious to see him – I think of Nonah so much & miss her so very much. There were so many little ways I used to be planning for her & thinking of her – and now that is all done. [14 February 1899]

Mrs. Pelly was just giving the little baby his bath when we got there. He is a lovely little boy. Mrs. Pelly & Hal both think he looks like his dear Mother, but I cannot see it. He has the bright sunny smile that was the greatest charm of Toby's baby face and he has Dick's forehead, but not atall Dick's or Toby's complexion – he is darker I think than either of them, though Mrs. Pelly thinks not – and I believe his eyes will be brown & his hair dark red. His eyes now are big grey ones – so pretty in shape & expression. He is a very fine baby, large & strong, & so good & happy. How Nonah would have loved to care for him and watch all his pretty ways & looks! Mrs. Pelly thinks he is prettier than either of the others, but I don't think he is so pretty as Dick. Of course he is only four months old and will change. Toby grows prettier all the time. Dear little boys! how I love them all & wish they were nearer. [26 February 1899]

Wese says little Dick is so clever he frightens her sometimes. It makes me long to see them when I hear of their sayings and doings. [14 March 1899]

I got one of the baby's little dresses finished today – it looks very sweet. I have the other one cut out, & will try to make it tomorrow. [13 December 1895]

I stayed at home and sewed. I have finished making Toby's little drawers. I have done five pairs for him, which will be enough I think for the winter ... I made a little white muslin pinnie[12] for Dick while they were gone. [6 November 1897]

I finished Toby's little brown dress today ... I made a broad white collar, with a bit of embroidery, to wear with his dresses – I think it will look nice. [14 December 1897]

Friday morning I cut out Dick's little pink gingham dress, & basted up my own print waist & made the sleeves, and swept all the house. I nearly made Dick's dress that day. [27 March 1898]

I cut out two little summer suits for Toby & began to make them ... Early after dinner I went for buttons & tape for Toby's clothes ... I sent Toby's little suits off on Tuesday. [23 April 1899]

   Harry did not have the heart to return to the Okanagan; he and Uncle had already decided to sell out:

Uncle came up to try & find a purchaser for the ranche. He & Harry would like to sell out altogether. I think Harry is really more attached to the place than he knows, and I half think he is foolish not to buy Uncle out, even if he has to mortgage to do so, but I don't like to advise and both Hal & the ones at home seem to think a mortgage would be foolish. I know it is hard enough to make ends meet now. [24 August 1898]

[Wese] says she thinks Harry begins to long to come back West. I don't think I quite realized how much I have missed him, until there is some chance of his returning. If he can only come & be happy I'd be so very glad. [17 March 1900]

   (Harry would not return until the summer of 1902, and then only for a few weeks, to see if he could make a go of ranching again. Having finally decided that he could not re-settle in the west, he returned to Port Dover for good.) Alice and her sister Wese were like twins in their close and loving relationship. To earn a little pin money, Wese used her artistic talents to make many beautiful articles, which Alice sold for her:

Wese sent the little photograph frames & court plaster cases which I asked her to paint for sale and they arrived safely today. They are very dainty and lovely. I hope they'll all sell – I sold two on the way to Mr. Taylor's shop – 75 cents apiece – & Mr. Taylor said he'd do his best to sell the others. [8 December 1893]

... I sent my last volume of diary to Wese last Thursday, hoping it might reach her on her birthday ... Wese talks more definitely about coming out, and says perhaps Father may come too. I hardly dare to hope that – sometimes the longing to see them all is very strong – indeed not sometimes, but always I think it is strong. [1 January 1896]

... Hal brought up two more frames tonight that Wese had painted for me to try to sell. They are lovely, particularly one with roses on. I will take them up on Monday to show Mrs. Martin. [11 January 1896]

My home letter last week contained a disappointment – Wese has decided not to come out this Spring. Harry & I are both very much disappointed, & I think Hal feels *nearly* as much so as we do. [28 March 1896]

Hal brought me ... two lovely paintings from Wese – a photograph frame & a letter case. The latter is lovely – the frame is pretty too, but the case is so dainty & lovely. I have looked at it ever so many times & would just like to keep it. [10 December 1896]

I had taken the frame Wese painted for Hal in to show it to [Mrs. Martin], & as I walked home yesterday I left it there until today. She was delighted with it – she has given me an order for another toilet set like the one Wese did for her some time ago ... [9 February 1897]

Mrs. Cameron heard from her sister in England, & she is in raptures over the frame Wese sent. [1 April 1897]

Wese is so good – she always writes no matter how little time she has. [9 November 1897]

I think the rooms will look very pretty when we have the curtains up & the piano in. We have such nice books and pictures – & dainty bits of painting that Wese has done for us. Wese & Clarence have beautified our home for us. I have Mother's little paintings up in my own room – & the texts that Wese has done for us. [22 August 1898]

This morning I ... dyed a pair of heavy curtains for the archway – they were red with pale pinky blossoms on them. I thought I'd dip them in yellow dye, as I knew Wese said that brightened up colors – so I washed them first & then dyed them, & they have come out a kind of sage green with yellow flowers. They go very well with the rest of the room, as carpet & blinds are green, but they were a great surprise to me – they have quite an oriental look. [31 August 1898]

I went first down to Mrs. Cameron's to show her the blotters Wese had sent – there was an extra one over those Mrs. Cameron had ordered and Mrs. Cameron begged to buy it – so I let her have the violet one. I liked it best & so did she, but Hal liked the roses best, & Lizzie the other pink one. They were all so pretty it was hard to make a choice. [9 March 1899]

Wese sent another little bundle of paintings yesterday, & I wanted to keep a couple of them myself to give away, but Mrs. Morris & Mrs. Cameron & Mrs. Henderson were ready to pounce on the package like hungry cats on a mouse & they coaxed them all away from me. I think the little address books were just lovely – and the other things too. [19 December 1899]

Wese sent some beautiful paintings on Friday, frames & blotters. She has such lovely ideas – her designs are always so beautiful & so much admired. [1 April 1900]

Uncle Henry remained at Mountain Meadow for two more years after Nonah Barrett's death. Despite the effort she made from the earliest days, Alice was never able to develop an amicable relationship with him:

Uncle was quite cranky all day yesterday – I think because he had so much to do, Harry being away. I have found out he does not like work – at night he was grumbling about Tiny keeping near the stable, and used very strong language. Harry didn't like it because, of course, the horses are his, & I did not like it either on Harry's account. So after listening a while, I just said "I don't think it is half so bad for a horse to stay where it isn't wanted, as for a man to use bad language." I was sorry as soon as I had said it, because of course he is old and I ought to be respectful – but I guess it did him good, for he was extremely nice to me last night and this morning came in & sat down to get up a conversation – said he did not know how it was he could not like horses – they seemed to aggravate him. Poor old man! There is nothing like living [in] the west to make one appreciate the wisdom which gave Adam a helpmate. [23 July 1891]

I have not been in a very serene temper lately – Uncle tries my patience terribly. Alec Scott was telling me a story of some old man who used to come to James & say of his son "Oh Jimmy, he do harass me so" and Uncle does "harass" me very much – sometimes I don't see how I can stand a whole winter of it, for I suppose he will be in the house all the time. [12 August 1891]

... tonight I quarrelled with Uncle about the Globe[13] & politics, which has made me ashamed. He is tantalizing – still I ought to know better. He does not mean to provoke me, but he does. [14 January 1892]

Uncle shows great partiality for Gulliver. He does not like poor little Jerry, & while he pets one, he cuffs the other. But Jerry has not a tender & sensitive spirit, and is well able to take his own part. [19 December 1891]

Uncle has been as cranky as "a bear with a sore head" as the saying is, for the past week. He and Harry had a hot argument at tea tonight, and everything either of us says, he contradicts. He makes me so aggravated I can hardly stand it. He is undoubtedly my "thorn in the flesh" these days. I thought I was getting to like him better – but it is a clear case of "too much familiarity breeds contempt." When he is away I like him well, but a week in the house with him strains the bonds very much. [19 January 1892]

Uncle was quite concerned about [my appearance]. This morning when I came out of my room he was alone in the kitchen, & put his arms around me & kissed me quite warmly, saying "You look thin, my dear." Poor Uncle! He often tries me – but after all, as Harry says, he reverses the general order. His roughnesses and ungraciousness are the veneer – the real refinement of a gentleman is underneath and peeps out sometimes. [28 January 1892]

Uncle went this morning to the Crozier's, where I suppose he will be till the end of the week. He may come home at nights, but I am rather hoping he won't. I enjoy these evenings alone with Harry. I feel ashamed even to own to myself that I have not grown atall fond of Uncle. I do try but love won't be compelled. I just begin to think I am getting to like him better, when he says or does something which hurts or vexes me so much. I am back on the old platform of simpler toleration. I don't attempt to deny that this year would have been a far easier and happier one for me had Harry been here alone – & yet that seems unkind & ungrateful, & I do feel glad that I have been able to bring a little comfort into Uncle's life – it has had few enough joy or pleasures – but I know it would have been so much better if I could have grown really fond of him. [7 March 1892]

Uncle is always nice & kind when anything goes wrong, and tries to do all he can to make matters happier. [19 November 1893]

Uncle stayed with the Parkes in Vernon from time to time and made himself thoroughly at home:

I think this has been the longest week I have spent for a long time. I will be so glad when Harold gets home again – the house is so desolate without him. I think even Uncle feels it, for he said this morning "This is an awful dull place." I think even he is getting tired of so much reading, & he has no cronies around town that he cares much to be with. [1 June 1894]

... I was much struck by one thought in that book "Beside the Bonnie Briar Bush" – the writer says, in describing a kind act & keen discernment of the village cynic "Such a wondrous tender thing is the heart of a cynic." It made me think of Uncle. His speech & his doings so often disagree. He says a harsh thing, while he is probably planning to do a kind one. I think these characters suffer more than the ones who are hurt by their sternness. Poor old Uncle – I don't believe he is very well. I ought to write him very soon. [8 November 1895]

Hal is roasted out of the sitting-room – Uncle does like the house very warm – I don't wonder, because he sits still all day, hardly putting his nose outside. [14 December 1897]

I think I have often said in my home letters that Uncle has been so much kinder and pleasanter down at Harry's since his return. I believe he must have come up here to "let off steam," for cantankerous is no name for his actions. He tries to get up an argument with me on every possible occasion, & he doesn't care what he says – I'm afraid I do answer back too much, for I really feel very sorry for him. I know he doesn't feel very well, and he has many really noble qualities of mind, but however one may admire the cleverness of a cynic he isn't always the pleasantest fire side companion.[14] I must say he makes Hal's very different characteristics show well by contrast. Uncle seems to take a pleasure sometimes in saying sneering, cutting things – while Hal is always so careful of one's feelings. The moralists say we are least tolerant always of our own faults in others – I do wonder if I am guilty of that heedless way of treading roughly on the tender spots of others. I don't think the life in California brings out the best in Uncle, and then one can fancy how a really loving heart would grow warped when the "dew of affection" was constantly turned in on itself, instead of refreshing some other life. [15 December 1897]

I have been away from Uncle a good deal since he came – I was excusing myself yesterday for going out to the garden and leaving him – and he said "Oh, don't apologize – I'm just as happy without you as with you" – so I am rather taking him at his word. I think ever since he came back from California this last time he has been more cranky & hard to get on with. I do try to be patient, poor old man. He hates to be old,[15] & I think it makes him cross. It is impossible to be loving in one's words to him – he meets all such advances with actual incivility – and yet I suppose he notices any failures on our part to be loving. [13 April 1898]

I don't know what is wrong with Uncle. He seems so low-spirited and unhappy. I feel badly for him, and very sorry for Harry & Nonah too. I know they both try to be patient, & to do what they can for him, but he is really very trying. I wish he could go away again. [28 May 1898]

Uncle went home this afternoon. I feel sorry that I couldn't feel distressed over his going, but really he isn't pleasant to live with. He seems to enjoy saying things that hurt rather than anything that is kind & cheerful. He told me today that it was altogether likely that Hal could lose his position, & went on to give me his reasons for thinking so – asked if he knew what he'd do in the event of the Government dismissing him. I did say at last that he seemed determined to make me as uncomfortable as possible over the matter . . . I couldn't help saying that, for it seemed to me so unnecessary for him to be looking on the dismal side, & trying to get me to do the same. I have tried to be patient with him this time, & I didn't argue with him once – though I think he tried hard several times to get up an argument. [27 August 1898]

Uncle . . . is very miserable – has a bad cold & cough, & a *very* bad temper. Poor old man! he won't be happy himself, & tries his best to prevent any one else being so. I do feel very sorry for him – but oftener, I'm afraid, I feel sorry for myself that I have to try to be patient. I wonder at Hal – he never says cross or nasty things to Uncle no matter what provocation he has. [21 January 1899]

Uncle really looks very sick – I don't much wonder, for he has a heavy cold, & he *drinks* cough medicine – not taking it by the spoonful as most people do, & last night he took seven big pills – I wonder he is not sicker than he is. I feel very sorry for him, for I know he is very miserable, but he won't let me do anything for him. [22 January 1899]

Uncle hasn't felt so well again the last two or three days and is rather cranky. Yesterday morning I made dough-nuts – he has been telling me lately how much he liked them. I finished frying them about eleven, & he came out in the kitchen & ate *four* big hot ones. Well, that was all right, but when we sat down to dinner at twelve, he gave a most superior look at the food & said "I am not a bit hungry – I have no appetite these days." I really couldn't help it – I laughed and said "Don't you think you spoiled your appetite eating dough-nuts." "Oh no," he said – very huffily – "that never makes any difference." However, I notice he munches away at them most of the time between meals and then proclaims his small eating powers at the table. It is amusing but it is provoking too. He says he is going down to the ranche to pack up his things when his cough gets better! – as he has had it for the last two years I am afraid it won't be cured soon. [9 February 1899]

Uncle got the money he has been expecting yesterday and he went down to the ranche today to pack up his books and other belongings. He said he'd be gone a few days and then come back here for a little while before starting for California. I feel guilty & ashamed of myself that I have not been more patient with him, and yet I do think it has been chiefly in my thoughts & my letters that I have been impatient. I have not said any thing disagreeable to him, though it has very often been hard to hold my tongue. I can't tell how much afraid I am that I have the same fault myself, of speaking harshly when I really don't feel angry, but just a little perverse – & the words sound more unkind than the heart feels. [14 February 1899]

Alice saw her uncle for the last time in February 1899, as he departed for his brother Joe's home:

Uncle left on the afternoon train. Hal went up to the station with him, but I said good-bye here. I hated to see him go, because I don't really think he wanted to do so, but I think it will be better and happier for him to be down in California. [26 February 1899]

I had a letter from Uncle yesterday ... [he] says he only weighs 134 lbs. – but the heat is intense there, 100 in the shade. [22 July 1899]

CHAPTER 8

Oh! I wish I could hear someone who would stir me up

Religion in the West

Alice Barrett Parke's passionate nature displayed itself most fully in the diary entries that described her religious feelings. A committed Christian, she needed food for her soul but was frequently disappointed in the preachers who served the valley. One man in particular made her hackles rise – the Anglican minister Mr. Outerbridge, whom she met soon after her arrival in the Spallumcheen.

Yesterday we were just going to dinner when Mr. Outerbridge,[1] the new clergyman, came along. Of course, he stayed to dinner. He looks very much like a Romish priest, and I strongly fear that the resemblance does not cease there. It was strange that my chapter for the day was that fourteen of Romans – if we could only all get the tolerance it teaches into our hearts, how much better work we would do. Mr. Outerbridge talks *church* so much. [5 October 1891]

We had the largest congregation I have ever seen there – thirty two. Mr. MacSorley played & we had the chants as well as the hymns. Mr. Outerbridge presided. We had a very good sermon, and the communion service. I was so glad we went – Mr. Outerbridge reads exceptionally well, and the service was very simple. [7 February 1892]

. . . I had to fly around and get something for [Mr. Norcross and Mr. Outerbridge] to eat. I was glad to do it though. It seems like helping the church a little bit to be kind to Mr. Outerbridge. I like him better than I did at first – still I don't *quite* like him, though he is a good conversationalist, and I enjoy a little talk with him. [28 March 1892]

Everyone laughs at the way Mr. Outerbridge mismanages his horse "Billie," and Mr. Norcross was telling us last night how it will bolt, the instant its driver gets in the carriage, so Harry said he would harness it, & start it off this morning. Sure enough no sooner was he seated, & holding the reins, than Billie made a start up the road, & Harry said he never drove a harder-mouthed animal . . . [Harry] says, though, that it is no horse for an inexperienced driver to handle, & they may come to grief. [9 April 1892]

Once he moved to Vernon, Outerbridge introduced a negative dynamic into the Anglican congregation there and offended Vernon church-goers as well:

. . . we went to evening service. Mr. Outerbridge gave us a great tirade – reproaching us for not coming to church – & defending himself against various complaints which had been made about him. [14 November 1893]

. . . Mr. Outerbridge . . . stayed a very long time, for we got interested in a conversation. He really believes in transubstansiation[2] and was trying to convince me. I think it is an awful belief, & directly opposed to our churches teaching in the [39 articles], besides having no warrant in scripture. Of course I could not argue as well as he did – but he could not alter my belief. [19 November 1893]

. . . Nonah and I went to church, & we had a great service. Mr. Outerbridge got angry because so many people were late, & wouldn't preach his sermon, & declared that he would preach here no more, as his teachings were plainly a failure. He went off immediately after the service to Enderby, and I don't know what the result will be, I'm sure. [4 December 1893]

. . . Mrs. Beckingsale was so taken up with Mr. Outerbridge's Sunday performance that she could talk of nothing else. There are a great many small squabbles and quarrels going on in the church – it is most distressing. [5 December 1893]

At Mrs. Spinks they were again talking of Mr. Outerbridge. Mrs. Dewdney had a telegraph saying he would be up on Sunday. I daresay the whole thing will blow over, & he will stay. [8 December 1893]

[We] are now waiting for church time to come. I don't know what we will hear there, whether Mr. Outerbridge will have reconsidered his declaration, and act differently – or whether he will keep up his vexation, & simply have the service, without preaching. Oh! I can't tell how often I have thought how wrong I was at home to get angry & impatient with Mr.

Newell[3] – & how thankful I would be to have him for my clergyman now instead of Mr. Outerbridge – who is a far more eloquent, clever man, & has had so many advantages which Mr. Newell has not had. [10 December 1893]

None of [the Gibbses] are going to the entertainment on account of its being Lent. I suppose Mr. Outerbridge won't like it that any of his congregation go – & I think it is a pity they did not wait until after Easter but I don't feel it wrong to go. So far as social pleasures are concerned people keep Lent pretty much all the year round here, so an occasional gaiety is not to be objected to. [15 March 1894]

... Mr. McGowan[4] ... was telling me of the vestry meeting they had last night. Hal wouldn't go – Mr. McGowan says he does not believe Mr. Outerbridge has any intention of leaving Vernon. All the talk at the meeting seemed to be on ways and means of raising money. [5 April 1894]

Mr. Outerbridge preached his farewell sermon – he leaves for Vancouver tomorrow. We will probably have no one for a time ... we are going to a farewell social for Mr. Outerbridge. He leaves tomorrow for Vancouver where he has had another church offered to him. He seems really sorry to go now that it is settled. He was here to see me this afternoon. Now that he is going I feel that I might, & indeed ought to, have been more patient. I am going to try to see some good in the new man – even if it be not easy. [16 April 1894]

Mr. Outerbridge did indeed leave Vernon:

We went to church in the morning, & quite liked our old clergyman – he is as great a contrast to Mr. Outerbridge as one could well find. Mr. Outerbridge always preached as though his hearers were highly cultured and intellectual while this old man speaks as if he were accustomed to talking to quite ignorant people. He explained each little point of history to which he referred, and used very simple language. Of course he is not nearly so eloquent as Mr. Outerbridge – not eloquent atall, in fact, but he read the service quietly and reverently, and preached earnestly. He is quite old – sixty I should think. [12 May 1894]

The Reverend returned after a short absence:

We hear that Mr. Outerbridge is likely to come back, and I am sorry. [22 June 1894]

They are decorating our church this week – I wish, so much, we had any other clergyman. I get homesick for our own service and yet when we go, Mr. Outerbridge is almost sure to say something which makes us feel sorry we went. I think we must go on Xmas Day any way. Surely then peace & good-will must reign in all our hearts. [22 December 1894]

They say that Mr. Outerbridge is going away, but I can hardly believe it. [6 January 1895]

I was glad Hal did not go [to church], for Mr. Outerbridge preached on that text "Let every soul be subject to the highest powers," and after dwelling at some length on the advisability of deference & obedience to civil authority – which was well enough – he said that the church was the religious authority to which all men should be subject. He denounced all brotherhoods & societies which in any way took the place of the church – & said that those who allowed these bodies to supersede (instead of merely supplementing) the church would be destroyed body & soul. One could not but think he meant a direct allusion to poor Mr. Girouard – and I could not help feeling grieved. It seemed so useless, so unnecessary. [5 February 1895]

Easter Sunday I went to our own Church. It was very prettily decorated. I lent all the white flowers I had, a lovely calla lily & some white geraniums – but I did not enjoy the service – it was all entoned & the sermon was very short. [16 April 1895]

I am particularly sorry [Hal] is not to be home tomorrow as we are to have service twice in our own church – some Englishman is to preach, & we hear that he would not be unwilling to accept a call to the place. I would be so glad if we got a nice clergyman. [7 September 1895]

… Mrs. Cameron was at her window, & she began talking to me. I am sorry the conversation came around to Mr. Outerbridge, & I said more than I ought to have done. I was quite sorry afterwards that I did not just keep still. Mrs. Cameron likes him I know, & I ought not to mention his name when I can't say anything good of him. It is a bitter disappointment to me that he has come back, for it is no use trying to join any other church. I couldn't be a real member, & I don't believe Hal could either, of any but the Church of England. I don't think it is because of Mr. Outerbridge's religious doctrines that we cannot agree with him. Though we do not think as he does, I could honour & respect and listen to a man whose ideas exactly differed from my own – but I have lost all faith in him as a Christian man. If we wrong him I do hope we may learn to see our mistakes. [1 October 1895]

I told Mrs. Ellison I was going to give up my [Sunday school] class at Xmas – she seemed very sorry and indeed I am too, but I think it is best to do so just now. I don't want to give Mr. Outerbridge any occasion to blame me more than I can help. I think the children will be sorry too. [30 November 1895]

While the Parkes lived at the BX Ranch:

... while [Hal] was out Mr. Outerbridge called! I was surprised to see him. He was very affable indeed and stayed quite a long time – he had ridden out – he wished me every success & happiness and said he was sure I must be delighted to get out of "that dismal Vernon." I said I had never found Vernon dismal but I loved the country, and would be hard to please if I did not think this a lovely spot. [27 October 1896]

[Hal] did not care to go to hear Mr. Outerbridge. We had quite a nice sermon. I never really enjoy the entoned service – I don't seem to be part of it atall, just a listener & on looker – and when the music is not always true, not even the senses are pleased, & I'm sure devotion isn't awakened, so I don't see what good it does. I suppose though, to people who are accustomed to it, the effect is different. [9 May 1897]

It was soon after Luc Girouard's death that the Parkes decided to become more eclectic in their church-going. From then on in the diaries Alice spoke often of regular visits to the Presbyterian and Methodist churches.

[Mr. Henderson] said it was nice to see us there again. Oh! how I wish we could go, but even lately we have heard more about Mr. Outerbridge which has made our dislike & distrust of him stronger. [19 February 1899]

Mrs. Cameron says Mr. Outerbridge expects to go to England for three months in the summer and Archdeacon Pentreath is to come here to take his place. Perhaps we'll have a chance to get another new clergyman, & not have to take Mr. Outerbridge back atall. [26 February 1899]

Mrs. Cameron said that Mr. Outerbridge was quite ill in church this morning, & tonight there is [a] notice on the church door that there will be no *service*. Mrs. Cameron says she thinks Mr. Outerbridge will have to be sent away for a change, & I am sure I hope he'll go, even for awhile. [3 September 1899]

At last we have a clergyman[5] – & we are hoping he may stay in Mr. Outerbridge's place. He is quite an elderly man, which is an added charm to my mind. He isn't atall a brilliant preacher, but both his sermons on Sunday were good & sound, quiet and reverent – & we like his way of reading the service so much. Of course I know he can't please every one – but so far I have not heard any one say they didn't like him. I think we are disposed to like almost any one who is atall likeable – but the worst of it is that Mr. Outerbridge has never resigned the charge, & the Bishop, of course, will not appoint any one else until he does so. [3 May 1900]

Alice wrote about many other clergymen:

We both went up to the Presbyterian church at night, & I disgraced myself by laughing out loud in the middle of the sermon. I really couldn't help it. It was a strange young clergyman who preached on the law of heredity, in which he is a very firm believer – so much so that he declared that we are not responsible for any evil actions which are the result of inherited tendancies. However, I won't attempt to report him for I couldn't do it justice on paper. I find even when I try to tell anybody what he said – it doesn't sound so funny as it did in church. One remark he quoted which wasn't bad. He said "Every man is an omnibus in which his ancestors sit." I don't think very many people knew that I was laughing for I tried to turn it off in a cough. [3 June 1895]

Young Reverend Wilson was a particular favourite:

… we went up to the Presbyterian Church, & heard a beautiful sermon. Mr. Wilson isn't clever or eloquent, but his quiet simple words come with power, for one feels that [one] has learned from the best wisdom. I often think of those words "Not by night, not by power – but by my spirit, saith the Lord" and surely the sword of the spirit must be a better weapon to fight the power of evil than the greatest human prowess can be. [18 June 1895]

… we all went to church in the evening to hear Mr. Wilson. He certainly does not speak with cunning words of men's wisdom, but he is so good & self forgetful that one always feels a desire to do better after hearing him – & I think his humility is a little infectious, though I am conscious that humility is a Christian Grace of which I am sadly lacking. [24 June 1895]

Mr. Wilson gave a very nice sermon on the miracle of feeding the five thousand. He gave us one beautiful idea. He said Christ often used his miracles as illustrations of the truth He wished to teach, and soon after feeding this hungry multitude He calls Himself the "living bread" which satisfied the hungry soul. Mr. Wilson said just as these small loaves fed the throng of hungry people, & still left more in fragments than there had been in the beginning, so the *life* of Christ has fed millions for centuries, & still it grows not less – but more. [31 March 1896]

[Reverend] Wilson came along, & was talking over the fence for awhile. He was distributing bills announcing a temperance lecture for tomorrow night. He is a young man with a great capacity for saying the wrong thing. I asked him to come in and he said "Oh no thank you, I have something more important on hand." Then, of course, he was covered with confusion, and tried to explain about business before pleasure etc. – but his heart was in the first expression, one could plainly see. [22 August 1898]

We had another Prohibition sermon. Mr. Wilson is not atall rabid – I think he tries to be very fair, but it is a hard subject to handle. [12 September 1898]

We went up the hill to church this morning, & had a beautiful sermon from Mr. Wilson. He preached from "Foxes have holes, & the birds of the air have nests, but the son of man hath not where to lay his head." It was all about the self denial & sacrifice which is demanded of Christians – the necessity for holding the things of this world, even its holiest & best affections, less dear than our duty & service to God. Poor man! he is in sore grief just now. His father is very ill – in Hamilton – they fear dying, & he is not able to go just now. He may go soon – his Mother is old & feeble, & the one sister at home is very delicate. I felt so sorry for him this morning – he looked worn & ill – but I never heard him preach so well, so earnestly and touchingly. [12 March 1899]

Other ministers received mixed reviews:

We had service in our own church twice yesterday and we did enjoy it. Archdeacon Mackay from Donald⁶ was here. He is a Scotch quarter breed – a dark quiet man, with not a very pleasant voice, rather flat – but he read the service so quietly & reverently and preached such earnest sermons that we both like him very much. He uses very good language and speaks fluently. [22 July 1895]

This morning we drove in to church. We had a stranger for a preacher & both liked his sermon – it was earnest & decided – the most orthodox sermon I have heard for a long time, and it seemed to me a rest, after the many new and unsettling opinions one hears, to see a man get up and boldly & confidently and *believingly* rest all his hopes & his faith on the old doctrines that made such good men & women in the days of old. To be sure one might, in some moods, be tempted to call what he said narrow – but today it just seemed strong & reliable. Hal liked it too. The preacher, Mr. McKay, is only a student and will just be here two Sundays. [21 March 1897]

Mr. Butler[7] gave us a beautiful sermon on Christ as an example of Godly living. He said Christ came to save us from the *committing* of sin, quite as much or even more than from the condemnation of sin. Mr. Butler has no pretence at being an orator – nothing bold or striking in his style – nothing very pleasant in his delivery – but I often think of those words "not by might, not by power" and it does seem to me that not often do the most gifted men, as to natural talents, do the best work for God in the way of preaching. Too often a clever sermon only pleases our brain, and leaves the heart untouched, while words that come straight from a humble earnest heart find their way to our deepest feeling. [7 May 1897]

We heard rather an extraordinary sermon, it was on the text "It were better for that man if he had never been born." He said the great question of this – of any – age was "is life worth living?" & no doubt in many cases it was not. At first it almost seemed as if he were upholding suicide, but then he spoke very nicely to the two cases of Peter & Judas. He said up to a certain point there was much similarity in their behaviour – one denied his Lord, the other betrayed him – but the great difference was that Peter went out from the presence of the priests & wept bitterly, while Judas went out and hanged himself. Both when conscious of their sin ended their unworthy life, but one ended it by repentance, the other by death, & he [died] for us all – an unworthy life was *not* worth living, but let us choose Peter's brave way of ending it, & not the cowardly way of Judas. [2 November 1897]

We went to the Methodist Church, and heard a very good sermon from the new clergyman, Mr. Robson.[8] His text was "Jesus only" – & he gave two very good illustrations, I thought, of the comparative insignificance of creed or sect, & the vital importance of love for Christ. He told the story of Diogenes meeting with Alexander, and his famous words "I beseech thee, stand aside & do not shut me from the sun." He said let us beware lest in exalting unduly the importance of doctrine or ritual, we deserve the reproof that *we* are hindering the *sun* from the soul seeking light. I thought it was a lovely thought. Alexander was a great king, & deserving of much honour & deference, but what was he, or his power, compared with the sun! Again, he illustrated the same thought by the story of the building of the Pharos – in Alexandria harbour – by order of one of the Ptolemys. How the king ordered the architect to carve the name of Ptolemy on the wonderful building, where men should always see it, & give praise to him who had done such a good work for the mariners, and how the wily architect did indeed put the name of the king on, but in plaster, where the years wore it off, and left underneath, carved in the solid stone, the name of the man who had indeed built the mighty Pharos, whose brain had planned, & whose hand had laboured. So with the churches – underneath the perishing name of church or denomination let there be cut deep the everlasting name of Christ – let the work indeed be planned by Him and the light shall shine afar to guide many safe into the Haven. [20 June 1898]

[We] went up to the Presbyterian church tonight, & heard rather an extraordinary sermon. The preacher, in all solemnity, chose as one of his illustrations of the parable of the lost sheep some lines from "Mary had a little lamb" – it came in so ludicrously that I couldn't help laughing. I do think that clergymen should remember that they must have some of the wisdom of the serpent – as well as the harmlessness of the dove – indeed, without wisdom, they must do harm. [26 June 1898]

The Arch-deacon of the diocese – Archdeacon Pentreath[9] – preached. We enjoyed his sermon very much. The text was "I have found the Christ." He is not an eloquent man but there was so much quiet power in his words. It seemed as if his thoughts were so eager to come out that he had not always time to clothe them in the most fitting words, and yet he expressed himself well too – only not eloquently. We will go again tonight – D.V. [19 February 1899]

[In Vancouver] we went to a little church nearby yesterday morning, and listened to a smooth-faced little man talk – not preach. Oh! I wish I could hear someone who would stir me up. [24 August 1891]

Mr. Wright preached another fire and damnation sermon – I wish he would not. I had a long talk with him coming home, and I told him I did not believe that many people were brought to love and serve God through fear. He was very nice and kind. [21 October 1891]

Harry & I went to the Methodist church Sunday morning – I was sorry the sermon was quite lacking in interest. It seems strange to me that with such a subject men can be so dull.[10] It is a pity that men who have not the gift of preaching are sent out as preachers – surely there must be some other work they could do better. [26 June 1894]

Sunday morning Lizzie and I went to the Roman Catholic church[11] – the singing was good – the music always is lovely, & it was very well rendered. The sermon was good too, from an R.C. point of view. It was on the Mass, and was clear & logical and pleasantly delivered. Of course I didn't agree with it, but it seemed honest & earnest, so one could listen with interest. The priest made one rather startling statement – I wonder if it is true. He said that in England for several years, the Roman Catholic church had each year received one thousand converts from the other religious bodies. [12 September 1898]

We all laughed a great deal – for Mr. Winfield was very humorous – & yet I liked him best when, at the end, he became serious, and spoke of the terrible reality of the degradation and even brutishness of the native tribes, & the great need there is for taking light to their darkness – liberty to their bondage. He is a tall, very dark man – a forcible, though scarcely a pleasing speaker. He has a very Irish look, & some Irish tricks of the tongue. Mrs. Cameron told me he is Irish-Canadian. He is nervous, & his voice is not musical, but he looks like a *real* man, with strong earnest convictions I should say, & some character. I daresay he would be absent-minded and peculiar, but altogether I enjoyed the lecture very much. I was introduced to him afterwards. He has none of the easy friendliness of his patron – indeed he seemed to me to have very much the manner of Bishop Baldwin[12] – too much taken up with the one thought his mind happened to be set on even to *know* – still less to notice keenly – the individuals with whom he came in contact – and yet I daresay he sees far more than one imagines. He is to give another lecture before he goes away – the subject is not yet decided upon. [22 December 1894]

I liked Bishop Dart.[13] He is a middle aged man with a very nice face, & he spoke very well in reply to Mr. McGowan's address of welcome, which was about as silly as it could be. He (Mr. McGowan) said he supposed his lordship in coming to British Columbia had expected to find people little removed from savages, who had almost no knowledge of religion – & so on – but he assured the Bishop that we did know something, and had a love for religion although to be sure it progressed but slowly, as we had "so many other denominations to *fight against!!*" and he hoped his lordship would "put his shoulder to the wheel" & bring about great & wonderful changes. Bishop Dart said he had not looked for the state of savagery Mr. McGowan described – for he had read the papers! I thought that was a very neat little take down but I don't believe Mr. McGowan appreciated it, for he looked thoroughly complacent. Then, the Bishop said that although, with God's help, he would try to put his shoulder to the wheel as Mr. McGowan suggested, & though he would try to do his work – we must remember that one man's efforts could not accomplish much – there must be cordial co-operation of clergy and people if God's work was to be properly done. [13 October 1895]

I forgot to say that yesterday just as I was ready to go out I had a call from the two Salvation Army leaders. They stayed over half an hour. The Captain is quite a talker – the other little fellow sat very mum in a corner, & once I caught him yawning, poor little man. He hasn't the happy expression that most of the Salvation people have. The Captain was telling me of an experience their "boys" had at Lytton. There is quite an extensive Church of England mission there among the Indians. It seems last year, a couple of Army soldiers were there having meetings in an old bar-room. The man who had kept it had become converted, and had turned it over to the use of the Army. Well! a good many of the Indians came to the meetings, & seemed interested – they were at the time building a small church, & in their desire to be friendly, offered the use of the church to the Army. The "boys" accepted, but had only held a few meetings when it came to the ears of the bishop, who was very angry, & wrote up to the Indians forbidding them to have anything to do with the Army. Captain Jarvis said he saw the letter, & the Bishop threatened that if they disobeyed he would excommunicate them from "the church militant & the church triumphant." It doesn't seem right to have a bitterness of spirit towards any who call themselves Christians – or indeed towards anyone – but least of all for those who profess the same hope that we have ourselves. [15 February 1894]

... I have learned since I came west that religion & church going are sometimes two widely different things. I think many men do not enter the churches, not because they disbelieve in God, or despise His worship, but because they find so little of Him in the churches & His professed followers. The Christlike lives are not always lived by those who know most of modern theology. I often think of those words "to do justice, & to love mercy, and to walk humbly with thy God" – & they seem a deep reproach to many of us Christians, where the spirit of intollerance, of harshness & spiritual pride reigns. It is all so different here from what it is at home. I sometimes think, there I was blind to much that was real in the world around me – & though one should indeed be thankful for keener vision, the operation which brings it is often a painful one, and it does not hurt to see the failure which so often attends the present system of the churches & the clergy. I don't think the teachings of our dear old church are wrong, but rather the men who attempt to represent them. [22 June 1894]

  While on a train journey, Alice wrote:

We have a comical looking child on board – a boy three years of age – red haired and freckle faced – a romping jolly little fellow, who has been gleefully playing horse with a band box belonging to one of the lady passengers. He insisted on rubbing it violently, as it had a sore back, & beating it fiercely until at last the porter hung it safely out of reach at the top of the car. His Mother told me that he is to be a preacher. His grandfather is the Rev. Leonard Gates (she seemed to think everyone had heard of him, but I hadn't – he is a Methodist and this boy also a Leonard Gates is to succeed his grandfather's fame!). [26 September 1897]

I am quite sorry we lost our little Methodist preacher. He was very amusing – I asked him if he had any brothers or sisters, and he said "No – all my Mother's other little boys and girls are in gopher holes on the prairie, and I don't know if we'll ever get any of them out." This was evidently a little fancy of his own, for his Mother seemed as much surprised and amused as I was at the notion. He was such a bright happy little chap – indeed most of the children are very good. [27 September 1897]

A man of Mr. Parke's ability

A Husband of Unusual Accomplishment

Everyone who knew and worked with Harold Randolph Parke came to like and respect him highly. He was well educated but felt stifled by the conventions and restrictions imposed upon him by eastern society. The attractions of unfettered life on the frontier, and the challenges it offered, were welcomed by this quiet, complex man.

Hal and Alice shared many fundamental beliefs. He was a loyal friend, devoted to his wife and committed to doing a thoroughly professional job in whatever position he found himself. After his marriage, he never again went into business for himself, seeking secure government positions and for a time working as manager of the huge BX Ranch. He willingly made entries in the diary when his wife was absent, and he chided her gently to make sure that she maintained the record. While not wealthy, the Parkes were members of the "Upper Ten" in Vernon society (we do not know the names of the others in this social set but can speculate that it also included lawyers Cochrane and Billings, Jack McKelvie, Commander Carew, Judge Spinks, the Price Ellisons, the Camerons, and government agent Leonard Norris).

Although reticent about writing overtly of the details of their relationship, it is quite clear that Alice loved her husband deeply and came to depend upon him for the support that was so important for her emotional well-being. He comforted her, gave her wise counsel, showered her with gifts, laughed with her, ceded domestic authority to her, but was stubborn in his refusal to move back to Ontario at her pleading. They settled down into domestic comfort, content to be Darby and Joan, working on their garden together, sometimes preparing food together, visiting friends, enjoying music, attending church, going for long walks, and spending evenings in wide-ranging conversation. In Hal, Alice had found her intellectual equal and, with him, explored the world of ideas; he was also the practical handyman about the house. Their partnership became the envy of the town.

Once Hal Parke entered the pages of the diaries, he remained a constant presence; after their wedding his first job was that of assessment officer for the newly incorporated City of Vernon.

Mrs. Martin said ... she believed we were "the happiest couple in Vernon." I don't know of course how much pleasure in each other's society the other people take, but I know that we have very much to make us happy and contented. [8 May 1897]

I expect Hal home any minute. He is having quite a lengthy Council meeting tonight. I suppose they are talking about the new roll.[1] We will soon have plenty of evening occupation going on with it – but it won't be nearly such an undertaking as it was last year. [22 January 1894]

We have been reading Martin Chuzzlewit since tea, & as we have just got with Mark & Martin, to Eden, it is rather dreary. [25 January 1894]

We have been working at the roll. It is not nearly so hard a job as it was last year, though there are a great many alterations to make of course. [13 February 1894]

Hal worked on the roll. I was supposed to help him, but he had so much calculation to do that I read nearly all the time ... I have left the plants in the window [while I'm away], I know Hal will take care of them and move them should it turn cold. It is very mild now, a regular thaw – I expect Hal will be pretty lonesome. [26 February 1894]

... we went to bed early, & Hal was sick nearly all night – nausea & vomiting. Of course I was much disturbed though he tried not to waken me – he seemed quite feverish too. We both felt rather miserable on Saturday. He was weak & I was tired, but I am glad to say since then he has not had a touch of indigestion, so he does not regret one night's discomfort. [7 March 1894]

... Hal thought it would be a good plan to get the tax notices out this week, as it is one of the weeks they send a report to the Government of the numbers of letters going through the office and, of course, two hundred and 24 extra ones will swell the list. So yesterday morning I began filling in the notices for Harold, & this morning I had them all done ready for his signature. He looks them over, & together we fold & address them. We have 50 done & hope to almost finish them tonight. Hal came home to work yesterday afternoon, but we had so many interruptions that we did not get on very fast. [15 March 1894]

Parke served the Vernon Council for fifteen months, and then:

... Hal has got Mr. Norris' old Government appointment [as provincial constable] and is going to leave the post office, and all his other business and go to the Government Office.[2] I am glad, for the salery is a good one – & sure, while all business is in such an uncertain state, with the prospect of still harder times for British Columbia it will be a comfort to have something settled. Then he likes Mr. Norris, & will be able to work comfortably with him, while there have been various unpleasantnesses connected with the City work. He has never said very much but I know often he disliked it very much indeed ... I want to write home to tell them about Hal's appointment. I am afraid it may seem to them a tightening of the links that bind us to British Columbia. If Hal could see any opening in the east, I know he would go for my sake, but it would not be right not to try to do as well as possible here, while we must stay. The only thing I don't quite like about this is, there is a possibility of our having to leave our pretty new home, & go to live in the Government House. Mr. Norris is not a married man, & he did speak to Hal about our coming to live there ... Of course it is a much larger house, but it is old, & not in nearly such a nice part of the town; however I won't cross my bridge before I come to it, & if we do have to go, I won't make myself unhappy over it. [13 April 1894]

Hal began his duties in the Government office that morning & was away all day. I'm afraid there won't be any more chance for him to run home in the middle of the morning or afternoon now, as he will have to keep to regular hours – but when they are not busy he'll likely get away from the office at four ... People have been very cordial in congratulating Hal on his appointment. He said Judge Spinks went in to the office & said he was very glad – that Hal was "Just the right man in the right place," but I haven't much faith in his apparent friendliness. I don't think he is a sincere man – I think he is just silly. Hal had to go out to the Indian Reserve this afternoon – it is a long ride – & he was tired when he got in ... [16 April 1894]

I went into the Gov. Office – Hal was alone there. It doesn't seem natural yet to identify him with the place. He likes it so well that I am very pleased. [17 April 1894]

Hal's handwriting began to appear in the diaries in 1894:

The Boss has gone to a Fandango at Mrs. Dewdney's and has left me at home with orders to fill in the Diary to date. As my pen does not flow like hers I will find it hard work to fill the gap. To commence with yesterday morning – we got up – and after partaking of Breakfast we went to church, and on our return ate some cold chicken – not much though, as we wanted to leave enough for the big nurse. In the afternoon Alice went to a christening and I went to sleep. Shortly after her return the nurses came (a big one and a little one). Mrs. Costerton also came to tea so we made quite a formidable party going to church in the evening. I don't think Mrs. Costerton will come again in a hurry, as the repast evidently did not agree with her and she had to leave church with a pain. The nurses however appeared to stand it all right so Alice comforts herself that the fault was in Mrs. Costerton's anatomy and not in the cooking. We walked home with the nurses and then came home ourselves, and soon after went to bed, which is one day accounted for. This afternoon Mrs. Dewdney sent a note asking Alice to spend the evening there (by the way she is much addicted to notes as the Boss herself) – with a faint addendum that I might come in at the tail of the hunt and escort the Boss home. The latter at once gave orders for me to write in the diary during her absence, and to come for her at the proper time. I of course complied and have done the first to the best of my ability and will attend to the latter if I don't go to sleep. I might say the family was all broke up today when Alice's letter from home informed us that Wese was not coming out this summer. We were quite set upon it, and the disappointment was consequently great. "Twas ever thus from childhood hour, We've seen our fondest hopes decay, And when we thought some one would come, Twas mighty sure they'd stay away."
Sic transit tempora Monday *and* Sunday. [14 May 1894]

It soon became apparent that, as provincial constable, Hal would be absent frequently while covering the area from Kamloops in the north to Rossland in the south. Because of her fear of being alone in the house, Alice always asked a friend to come over while Hal was away. She did not take kindly to these absences:

I had only been home few minutes when Hal hurried in, & asked me to give him something to eat quickly – he had to start off again for Enderby. Of course he would be gone all night, so after he had had his tea, & got started, I went over and asked Miss Kape to come and sleep with me. [25 May 1894]

I don't wonder Hal does not like it when I am away. The house hardly seems bearable when he isn't here. I don't believe I could live alone – I'd sooner work for somebody for nothing than live by myself . . . I have had that regular old fashioned homesickness today . . . I know it is because Hal is away. [29 May 1894]

I think this has been the longest week I have spent for a long time. I will be so glad when Harold gets home again – the house is so desolate without him . . . Yesterday I was anxious to get on with my sewing . . . [I] want to dress in my new "duds" tomorrow afternoon if Hal gets home, to show him how nice they look. [1 June 1894]

I was so thankful that Hal got home safely yesterday . . . [he] says there is hardly a bridge left in the lower country, & one little town over in Washington (Concounlly) has been completely washed away by a cloud burst. It was built at the opening of a gulch, & a cloud burst up in the mountains, & the water rushed down the gulch like a huge wall carrying away the whole town. One house was left standing – only one woman was drowned. The people saw the water coming, & made for the higher ground, so all were saved but one poor woman – but of course they only escaped with their lives. It makes one feel we should not be complaining because the drought & late Spring are likely to make hard times for this country . . . Hal did not fall in love with the Lower Country, though he says there are some splendid peach orchards, & other fruit. The finest land is on the Indian Reserves. [3 June 1894]

A year & five months today since we were married. Sometimes it hardly seems that, & then again I feel as if I could hardly realize that Hal & I had not always belonged to each other. [4 June 1894]

Hal is down at the office. He always has to go to see that everything is all right at the Jail. I don't suppose there had to be any Jail in Utopia, but if there had been, I'm sure it would have been conducted something as this one is here. They have had two prisoners in for some time. One is a half breed,[3] sentenced to six months for giving liquor to Indians – the other is a young Belgian, a harmless half witted fellow who is in jail more for safe keeping than anything else. He was hanging about the ranches, & the owners were afraid he might set fire to some buildings. He was to have been sent to Kamloops, but no opportunity has offered to send him, so he is kept here and certainly he is better off. Hal locks them in at night, but opens the jail at about eight in the morning, & they work about the place, saw wood, care for Mr. Norris' horse, wash windows, scrub the court house etc. – as any ordinary hired man would do. One of them goes over to the hotel & brings the food over to the jail where they have their meals. They get "whatever is going" at the hotel, except that a fresh pie or cake is never cut for them, and Hal has supplied the Belgian with tobacco. He begged for some – said he was "dying" for a smoke – so I don't think they have much to complain of. Of course there is occasionally a prisoner who has be more strictly watched. There is a corner of the office filled with shackles & handcuffs, which have to be used sometimes. [9 June 1894]

Hal & I are going down to Government House to sleep tonight. Mr. Norris is away and they thought it hardly safe to have no one near the jail – for if a fire should break out, the poor prisoners might burn up before anyone could get up here for the keys to let them out. They have five in now, but they are a quiet ("respectable"?) lot of men – that is respectable compared with the kind of men one usually pictures as belonging to a jail. [18 June 1894]

I wonder how Hal has got on all this week without me. I have thought of him all the time. [4 July 1894]

Hal met me at the station. I was so glad to see him again and when we came home I found everything looking so nice & cosy. Hal had had a woman in to clean and tidy everything; the plants were looking well and everything gave a warm welcome. [1 November 1894]

Alice played a pivotal role in solving a poignant mystery that played itself out between the fall of 1894 and the following June. It was Hal's duty to investigate a gruesome discovery made in the mountains near Cherry Creek by miner Bill Hollingsworth. One day late in 1894 Hollingsworth brought an old flour sack to the government office; in it were the remains of a human skeleton, some tattered clothing, and a small notebook:

I have been very much interested over a little book Hal brought home to me. A man brought it in to the government office having found it on the hills, about 9 miles up the North Fork of Cherry Creek – he found it beside a little pile of human bones – also he found a pair of spectacles and a few camp utensils beside it. It is a note book very much spoiled by the weather. The leaves were stuck together, the pages torn & in many places the writing undecipherable, but we have made out a good deal. The writer was evidently lost on the mountain, & slowly starved to death – some of the entries are very pitiful. I cannot get it out of mind. He has tried so hard to leave word for someone – but we cannot quite make out the name, though an address is written in three separate places. It is Miss Agnes – I think Byam, or Blyam – then the name of the town is indistinct, Sussex, England. We are going to look at the list of P.O. in Sussex, & if we can find one atall like the word we fancy, write to the Postmaster. The poor man was evidently well educated. He tells of losing his way – evidently he had a companion with him, though no signs of another man were found – for he always writes "we." One entry is "Had to kill Willie, the dog" – then "Found a few berries" – "Weaker & weaker" – "Ate last of dog – the end must come soon – but God is good, something may turn up." It begins while they were in camp with a lot of others – then where they tried to get over the mountain and so on, gradually getting sadder. I wish I could make it all out. It is dreadful to think of someone waiting & watching for news that never comes – at the last is "Love to Agnes" – "Visions of food are constantly before us" – "Weaker" – & the last I can make out is "Cold." [1 November 1894]

We were talking about the book found on the mountain. Mr. Norris wants me to go on trying to get the other leaves apart – he thinks it will be a good thing to advertise in some English paper. [6 November 1894]

Hal Parke, knowledgeable in postal matters from his earlier work in the Vernon post office, wrote instead to the postmaster in Cuckfield in the hope that the Parkes could learn more about the dead man and his family. The Parkes received letters from both the postmaster and Agnes Byam:

> Woodlands
> Cuckfield
> (Near Hayward's Heath)
> Sussex
> England
> November 26th 1894

Dear Sir,

The Postmaster of Cuckfield brought us your letter of Nov. 10th on the 24th, & it seems very probable, from my name being mentioned in the memorandum book found with the remains, that they were those of my brother, Arthur M. Byam, especially as my last letter from him was dated April 25 1893 from Spokane Bridge Washington State, where he had spent the winter with a friend, T.W. Galbraith, and intended starting thence for Lake Kootena June 1st since when I have written several times to him to the c/o of Mr. Galbraith.

Therefore would you kindly forward to me as soon as possible the memorandum book, that we may be able to identify our brother's writing, & if there should be anything else, or any other clue you could give us, we should be truly grateful. My brother's hair & beard were dark, thick & abundant, if that remained.

And would you kindly let me know if the remains were reverently interred, and if we are indebted to you for that, or any other expenses, & if we could give any reward to the miner Hollingsworth, who brought them in. And also if the man, Jim Stevenson should have survived, and ever turn up at Vernon and you could gain any further information about my brother's death (supposing always it should have been him) we should feel still further indebted to you. And now thanking you much for the kindness which prompted you to write in such detail, & so very sympathetically, believe me
Yours very sincerely,
Agnes W. Byam

P.S. Would you also kindly tell me where abouts Nakusp and Vernon are, as to the mountains & near rivers, as the maps we have give so few towns in British Columbia, except along the lines of Railway or the large rivers, & I can find neither place marked. [15 December 94]

Hal Parke reacted with his customary kindness and sent Miss Byam a package of information on the interior of British Columbia, and she was effusive in her thanks. Thus it was learned that the dead man, her brother Arthur Merrick Byam, was the third son of General Byam of the 18th Hussars and Elizabeth Augusta, daughter of Sir Grenville Temple, Baronet, and that he was about fifty-five years old when he died.

Hal got another letter from Miss Byam today. I will copy it here, as all who have read the story so far of her brother's death will be interested in it. Hal told her that I had done most of the work in deciphering the writing in the little book that was found. This is her letter:

January 15th '95

Dear Mr. Parke,
    You & Mrs. Parke have indeed been kind & thoughtful in this sad matter, you in writing so fully & sympathetically, & your wife in having taken so much trouble in deciphering my name in the memorandum book. Yes, it is indeed my brother Arthur Byam's hand writing – just the clear neat hand he always wrote since his boyhood – it never altered since then although he would have been 55 years of age Nov. 30th '93, & although his right hand was fearfully burnt 13 years before – the fingers being all crumpled up together, & for some time powerless – even after having been straightened out in Guy's Hospital, still he told me he had recovered the use of that hand after his return to Canada, & wrote as well as ever with it, but would signs of those once distorted fingers still be visible? They have done their work in sending me kind messages while he could write. The great comfort to be found in those touching entries is untold – there is not a word of complaint throughout and the words "God is good" are most consoling.

I have copied all I could decipher, but it is very difficult and makes me feel the more grateful to Mrs. Parke for having done so first for me, & I do thank her most sincerely for her kindness, & you also, for telling me all you possibly could. It seems to me now that there is no doubt, but I leave it to your judgment whether it would be better to wait until the miner, Hollingsworth, returns next Spring, in case he may have found the other remains, & the identification be complete; & then I should indeed be grateful to you if you would have the bones interred reverently, & a stone cross erected to my brother's memory.

. . . I must again thank you & Mrs. Parke for all you have done for us in every kind way, & for the map you so thoughtfully sent in your letter. I will write what I would wish inscribed to my brother's memory, whenever you feel a certainty about the matter, & trust you will let me know all & every expense incurred – & with many best wishes for you and Mrs. Parke, for many happy New Years. Believe me

Yours very gratefully

Agnes M. Byam

The inscription for the stone is to be as follows

In loving memory of
Arthur Merrick Byam
third son of General Byam 18th Hussars
of Warblington, Hants, England
and of
Elizabeth Augusta
daughter of Sir Grenville Temple, Bart.
Departed this life in the Woods
between Vernon & Nakusp
October 1892 – Aged 55 years

"But God is Good" [30 January 1895]

In May 1895 Reverend T. Williams Outerbridge officiated over a Christian burial for Arthur Byam in the old Vernon cemetery, just west of Old Kamloops Road. Byam's name is among those listed on the bronze plaque adorning one of the ornamental lamp standards at the entrance to the old burial ground. There is no record, however, of any headstone for his grave, and Alice doesn't mention one; indeed, when the cemetery was closed in 1904, and the graves relocated to the new cemetery on Pleasant Valley Road, it appears that Mr. Byam's remains were not exhumed. It is probable that he still lies in his old resting place.

Hal Parke continued to act as constable for the city of Vernon:

I don't wonder that Hal does not like to have me go away. I really don't think I could stand it for two months without him. One day is bad enough. [6 November 1894]

... at seven Hal came in. He was pretty tired & stiff – having ridden seventy miles since he left home, & having had very little sleep the night he was away. [17 November 1894]

My cold is getting much better ... Hal says he has taken me in hand now and won't let me go out until I am well. [9 November 1894]

Hal has a nasty cough – I am going to dose him with hot lemon-aide tonight. He is always very ready to get medicines for me, but not so anxious to take them himself. [10 December 1894]

In the evening we went down to Mr. Norris – ... We had quite a pleasant evening – played whist & talked. Baker[4] – one of the prisoners – presided over the coffee, & had a fine time out in the kitchen. He is in jail for keeping an illicit still. Hal says he is quite a character – an Irish Catholic from Inchee – talks French as well as English, and makes himself equally plausible and roguish in either. He is a very useful man about the premises – & as he is alone in the jail just now, he is thoroughly satisfied with his comfortable quarters for the winter ... Hal ran in to say he had to go down to Kelowna to collect the agricultural returns, and would be gone all night. [19 December 1894]

Xmas morning ... Hal gave me a lovely silver toast rack ... I gave Hal a pipe, and subscribed for a paper for him. I didn't dare to tell Wese I gave him a pipe – but I believe even she would relent if she could see how he enjoys it ... When I got home Hal was here, & had the fires going famously. [27 December 1894]

Hal has been teaching Nonah solitaire and now we are going to have a game of whist. [1 January 1895]

Right after tea we laid a cloth on the kitchen table, & put out the dishes we needed. Hal sliced some spiced beef, and ground the coffee. [3 January 1895]

Hal is sitting by the table reading some book on Psychical Research which Judge Spinks left him, and he says it is "bosh" – but the Judge urged him to read it. [3 January 1894]

Hal suffered a serious accident at the beginning of 1894:

About eight I heard sleigh bells, & presently some [one] came in the door

– it did not sound a bit like Hal, so I went into the hall, & was surprised to see that it was he. I said "Did you drive home?" and the minute he spoke I knew something was wrong, and asked if he was hurt. He then came in the dining room looking very white & faint, & told us he had hurt his leg, & Bill Martin drove him home. Mr. Jim Martin followed him up very soon to see if he could do anything. At first Hal thought the bone was broken – he stepped in a hole, & was thrown over. He could not get up. Mr. J. Martin and Mr. Crowell got him into the sleigh, but when they got to our door, he found he could walk into the house. However he was sick and faint with the pain so we got Mr. Martin to go for Dr. Morris. He said one of the fibres of the muscle was broken, and said Hal must keep very quiet for awhile – indeed he advised staying in bed – but Hal can't stand that. He went to bed Friday night as soon as he was able to get upstairs, and had rather a wakeful, painful night. The doctor sent lint and lotion which soothed the pain somewhat, yesterday morning. I insisted on getting up & lighting the fires. The leg ached a great deal all day. I had to go down in the morning to the office to tell Walter Dewdney Hal wouldn't be down. It fortunately happens they are not very busy in the office as Mr. Norris won't be back before tomorrow. Walter came up for instructions, & was in again after dinner. [6 January 1895]

... Hal is very lame yet – and I know it hurts him a good deal to walk, but he makes as light of it as possible. He got a drive down to the office this morning, but walked home at noon, & back again after dinner. [9 January 1895]

Nonah & Harry wanted me to stay until Monday, but I felt I ought to come home. I was uneasy about Hal's leg – he makes so little complaint, but I know it bothers him a good deal. He has not looked well ever since he was hurt – such a white look comes over his face sometimes. [12 January 1895]

Hal would have gone, but he had to drive out to the Lake. Some building has been broken into there, & things stolen, and Hal was to go & investigate. He had to turn back however as the road was impassible with a cutter – so he came home, & sent a man out on horseback. He is not able to ride yet. [13 January 1895]

Hal's leg has pained a good deal today, but he will walk about a great deal. [12 January 1895]

When Alice went to sit up overnight with Mrs. Shatford:

Hal wouldn't let me even wash the dishes. He said he would do them when he came home ... Hal had washed the dishes, got his own tea, and made meat balls for breakfast. [22 January 1895]

Hal had got himself some dinner in the kitchen and was eating it out there. I had to "do the polite" to Gertie & Mr. Horseley, & all the time I did want to get out to the kitchen to see if Hal was all right. [26 January 1895]

Hal & I were alone, it was so long since we had had a quiet time to talk, that I did not write much ... I had just finished this afternoon when I heard Hal's whistle, & looking out saw him at the gate with horse & cutter, to take Annie & me for a drive. Of course we hurried on our wraps, & were ready very promptly. [30 January 1895]

... Hal was home all the afternoon, so I couldn't bear to go out ... Hal played chess with me and we talked & read – a thoroughly lazy, but lovely afternoon. [2 February 1895]

Just two years ago today since I came to Vernon to live – oh! how cold it was – and the house, of course, wasn't a bit settled, but it has always been a real home wherever Hal was ... [6 February 1895]

Yesterday afternoon Hal put up some plant shelves for me, in the little dressing room – one high & one low – so the window looks quite pretty. [9 February 1895]

Hal is engrossed in a story. I have addressed two or three remarks to him without getting an answer. It does me good to see him so taken up with what he is reading, for I know he must be enjoying it thoroughly. [12 February 1895]

[I] was quite rushed at dinner time, but Hal never makes any extra fuss or hurry when he gets in – he helps if things are not ready. [13 February 1895]

I was tired last night, and Hal laughed & said it was because I hadn't had a chance to say a word [while Mrs. Wilson visited] – but it wasn't that ... Hal always knows the right thing to do ... [21 February 1895]

... by five we were both nearly ravenous. Hal said he'd do the cooking if I'd lay the table and we had a great repast. [24 February 1895]

Monday Evening we went to the Minstrel Show[5] and Hal & I almost registered a vow that we will not go to any more amateur performances – it wasn't very nice, though there was a large & most enthusiastic audience. [27 February 1895]

It is seven o'clock, and Hal and I have just come in and lighted the lamps.
We had an early tea, & have been working out doors since raking up rubbish – and Hal has been spreading some rich earth – half manure – over
the beds. He is having three loads of it brought, and will spread some on
the grass too ... [4 March 1895]

Early in March 1895 Hal Parke went off on a search for a wanted man;
his secret service involved hunting a criminal as far east as Montreal, an
assignment that lasted almost a month but that proved fruitless:

I must try to write regularly every day now, as Hal is away, and I'll want
him to have a full and particular account of all that I do during his absence
– more especially as he is off on "secret service" and I may not write to
him, as he does not want anyone here to know where he is. I addressed
some envelopes to myself, which he has taken with him, and so will be
able to write to me. He will be gone two weeks, and possibly longer. It
seems a dreary time to look forward to; and I'll be very thankful to have
him back safe and sound. I try not to be uneasy, but this is about the worst
time of year to be going through the mountains, and this trip is not without other dangers, still I will try to be trustful. [12 March 1895]

I can hardly believe that Hal has been gone two days – this will be the
third night.... I have got so used to letting [Hal] bear more than half my
cares, that I feel the weight of them doubly when he is not at home ... I
wish I knew just where he is tonight, & *how* he is – indeed I wish this trip
were safely and satisfactorily accomplished – but I must have patience. [14
March 1895]

I have missed Hal dreadfully. At any time it is hard to do without him, but
now that my heart is sad and my body is sick (for I have some way caught
cold) it is doubly hard to have him away. I do feel a little anxious over him
too, and wonder how his business will turn out. [17 March 1895]

I half hoped Mr. Norris might hear from Hal today – surely a telegram
will come tomorrow – if not, I'll be afraid the business has not been successful, and he may [be] away longer than we expected at first. [19 March
1895]

It seems such a long weary time since Hal went away – I hope he won't
have to take another trip very soon. I feel uneasy about him too, & will be
until he is safe at home again. [20 March 1895]

I did not write last night. To tell the truth I feel rather down hearted. I
had been so miserably anxious all day, watching each minute for Walter

Dewdney, as Mr. Norris promised me he would send him up if any telegram came. The whole day passed without a message, and I had all kinds of fears about Hal's safety ... [22 March 1895]

I find it very hard to wait patiently – I long so much to have him home again. [25 March 1895]

I really don't know whether I miss Hal most when some one comes in, or when I am alone. I think of him most of the time any way. Yesterday I was very busy – I took up the parlour & dining room carpets, & washed the margins, got the carpets down again, gave a thorough dusting, and put up clean blinds and curtains, so it looks very spic & span. Today I did my room. I wanted to get it all done before Hal gets home, both that the house may be as attractive as possible, & also that I may be lazy if I want to ... I did not sleep much. I felt nervous and frightened all night, & began worrying about Hal, & wondering where he was – so I got up this morning rather unrefreshed ... It makes me a shade more lonesome that I can't even write to him. [27 March 1895]

I had a letter from Hal in the morning – he is longing to come home as much as I am to have him. I think I could bear his absence better if I knew he was having a pleasant time, but I know he is worried and disappointed over the turn affairs have taken. He did not say anything about the business to me but Mr. Norris had a long letter from him, and kindly brought it up for me to read. I feel so sorry that he hasn't been successful for his sake – but Mr. Norris seems to think the trip has not been fruitless any way. [30 March 1895]

I can hardly wait for tomorrow morning, as I am hoping Hal may be home ... It will soon be three weeks since he left – and that is pretty long. [31 March 1895]

I have been so happy yesterday and today, for Hal did get home yesterday morning, & I *was* glad to see him. He wasn't sorry to be home either. He looks well, in spite of rather a hard trip. Until Sunday night at Sicamous, he had not had his clothes off for eight nights. He went trying to catch a man who is wanted here, & though he was on the right track some one had warned the man, & he had escaped. However the trip was not fruitless, as Hal succeeded in getting the C.P.R. to take the matter up, & they hope to catch their man eventually. It may mean another trip east for Hal – I hope not. [2 April 1895]

Immediately after his return from the east, Parke set to work:

When we came home Hal was here. I put in some sweet peas – Hal had the front bed beautifully prepared. [3 April 1895]

Hal had to go to Kelowna today, & will be gone until tomorrow night, possibly until Wednesday . . . He just has to act as Clerk of the Court, & will have pleasant companions during the drive. [8 April 1895]

I don't think gardening agrees very well with diary writing. Hal has been helping me a lot lately – or rather I ought to say I have been helping him. . . . about half past ten I heard [Hal's] step and whistle – & glad enough I was that he got home. He was drenching wet and rather cold – fortunately the fire had not gone out. I got up (in spite of Hal telling me not to), slipped on a dressing gown & slippers, & came down stairs to help get a bit of supper ready in a hurry, & soon Hal was warm & comfortable. [15 April 1895]

Hal was home this afternoon and took down the storm porch, besides some other little jobs. [29 April 1895]

We wandered about the garden. I think we almost count the leaves on each growing thing . . . [16 April 1895]

Once again, Hal Parke took up his pen:

Tuesday Evening, 30th April 1895
The "Wandering Jew"⁶ has apparently superseded all other considerations in the estimation of "The Boss," for the last three days she has been so completely immersed in it that she will neither talk, play 66 nor write in the diary, so rather than have the poor thing die altogether for lack of attention, I will try and fill in a few pages, until The Boss gets through her ordeal, which I now have some hopes of her doing, as she's well into the third volume, she certainly has great powers of endurance! . . . I will endeavour to chronicle the events of the succeeding days. On Saturday we worked a little in garden, and in the evening The Boss commenced reading The Wandering Jew . . . We intended to go to the Presbyterian Church in the evening but it looked like rain, so we stayed at home, and the Boss read The Wandering Jew.
On Monday she rushed through the washing and house work in double quick time – and read the "Wandering Jew." On Tuesday she ironed, made pies, and is still reading The Wandering Jew.

Our irrigation ditch is a great success. Hal has dug in part way around the garden, & now I ought certainly to have pretty flowers this summer. Hal means to have [the backyard] in corn this year to work the soil up to have it in good order for fruit trees this fall. I will have a corner for peas & tomato plants. [2 May 1895]

Hal had to hurry away afterwards to see if everything was all right down at the office, & the jail. They have just one prisoner in now – a Siwash called "one-eyed Louis," in for horse stealing – quite a young man. They are not much afraid of his attempting to escape, as he has a good ranch out at the reserve, and has not very much more time to serve. [15 May 1895]

I had a cake in the oven almost baked when I heard Hal whistle and there he was at the door with a nice horse and covered buggy ready to take me for a drive. He had to go to the Reserve, and said he could take me as far as Mrs. O'Keefe's ... [later] we both went out & worked in the garden until tea time – & were out again afterwards until nearly eight. [7 June 1895]

Hal has been so busy that we hardly have seen anything of him this week. Monday night he did not get home until eleven, Tuesday night 11.30 and only rushed home to swallow something to eat both at noon & at six o'clock. They hope Court will be over tomorrow, but Hal thinks he'll probably be very busy all the rest of this month ... [13 June 1895]

Hal is still very busy in the office. He has all Mr. Monteith's assessment & tax work to do, & this is the busiest month of the year for it. [21 June 1895]

Hal said at noon he expected to go to Kamloops by the afternoon train. He has not come back from the office – he generally does run over before starting away, but perhaps he hadn't time. [18 July 1895]

We have just come in – we were sitting out on the porch after watering the garden – until darkness & mosquitoes came together & drove us in ... Mrs. Cameron had given Hal the receipt [for spiced currants], and as he is fond of sweet pickles I thought I'd try it – however we don't care very much for it so I am glad I only made a small quantity ... Hal bought a little coal-oil stove, so getting tea isn't much trouble now. [22 July 1895]

It is dreadfully lonely tonight. Hal had to go off to Rossland this afternoon. They think some man is making counterfeit coin down there and Hal has gone to investigate. He will be gone a week anyway and possibly longer ... [7 August 1895]

[Hal] has been very busy lately. They have caught the man he went to Rossland for – the trial comes off tomorrow and Hal has been busy preparing evidence ... He had to go to the office again tonight. [19 August 1895]

More excitement occurred when the local butcher escaped from jail:

A few minutes ago some one came for Hal & he had to go down town.
He has been nearly rushed off his feet today. Poor Jack McKinnon[7] has
been arrested for cattle stealing and is in the jail tonight. They have put a
special constable on guard at the jail, for Jack has many friends & sympathizers in town, & Mr. Norris & Hal feel that he would run away if he
could – for I am afraid there is no doubt of his guilt; indeed everyone
thinks he has been at it for a long time, but has been clever enough not to
be caught before. The trial will be on Monday ... Hal generally has Saturday afternoon at home, but he has been rushed all day today over this
case ... Hal came in, in a hurry for his tea. I know he is sorry too that
McKinnon is guilty of such practices, for he has known him for a long
time – and one naturally hates to believe evil of an old acquaintance even
if he be not a friend. Hal went back down town immediately after tea ...
[24 August 1895]

Hal & I had just settled down for a home evening when we heard a man
running up the sidewalk, & coming in our gate. Hal hurried to the door,
& the man breathless gasped out that McKinnon[8] had just broken out of
the jail and had made into the bush. Walter [Dewdney] was on guard &
I suppose must have seen him, but I am afraid he will never be caught.
He has so many friends & well wishers who will be on the look out to
help him. Of course Hal had to hurry right down, & I haven't an idea
when he'll get back. He may be gone all night. I am sorry the man was not
sent to Kamloops. We thought surely he'd go today, but he was again
remanded till Saturday for further evidence. He evidently saw that there
was no hope of his being proved innocent, & has made a desperate effort
to get away. Hal was down at six o'clock, and every thing was all right. He
gave the keys to Walter, & put him on guard, and we came home (I was
down at the store) and at a quarter to eight the alarm came. I am very
sorry, & I do hope they will catch him, but I have very little hope. Hal isn't
fit to be out tonight. He is really very miserable, & I know he will be very
much upset over this. [4 September 1895]

Walter Dewdney ... told me too how the escape happened. Hal had been
down at half past six, & found everything all right in the jail. He then gave
the keys to Walter who was on guard for the night. At a quarter to eight
Walter went in to lock the cells. McKinnon asked him to please hand him
a blanket. Walter turned to do so, & so had his back to the door. McKinnon made a dash out of the door and reached the woods at the back before

Walter could get near him. Walter fired three times but evidently failed to touch him, as the man had made good his escape. Evidently some friends had managed to get files in to him, for his shackle was filed off between the time Hal had seen him & when Walter went in – they found it in his cell. I think I have thought all along that the two drunken men who were run in on Tuesday did it on purpose to aid him, & probably if Walter had been keener & quicker there would have been rough work to silence him. As Hal says "Give the devil his due." McKinnon might easily have given Walter a knock on the head but he risked being shot rather than hurt the boy. I felt sorry for Walter – he seemed very shaken and nervous ... at half past two Hal came in. Of course they had not found Jack, & I don't believe they will – for nearly every one sympathizes with him & would help him. Hal said they could not get a man they could trust in town to go out & help in the search – every one laughed & said they hoped he'd get away – even Mr. Tronson, a magistrate, did not conceal his glee. Hal hopes they may catch him again, but this is an ideal country for a hunted man, especially when he has helpers on every hand. Hal only slept until five when he went out again. I was very uneasy to have him tramping round so much when he was not feeling well, but the excitement seems to have made him better instead of worse. [6 September 1895]

Hal got me a lovely new wrap today. I will be very swell with it on, but I feel a little afraid it was extravagant. [10 September 1895]

[Hal] ... helped me get tea. I made biscuits, he ground the coffee, & then we laid the table. I was hungry so was glad we had a nice tea – cold tongue, governor's sauce, plum jam etc. We both did justice to it. [12 September 1895]

Hal had dinner all ready when I got home – the table laid & everything so nice – flowers on the table. I had cold meat, but he had cooked corn & sliced tomatoes & potatoes, and it was very nice to find it all ready to sit down to. [16 September 1895]

Last night I went up stairs soon after eight, & Hal came up to rub my shoulder with turpentine. [18 September 1895]

Hal was home all the afternoon, & we worked out doors for quite a long time fixing up the bay-window bed, transplanting some roses, & putting out some more strawberry plants ... We were alone in the Evening, and Hal gave me a shocking beating at chess ... [22 September 1895]

I feel quite shakey tonight. I was frightened this afternoon. We had rather a scene with our horse when we were leaving the grounds. He lay down in his shafts, nearly upset the buggy. He would have quite done so if Hal had not known exactly what to do … Hal told me to jump, & I flew out. I hardly knew myself how I managed it – then the buggy went more over, & Hal jumped himself, & two men came up & between them they righted the buggy, undid some straps & managed to get Jimmy up with nothing broken. My knees felt very weak, however I got in again & we drove into town. Walter stopped us near the Court House, and Master Jimmy (the horse) began his prancing again. Hal said to me "Get out" in far the shortest tone he ever used to me, and I didn't lose any time in obeying, & then he gave Jimmy a lesson. [12 October 1895]

Hal had to get ready all the evidence in the Smart case. He was all one afternoon in the witness box, telling about the case, & afterwards he said Judge Walkem[9] came into the office & held out his hand & said "I must congratulate you on the manner you presented that evidence." He then went on to say he had presided over many Courts of Justice, but he had *never* had the evidence put in so clear and unprejudiced a manner. Mr. Tronson told Hal he was talking a lot about it. [21 October 1895]

Hal is cutting a pattern for me, of my little spool stand. I want to make one for Nonah for Xmas if I can possibly get time … Hal brought me a new book yesterday – "The Days of Auld Lang Syne" by Ian Maclaren. I am looking forward to a treat. [15 November 1895]

Another entry by Hal:

The Boss went down to the Ranche yesterday and before leaving gave me strict orders to write in the Diary while she was away. Though what I am to write about is more than I can tell. One of the old timers of the Okanagan was buried yesterday – Peter Bassette.[10] *He had been here for over twenty years and was liked and esteemed by everybody. His wife died about four months ago – there are nine young children. Pete was a French Canadian and was looked upon as the representative of his people here, and had helped many a one both French and other in making a start here. Tomorrow will be Thanksgiving Day. I suppose it will be a dull sort of affair for me as the Boss is away. If I want to do any feasting I'll have to do it at a Hotel – most likely I will have a cold snack at home.* [20 November 1895]

It is nearly a week since I have written a word in this, and Hal didn't quite follow out my instructions, as I told him to write *all* that happened while I was gone. [24 November 1895]

I don't think anyone could lose hopefulness with Hal for a daily companion.

He is the most hopeful man I ever saw, & no doubt that is why he keeps so many youthful thoughts & ways. [26 November 1895]

... the diary will doubtless be dull tonight and tomorrow may be even worse, for I won't have Hal atall ... [Hal] brought me a new book – "The Golden Age." I have not read it yet, but we saw a review of it not long ago, which made me want to read it ... Hal often tells me I am "only a kid" ... [29 November 1895]

... as I told Miss MacIntyre when Hal is away I feel much as if I had (mentally) a bad cold in the head – every thing has lost its flavour. I go on with the daily doings because I must go on – but one thing is much as another and I can't do my work half as well. I always get much more homesick, too, when Hal isn't here. [11 December 1895]

It does make such a difference in the house when he is here. It seems so much more worth while to do everything. When he is away the daily doings are something like bread without salt – so flavourless ... [22 August 1898]

I am going to make head-cheese in the morning (D.V.). Hal cut the head up for me tonight. [16 December 1895]

Hal soon came in & I got him to distribute my gifts round town ... Hal gave me a splendid pair of scissors and a very pretty leather card case – I had worn my old one quite out – Hubert gave it to me long ago. I gave Hal a pair of gloves, two books in a set & a couple of washing ties – he is well off for neckties now with the pretty one Mother sent. [25 December 1895]

At noon when Hal came in, he told me we were to have a piano in the afternoon. We have it on trial for a month, & may continue to rent it, or perhaps buy. We like it very much indeed ... I spent most of the Evening playing, and Hal sang a little ... [1 January 1896]

I always get a genuine good fit of homesickness when Hal is away, and today has been no exception.[3 January 1896]

I played a little for [Hal] before tea, and afterwards ... we just spent a very lazy evening. [7 January 1895]

Hal is cutting a pattern for me. I want to make another patch work quilt ... Miss Norah [Cochrane] said to tell Hal she had a new set of whist markers, and wanted him to come up some Evening soon & christen them – but I know he enjoys better sitting at home helping me with my patterns. [9 January 1896]

Hal has been down town to get me some quinine, for I feel a little afraid that I am taking cold. [13 January 1896]

... we went to an entertainment in the Methodist church – magic lantern views[11] & singing. The showman, a negro named Ball,[12] used to live in St. Catherine's. Hal knew him when he was a boy and says Ball is the first man who ever shaved him. He is getting on in years, but still has a very sweet pleasing voice. [26 January 1896]

The young people were having their little dance & wanted us to go, but I did not care to go, & Hal is never sorry to stay home. [30 January 1896]

Hal Parke's diary entries continued:

The Boss has gone to the Ranche today leaving orders for me to write in the Diary during her absence. I am quite satisfied of one thing and that is that I have nothing to say and the question is how am I to say it ... I am sticking to my resolution of not going out of the house today – it is quite a novel experience for me. I cannot remember when I have tried it before except when I hurt my leg last winter and simply couldn't walk. I think if I had much of it to do, even I would become a diary writer. [9 February 1896]

Had breakfast at the Vernon[13] – took cold scraps for Lunch at home. Came from the office at 4.30 and invited Kerby to come to tea with me. Had Sausages, Slumgullion of Potatoes and onions, Bread and Butter, Lemon Pie, Doughnuts and coffee. He has just gone away as he and McKelvie are going to the Martin's – so I am left to my own devices for the balance of the evening. [10 February 1896]

Tuesday Night. Took breakfast at the Vernon again this morning – had dinner at the Jacques, and Kerby was over to a bachelor tea with me at home ... I suppose the Boss will be back tomorrow morning and in all human probability will bring a bad cold with her, that being the general result of these ranche expeditions ... I suppose I am trespassing on the Boss's ground in writing about what is to take place tomorrow so I will stop as there is nothing more to tell about today. [11 February 1896]

Hal was better than his word to make a daily entry in the diary ... he has done so well that I think I must often get him to be my substitute ... I came home to find everything all right – plants, cat & all in good order, except poor Hal himself – his cold isn't gone. He does not look very well though he says he is better. I guess he is glad I'm here. [12 February 1896]

... Hal is determined [my cold] shall not develop into a bad one if he can help it, so has ordered a programme for me to follow, and one item is to stay indoors ... Hal gave me a great dose for my cold & wanted me to stay in bed today ... I did manage not to get up until breakfast was ready ... [23 February 1896]

Hal thinks he may go to Vancouver a week from Tuesday, to be gone a month ... If nothing turns up in the office in the meantime to prevent, Mr. Norris thinks he can get away. He will enjoy the holiday. He has not had one since he went in the Government Office – not a real holiday, though he has had a good many trips to various parts of the Country. [29 February 1896]

I promised Hal to have a good lot of diary ready for him to read when he got back, and so far I have not written a great deal ... It is getting very lonely – more so each day. [14 March 1896]

[Hal] brought me two pairs of kid gloves, a lovely pair of boots & a pair of slippers, also three fine hardy hybred roses for the garden, & he hardly got any thing for himself atall. I think he was glad to be home ... Hal & I had a cosy time together. I played for him, & then we had a game of cards ... [19 March 1896]

Hal has caught a little cold some way, and has a pain in his side, so I thought we'd stay at home – we have been quietly reading. [5 April 1896]

There is so much to do [in the garden] one scarcely knows what to begin at. When Hal came home he was working at the walks and I was out looking on ... Hal was busy at the walks till dark – we are having more gravel put on – they will look very nice when finished. [11 April 1896]

We were up very late, & had a very swell breakfast, as Hal got it ready. I was so sleepy I did not get up till Hal had the breakfast cooked, & then we all did full justice to it – it was nearly ten when we were finished. [12 April 1896]

Hal says it is just five years ago today since he first saw me, but I didn't see him. Harry & I had driven in to Enderby to one of those dances they used to have and Hal was in Harvey's store & saw us come ... Hal has been doing a lot of work in the garden lately, and is making it look very nice. He got a lawn mower lately, so we hope to have a fine lawn this summer. [19 April 1896]

... my eye got sore and at tea time I could not open it. The eye was so much inflamed that Hal insisted on getting the Doctor ... Hal was home all day Friday & most of Saturday – his eyes too being inflamed. We couldn't go out, we couldn't read, we couldn't write, we couldn't sew and we really got, for once, pretty well talked out. [27 April 1896]

Sometimes I feel guilty in not having [Lizzie] board here, because I know she'd like to come, but it is so nice for Hal and me to have our home to ourselves, & we are always pleased to have her come over & see us every day if she likes to do so. [20 June 1896]

Sunday was a frightfully hot day. We did not try to go to church – Hal dressed himself in his nightshirt & lay on the lounge for a good part of the afternoon. [9 July 1896]

Hal has to go to Mara tomorrow afternoon, back Tuesday morning, & then probably down to Penticton on Wednesday morning to be gone until Saturday. [31 July 1896]

... with the prospect of Hal's being away so much I feel as if I'd like to spend all the time we can at home. [2 August 1896]

Hal Parke applied for, but did not receive, the hoped-for position of road superintendent:

When we got home I found a note here on the table from Hal, saying that he thinks Mr. Cuppage has got the appointment of Road Superintendent after all. I think he was a good deal disappointed. I am longing to see him & talk to him about it. The house *is* so lonesome without him ... [8 August 1896]

[Mr. Cuppage] wants to give up his appointment in favour of Hal, so it is again undecided – and Hal is feeling rather unsettled. They are reducing the salaries of all of the Pro. Constables – quite a heavy reduction, so I don't know what the end of it all will be. Of course it is a worry to Hal I know and I am sorry he is worried – perhaps it is hard for me to realize how heavy money worries can be, as some one else has always borne them for me – but I don't ever dread being a little poorer than I am if I have those I love left to me. [15 August 1896]

Hal is away again, and of course, the house is desolate. He went to Mara by train yesterday ... [18 August 1896]

I was so glad to find Hal had the fire lighted – he knew I wanted to cook the apples. He cut them up for me while I made biscuit ... [28 August 1896]

After tea Hal & I went for a little walk, then I wrote home & played for a long time. Hal sang a couple of songs. He has quite a sore eye, but tries to make out it is nothing. If mine were as sore I'd be making a big fuss. [3 September 1896]

... Hal stayed in all day – the doctor had given him a strong dose Saturday night which made him perspire very freely, and he was so weak on Sunday that he stayed at home all day. We did not even go to church, but read to each other. [8 September 1896]

I did not write last night because Hal & I were here alone, so we talked & read to each other – or rather I read a little while to him. He has a very sore eye. The drive down to Enderby in the dust made it much worse. He has been at home all day today – it is swollen almost shut ... and yet Hal makes so little of it. Indeed it was hard to persuade him to stay home from the office. [10 September 1896]

I didn't feel like working this morning, so nothing was easy, and my fingers were very awkward. I made a tart, & as I took it out of the oven it just slipped out of my hands upside down on the floor! Hal was standing by the stove & looked at me in a pitying manner. I was cross & own that I stamped my foot with vexation. I was ashamed of myself the next minute, but it was disappointing. I said to Hal "Well, I am ashamed that I showed temper" and he said quite comically "Oh, I thought you behaved beautifully – I expected to see you jump on the pie!" [11 September 1896]

[Hal] isn't a bit well, & he won't do anything to make himself better. He tries to *pretend* he is well, & though the will and the imagination are no doubt great helps in fighting disease I think it is sometimes necessary to supplement them with quinine or some other drug. I am coaxing him to go out tomorrow & gather wild sage to make a tonic. [12 September 1898]

After dinner I got my patchwork quilt out ... & when Hal came home he fixed it up in a kind of frame for me. We were busy at it when Lizzie came in from school, and she helped me tie it ... We had it up stairs & Hal stayed with us, & acted *overseer*, so we finished before tea and now I only have to finish off the edges, and it will be done – it is a very pretty one – & so warm. [15 September 1896]

[Hal] drove Lizzie & me out on the hills & we gathered some wild sage, which Hal says is a splendid thing to use to make a herb tea for a tonic. I have been steeping some, & if its virtue is in any proportion to its vile smell, it ought to be extremely useful. [19 September 1896]

CHAPTER 10

I have been as busy as I could be

Life at the BX Ranch and Encounters
with the Chinese

At the end of September 1896, Harold Parke found himself unsettled – disappointed by his failure to obtain the position of road superintendent for East Yale and facing the prospect of a reduction in pay as a provincial constable. His wife had become increasingly dismayed and disenchanted by the frequency and length of his absences from home and so offered her full support when Hal decided to take the position of manager at Francis Stillman Barnard's BX Ranch, two miles north of Vernon. The Parkes were able to rent out their Vernon home while they lived at the ranch, and Alice began yet another phase in her life in the west, which lasted from October 1896 to May 1898.

The six BX diaries offer many insights into life on a large spread. The circumstances of her stay at the BX were very different from those in which she had found herself five years earlier. This time she was the wife of the ranch manager and so had no responsibility for outside work other than what she chose to do. Meals were prepared for her, and, once again, the ranch hands she grew to know reacted readily to her sympathetic and motherly attitude.

Francis Stillman Barnard was one of the wealthiest men in British Columbia at the time, and he stocked the ranch with horses to be used by his express stage line.

Hal came in, and asked me if I would be willing to come out here to live. Mr. Ellison was talking to him about taking the position of manager, & wanting him to see Mr. Barnard[1] (who was in town) about it. I said I'd be

quite happy to do whatever he liked – so Saturday morning Hal inter-
viewed Mr. Barnard & accepted the position,[2] & here we are! Mr. Barnard
wanted Hal to come out at once, but he would not leave Mr. Norris until
the assizes were over ... [22 October 1896]

Hal had such a nice letter from Mr. Barnard yesterday. He enclosed a
cheque for $500.00 which he said Hal might use "for petty or interim
expenses." He usually sends cheques for each bill as needed, but sometimes, of course, it is awkward to have to wait for an answer from Victoria before settling a bill. I only thought how nice it is to be able to think
of $500.00 as a mere "petty" expense – but really the money paid out here
is something enormous. I certainly don't think ranching on a large scale a
very paying business – unless the management is something phenomenal.
I only hope we'll be able to at least make the returns meet the expenses.
Last year Mr. Barnard was out of pocket on this ranch – it is well he makes
money otherwise. This is only a small iron in the fire with him.[3] [26
November 1896]

Once again, it is the portraits of people that interest the reader. Almira
McCluskey, the widow of a former ranch manager, lived close by and was
trying to raise a large family while almost destitute. Frequently, she had to
rely upon the charity of others. It is in these passages that we see Alice at
her least charitable. She always preferred to be the one who made an offer
to help, and it is apparent that she considered Mrs. McCluskey a brazen
scrounger:

Mrs. McClusky came & stayed for quite a long visit. She is a loud voiced,
very talkative woman – I don't care for her atall. I am sorry she lives so
near. She was telling her grievances, & she seems to have trouble with
every one she has dealings with. I am afraid she will want to be a borrower
& I must not let her begin that. [Later I saw] Mrs. McClusky was at her
door – she lives just outside the gate – and invited me in. I was afraid of
offending her, so I went – for a little while – I have had enough of her
today. [27 October 1896]

I have a head ache tonight. Mrs. McCluskey was here this afternoon and
talked until she made my head ache. I didn't get a thing done but listen
to her; I had just decided to have a good long afternoon's reading when
she came and it was dark before she left ... as I said, I thought I'd read. I
was disappointed that I couldn't, especially as I don't care atall for Mrs.
McCluskey. [11 November 1896]

Mrs. McCluskey came – she came in & stayed ever so long. She wanted all sorts of things, to get feed for her cow, or else to have us keep her cow and give her milk all winter – then she wanted something about calves and was hinting around to get onions & apples – altogether Hal is afraid she will be a great nuisance. One feels sorry for her little children, but really we dare not help her much, or there would be no end to her demands. She is never satisfied, and is so bold. [18 November 1896]

I went down to Mrs. McCluskey's with some cough drops for her children. They all have very bad colds and though I don't care for their Mother, I feel sorry for the little children. They are attractive little things too – one little boy in particular – he has such a solemn chubby little face. [1 December 1896]

We were ready to sit down and Lou-ee was bringing in hot fish balls, when Mrs. McCluskey came to the french door – she stayed on & on for nearly an hour, though neither of us were very cordial. I knew the tea was all getting cold, though I had put the hot eatables on the damper, but I wouldn't ask her to stay, for she takes an ell without being even given the proverbial inch, & where her encroachments would end if she did have encouragement it is impossible to tell. I hate to be inhospitable to any one, but it is really necessary sometimes. [3 December 1896]

Francis Barnard and his wife decided to build a summer house there, and the pair paid several visits:

Mrs. Barnard is pretty & looks young – I did not think she was any more than twenty four, but she told me she had been married fourteen years, so she must be older than she looks. She is very bright – & was exceedingly nice to me – still I was glad they didn't make a long stay until their own home is ready. They are intending to build this summer & will have their new house finished before they come for their long stay in the autumn. [29 April 1897]

Mrs. Barnard, her two sisters & Miss Dunsmuir[4] are still here at their cottage – the young ladies are the very gushing style – they are all nice happy, giddy girls, but a little too "awfully" intense & emphatic for really good style. Mrs. Barnard is the prettiest & has the best manners I think. [30 September 1897]

Mrs. Barnard was in just now asking if she couldn't have an afternoon tea up at Brookside next Saturday, however the house is in such a dirty state and no seats up there, so I really couldn't do other than offer to let her use this house. She didn't ask, or even hint for it, but she seemed pleased when I offered, so I suppose if the day is fine we will have them here. There is to be a riding party first – of course they will take all the trouble – I'll only give the use of the house, & do what I can to help making it pleasant – but I won't need to do much, for they are all great talkers and well used to entertaining. [2 October 1897]

Mr. Barnard told Price Ellison his ranche had never looked so prosperous, & everything so well looked after, that he couldn't have a better manager. I think myself he is right, but it is nice to know that he appreciates his blessings. [6 October 1897]

Alice had been apprehensive about living in close daily contact with a Chinese cook. Her early contacts with the Chinese had been from a distance, and she viewed them as odd curiosities. She had visited the Chinatowns in Victoria and Vernon but had never yet attempted to develop a closer acquaintance:

It was the Chinamen's New Year, which is, with them, a season of great festivity, shown chiefly in the setting off of fire crackers. We went down through Chinatown.[5] The buildings are all rather small, shops & laundries principally – few of the windows had any curtains, so we could see the interiors, dirty cheerless looking places. In one – a gambling house[6] – two white men stood among the crowd of Chinamen round a table – some of them were smoking opium.[7] Hal says very few of the Chinamen here are free men – they are owned by some "tyee,"[8] & work under him. It seems dreadful to think there is a class of heathen slaves in our midst, & we grow utterly callous to it. I confess, while at first it was a trouble to me, latterly I am getting used to it, & say like all the others, "What can we do?" and there it ends. All this shooting off of fire crackers is their attempt to scare the devil away – who they seem to think is specially near on New Year. Perhaps he is specially near us all at times for fresh beginnings, & we do little else than set off some spiritual fire crackers. Tomorrow Lent begins & the Salvation Army are having a great meeting tonight. I think we will go. Will it be only a fire cracker? [6 February 1894]

When we got home Hal wasn't here. A Chinaman came – Sing Lee – who was very anxious over one of his friends who has got into some trouble. Sing wanted to see "Missie Pak" & came twice in vain, so the third time he approached I invited him into the kitchen to wait & had quite a long "visit" with him until Hal came home. He kept assuring me that the man in trouble (accused of stealing a valise) was a "welly good boy" & wanted me to tell him if he couldn't "get him out." Hal has gone down since tea to see what can be done about it. [18 January 1896]

Mr. Norris' Chinaman, Charlie, just came up with a loaf of lovely fresh bread for me, which he said he baked himself, and he looked very proud of it too. He had not baked for a year, he said. He is such a nice little Chinaman and talks very good English – not the broken, babyish kind that most of them jabber. I think it half the fault of the white people, nearly every one talks to a Chinaman as if he were a baby, or half foolish. [18 August 1896]

Hal Parke wrote his own observations:

Tomorrow will be Chinese New Year and if there is any virtue in fire-crackers, the Devil will no doubt be badly scared. I think they are all too poor to make many presents this year, but they must have fire crackers if they have to starve for a month to make up for it. There will likely be over a hundred dollars worth of them burned in this small place tomorrow, and large places in proportion. [10 February 1896]

At the BX Ranch Alice met a man who was to be pivotal in her intellectual and emotional development – her cook, Lou-Ee. (Once again, the spelling of his name fluctuated from volume to volume. As with many others of her acquaintance, she had some initial difficulty in ascertaining the correct pronunciation and spelling of Lou-Ee's name. In her pages he was at first Lou-Ee, then Loo-Ee, before finally settling in as GooEe.) Her relationship with this man demonstrated a definite and permanent change in her attitude towards another race. Ever willing to learn, she was eventually able to acknowledge that Lou-Ee's humanity mattered more than the colour of his skin. For her, this was a huge step, since it caused her to question much of her early conditioning. During her stay at the BX, Alice's attitudes towards the Chinese underwent a lasting transformation.

She had the same effect on Lou-Ee as she had on most of the other young men of her acquaintance; he came to admire and respect her, and their association became one of the most rewarding experiences of her life. She soon came to admire his lively sense of humour, his work ethic, his dependability, and his eagerness to learn; she also took on a new challenge when she agreed to teach him English. Once decided upon this course, she set about it with her usual thoroughness and determination, writing away to friends in Toronto for help in finding appropriate reading material for her pupil. Alice and Lou-Ee enjoyed a mutual admiration and affection that lasted throughout her time at the BX Ranch:

Then I showed Lou-ee how to make head cheese. [26 October 1896]

Lou-ee cooked everything for me & brought it over. He had so many good things for us, we scarcely knew where to begin. [27 October 1896]

I can't help thinking Lou-ee is a little extravagant in the fare he gives the men,[9] but I'll have to begin my reforms very gradually. I wish he could talk English. I believe he understands me better than I do him and I can see that he is mortified when I fail to get at his meaning. Nearly every one talks a kind of broken English to Chinamen, so I don't wonder they never learn to speak really well. I cannot do it, though I did say to Lou-ee yesterday (when I was trying to explain something to him) "Do you sabe?" – & he said "Oh yes I *know*" so I believe he likes to be spoken to as if he were a white man. I wish I could get over my prejudice against Chinamen.[10] I know it is a prejudice, for any that have worked for me – my different washermen in Vernon and now this man – have been most polite and obliging – still I don't enjoy having them around & would feel a good strong servant such a comfort, though I suppose here with all these men a Chinaman is really best. [28 October 1896]

It was nearly twelve when we got here, & it was nice to have a good hot dinner all ready when we were ready for it. Hal says I have certainly won Lou-ee's heart, for he always has some extra little dainty ready for our table, without ever being told to do so. [31 October 1896]

I asked Lou-ee yesterday if he would like to go home to China and he shook his head sorrowfully & said "No good, costs too much" – but he seems very happy and contented, though he works all the time. He generally goes to town Sunday afternoon but today was too muddy, so he has been busy in his kitchen. I often think he must be lonely – not one of his own people to speak to all the week – but no doubt natures are different, & perhaps he does not miss it so very much. I am beginning, though to think that perhaps Chinamen are not as bad as they are painted and probably the reason they act so little like other citizens is because they are treated unlike them. [8 November 1896]

Hal went in to town for the mail & suggested my going with him, but I had promised to show Lou-ee how to make a fruit cake, & I was afraid we might be late if I went to town. [18 November 1896]

We will have good beef now – the last we got from Knight was very tough, and Lou-ee had to exercise his ingenuity to make it palatable. [19 November 1896]

I had promised Lou-ee to show him how to make some mince meat, so I set him at the suet, raisins etc. before I left, & since I came home have put in the spices etc. He is going to make a pie tomorrow to try it. [25 November 1896]

Lou-ee had a very nice meal for us this Evening. (We had asked Mr. McKelvie out & expected him – for he told Hal yesterday that he would come.) We had roast chicken and a mince pie, besides vegetables. [26 November 1896]

I helped Lou-ee make two plum puddings today. They look & smell very nice – but Lou-ee is almost afraid they are not big enough. He says "Men heap likey – eat lots." We had quite a conversation. He told me he had a brother & two sisters in China. I find it rather hard to understand him, & I don't think he finds it very easy to understand me, but we make brave attempts. [12 December 1896]

Tonight Lou-ee came to me & said he would do my washing tomorrow. He knew I had hurt my hand, & he offered. I think it was so kind of him, because of course he is not supposed to do that kind of work for me, being very busy in his own kitchen. It just shows that Chinamen have the same feelings and natures that other men have. We have always been kind to Lou-ee, & he is willing to go out of his way to return the kindness. So many people advised me when I first came to be very strict & exacting with the Chinaman – they said "You can't give them any privileges, or they will impose on you" – but I think it is a mistake, & I often think where their knowledge of our language is so imperfect we cannot preach or teach Christianity to them except through our actions – & if these have not even a basis of "brotherly kindness" how can we claim so much as toleration for our religion, to say nothing of respect and belief ... Friday Lou-ee did the ironing for me. [19 January 1897]

[Lou-ee] ... had been to town & he brought us some New Year's presents – Hal a box of cigars & a beautiful big white silk handkerchief, me two embroidered silk handkerchiefs, a pot of preserved ginger & some oranges. Hal says he must have spent six or seven dollars on the things. I am sorry he got so much, but it was very kind of him. I thanked him very cordially, & he said "Oh not muchee, only little bit" – meaning that his gift was small. I suppose he'll want to go off for the afternoon on Monday – that will be China New Year – & they always go through some very noisy rites, firing off crackers seems to be the principal feature. [28 January 1897]

This morning I went in to Lou-ee's kitchen, and he gave me three more silk handkerchiefs – a beauty for Hal & two little ones for me – and after dinner when I went in I was astonished to have him bring out two black bottles with the request "Missee Park, you gin up?" One bottle he said was whiskey, the other Chinese wine. I thanked him, but declined – he kept urging me "oh yes, you gin up." I said "Oh no, Lou-ee – you keep it." He shook his head & said "Me no drink – make my head too sore – you & Mr. Park gin up." He pressed the bottles in my hand and, despairing of explaining to him any more clearly, I brought them in our house. I came in with a black bottle in each hand, laughing so that I could hardly explain to Hal & Lizzie the invitation I had had. Poor Lou-ee evidently thought he was using quite correct English when he politely invited me to "gin up." I don't know what I'll do with the stuff. The wine would have been very good to put in mince meat if it had come early enough. The Chinamen will have great excitement tomorrow with their celebrations. Lou-ee has asked to go to town in the afternoon & be away at "supper time." He said he'd lay the table & have everything cooked ready and I promised to make the tea. The men won't mind waiting on themselves for one night. They are all good natured and like Lou-ee. He said he'd wash the dishes when he got home. [31 January 1897]

We let Lou-ee go before dinner. Indeed we are fortunate that he only wanted one day. A great many Chinamen go off for four or five days. Mrs. Cameron had to let hers go for Sunday & Monday, & Harry Hann says the one they had last year went off for five days. Lou-ee only asked to go in the afternoon, but I offered to get the dinner & let him go in the morning – at first he said "Oh no, too muchee work for you" – however, he got everything ready & went off quite happily at ten. He came home some time in the night and is quite smiling and busy today. They have feasts every few hours all through the night and send off innumerable fire crackers – these are to drive away evil spirits. It seems dreadful to think of these poor creatures right at our door, right in our households, having no real knowledge of the true God – & still more dreadful to think that even if one could make preaching comprehensible to them, they are so keen to see our failures in practice that it is hard to make them believe in the power of Christianity. I did not have a great deal to do yesterday in Lou-ee's kitchen ... [2 February 1897]

It is so nice, when one comes in tired, not to have to think about what to prepare for a meal. I just lay my table, and Lou-ee is sure to bring in some appetising little dish. [9 February 1897]

I did not go to town with Hal because I had set Lou-ee to clean his big pantry, and wanted to be here to overlook him. [12 February 1897]

There seems quite an excitement again in Vancouver over the Chinese tax.[11] A great many people want to raise it to $500 a head – it is now $50. For my part I don't think it is right to tax them atall. One cannot help seeing that it is a "curse come home to roost" on the Chinese themselves. For so many years they closed their ports to foreigners and now the boomerang has returned to give their own head a blow. Still, I don't think it is the right policy for us to adopt. We despised and blamed the Chinese in former years for being so narrow and selfish & now we turn around & follow their example. If white men & women can't compete with Chinamen, why sooner or later (in spite of any restrictions) the survival of the fittest will result – & if we have awakened their hatred and antagonism it isn't going to make matters any better for ourselves. If, on the other hand, we are well able to hold our own in spite of cheap Chinese labour (and I believe we are) I don't see any sense in shutting them out.[12] I suppose I have not enough knowledge to be a judge in these National problems, but I confess I don't like National selfishness any more than individual selfishness & I think some time – if persisted in – it has the same weakening effect on a *Country* that it has on a single individual. Surely we don't want the character of our country to become altogether self seeking and narrow! [17 February 1897]

I have begun to teach Gou-ee to read and write English and an apt pupil he is. We only began Monday night. He did not know one letter from another and already he reads the first 6 lessons in the primer and writes all the words besides writing & spelling his own name. He says he went to school eleven years in China, & there they go to school at 5 A.M., go home at seven for breakfast, back to school again at half past seven, home at twelve for half an hour, back to school and remain until seven at night. I wonder how our school children would like those hours! I teach Gou-ee for half an hour after his evening work is done. He seems delighted at the idea of learning to read. [4 March 1897]

Gou-ee came in for his lesson, and I played a game of cribbage with Hal, then wrote my letter, & after reading a little while it was bed time … I went in to Gou-ee's kitchen for some bread, & he was most anxious to get my breakfast for me, but I didn't let him … Gou-ee has been here for his lesson, and has gone off now having had a good long one. I asked him how long it took him to learn to read in Chinese, and he said seven years! I have heard that the letter "I" has over a hundred different sounds & meanings, & that there are several thousands of letters – so if they all have different meanings it is not wonder Gou-ee finds English easy. He says his brother went to school twelve years – but then he stopped as they couldn't teach him anything. Fancy taking twelve years to find it out! [6 March 1897]

Last night I wrote to Mother, Father & Harry – gave Gou-ee his lesson & played a game of crib with Hal, so there wasn't any time left for writing in this. [9 March 1897]

Gou-ee had tea ready, & I wasn't sorry that I didn't have to get it myself, for I was quite tired. It is nice to be able to stay out as late as one likes, and be sure to find the meals ready when one comes in. [27 March 1897]

In the evening Goo-ee did not come for a lesson – he was cleaning his stove ... Hal helped me carry down the plants and Goo-ee & Harry Hann shook the carpets. [8 April 1897]

I had left the tea table, thinking I'd just pack up the dishes when we got back, & wash them tomorrow morning, but when we came along I was surprised to see a light on in the kitchen, & there was Goo-ee washing the things for me. He had them nearly done when we got here. I gave him his lesson & have been reading a little since ... Goo-ee was sick. I went in to his kitchen in the morning & found him with a great white cloth around his head, looking very miserable. He said "All same knives sticking in my head." He was sick at his stomach too. I asked him to let me help him, but he said no, he hadn't much work to do today & could manage it all. I did help him wash the dinner dishes and then he went to lie down until after four, when he said he was better, but he is not going to take a lesson tonight ... I was glad [our visitors] didn't stay to tea, for poor Goo-ee was so miserable I didn't want to give him extra work. [8 May 1897]

I had told Goo-ee that we would just have a cold lunch, but he had kept dinner hot. He is better today, but not very well. [9 May 1897]

I was pretty tired when I came home, but I gave Goo-ee a lesson after tea, and watered the flower garden ... The Chinese book came for Goo-ee yesterday. He has had the lessons from it and is greatly delighted. I think he will learn very fast now ... [13 May 1897]

It was after twelve when we got started for home, so of course we were a little late for dinner – however Goo-ee had everything nice & hot . . . I did not give Goo-ee a lesson tonight. He came and told me he wanted to go to town. He is getting quite proud of his English and explained that he wanted to go "to get a little more something" and evidently thought he had been quite communicative. [22 May 1897]

I gave Goo-ee a lesson at night. We have a new Chinaman in the Garden – Chung – he is a comical man. He insists on watering & weeding my flower garden & he has made the paths beautifully trim and tidy. He reads English quite well, & uses the longest words he knows how. It sounds quite funny. He is much more inclined to be bold than Goo-ee is – still he is very kind and a good worker. [10 June 1897]

Goo-ee excelled himself in the dainties he prepared for us. He made ice cream in the afternoon. I didn't know he meant to do it until it was done. [21 June 1897]

In the morning I went over to the garden to pick some strawberries for dinner and Chung came with me and offered to help. He asked me who the ladies were who came to see me the day before. I told him my brother's wife & her Mother. Presently he said "Your brudder's Mamma-in-law very young-looking – she very elegant lady – very nice-looking" – then he went on to dilate on how old white people were before they married. He said in China you never saw a girl of seventeen who wasn't married – he said he has a sister who is only nineteen and she is a widow with two children. "She very good at embroidery. You save embroidery?" Then he suddenly said "How old were you Missie when you were married." I told him 31 – he gave a great chuckle, and exclaimed "Oh all same Spinster s-p-i-n-s-t-e-r spinster." He seemed to think it a great joke. [23 June 1897]

In October the Barnards came to visit their property:

I am quite amused by Goo-ee. He does not seem atall pleased that I don't take part in all the gaiety of Mrs. Barnard & her guests, and he is determined to give me all the waiting on that he can. They are going to have a picnic tomorrow and asked to have a turkey killed & cooked for it. He asked me if I was going. I said no – I did not go to picnics on Sunday. He didn't seem to approve of their having a turkey which Hal & I were not to share. Mrs. Barnard asked him to make tarts for them – he didn't do it with a very good grace, but he made them & brought some in for our tea! [2 October 1897]

Mr. Barnard is going to build a new kitchen and men's dining room with a pantry & room for Goo-ee. It will be so nice ... Goo-ee seems very happy & good-natured tonight & said to me "Oh! not much work now." I think he is glad the Barnards are gone and I don't wonder that he is. [10 October 1897]

Friday I was as busy as a bee getting ready for the dance. Goo-ee had made five cakes but I was so afraid it wouldn't be enough that I made two more on Friday morning. [17 October 1897]

Since tea I have given Goo-ee a lesson. He seemed glad to begin again & I hope we'll be able to do the lessons regularly this winter. [20 October 1897]

Tonight we are alone, except that Gooee has just been in for a long lesson. I was trying to teach him the different parts of "to be." I think he grasped the idea of different tenses in English – or perhaps only in part – in Chinese exactly the same character expresses is, am, & are. [29 October 1897]

I didn't give Gooee any lesson tonight. He has been moving in to his new kitchen today and had too much tidying and settling to do to have time for a lesson. I think the new quarters will be very pleasant and warm. [3 November 1897]

Goo-ee is having another holiday tonight. A cousin[13] who is going to China came to see him today. He came before dinner and I could hear their voices nearly all the afternoon. They talk more as if they were singing – or intoning – they ought to be good at a high church service. Gooee has gone off to town with his cousin tonight. [4 November 1897]

Gooee has gone to Penticton to visit his cousin, Ah Jim, who is going to China, so we have another cousin – Sing – in his place for awhile. Gooee said he would be back Saturday or Monday. I do hope Jim won't persuade him to stay in Penticton. He gets $40.00 a month for cooking at the Hotel there and we only give Goo-ee $25.00, so I often feel afraid he will be coaxed away. Sing is quick & cheerful and seems to do his work well, but of course I like Gooee best. [9 November 1897]

I do hope Goo-ee will come back on Tuesday. Sing is a fairly good cook, & seems good-natured and pretty clean, but I don't like him nearly so well as Gooee. I suppose a good many people would laugh at me for saying it, but I think Gooee is a natural gentleman. His ways are so nice. Sing was watching me put some pictures up in the men's dining room – one was a battle scene. He was chattering away about it & asking questions. He said "White men fight all same Chinamans and Japs?" I said yes. He said "Me in China when Chinamans fight Japs." I asked "Did you fight?" He showed all his white teeth (& they *are* white) in a very knowing grin, and shook his head. "Oh! no, me no fight – me scared, me fled." It sounded so funny, the way he came out with that "me fled." He told me today that he is a Christian,[14] that he had been to school in Victoria and had been baptised. [4 November 1897]

I am rejoiced to say that Gooee came back today, & Sing has gone. I think Gooee is glad to be back. He filled the wood-box to overflowing, got a basket of lightwood, & did all his little chores promptly and well. I know the way one renews old duties, after a rest. He really seems glad to be here again and I know without a doubt we are glad to have him. He brought me three Chinese lily bulbs. He had a lesson tonight. [17 November 1897]

I have given Gooee his lesson – he generally goes to town Saturday night, but I fancy he had enough visiting in his Penticton trip to last him for one while. [20 November 1897]

I went into the kitchen this morning to oversee the mixing of the mince-meat & cut the suet. Gooee stoned the raisins last night. We have it nearly finished, will put on the touches tomorrow. [1 December 1897]

[I] helped Gooee make the plum puddings. He isn't coming for a lesson tonight, as he is going to ice the Xmas cakes – I am going in to watch him do it. [10 December 1897]

Gooee didn't come for a lesson tonight, as he had the turkeys to clean. [16 December 1897]

I gave Gooee a good long lesson tonight. He didn't seem as quick as usual tonight – maybe I wasn't just in the humour for teaching. I think a teacher's mood very soon reacts upon a pupil. [21 December 1897]

I gave Gooee a lesson every night last week too, for he is so disappointed when he has to miss [one]. [9 January 1898]

Yesterday I got a most gorgeous present from Gooee – two huge bunches of the wonderful Chinese paper flowers. They are marvels of workman-ship but oh! so distressingly ugly, & I can't hurt the poor fellow's feelings by hiding them away at once, for he sent all the way to Vancouver for them and paid a pretty penny too. I know that for they came by express, & he gave Hal the money $10.00 to pay for the parcel & bring it to him. I feel really sorry that he spent so much money. Next week will be their China

New Year, & they always give presents then. He gave me some lovely handkerchiefs too – two of them are exquisite, & two very elaborate. He has gone to town tonight. He expected some letters from China and they don't come addressed to himself[15] – I think the Chinese store keeper gets all the Chinese letters & they go to him for them. [14 January 1898]

Hal & I were both quite sick in the night – coughing & feverish with our colds. I think it has really been Grippe this time. Hal made me stay in bed yesterday morning, & strange to say I didn't rebel. For the first time in my life I was quite content to lie in bed. Hal is a very good nurse – he stayed home to look after me, and Gooee sent in wonderful trays of food, which I didn't want. [27 January 1898]

I have scarcely been out of doors for a week – not at all until yesterday, when I went in to Gooee's kitchen. He, poor fellow, has a nasty burn on his thumb. I cut him a finger out of a kid glove to put on when he goes outside. [30 January 1898]

I turned out the parlour, gave it a thorough sweeping and dusting. Gooee shook the carpet for me, & I washed the margins. [19 February 1898]

We went to church in the morning, and came home to dinner. Of course it was a little late, but Gooee had everything nice and hot for us . . . I have been interrupted by giving Gooee a lesson. We have a lesson on the Geography of China occasionally, and I am sure I am learning more than he is. He tries so hard to explain about the places to me, but his English is not very fluent yet. [12 April 1898]

The Barnards were expected to make another visit, this time to stay in their newly built house:

Gooee washed the dishes and put them on the pantry shelves [in the Barnards' house]. I was distressed when the extra Chinaman we have had since Monday didn't come this morning. He still had three rooms to clean, and up to noon there was no sign of him. Gooee said he was smoking opium all night last night – he (Gooee) was in town till pretty late. The poor thing. Tiny, the new Chinaman, is a miserable specimen any way – he is small & thin & old looking. Monday night when he was going back to town he came to the door, and asked to see me. Hal called me, and all the creature wanted was to say good night. [5 May 1898]

I had the Chinaman from town working at the [Barnards'] house, & had to make a good many trips over to look after him. We have the house as well settled now as we can before they come. Gooee has been doing some cooking for them today – a cake, a beef-steak & kidney pie, boiling a ham, making bread etc. I want them to go right to their own house. I had the boys take over quite a lot of bottled fruit for them today, and we have been getting flour, oat meal etc. in their pantry. It takes quite a lot of work & there will be a great deal for them to do after they come in the way of settling, but they will be able to go right into the house. [6 May 1898]

Within a year, despite Lou-ee's attentions and the devotion of the ranch hands, Alice was expressing dissatisfaction with life at the ranch. She found herself totally isolated, removed from her friends and social rounds, and considered the BX landscape gloomy and claustrophobic in winter. She longed to re-establish her regular interactions with friends in Vernon. She continued to visit Harry Barrett and his family at Mountain Meadow, leaving Hal on his own. The solitary Hal was himself going through a period of depression that was totally at odds with his usually optimistic and energetic outlook. He would go to great lengths to please his wife.

Mrs. Burnyeat returned today from her visit to her friends in Nova Scotia. Query! why do women want to go away at all if they think enough of the place to come back from that distance? . . . I don't think Diarying is my forte so I will strike. [24 November 1897]

. . . the Boss won't object to having her visit extended for two or three days – it is not so lonesome for her down there as at the B.X. I suppose she will come up by the train on Monday to see why I have dared to disobey her orders. I got one egg in the chicken house yesterday – the first for nearly a month, but by way of correction in case I should feel too exuberant over the egg I found a dead chicken in the same nest today. [26 November 1897]

This has been the coldest day we have had so far and it bids fair to be the coldest night – I would not be surprised if it reached the zero mark before morning. I got one more egg today and wonder if it will be followed by a dead chicken tomorrow. [27 November 1897]

If I am not any more agreeable company for the Boss than I am for myself, I do not wonder at her finding it lonesome here and wanting to go away visiting . . . Harry Hann raffled off his Bicycle and is going to start for Ontario in a few days. I only wish the raffling of a Bicycle was all that stood in the way of my going there and staying there. The only possible road I can see leading to Ontario is by way of the Klondike and either leave my old useless bones there, or make enough to live elsewhere. Strange to say I got another egg today instead of a dead chicken – the law of compensation must have gone wrong somewhere. [28 November 1897]

Hal Parke resigned from his position as manager in May 1898, when he was able to secure an appointment as superintendent of roads and bridges for East Yale. Lou-ee and the ranch hands were deeply saddened and unsettled by the Parkes' departure.

Poor Gooee! I was quite touched last night – he said "I so sorry you go away. I all same sick here" laying his hand on his breast. Charlie (Mr. Norris' Chinaman) told me that Gooee was in town last night & said he thought he'd leave the ranche, for he didn't think he'd get another "boss man" like Mr. Parke. [18 May 1898]

I saw Percy Mark yesterday. He says he has left the B.X. & so has Nick, & Gooee told them he would soon leave. Mr. Barnard is still managing it himself. [9 June 1898]

... we were out on Friday afternoon, & wasn't Gooee delighted to see us. He brought out all the dainties in his cupboard and wanted to feast us with them. Mrs. Barnard was very nice too, but already my pretty little garden out there is over run with weeds & looks so neglected. Snowball the cat knew me – Gooee is taking good care of her. [13 June 1898]

Alice made contacts with other Chinese in the valley. During a visit to Kelowna:

When I got [to Mrs. Wilson's] I couldn't open the gate. It was a great heavy gate, & the hinges seemed broken. I was just thinking I'd have to climb over when a Chinaman came along and very gallantly opened it for me, took off his hat and was most polite. [3 July 1898]

After the Parkes returned to live in Vernon, Alice did not cut her ties with the Chinese community; she volunteered to teach English classes to some of the Chinese men in town:

Wednesday Mr. Robson came to ask if I couldn't go down to the Chinese school that night, as he hadn't been able to secure any teachers, so Hal went up for Mr. Billings, and both of us went down with him ... I quite enjoyed my evening at the Chinese school. We had nine Chinamen there. I taught three who knew nothing, not even their letters, but they seemed very anxious to learn. Mr. Robson appears to know their ways well, & how to talk to them. [8 May 1899]

Tuesday was my night at the Chinese School. Mrs. Billings called for me, and as Hal was going to a Water Works meeting I went home with her & stayed until Hal called for me. We got out of the school about half an hour earlier than he did. [14 May 1899]

Monday night I wrote some letters & last night was my night at the Chinese School ... [7 June 1899]

... we went to the Chinese School. I took down some maps of China and we had quite a talk over Geography. The Chinamen seemed so interested ... [14 June 1899]

Last night was our night at the Chinese School – the attendance keeps up well & the men seem so interested. [21 June 1899]

It is my night at the Chinese School. It always rains lately on Tuesday night. [4 July 1899]

... [it] rained heavily last night. I went, however, to the Chinese School, thinking I'd probably be the only teacher, but Mr. Wilson & Ada Gould both came. We only had four pupils ... [5 July 1899]

I ... went to Chinese School in the evening, & had just two pupils, Charlie and Wing. Charlie says not many Chinamen will come in the summer. [13 July 1899]

The Chinese learners did indeed take time off during the summer:

Mr. Robson came in in the afternoon to say that Mr. Winchester[16] (who works among the Chinamen at the coast) would like to speak to those who were interested in teaching them here. Mr. Robson asked all the teachers to meet him, but only himself, Elsie French, & I were there ... I don't think any definite plan was arrived at about beginning the school again, but I hope we'll be able to do so. I am afraid it will be very hard to find teachers. Ida Birnie is gone. Miss Glover has gone away to teach school, and Mrs. Billings can't help this winter – so it will be harder even than it was before – still, we may be able to have it open for three nights in the week. [1 October 1899]

I do hope we'll be able to re-open our school. I asked one of the Chinamen yesterday if they'd like us to, & he said yes – so we may begin again soon. [5 October 1899]

The Chinese school did not reconvene. But such was Lou-Ee's influence that Alice paid her first formal call upon a resident of Vernon's Chinatown, and she continued to hire Chinese laundrymen, cleaners, and gardeners from time to time:

Today I went down to China-town to see a little Chinese woman who lives there – the wife of Kwong Hing Lung[17] – their Chinese merchant. She is a nice little thing eighteen years old, & talks pretty good English. She seemed quite pleased to see me, & asked a great many questions about my dress, whether I made it myself & what it was made of, & how old I am. She begged me to come again – I wish I had time to offer to teach her English. Kwong Hing Lung was most attentive. He brought a great tray of candies to treat me, & when I was going gave me an orange and a box of most delicious preserved ginger – dry – like candy. It is too rich to take much more than a taste. [17 March 1900]

I came up stairs, & began to get the two front rooms ready for cleaning. I expected a Chinaman yesterday morning, but he didn't come, so I went on, & did what I could myself. I got a good lot done, but confusion reigns in the front rooms yet, so I haven't been able to do much settling, however I hope to have everything but the dining-room done this week, & I must have a Chinaman when I attack this room, as the carpet is so dreadfully dusty. Hal helped me all he could, but he had to be in the office nearly all the time. He took down the pipe & moved the piano, & put a hook in the parlour ceiling for a hanging lamp ... We got a Chinaman in this morning to dig the little beds in the back garden, & we got some hop roots, to put in by the stairs. [11 April 1900]

CHAPTER II

There is much of the untamed animal nature in me

Confessions to the Diaries

Throughout the diaries, Alice Barrett Parke reflected upon a host of different topics. These reflections appeared at random, in response to people and events. They reveal the basic ethical and philosophical beacons guiding the young woman who was committing them to paper. The diaries were a safe, uncritical repository.

AFFECTATION:
... I often think though affectation is very contemptible, & much sneered at, it is perhaps quite as grave a fault not to try to really rise to grace whatever position one may attain to. I think no one detests snobbishness more than I do, but I see no reason why one should not strive to adopt a lady's manners and a lady's speech even if one were not born to it, when circumstances call one to a position of wealth & influence. I suppose though, it isn't an easy matter – & so many people just do what is easy. I believe that all lofty living is hard to attain to and I earnestly think that sloth is a harder enemy to fight than sin; I know lately I feel that in myself. [16 June 1894]

AGING:
... I was thinking of how tired my body gets sometimes now – & I was confessing to myself that I don't in the least dread growing old, in so far as looks or mental growth are concerned. But sometimes I do wish my body could always keep the spring & elasticity of youth. I don't believe my heart does grow old. Hal often tells me I am "only a kid," and I think

little pleasures and little pains are very keen to me, as to any child.
[29 November 1895]

It is quite a pleasure to see [Mrs. Mildmay] – there are so few old people
out here, and I think it does one good to see a pretty gentle face that has
grown old gracefully, with refinements & patience expressed differently to
what it ever can be on a young face. [22 May 1897]

AMERICANS:
I don't know why it is, but it seems to me Americans have a very original
way of talking. [Marshall] makes me think of Mrs. Perkins – the same
alertness of thought – they never seem to have to feel for an idea, or
for words to express it. It is the same tone of mind that one finds in their
writers too – Holmes, Emerson, Lowell – such kindly keenness and
shrewdness combined with true poetry of thought. I have not had a wide
experience of men & manners, but I think in each individual national
characteristics are strongly marked. I suppose I see fewer peculiarities in
Canadians because I am one of them. [15 February 1898]

GOOD FORTUNE:
I was just saying to Hal I feel I have so many blessings – none of those I
have seen are so well off. I have such a nice home, and everything I need
for comfort, & that one time I was ill since we were married Hal took such
good care of me – no nurse could have been better ... [8 November 1894]

PERSONAL HABITS:
... I always feel ashamed of myself when I am bored by any one. It must
be that my sympathies are not broad enough – for their plane of thought
is interesting enough to themselves, and should be to me, if I could only
get up – or down – to it. [12 April 1898]

... when I was cutting the bread to make toast for breakfast I cut my hand
and it was a little troublesome. Hal says I and a knife are a "fearful combination" at any time. I believe I am very awkward with any kind of a tool
except a needle! [7 November 1895]

I have a sore finger – I burned, bruised and skinned it all in the same spot.
Hal says the reason is, because when I start for any point I go straight
there, no matter what obstacles intervene; & I suppose I am rather careless. [21 February 1895]

CHILDREN:

I often long so much for Mother or Wese to tell me what I ought to do. I wonder if little children feel the same shrinking from physical standing alone that we more mature learners do from the mental attitude. Poor little souls if they do – I pity them. [25 June 1891]

I do believe that love counts for more than anything else in the training of children, because it is love that underlies all the Heavenly Father's teaching of his children – and in this, surely
"It is the heart & not the brain
That to the highest doth attain
And he who followeth love's behest
far exceedeth all the rest." [17 September 1891]

... I never have had any liking for the notion of adopting a child. I have a good many to love. Indeed I think I am very very rich in family ties, & "Blood is thicker than water." I think the only stranger that I have seen out here that I could really love, and delight in caring for, is little Alfy Postill. [15 March 1896]

Sometimes I wonder how people do manage, who have so many little children. I often think I lead a busy life, & yet of course one little child makes more work that *must* be done than any thing else does.
[19 March 1896]

... I do like young voices. There is a brightness in them that dies out of ever so good a voice when youth is gone. [29 March 1898]

BRAVERY:

It is getting dark, and I am getting a little bit frightened. It is queer how my courage all flies when night settles in. I think there must be truth in Ruskin's idea of the "power of the sun" over our spirits and bodies both. [7 December 1891]

I wish I were more brave, but I think I grow less so. I just get a weak, terrified feeling when the darkness closes in, & it doesn't seem to be much use to fight against it. Miss Godwin will soon be here now – she is very good protection. [9 April 1895]

I couldn't sleep – I got one of my frightened moods. I have been braver lately when Hal has been away, but last night I heard so many noises, which were all suggestive of midnight horrors, and I thought of all possible misfortunes & dangers to all my loved ones, altogether I had a very miserable time – & consequently have not felt as brisk as usual today. Lack of sleep wears me out more than any thing else. [31 March 1896]

I am thankful to say I am not nearly so nervous about horses as I was before I went away – I seem to have gained courage & often drive through the gate now, & I even forget all about the horse sometimes as we are going along, so I am able to enjoy what there is to be seen. [29 October 1897]

I daresay I make a lot of fuss over a small ailment, but this pain makes me feel too dull to be pleasant company. [17 September 1895]

I think [Hal] is very different from me about physical pain. I often remind myself of a child – I just "cry when it hurts" – I don't seem to have any fortitude in bearing physical pain. I resolve & resolve that I won't murmur, but as soon as a little ache comes I am possessed with a mighty desire to share it with some one else – while Hal doesn't seem to want to talk about his afflictions – he just "grins & bears it." I can bear it twice as well if I don't try to grin. [4 January 1897]

When I came home one of my feet was very cold. It ached so when it was getting warm that I fairly cried. It made me think of when I was a little girl & used to come in from Miss Emma's school with toes aching from the cold, & father used to take off my shoes and warm my feet in his hands. I think the tears yesterday came half from the physical pain and half from the memory of the old days that are so far away – those dear childhood days so full of love & tender care. What a Father & Mother we have! I never remember when either of them treated us selfishly or even thoughtlessly. I was ashamed of myself yesterday for whimpering over cold feet – I don't seem to have any courage atall to bear a bodily pain. If I had to bear what Nonah has gone through with her ingrowing nails I don't know what would happen to me. Sometimes I just think I *couldn't* bear a bad pain – I believe I'd die. [9 November 1897]

DEATH:
I am sure it is better for people who can talk to any one of their griefs – but someway it seems so impossible to me. I suppose there is much of an untamed animal nature in me – I can more easily understand the wounded brute that steals away to be alone with nature, than I can a human being who lays bare its bleeding heart to every eye – but such people do grieve in their own way ... [Gertie] talks so freely about her [sister] being "dead" – a word I never can bear to use in speaking of anyone I love. It hurt me today to hear her talk. [16 January 1894]

Why is it we long so to keep our dear ones here when we believe that greater happiness awaits them in the heavenly home! Partings are so hard to bear. [12 December 1894]

I had one such strange dream, & a very unpleasant one. I was dreaming about being home & seeing all the old friends, & being so happy among them, but in every place I went there was a mysterious figure with a veil over its face. I seemed always most curious to know what was behind this veil, & often asked the figure to remove it – but vainly. No one else seemed to notice anything peculiar. At last one day I found myself alone with the mysterious stranger, & then for the first time a feeling of fear seized me, which became almost a frenzy when suddenly it turned on me saying "Now you shall see my face." I thought I begged and prayed not to see, but the creature seized me fast, & in spite of my struggles, tore the veil from its face, & turned my unwilling eyes upon it – & then I saw – Death! [18 September 1895]

... I cannot take it in that I am never to see [Aunt Rose] any more. She died very peacefully indeed ... she was so willing to go, and had lost all her old clinging to her possessions, planning with such pleasure to give them away. Often I think I am like her in the way my love winds itself around inanimate objects – if I had the same loneliness that she had I daresay I'd get even fonder of my household goods. [2 March 1898]

ENTERTAINMENT:
The band is giving a concert tonight but I did not care to go, they are to have a "side splitting" farce and one of the performers is too often rather vulgar, so I'd rather stay at home. [17 February 1895]

Thursday night we went to the social ... Why they call those affairs "socials" I can't imagine. Every one looks bored to death, and I never do believe in trying to mix all sorts and conditions of men and women. It is far better to let people arrange themselves into little circles that are congenial and not attempt a general mixture. [27 August 1898]

HER OWN CHARACTER:
I wish I could clear all the rubbish out of my mind & heart too. It is easy to have a "spring cleaning" in one's house – but in one's heart alas! the dust of old worries, the specks of present defilement stick so firm and fast that it is not so easy a thing to get rid of them. [15 April 1892]

I know that "it takes very little talent to find fault" – but even where one knows ones self faulty it is possible to see failings in others. [6 November 1894]

I had hardly got well started at work again when Mrs. Poulin called. I'd rather almost any one else had caught me in such an upset state – I can't be the pink of perfection when I am at such work. [31 March 1896]

[Hal] often makes me ashamed, because I know sympathy is so dear to me, I always share every little woe with someone I love, thinking of my own comfort rather than the pain I give. [22 January 1895]

I do like Mrs. Martin & Miss Macintyre, but they seem rather helpless in some ways. I suppose I can't understand it because I am so self confident (that sounds better than conceited!). I never am afraid to undertake whatever presents itself, even though experience had taught me that I don't always make a success of my undertakings. [7 April 1894]

I am getting worthless to sit up late; I cannot do it without being tired all through the next day. [25 April 1894]

I am a great believer in what Ruskin[1] calls "the power of the sun" in our work. Nothing is so well done, I think, as that which we do in the first morning hours. It is rather bad management on my part perhaps to generally devote that time to cooking & housework. I wonder if our social intercourse would be more elevating if we took the morning for it instead of afternoon or evening! [15 December 1894]

I was quite sorry Mr. Tronson asked me to play a game of whist. I did not like to refuse, but would have much preferred flying around talking to everyone. [17 March 1894]

. . . I wasn't just in the humour for teaching. I think a teacher's mood very soon reacts upon a pupil.
[21 December 1897]

I couldn't stand [the gypsy] life for a month. There isn't anything of a Bohemian about me. I suppose there is no genius, & very little originality, for I do like well-beaten paths – and established conventionalities. Of course I would not like to be slave to them, & never be able to get over the fence of custom, but one feels safer in the main on a thoroughfare than in a lonely way. It takes so much courage & self-reliance to choose out a new path, & sometimes one finds after all the hard struggling that it doesn't lead to anything so good as the old beaten way reached. [25 April 1892]

I did not enjoy [Mrs. Burnyeat's tea] very much as the whole conversation was about the tableaux[2] the night before, and as I was not at them, & did not care to obtrude my opinions about church entertainments, I was necessarily rather dumb & I don't quite enjoy that. [17 January 1895]

I know I, myself, so often regret a speech as soon as I have made it, that I can feel for her. [14 February 1895]

I have a long evening before me, with probably as much quiet as I choose for writing, and such is the perversity of human nature I don't feel like either writing or reading – I am too lonesome I think. [9 March 1896]

I am learning rather to distrust my own judgment in business matters. I used to think I knew a good deal about every thing, but I have found myself mistaken so often that I am not quite so self confident now. [24 August 1898]

FORTUNE-TELLING:
I think I'll make [the young people] happy presently by telling their fortune – strange how we all love to hear about our own future, even when we haven't any faith in the foretelling. [27 September 1897]

GARDENS AND FLOWERS:
I suppose it is early yet to sow seeds, but I thought there wouldn't be any harm in putting in a few sweet peas – & one does long to be "pottering" over the earth when the air feels spring like. [3 April 1895]

... I do rather grudge time spent in doors once the Spring comes. [16 April 1896]

Whenever the Spring comes I think of Abraham Cowley's[3] wish "Let me a *small* house and *large* garden have," and echo it. One longs so to be out of doors, & yet there is so much inside that must be done, before one can turn with a clear conscience to the pleasant outside work. [19 April 1896]

I could spend half of each day out in our small garden and still see work to do ... The whole place is sweet with the perfume of mignonette, sweet peas, petunias etc. and I have a few double stocks – not many though, the seed did not do well. [13 August 1896]

Wese's letter was sweet with the odour of violets – how I love their smell. [18 May 1897]

I was reading yesterday that a love for flowers refined and elevated one's tastes, that one could not love Nature and her works without being uplifted. It sounded very nice but I couldn't help thinking of old [Iniw],[4] and how – to all appearances – he wasn't much improved by the hours and days he spent alone with Nature. I think a garden is very enticing – we spend a great deal of time in our little spot. [15 May 1895]

This morning I washed and rearranged all my plants. I always linger over them; they look and smell so nice when the leaves are wet. [29 November 1895]

GOOD MANNERS:
Mr. Smith and Mr. Fleming came to tell me about a social they are getting up for the Odd-fellows next Thursday night. Of course I knew they had come to ask me to do something and they seemed so very reluctant to tell what it was, that I was imagining all sorts of requests. I thought probably they wanted to borrow the piano – they were very anxious to know if I'd be sure to go and at last brought out the important request that I would "make myself agreeable, & help things along." I really could hardly help laughing to think that was all they wanted. It didn't seem very flattering – one might hope the "making oneself agreeable" would be a foregone conclusion. However I said of course I'd do my best if we went. [15 February 1896]

HARDSHIP:
I [feel a] real thankfulness that my lines have fallen in the pleasant places they have – "neither poverty nor riches" is indeed the prayer of a wise man – so great temptations come with either extreme few natures can live among them without being really evil. It is terrible to think of the hardships so many have to bear. [16 November 1899]

DOMESTICITY:
There is certainly a charm about "our ain fireside" that cannot be found anywhere else. [21 November 1894]

I did think perhaps I'd go & see Mrs. Cameron and Rosie dressed, but I don't believe I will – it is pretty cold and our "ain fireside" is so cosy & attractive – I don't wonder Hal hates to leave it. [14 February 1895]

It … is so wet & dismal I thought lights and a fire would make it more cheerful. This is just the kind of evening when home is so delightful if one has all the home ones at hand – but it is indescribably gloomy when they are away. I think I miss Hal more every time he goes away … [7 September 1895]

HOMESICKNESS:

I hear the train whistling and it does sound nice. I never thought I'd get up any sentiment over an engine whistle – but when one realizes that it is the nearest approach we nineteenth century people have to the wishing coat which transported its wearer to a distant spot in a second of time, one values it accordingly. I suppose at the time our fairy stories had their origin a railway would have been thought quite as marvelous as Alladin's geni. [29 June 1894]

It seemed a shame for me to be amused, even in my mind, by the old man's (Mr. Baldwin's) peculiarities of expression when he was so honestly glad to see me, & so communicative over his troubles. He said, "Your visit has quite *rose* me up and I was feeling very low." I don't suppose my few weeks of strangeness here when I first came have made me quite able to realize what it would be to live on month after month, feeling a stranger in a strange land; but at least they have made me able to sympathize with and long to help those who do feel strange. [26 January 1894]

Of all principles of philosophy I think I most deplore the one which requires that "One thing (or person) cannot occupy two places at the same time." (I'm afraid I have transposed it a little, but never mind.) I often wish I could fly from one spot to another without losing any time by the way ... I can't understand anyone living long in one place, & leaving it without regret – I couldn't even leave Vernon now without feeling very sorry to part from some of the people – & there would be a real pang in giving up our happy little home for some one else to inhabit. Of course, if we were able to go back home to live the compensations would be more than adequate, still I freely confess some of my heartstrings are quite firmly caught here. [7 May 1895]

It is seven o'clock here – ten at home. I wonder what they are doing & who all are there – Mother, Father, Wese and Hubert – maybe Maude & the baby & probably Walter, Roy & little Louise. I can picture the dear old dining room, & each familiar face, & how they would look if I were to surprise them by walking in at the door – but I'm afraid it is only into their thoughts I can enter for some time – & I feel sure there is no surprise connected with that entry – it takes place too often. [1 January 1897]

The other day I was lamenting the necessary move from our pretty little home in Vernon, & I asked Hal if he didn't sometimes get homesick for it. He said no – he was satisfied here – and I said "I don't believe you get as much attached to places as I do." His answer made me feel very shamefaced, all the more because he did not in the least mean to reproach me – he just said very quietly "Oh yes I do, the only difference is, I get attached to the place where *I am,* and you are attached to the place where *you were."* I know there was a great deal of truth in it. I am too apt to try to have the past as well as the present, & to mourn because my hands cannot hold fast all the joys which pass through their grasp – instead of being thankful that there is always room in ones hearts to store all the love and blessings of a life-time – even though they are not held close in our clasp each day. [18 May 1897]

There is a glorious sun-set across the bay, but sea-sickness and home-sickness combined are great deadeners of appreciation. I feel if I could only have the ones I love with me any natural objects would be vastly brightened. After all, human companionship is the greatest joy and satisfaction. I mean real companionship & not just society. [25 September 1897]

The present holds much of joy and restful happiness for me "but the tender grace of a day that is dead can never come back to me." Those days were gleeful, where these are quietly content. One who has a happy youth to remember has a possession that none can take away; but pain & pleasure are sometimes so closely intermingled that it is hard to analyze them. [20 June 1894]

HOUSEKEEPING:
... I had a great cleaning up in the kitchen. I do think one enjoys the parlor more when there is a consciousness that each corner of the kitchen would bear inspection – & that's a way I don't always feel. I know quite well I am not what would be called a good housekeeper[5] – but Hal says I satisfy him – & I know if I never neglected my house I'd have to neglect all outside interests. [11 April 1894]

Hal says he used to think I exhibited simply eccentricity in always putting articles in a new spot; but now he knows it is genuine, the number of places I can find in a small room to put things. He has just been having a great hunt for his overshoes. I really have no bump of order. I don't believe I could endure the monotony of having everything in its place all the time. I suppose systematic workers accomplish more in a given time – but the enjoyment would be taken out of labour if I had a certain day and hour for each occupation. As it is, I enjoy doing my work, for I do each kind just when I feel disposed. It is well for me that Harold is not a man who cares more for his dinner than anything else, for when the sewing mania seizes me – today for instance – I just get whatever happens to be in the pantry, and at other times I quite enjoy cooking a lot of good things. I sewed all the morning, & after dinner until nearly three. [12 December 1894]

I do think it makes a room so cheerless to have wet clothes hanging around – they are sure to switch against one in a sudden movement. [21 February 1895]

I did up my room ... I must try not to get any spots on anything. It does make one feel better to see everything white and clean – soap and water are very mighty factors in the world's economy. [27 March 1895]

I ... have been three times down to the ranch since the end of June, and when I was at home I was busy preserving ... [I] have made strawberry, gooseberry & black currant jam, and have sealed down raspberries and ollallies. I am hoping to make red currant jelly tomorrow. The preserve closet already looks fairly well ready for winter, and I expect to be able to get some fall fruit this year. Last year, of course, I was at home and did not get any at all, as everything was frozen up when I got back here. I think I quite like preserving, though it is hot work. [18 July 1895]

I remember Miss Higman used to think cooking, & talk of cooking was very groveling work, but if she lived here she might come to think it quite elevating to the mind. The health of the body cannot be maintained without wholesome viands – so it isn't atall unimportant to be a good cook ... This morning I made pies and a cake & then tidied the kitchen pantry – and gave a great cleaning up to the kitchen – so I have the satisfactory feeling that tomorrow I won't mind what corner of the house any body spies into, for it is all ready for inspection ... [24 August 1895]

I was busy all the morning arranging things in my new porch. It is almost too large to be properly called a porch – more a shed I suppose. Hal says I am like a child with a new playhouse, & I confess I have found great satisfaction in establishing authority over this new domain, if it be only a kitchen porch. I am afraid some of my tastes are decidedly plebeian, for I do enjoy work, and the details, rather than the theory of domestic economy. Indeed I don't think I have any theory ... I let my next idea come to me as I work, & have no settled plan for any day's proceeding. [8 November 1895]

... [upstairs] seemed to me crying out for sweeping, dusting & a general cleansing. I turned out the clothes closets & hung all the clothes on the line – one never realizes how rich one is in possessions until housecleaning or moving is undertaken ... I think six hours a day is about all I care to work, then I want to rest, as I have worked with all my might. It is only at extra busy times that I work more than a couple or three hours. [31 March 1896]

Hal always laughs at me for having a general "cleaning up" whenever any visitors leave – but indeed the house always needs it, for I neglect everything I possibly can, so that I won't have to work all the time. [21 June 1896]

I trimmed a lie back collar with cream lace & made a black velvet girdle – tight sleeves with large loose frill over the shoulder and a little fullness in back and front of [the] waist. It is really quite pretty, but I do find it so uninteresting to sew for myself. I don't enjoy it atall. [4 March 1897]

I have worked so steadily I think it would do me good to take a rest – & yet the embroidery is very fascinating – I hate to leave it when I once get seated at it. [15 March 1898]

I have had such a bustling week. I suppose it is because we live rather quietly – but confusion makes me far more tired now than actual work does. [2 October 1898]

I have been adding up my accounts. I never come out quite right – generally I have a few cents too many or too few in my purse, and Hal rather laughs at my attempts at book keeping, but I am often glad to know just how the money has gone. [14 March 1899]

LAUGHTER:
... it kills all the joy in many a life – not being able to see the merry side. I think out here there is very little joking – and laughter – honest joyous fun is truly a great sweetener of home & society. I think we usually look to those who thoroughly sympathize with us for participation in our merriment and here there are so few family circles – the country is so largely filled with solitary men or young couples. It is a real treat to get in a real home nest like the Pellys, where, for the younger members, at least there are none of the hidden, hungry longings for other days and other places, which must tame, even if they do not sadden, the spirits of us older ones. [7 March 1894]

CORRESPONDENCE:
I did not get my usual home letter yesterday, & ... I think of all sorts of dreadful possibilities, and have found it really hard to be bright & cheerful yesterday and today. One's imagination has much to do with one's happiness or unhappiness. [21 February 1894]

Hal says when I get to be an angel he is afraid I'll use up all the feathers in my wings making pens. He has warned Nonah not to fall too readily into the Barrett way of writing so many letters. He says he never saw any-one to equal us – but I notice he always enjoys having me read the home letters to him, & wants to see the diary every night – so I don't think he considers our writing so much a very grievous failing. [3 January 1895]

I have been writing to Frank and to Uncle Harry – and feel as if I had nearly exhausted both my fingers and my thoughts. [27 November 1895]

I never seem satisfied with my letters – I am insatiable in my hunger for home news. [13 December 1897]

THE WEST:
For [this] new wild life a man needs a peculiarly strong and yet flexible character. If he be of a nature that too readily can suit himself to circum-stances he is apt to sink to fit his surroundings. On the other hand, if he cannot put up with the absence of luxury & refinement his life must be a kind of purgatory. Very few are able to raise their surroundings to meet them, though, thank God, there are both men and women who live noble, loving, true lives in [the] Wild West as in the older East – in backwoods as in cultured drawing rooms – & they are a boon and a blessing wherever they are. I think, though, that even the strongest feel a longing sometimes for the ease and rest that wealth and luxury (in its ideal sense) bring. [26 January 1892]

We had quite a discussion – Hal & Mr. Fortune for the west, & the rest of us "contrary." I know very well Hal doesn't admire it out here as much as he sometimes pretends to. A good many people have to persuade them-selves that grapes out of reach are sour – but I know if this particular bunch (Ontario) should fall to us, we'd devour it with delight. [15 March 1894]

LITERATURE:
If [Kipling] would not so often be so disgustingly vulgar & profane he'd be much pleasanter reading. I think he spoils his books by such rough lan-guage. People excuse old writers for coarse language by saying it was "the times they lived in" – & yet there were clean – as well as clever – writers of the same date – and so they say of Kipling now "oh it is true to the life he pictures" but I'm sure quite often his portrayals could be as strong and telling with much of the bad language left out ... in Wee Willie Winkie there is a real understanding of child nature, & not much that is objec-tionable. [6 August 1899]

What a blessing the world of fiction is to us, often taking our thoughts from our own worries and teaching us many lessons of hope & trust. I have needed those lessons lately – I have been a good deal troubled & perplexed. I know it is not right to weakly hide ourselves behind the words "all is for the best" when our own mistakes or wrongdoing have brought us into trouble. Evil cannot be "best" ever – or anywhere – but surely when our eyes seem blindfolded, just when we have to decide which of two ways to take, if we put our hand trustingly in the Father's hand, He will not lead us astray. Perhaps He may not lead us into green pastures or still waters, but if *He leads,* we can bear all else. [24 November 1891]

I am getting to have a more voracious appetite for reading than ever, & I never did need to improve that appetite. Perhaps I care too much for the puddings and cakes of literature, and not enough for more nourishing food. [5 December 1895]

I have been absorbed in The Wandering Jew – I think it is the most interesting novel I ever read. Not only is the plot thrilling and exciting – but the insight one gets into the manners of the times in all classes of men – the enlightened view taken of the rights of labour – and above all the exposure of the violence of the work of the Jesuits – keeps one's interest & attention always excited. [1 May 1895]

I often wonder that I don't read Scott's poetry more often. It always does me good. It is so wholesome. No morbid sentimentality, no bitter sarcasm, but plenty of excitement of an honest healthy kind. [25 March 1892]

... I went to lie down with the newspapers. They were so full of horrors that I didn't have much comfort – R.R. accidents, cyclones – murders – everything distressing. [22 July 1895]

LIVING ALONE:
I think it must be dreadful to live alone – I really don't believe I could stand it. Little duties that are interesting and pleasant, when one feels that some one else will share the comfort they bring, become positively irksome when done for one's self alone. [19 December 1894]

LOVE:
It is only to the eyes of love that our little homely, everyday happenings would be interesting, but at home they like to hear all that we do & say, & there is so little I can do – all these weary miles away – to help or cheer them: that I am glad to do anything which I know pleases them. [6 February 1894]

I think I am truly thankful for all the good things God has given to me. I remember an old song "Tis the heart makes the home" and when there are love and peace within the walls it doesn't much matter about the walls themselves. [13 April 1894]

MORE ABOUT PEOPLE:
It seems a mistake, but it never does any good for an outsider to meddle – [people] will manage it their own way any way. [18 January 1894]

I often think, to people who like excitement & novelty, a monotonous every day life is very trying. I believe it is much harder on their nervous system to have enforced quiet, than it is for a quiet nature to be forced into gaiety – because we can be quiet and self contained even in a crowd. But the merry, pleasure loving soul cannot always find the companionship it needs any where except in a merry making throng. [4 February 1896]

I wonder if the people who have the reputation of being "always the same" really have no ups & downs of moods, or if it is that they are quite as much moved "in the depths" but are about to present a smooth surface. I am conscious that both without and within I am very variable, & more than any thing else, the frame of mind of those I am with affects my mental attitude. Hal has been worried & bothered over several things today and I, consequently, feel very quiet tonight. I feel so useless in the way of giving helpful council when difficulties arise. I distrust my own way of looking at things, for I know I am hasty in my judgments – so sometimes the best thing I can do is to keep quiet – but I really think that makes me more tired than any other effort I can make. [5 October 1897]

It seems queer to be right in town, as we are [in the Post Office] and yet have no neighbours. No friendly back yard to view, & be viewed by. Sometimes it is an advantage – sometimes not. [11 August 1899]

RELIGION:
... I have not as hard a spirit, even against Romanists, as I used to have – individually I like some of them well, but one feels the instability of a friendship with them if they are completely under the domination of the priests. [17 February 1894]

I do think one has to live in a house for some time before it gets an air of home. Perhaps the Christian Scientists[6] have some right in thinking that we write our individuality on the inanimate things about us. [14 November 1894]

If the Christian Scientist theory is true, I ought to feel very young. They say when one puts on any garments one renews the sensations felt at the time of wearing. [2 November 1897]

Everybody has a "but" – & the "but" in this case is that we can't have those we love near us. I suppose one of the many pains Christ bore to leave us "an example of Godly living" was this homesickness for the Father's house. If we can yearn so for the old earthly home, which we know is only for a time in existence, & if we can miss so sorely the rest & comfort of a parent's love, what must He have felt in leaving the house not made with hands – and the Almighty Father's presence. I don't think it is irreverent to feel that He will know how to make Heaven all the more homelike to us, because He knows an exile's feelings. [18 May 1897]

The Church of England people had a dance on Tuesday night ... It seems to me such a wrong way to get money for God's house. The church ought to wean us a little from the world surely, instead of encouraging the intimacy. [9 April 1899]

We went to the Salvation Army last night, and there is to be a social in the Presbyterian Church tomorrow night to which we may go, so we have quite a variety this week. Harold wanted to go to the Army, so of course I went with him – having none of the contempt for these people & their mode of working, which so many have. They seemed very earnest & hearty: of course they are largely uneducated people & many of their ways and words grate on one – but more, I think, because they lack refinement than because they lack reverence. I often think of that beautiful collect we pray "Stir up the will of thy faithful people, O Lord," and yet when there is a stirring up, we are apt to be distrustful & call it excitement. I think I love the dear old church better after any visit to another denomination – just as one comes home with renewed appreciation of its love & helpfulness after staying somewhere else. But I think, too, I can see that the Church of England never could be a spiritual home for some souls ... Heaven is, after all, the one grand house we travel to, and the churches are only inns for refreshment by the way side. [7 February 1894]

... I really live two lives – one at home, in Dover, where each little doing is full of interest – & also at home, here, for I think one can hardly live anywhere for a whole year without finding many to interest; & some to love. Then there is the ranch too, where I seem to belong. I wonder if

Solomon would have been wise enough to divide me up with satisfaction to all claimants. I am not a Solomon, & I do find the conflicting claims rather a tug on my heart strings – but I often think of that sentence "Thou camest not to thy place by accident." God knows what is best for us – but I do think if only someone – more capable – were in my place, so much more might be done. I seem to have so many more opportunities for service both for God & man than I fulfil. [26 January 1894]

... it never seems to me so sad for a young life to be transplanted to a brighter & purer home, before cares and sorrows have blighted or broken it – as it is to see an old life lasting on, withered and uncared for, as alas! the lives of some people are. Sometimes I think it is very beautiful to think of those young spirits, to whom *this* world has been all joy and hope, just moved to the other world where everything will be fulfillment not disappointment. Of course the hearts must ache that are left behind. [3 September 1896]

I was reading Macbeth this afternoon, & wondering what sort of an essay I could write on his character ... I'd be afraid even to attempt it. It seems essays on Shakespearean subjects are something like so many of the sermons we hear – just the reading of the text would be so much more effective. [19 November 1895]

This is Ash Wednesday Evening – the beginning of another Lent. I wonder if I will be able to fast from any sins this year! There are so many which "so easily beset me" that I don't know where to begin.
[19 February 1896]

If the soul grows strong in solitude there ought to be a good tough strain in mine just now, as I have been alone all day, except for a little while this afternoon. [15 December 1895]

SEASONS:
I do think Spring awakens old memories more than any other season.
   "When swallows build & leaves break forth
   My old sorrow wakes and cries"
and not only our old sorrows, but the joys of other years seem to stir anew in our hearts when Spring comes. We have had that lovely bright weather lately which makes one long to grow, as all outdoor things do. [17 March 1892]

SOCIALIZING:
I know [Hal] does not care for going out, & sometimes I feel very selfish in wanting to go – then again I feel that it is really better for both of us to get shaken out of our jog-trot now & then. It is a very happy contented jog-trot I will allow, but the social instinct should be encouraged out here. I am sure we are too apt to look for all our happiness just inside our own home – and it isn't fair to ourselves or our neighbours to narrow joy down to that one spot. No doubt a life cannot be a happy one unless home is the fountain of its peace & refreshment, but we don't want to keep all the waters of a fountain shut up in their source – it would be of little use then, and so I think a happy home ought to strengthen and beautify our character that its influence may be more wide spread. [28 November 1894]

VISITING:
I hope we'll be alone, for of course, if visitors come in it puts a stop to everything. [4 December 1895]

I am not nearly so fond of going out as I used to be, though I still enjoy seeing different people. [9 January 1896]

It is so nice to be quiet that I hardly like even to write. I just like to enjoy the restfulness of the house – not that I dislike having visitors – I really enjoy it – but there has been such a confusion and bustle lately that we appreciate quiet. [9 January 1898]

WAR:
My interest has been divided lately between wondering if Spain & the United States[7] will fight, & if my hen will bring out any young ducks. I can't form any decided opinion on either question, but think tomorrow will tell. I hope there won't be war, and that there will be ducks, but cannot do anything but wait & see in either case. [12 April 1898]

War is really declared. Rumour says that the Spaniards have captured a large American liner "The City of Paris" & the Americans have taken two Spanish merchant vessels. I dread this war – I fear so much that the other nations will be drawn in before the trouble is ended. The world has been a long time without a big war now – & fighting is very catching, besides it seems to me there is such a spirit of unrest abroad – men only too ready for excitement and adventure, even the terrible excitement of war. [26 April 1898]

POVERTY AND WEALTH:
I was reading some old Scotch proverbs, and was much struck by one "God help great fowk, the poor can beg." It seems to me that the needs and longings which come with riches are harder to bear properly, than the necessity of poverty. It is better for us to have to work for common needs – less time is spent in vain & useless work. [11 April 1892]

Mr. Crozier had some funny stories to tell of the "green hands" up there [at the Guisachan Ranch]. One cannot help laughing, & yet it is pitiful, too, to think of the discomfort many of them go through for want of tact & adaptability. Perhaps, in a workaday world, being bred to the purple isn't such an advantage as many of us try to believe it is. For my part, I think the prayer of Agur was a wise one – "Give me neither poverty nor riches." [7 January 1892]

I was so pleased to get the toast rack [for Christmas] – I have wished for one very often, but hated to say so, because I have so much, it seems very selfish to draw attention to the few little things which are lacking. [27 December 1894]

After dinner I went down to Mrs. Crowell's house to help them cut sand- wiches for the Odd fellows social ... It is a lovely house – I only wish we could afford to buy it, furnish it properly & keep it up nicely – but then, if we could afford that we could afford a still better scheme – to go home to Dover to live. [23 February 1896]

WEATHER:
I do rather dread the heat but I try not to think of it very much – perhaps it won't be so hot & dry as it was last year. [8 April 1895]

It is very hot, but I have to light the fire, for I have steak, new potatoes and cauliflower to cook. [9 July 1896]

Mrs. McLeod called, and it made me hot to look at her. She had on a tight black dress. I don't think of dressing in any thing but cotton since this heat came, and indeed very little of that. [9 July 1896]

Of course the muddy roads & mild weather are bad for trade and the merchants grumble but one cannot help thinking how much easier it is for poor people. They do not need much wood, or nearly so much food and clothing as they do in bitterly cold weather and for us, it has been nice, because we have been able so far to use the little back kitchen for all kitchen work. [30 November 1899]

WEIGHT:
I am afraid I am going to be enormous when I get old. I used to laugh about growing fat, & say it was my great desire – but I don't know now whether I do long for it so very much. [18 November 1895]

Hal went with me in to Martin's and weighed me, & I weigh 130½ without my cloak. To be sure my clothing is heavier now than in the summer, but I think I have gained in weight – any way I haven't lost any thing. [24 November 1895]

THE ROLE OF WOMEN:
Mrs. Offerhaus was holding forth the other day on the necessity of "training" for girls, but I do think boys need it almost more. Mrs. Offerhaus says if she had a dozen daughters, they should all be trained to some useful occupation so that if chance threw them on the world they might be self reliant and self supporting. I did not agree with her – in general – and probably fell in her estimation when I affirmed that I was not fitted for any particular branch of work or business, and yet if occasion required I would not be afraid that I could not get through the world, usefully too, without being a burden on anyone's pity or charity. It is more in the nature than the education after all. I was reminded of the old fable of the fox & the cat. The fox was boasting how many ways he had of avoiding danger while poor pussy only possessed the one power of getting up a tree, and yet when the dogs came, while the fox was debating which way he should take, the cat watched his capture and death, safely perched in a neighbouring tree. Not that I would insinuate that women have but one escape from trials & tribulations (marriage) – I mean if a woman can climb, she will surely find a perch. [8 April 1892]

I really believe I . . . could turn lecturer with a little study, but I do feel terribly sorry for a woman who earns her living in such a public way – & I couldn't help thinking does she really earn her living – for after all, the success of such a line of life depends on people's interest in themselves, & it seems to me true teaching & true wisdom always tend to make us forget ourselves. I never have believed much in the merit of self-examination, except where it directly produces repentance & humility. [1 April 1894]

YOUTH:

... I don't believe any of us would love the young as well if they were always wise and reasonable – their varying moods form their great charm. [22 July 1895]

I hardly know whether to pity most the young or the old when unhappiness comes – the young feel so keenly, but then hope is often stronger – the old suffer more patiently, but often more despairingly. [26 November 1895]

CHAPTER 12

The women work much harder than the men

Attitudes towards Other Races

For the contemporary reader, Alice Barrett Parke's attitudes towards the local aboriginal population are problematic. Like the average colonist, she viewed herself as culturally and morally superior to aboriginal peoples in the area and referred to them regularly as "Siwashes" and "Klootchmen." She had no ethical reservations about the belief that Whites had the right to usurp aboriginal land, subjugate the aboriginal population, take advantage of them in trade, and belittle their social systems. In the course of his job as provincial constable, Hal Parke came into frequent contact with the aboriginal people who lived at the Head of the Lake Reserve; Alice's interactions with First Nations peoples, however, were limited and were never intimate. For the most part, they were remote from her daily existence and could be ignored. As a result of her husband's interaction with the Okanagan tribe, Alice came to associate First Nations peoples with unlawful behaviour and untrustworthiness.

The passages in her diaries that describe the local aboriginal people showed a fascination with what she considered to be the "oddities" of the Okanagan tribe's culture. She was typical of her time in that her writing was patronising much of the time; she could not ignore what she perceived to be the dirtiness of the aboriginal encampments she visited, and she was contemptuous of a work ethic so different from her own. She displayed an arrogance born of the assumption that aboriginal peoples were beneath her – a typically middle-class supremacist attitude that remained unshaken.

She could, however, evince surprise and gratitude for acts of kindness she received from aboriginal people, but she made no effort to develop a closer acquaintance with them. She was content to view and comment upon them from afar:

I was introduced to Mr. Tronson,[1] such a nice man, so gentlemanly & fine looking – he is married to a squaw![2] – lives in Vernon. [19 July 1891]

Lizzie was struck, as all newcomers are, by the dirty look of the store, asked me how often they shoveled it out! To make matters worse, it was full of Indians, squaws and little papooses.[3] One tiny little girl with her dress pinned up with about two dozen safety pins was flying round in everyone's way, and she was so small she seemed under one's feet before she was noticed ... I ... was wakened in the middle of the night by the greatest babel of voices outside. I could tell it was Indians talking in Chinook. Harry was answering them, but all I could make out was "Halo Halo" (no-no). A papoose began to cry and at last they moved off. I called out to know what it all meant & Harry said they wanted to put their horses in the stable. He had no room, so they went a few yards down the fence & camped. They were there this morning when we got up ... [21 November 1891]

During the cross-Canada journey after her marriage she had written:

The porter was telling [Hal] this morning that if white men & coloured people had stayed where Nature meant them to, no-one would have suffered last night – for this country was only meant for Indians and buffalo. [31 January 1893]

Once back in the Okanagan she continued to record brief encounters:

The walking was slippery & I was wishing someone had been driving our way. We had, however, reached the boundary of Harry's ranch, about half a mile from the cabin, when we heard sleigh bells behind us. It proved to be a hay rack driven by a Siwash – he however very politely stopped and asked if we would ride – so we perched ourselves on behind & gaily drove up to the door, where our cavalier very politely touched his hat & said "good day." [1 March 1894]

Hal has gone down town to see if Mr. Millar[4] is back – Mr. Norris sent him out to the reserve to serve a warrant on a half breed. They expected him back by noon, & at six tonight there was still no sign of him. I do hope he has not got into any trouble – Hal says he has made all the Indians dislike him. He is afraid of nothing, & is rather inclined to be quarrelsome. [5 May 1894]

Hal did not fall in love with the Lower Country, though he says there are some splendid peach orchards, & other fruit. The finest land is on the Indian Reserves. [3 June 1894]

Thursday afternoon Hal drove me out to Mrs. O'Keefe's. He had to go on to the Indian Reserve – there was some trouble among the Siwashes – so he left me at Mrs. O'Keefe's while he was gone, about an hour and a half. [16 June 1894]

We went through miles of fine country – all Indian reserve. There were two little bunches of houses, one they call Black-town[5] – and the names suit in many respects. [4 July 1894]

... at seven Hal came in. He was pretty tired & stiff – having ridden seventy miles since he left home, & having had very little sleep the night he was away. A half breed, Isaac Harris,[6] went with him as guide. They struck the camp on Short's Mountain about 7 o'clock. Hal said it was quite a picturesque sight the bright camp fires, and the tents – they surprised the man they were after and took him prisoner without any trouble, but had to watch him all night. He is accused of the very unromantic offence of stealing pigs! Isaac is a fine looking fellow, he has been here to see Hal. He is a very respectable Siwash, & often helps the Government to keep order on the reserves. [17 November 1894]

Hal had to go out to the Indian Reserve right after breakfast. They were fearing a grand Xmas carouse, drinking and consequently fighting, but Hal found all very quiet. He saw the chief – Isaac – & indeed most of the Indians – as they were just gathering in to church. Bazill,[7] a big Siwash, who has more than once given serious trouble, was ringing the bell, looking as solemn as a Bishop. [24 December 1894]

We had to go out to the Reserve near O'Keefe's before coming on home, to see some Indians. While we were waiting at the door of one of the houses, (Hal talking to a couple of the Indians old Chewile & Francis) a woman, squaw, came out on the step, & looked at me for a while – then slowly came over to the buggy, & smiled & held out her hand; such a little brown hand. I shook it of course, & smiled back at her and said "Good-day" but she didn't seem even to understand that. Nearly all the men talk more or less English but the squaws don't even try to. [16 April 1895]

Kelowna is on Lake Okanagan – a flat spot in the midst of hills – opening towards the Lake. The opposite shore is not far away, & rises up in a high, thickly wooded mountain, with one beautiful point of land which is Indian Reserve – more than a thousand acres of good farm land which lies idle, as the Indians are not numerous enough to work it. [19 May 1895]

[Hal] sent young Tronson down to [jail in] Kamloops. He said he felt sorry for Mr. Tronson – he seemed quite "broken up" over his boy's bad actions. One of his little grandchildren died yesterday. I often feel very sorry for Mr. Tronson. He is undoubtedly a gentleman by birth & education, a very nice man to talk too – but this unfortunate marriage with a squaw must be an unceasing source of trouble & disgrace. He has a good many boys, & they all are wild reckless fellows. Mr. Tronson appears to be fond of them, & to give them a great deal, but I don't think he has tried to train or guide them. Often it seems to me that some men's punishment is out of all proportion to their offences. No doubt it was foolish & wrong of him as a young man to become entangled & to drift into this companionship & marriage, but many men do so much worse, & appear to go free from evil consequences. Of course we cannot see the inner life – & there must be more justice than we know in the way events fall out. [25 September 1895]

[Hal] had to go out to the reserve immediately after breakfast this morning, to see why the prisoners had not been sent in as promised. He says the old chief, Louis Jim,[8] has them tied up, but will not let them be brought in until the stolen goods are identified. [30 January 1896]

Hal did not get home from the reserve until after six. I was getting quite anxious – I could not help fearing there had been some trouble as I knew the old chief did not want to give the prisoners up. Mr. Lowe went with Hal – they had quite a long "wak-wak" at the old chief's (that means "Council"). Hal said the chief did not want to give up the prisoners – he wants to punish them himself. He is a regular old heathen & does not like to give up any of his ancient privileges. Hal said about thirty Siwashes were at the Council & they argued the matter for three hours and a half. At last Hal said "Very well! If you won't give the men up, the Queen will send men enough to take them prisoner and you too will have to come to jail." But the old chief warily said "Well, I don't think the Queen and I are very good friends any way, I have never been baptized or married – & my land isn't baptized either. And who will know that I am a chief if you take my prisoners away from me?" "But," said Hal "that is just what will show you are a chief if you give them up to me. If I take them & you to jail, then everyone will laugh at you and you will no more be a chief." The reason he says he isn't a friend of the Queen's, & isn't baptized, is that he won't have the church (he has built one) consecrated, or let the priest go in it. He lets the people, who are all about half converted to Roman Catholicism, go in it & pray, and then when they come out he harangues them, teaching them their duty according to his lights. Hal & Mr. Lowe could not take the prisoners, as in the first place they did not know which house they were confined in, & in the next they need the evidence of the other Siwashes to prove the theft, so fair means were the only ones that could result in success. Hal said he was afraid he never would have been successful in the end, only that two half breeds stood with him right through and pleaded well. One man, the Chief's Captain – Camaskit – was very much opposed to giving up the men. He said "We might as well die at once as give up all our rights," but Long Edward[9] rose and said "You may die if you like, you are not much good any way, but I and my family will not be fools enough to die fighting the Queen." Hal says he was rather surprised at Long Edward being so friendly to him, as he once had to be brought in on a summons himself. I suppose it is hard for them to understand the complications of the law. The old chief couldn't understand why the Queen wouldn't be satisfied if he would make the men give up the stolen goods, & he would punish them. He said "I'll punish them hard enough – she needn't be afraid of that!" Hal said it was comical, & yet pathetic how he clung to what he thought his rights, & how he evidently felt the responsibility of his position as chief. His final argument was "When I go up to God & He asks me what I did with my prisoners, it will shame me to say I gave them up to the White man – and what shall I say to Him?" However, after it all he said "If I bring them in to you, will that do?" and Hal said "Yes" – so he has promised to bring them in on Tuesday, when the accuser is to come up from the lower country. Hal said as they rode home Mr. Lowe said "I declare Job isn't in it with you for patience – I never could have stayed to talk[10] so long" – but it was well worth while to win the result peaceably. Hal came home very well pleased. He says he was well satisfied with the general feeling among the Indians – they did not oppose their chief, but the large majority were plainly desirous to give up the prisoners quietly. When the Indian Agent was here last fall he went out to see this Chief and he told Mr. Norris that he very much feared there would be serious trouble if any occasion arose when the Authority of the Government & the Chief came in opposition to each other – so it is quite a feather in Hal's cap to have managed it peacefully. [1 February 1896]

Hal has brought a Chinook dictionary home & is studying it. It is very useful to master the jargon if one has much to do with the Indians. [4 February 1896]

We drove first down through the Indian Reserve which lies along the west side of Okanagan Lake. When we had driven through about a mile of Reserve we saw an old Indian with glasses on clearing small trees away, and Hal said he was at one time quite a noted character. He came from the American side of the boundary and in early days killed many white men (he did not look exactly tame yet). Seven miles farther on we came to Blacktown – a bunch of shabby looking houses. A good many Klootch-men[11] in very ragged clothes but with gay silk handkerchiefs tied around their heads were sitting or standing about their doors. None of them seemed to be working except one woman who was washing, and I never knew before that one could wash clothes and look idle. Several pigs with very sharp snouts and large families were eating what ever they could find, and a great many dogs were barking around, but we did not see any men. I suppose they were in the fields. We drove on a couple of miles farther to the place of a Siwash named Lame John. He had been fencing up the road and Hal had to go out to investigate. He was not home so we came back to the Reserve at the Head of the Lake, just opposite the O'Keefe's, but first we stopped under a big tree and ate our lunch. Hal saw the man he wanted and we drove on to the ranch, reaching there a little after three. I was tired but enjoyed my little visit there very much. [27 April 1896]

While living at the BX Ranch:

I was a good deal amused this morning. A Klootchman rode up with a string of fish and was trying to get Lou-ee to buy them from her. It is hard enough for us to comprehend either the Chinamen or the Siwashes, but it is a shade worse when they are trying to hold a conversation with each other. Hal was standing by on the veranda letting them do the bargaining, & I was peeping from the kitchen window quite enjoying the scene. Lou-ee's look of superiority when he would offer the woman "haf' a dolla" and then turn to Hal with a smile of pity when she seemed not to understand but jabbered away, evidently extolling the "good salmon" as she called them. However in the end Lou-ee decided the fish were no good, so she did not make a sale. [8 November 1896]

At noon a Siwash came out with a horse from Mr. Norris (one he had promised to send). The Siwash, Johnnie Pierrot,[12] is a prisoner in the jail – he works about outside the place, splitting wood etc. but it did strike me as funny to send him out of town on horseback leading another horse. I wonder if there is another country under the sun where justice is thus administered! – where prisoners are sent alone on horseback on important messages. [29 January 1897]

The other morning when Hal was in town, a big, fine looking Siwash rode up & asked to see him. I went out to the gate to speak to the man & he dismounted & held quite a long conversation with me – he wanted to get the job of breaking horses. He talked very virtuously of how well a man could get on with a horse if he treated it kindly, & didn't drink, or ill use it etc. etc. He waited to see Hal, & I was rather surprised to hear when Hal came in the house that it was the famous Bazille I had been talking to – the winter I was at Harry's he created a great excitement on the reserve, by attempting to kill the chief. He wanted to be chief himself as his father was before him – but his own wild ways & bad habits made the Indians choose another man to succeed his father. I think he is steady now, but he isn't exactly a model of all the virtues. However, he is really a handsome man, and a perfect rider. [20 May 1897]

Yesterday there were a great many Siwashes about all the afternoon. Isaac Harris came out in the morning, but the others didn't come until afternoon as they had all gone to a funeral in the morning. They took 10 horses to break for saddle work. [22 May 1897]

... Isaac Harris came to say that the Siwashes would be here that afternoon to bring back the horses they had been breaking ... [3 June 1897]

We did not get any strawberries picked today – it rained a little early in the morning and made everything too wet for the Klootchmen to pick. [30 June 1897]

While [Hal] was in town a queer trio of pickers came to be paid – an old white headed Siwash with a blue handkerchief tied around his head & a very dirty piece of white cloth flapping down over one eye – with him an old wrinkled Klootchman and a young girl about 14, dressed in the queerest collection of rags that I ever saw. None of them could – or would – talk English and I couldn't speak enough Chinook to make them understand very well. However, I got them persuaded at last that Hal had gone to town, so they would have to come back later on. Quite a gang came just as it was getting dark, & there was quite a picturesque scene out in the yard. Hal had his lantern on an upturned barrel, and all the oddly dressed group were gathered around while he paid them. However much ignorance they may assume (for it is more often feigned than real) about speaking English, they are all uncommonly sharp when it comes to dollars & cents. Each one knew exactly what was coming to him or her. One little incident amused me very much. The last to be paid were an Indian, his squaw and their boy. The man & boy both had a good deal to say about the amount and the change. Hal was short of small change so was going to pay the three in a lump sum. It came to $18.50 – he counted it out carefully – the man stood lighting his pipe with a very swaggering air, & the boy quite consequentially reached over to pick up & recount the money, while the squaw with an indifferent mournful expression stood silently by. I thought how hard it seemed that she should have none of the money, for the women work much harder than the men and I was wondering if they wouldn't give her something when I saw her quietly reach out her hand and take the 50 cent piece which the boy had left on the barrel while he folded up the bills. I felt quite pleased thinking she was going to get that much any way, but when the boy had carefully & slowly folded the money, again out came her hand and she took it *all!* – the man and boy looking as if that was quite what they expected. Hal says the women do get hold of most of the money, and that they are inveterate gamblers, particularly if a horse race is going on – they will bet every thing they possess. [26 October 1897]

Hal took the road foreman on to the Reserve to inspect a road. One of the Indians was making trouble over the road and Hal had to interview him. [13 June 1898]

... one of the Indians told Walter Cochrane that every man, woman & child on the Indian Reserve was coming in to see the [circus]. [24 August 1898]

There was a tremendous crowd in town – I never saw so many people gathered together here. Indians, Chinamen and Whites – men, women & children. [1 September 1898]

Lizzie came down after tea, & went with us to hear Pauline Johnstone.[13] We called for Mrs. Cameron too. We all thought Pauline was very good. She is certainly clever and entertaining. [16 April 1899]

After Hal took up the position of postmaster in 1899, there was no further mention of "Indians."

CHAPTER 13

Hob-nobbing with a Countess

Early Feminism in Western Canada

In January 1892 Alice had first become aware of Lord and Lady Aberdeen's connection with the Okanagan Valley. Two years later, in November, she made the acquaintance of one of the most remarkable figures ever to grace the political stage in Canada. Ishbel, Countess of Aberdeen, and her husband, the governor general of Canada,[1] owned ranches at Guisachan in Kelowna and at Coldstream[2] east of Vernon, and they headed the effort to establish orchards and hop fields in the area. Politically Liberal and a staunch feminist, the Countess set about organizing the women of the area as social activists, and the establishment of Vernon's first hospital was inspired by her efforts and encouragement. Men and women alike found her exhortations irresistible.

Despite a preference for individual and independent works of charity, Alice found herself drawn into Lady Aberdeen's circle and agreed – reluctantly – to become a founding member of the Vernon chapter of the National Council of Women. Her fears about committee work were to prove well founded:

Mr. Crozier ... says the Earl of Aberdeen is doing a lot of work on his ranch,[3] employing a number of men & putting up a lot of buildings ... Mr. Crozier had some funny stories to tell of the "green hands" up there. One cannot help laughing, & yet it is pitiful, too, to think of the discomfort many of them go through for want of tact & adaptability. Perhaps, in a workaday world, being bred to the purple isn't such an advantage as many of us try to believe it is. [7 January 1892]

Vernon has had a visit from His Excellency the Governor-General & Lady Aberdeen,[4] and everyone has been delighting to do him honour. They held a reception in the court house to which all the world and his wife went, and on Monday they had a public meeting to try and persuade the citizens to establish a public library, as Lord Aberdeen has given a building & stoves, & Mr. Ellison has promised fire wood for the winter. It has been determined to make an attempt to establish one on a small scale.[5] Hal is one of the committee, & is very enthusiastic over it. It would, I certainly think, be a good thing for many a homeless young man to have a warm comfortable place to spend his evenings. [1 November 1894]

[Mrs. Ellison] wanted me to go with her to Mrs. Cameron's to see about this concert they are getting up for the benefit of the reading room. I am not on the committee and Hal had fought well for me to keep my name out of it, because I impressed it on him that I have no talent whatsoever for organization, but I did not like to refuse to go with Mrs. Ellison, so I went & we had quite a conversation on the street as we met Mrs. Cameron, Miss MacIntyre, Mr. Hankey and Mr. McKelvie. I don't think any of them know exactly what they want, & they talk too much with no definite idea to work upon. I know that "it takes very little talent to find fault" – but even where one knows ones self faulty it is possible to see failings in others. After much talk they thought of several who might be asked, & I invited the ladies of the committee to come here tomorrow afternoon to tell the results of their efforts. [6 November 1894]

Mr. Wilson … came to say that Lady Aberdeen wants to get up some Woman's Council[6] here & he wanted me to help. I don't know, of course, what they want me to do, but I won't take any leading part, for a good many reasons. First, I have sense enough to know that I have no executive ability – I mean for business meetings and organizations, & managing & leading others. Then I really haven't time to give to any public working – I have my house to look after – Harry & Nonah to help sometimes – a frequent neighbourly kindness to do, many little calls on my time which I don't think it would be right to neglect … Then my last reason, & perhaps my strongest, is that I do not whole heartedly approve of "Associations" & "Societies." I remember one remark made by Dr. Battersby of Chatham. I never thought him a very clever man, but I don't forget one thing he said. He was speaking of a lady who had come to Chatham to organize a branch of The King's Daughters, & had asked to be allowed to speak in his church, & to have his help in her work. He said half comically, half exasperatedly "The world is organized to death" and I think he wasn't wrong. So little is done now by individual effort – no doubt unity is strength but there is the other side too. Supposing something *does* break down the union, the scattered remnants have no individual strength. It's hard to know what to do. I suppose the trend of the world is all towards amalgamation, but I think enough of the old fashion is left to last my life in spite of co-operative kitchens. I am still able to cook my own dinner – in spite of clubs & societies and lodges we spend our evenings in our own home – & in spite of kindergartens, if I had any children they'd be brought up as an individual and not by wholesale on a system. I suppose if I were to see Lady Aberdeen I'd listen meekly to all she has to say, & never air one of my old fashioned notions – but I'd "scissors" to myself just the same. I think she is a good woman, with an honest desire to improve & to help those she is among, & I wouldn't want to discourage ever so little (for of course my opinion would be "ever so little") any thing she may attempt. So I was not sorry I had rheumatism in my shoulder, which, for the present, makes a simple & conclusive excuse for taking no active part in her efforts. [19 September 1895]

There is to be a much talked of marriage tomorrow – Beatrice Myott, a protégée of Lady Aberdeen's, is to marry Mr. Lowe the Deputy Sheriff. Lady Aberdeen is giving a wedding breakfast at the Kalemalka for them. We were asked, but are not going. My shoulder is still too lame for me to enjoy sitting up stiff & straight for a couple of hours with a light dress on, & we are only too glad of an excuse. [25 September 1895]

... Mr. Outerbridge came to ask [if I] wouldn't allow my name to [be] given in to Lady Aberdeen as [one] who was willing to help in this Woman's Council. I resisted [for a] long time, but at last he [gained] a half hearted acquiescence [from me] and went away ... After tea we went to Lady Aberdeen's meeting. I won't attempt to report her speech. I was convinced that I had a wrong impression of the aim & objects of the Woman's National Council. It in no way promotes "Woman's rights"[7] in an offensive acceptation of the phrase – nor does it encourage the new woman[8] in the very slightest. It seems to me simply a movement to promote greater unity of feeling between women of all sects and denominations by affording a platform of common interests upon which they may meet and confer together – and to awaken and strengthen patriotism by making women in all parts of the Dominion cognizant of, and interested in, the good works in which the different provinces are concerned. Hal says he thinks it is a splendid scheme. Of course we do not hope very great things from our own little local branch (for one has been established here) but "many a mickle makes a muckle" and we can but do our best. [6 October 1895]

Miss Phipps ... wanted to go with me to Lady Aberdeen's meeting. I forgot to say that Saturday night they appointed a committee of ladies to meet her excellency yesterday afternoon & consult as to the advisability of establishing a branch of the Council here. I was one of those chosen. There were twenty-two altogether. We met in the Reading Room, and had a very enjoyable meeting. It is a pleasure & a privilege to be associated in any way with a woman like Lady Aberdeen. I believe she is very good – & though I can't exactly say that I am very hopeful of any great results from this Vernon Branch still I think we ought to try. After all my protestations I have accepted a place on the Committee – that of Corresponding Secretary. Miss MacIntyre is Recording Secretary, Mrs. Cochrane President, Mrs. Harber Treasurer & there are 7 Vice Presidents. We talked so long & so late that I did not get home until nearly six. [8 October 1895]

We stopped at ... at Mrs. Greenhow's ... I wanted to speak to her about the woman's council. She & Mrs. O'Keefe intend to come in on Tuesday, as they want to meet Lady Aberdeen. Of course the Tuesday meeting is really a Committee meeting, and should be private, but, under the circumstances I think it is all right for Mrs. O'Keefe & Mrs. Greenhow to come, as they were unable to attend the last meeting. [20 October 1895]

All of yesterday afternoon was taken up with the meeting of the Woman's Council. I did not get home until nearly six, & found Hal here with tea all ready except laying the table. I am afraid it looks a little like Mrs. Jellaby's[9] actions – but after we have settled down to regularity I think we won't keep our meetings up quite so long. Of course, when Lady Aberdeen is here no one can suggest breaking up the conference until she is ready to do so. We had quite a nice meeting – the only thing that troubles me is that everybody seems so anxious to do something at once that I am afraid all sorts of schemes may be started or at least attempted. We are to have a public meeting on Tuesday next & I have to read a report of what has been done, so [far]. I did not do any writing last night in this, for Hal & I were talking over the Council, & I had a couple of letters to write for it ... I had time to go & see Mrs. Harber & Mrs. Ireland. Mrs. Cameron came to the latter's while I was there and of course the conversation was on the Woman's Council – more particularly about the scheme of a cottage hospital which a few people here are most anxious to begin. I don't see any hope of raising enough money for the purpose,[10] & I think it would be worse than foolish to begin such a work without a good guarantee of funds. [23 October 1895]

About five I had a visit from Lady Aberdeen. She drove up in great style, with her coachman and footman, and paid me quite a long visit. Of course it was all about the Woman's Council, but Hal laughs at me & says I'll be very puffed up after "hob nobbing" with a Countess. It really is a pleasure & a privilege to be associated with a woman like she is – but oh! she is large![11] I felt quite like a pigmy beside her. She is so tall, & stout as well. When she left it was time to get tea. [25 October 1895]

We have been down to Mrs. Cameron's since tea. I only wanted to see her for a few minutes on business – Woman's Council again. I will be glad when it is in good working order, though I suppose it will always take up a good deal of somebody's time to keep it so. [26 October 1895]

I had a letter from Mother today. She is quite distressed that I have anything to do with Lady Aberdeen's Society. I confess I feel a little distressed myself over the thought of having to read a report in public – however perhaps there won't be very many people there and I am not going to usurp any of men's duties & responsibilities I am sure ... Mrs. Ellison ... had asked Mrs. Macdonald & Mrs. Cameron to meet here to talk over the getting up of an entertainment for the reading room. I dislike these entertainments most cordially, but I can't always refuse to have anything to do with them, so have agreed to do what I can to help. They are to have a kind of social evening in the hall – an informal programme & cake & coffee. It will be a failure I am afraid – I don't see why people are so crazy for entertainments. [28 October 1895]

We had one Woman's Meeting in the afternoon, in the hall, & there wasn't any fire in the room. As we were there from three until nearly six we all got pretty well chilled. The meeting was a disappointment to me – I had expected it to be managed somewhat differently. All the interest seemed to be centred round the scheme of a hospital and I did not like the idea of the Council attempting any work just yet. It seems to me that we need to know each other better before we can hope to work together. We are to have another meeting next week at Mrs. Cochrane's. We have already had three this month, & the idea at first suggested was to have three in the year! [29 October 1895]

Miss Godwin came at two, and Mrs. Macdonald soon after. We got to work, and had more than half the sandwiches cut before Mrs. Macdougal & Mrs. Harber came. We cut up 7 loaves of bread. Mr. Ellison & Mrs. Wilson were both in during the afternoon and Mrs. Jacques & Mrs. Somerville came to help, but they were so late we said it wasn't worth while for them to stay. They stayed however, quite a while – to talk, not to work. I was quite tired at tea time, for of course, after they left I had the kitchen to clear up. I lay down for a little while before tea. We did not feel very much like going to the social, & I did not anticipate any enjoyment. However, we went down at eight, & had really a very pleasant Evening. I think everyone quite enjoyed it – and we made somewhere about 50 dollars for the Reading Room, which was better than we expected. They do not know yet exactly what the expenses were, but I think nearly $50.00 will be cleared. Lady Aberdeen read "The Vision of Sir Lancifal"[12] and read it very nicely. I couldn't help thinking that it seemed to fit her own life. I do believe she is a thoroughly good woman. I think I like her better than I do the Governor-General – he is so nervous. Their children[13] played a duett on the guitar & banjo, & Lady Marjory[14] sang very sweetly – she hasn't a strong voice, but it is sweet & well taught. Dr. Gibson[15] played & Gertie played, & Mrs. Muir gave [a] short selection on the violin. Mr. Abbot & Mr. Henderson[16] sang, & Lord Aberdeen read. Everything was nicely done – nothing extraordinary but pleasant to listen to. the only thing I didn't like was Mrs. Ellison's reading – "Miss Maloney on the Chinese Question."[17] I did not like the selection, and was disappointed in her reading – I have heard her so favourably spoken of, I expected more. Oh! & two Japs[18] sang a hymn in their own language and in native costume. It was funny but not very harmonious. Then we had refreshments and it wound up with [a] dance – but we did not stay to it. I had another talk with Lady Aberdeen, and was able to introduce Mrs. Perry to her, greatly to the old lady's delight. [3 November 1895]

I ... went to the Council Meeting at Mrs. Cochrane's. We did not accomplish very much, simply appointed a committee to find out what subscriptions could be hoped for a hospital. Miss MacIntyre was very hostile over the matter, & didn't want to even agree to the canvass, but although I am by no means in favour of the hospital scheme I think it only fair to let its advocates see what can be done. [5 November 1895]

I met Mrs. Cameron, & we had a long talk – she came over home with me. We had various subjects of conversation – Woman's Council, Hospital, Christmas trees etc. ... She says, so far, they hear very encouraging opinions as to the wisdom of starting a hospital. I am not going to say any more against it – I have relieved my conscience by saying that I shirked any responsibility in the matter, and now I can afford to be agreeable over it. Anyway I wouldn't like to hurt Mrs. Cameron's feelings, and she is so enthusiastic that I will just keep still. I wish I could keep still oftener, any way – I speak hastily, & regret it for many days. [9 November 1895]

I had a letter from Lady Aberdeen yesterday, acknowledging mine telling her the result of our Executive meeting. They are to be in Vernon again next Friday – I think only for a day – before they return east. [16 November 1895]

Mother is distressed over my belonging to the Woman's Council but she need not be afraid that I'll be one to go too fast and furious into all these new schemes. Instead, I believe I am considered as rather a break [brake] on the wheel of progress – & of course [those] who think their efforts are to lead *up hill* are rather disgusted with me – but I may prevent a smash up. I get quite a lot of fun out of the unbusinesslike business we transact, & would be thoroughly amused if I did not get a little impatient. As far as a Hospital is concerned I don't think it will amount to anything in the near future. [18 November 1895]

Mr. McKelvie was trying to make me talk about the Woman's Council, teazing me I think – in fact he confessed that he just contradicted to see what I would say.[19] He said Mr. Wilson told him that he always talked so much here that I had a way of "drawing him out," & Mr. McKelvie thought he'd try & turn the tables, he said . . . Old Mrs. Postil[20] was on the train. We had quite a conversation. The Governor General's car was on that day, & we naturally talked about the Aberdeens. She said "Ah, what a fine woman Lady Aberdeen is. I felt her ribs well, & I said 'Ah Lady Aberdeen – what hips you've got! – but I don't think very much of *him* – you don't feed him enough porridge.'" Lady Aberdeen laughed & said *he* got as much as he wanted. [24 November 1895]

I have to go to the Woman's Council . . . I hope the meeting won't be a very long one for I really have a great deal that I want to do, & hardly feel like sparing an hour that isn't positively needed. [8 December 1895]

I had to go to a Woman's Council meeting at three on Tuesday afternoon, at Mrs. Cochrane's . . . [11 December 1895]

I also had a very pretty calendar from Lady Aberdeen and a card for Hal & me from "The Governor General & the Countess of Aberdeen." I think it was very nice of her to remember us. [3 January 1896]

I ought to write my report for the Woman's Council tonight, but I don't think I will attempt it, for I don't feel very bright mentally. [14 January 1896]

Mrs. Poulin came in and she stayed and went to the Council with me. We were kept there until five o'clock, & all that was done might have been settled in a much shorter time – still I suppose wherever there are a good many people there has to be a lot of talk before any decision is arrived at. However, I am glad to say we passed a resolution dropping the hospital scheme for the present at any rate. [22 January 1896]

Right after dinner today I dressed & went up to Mrs. Cochrane's – I had to see her about some Woman's Council business. We will have to have another meeting of the Executive next week. Mrs. Cameron has sent in her resignation – I think it was rather a pity she did so, just because matters did not go the way she wished. It reminds me of when we used to play hide & seek & one sulky child would say "I won't play if I can't be *it*." However I freely confess that I would rather like to follow her example – still, as Mrs. Cochrane says, we'd better all stay in office for the year, & just keep as quiet as possible & do as little as possible – & then we can all refuse re-election. [22 January 1896]

Miss MacIntyre ... came to tell me about the Woman's Council meeting which was held yesterday. I did not go to it for I had succeeded in nearly curing my cold & did not want to increase it, so I stayed in all day. I sent a note to Mrs. Cochrane, explaining why I did not go, & telling her not to let them put my name on *any* sub-committee. Miss MacIntyre tells me today that they insisted on putting my name on the committee to confer with the directors about the Fair, & I will just refuse to act. The other members of the Committee are Mrs. Ellison, Mrs. Cameron & Mrs. Burnyeat, and I know it *will* never work well together, so I am not going to enter it – for I like them all too well to want to disagree with any of them, and I can't & won't keep still & let people do things I think foolish & ill-advised, without at least uttering a protest. What I would like would be to just help the directors quietly, letting them still have all the apparent management of the thing, while we did what we could in the way of suggestions. [25 February 1896]

I went up to Mrs. Cochrane's to see about a Council meeting this week. [15 March 1896]

I was up at Mrs. Cochrane's all Friday afternoon at a Council meeting. There were only five members there – the smallest number we have had at any meeting. [25 March 1896]

We are to have a meeting of the Woman's Council here this afternoon, & the ladies may arrive at any minute now – so I must stop. [3 July 1896]

I ... got my books, and went to a Woman's Council meeting where we were deciding what was to be done at the Fair. Miss MacIntyre had put a notice in the paper, asking that all who were willing to help in the matter would come – so we had reasonable expectations of a fair sized meeting, and we had four! – Mrs. Cochrane, Mrs. Latimer, Miss MacIntyre & myself. We did what we could, which wasn't much, towards arranging some sort of a definite programme of work to be undertaken. I think we have settled it fairly well now, and not much more can be done before the 1st part of October. My year as Sec will be up in October and I will then resign. I am not fitted for *society* work – I am not tactful or enthusiastic enough to be a leader and not humble enough to follow without arguing, so I'd better give it up. [8 September 1896]

... Hal had to go out to the Aberdeen hop yards to see the Indian interpreter. There was some trouble among the pickers. Lord Aberdeen employs between four and five hundred Siwashes[21] there as hop pickers & during "the season," which lasts about five weeks, the town here is constantly filled with men, Klootchmen and "tenas Klootchmen" (children). Some of them come from across the American boundary & they look quite different from our Indians. [29 September 1896]

After the Parkes moved to the BX Ranch:

It was nearly four when I had my preserving done and before I had got dressed I saw Lady Aberdeen & Captain Sinclair[22] (their aid) ride up.[23] I rushed into my dress as fast as I could, & got to the door in time. They came in, & presently Lord Aberdeen and Lady Marjorie came too. They stayed quite a time. Lord Aberdeen went around with Hal a little while. Her Excellency talked Woman's Council to me, & then they all had a cup of tea before they left, when it was nearly tea time. [26 October 1896]

I formally resigned my office, and they put me in as one of the Vice Presidents. I didn't mind that, as I won't be obliged to go to the meetings & yet I can do so if I really wish to do so. [10 November 1896]

Mr. Ellison, too, was telling Hal about [the ball]. He & Mrs. Ellison took Lizzie with them – he said she got lots of dancing, & danced well. They kept it up till three o'clock this morning. Mrs. Jacques said some of the dresses were very gorgeous – I wonder if Lady Aberdeen wore her beautiful earrings. [20 November 1896]

Miss MacIntyre & I went to Mrs. Cochrane's at half past two, where we had a Council Meeting. It passed off quite amicably. I have made up my mind not to say or do much. I hold up my hand with the "yeas" and – in short – drift with the tide, feeling quite confident it isn't strong enough to do more than strand us on a level shore. I tried when I first joined the Council to be active – but I don't approve of most of the schemes proposed – they are too impracticable – and I found that by strenuous opposition I was only likely to offend my friends without changing their opinion, so I do nothing but smile & try to pour oil on the troubled waters when the others begin to quarrel. I'm afraid I am not well fitted for the role of peace maker, being by nature really fond of a wordy scrimmage – but I believe it is only between very old & tried friends that a hot argument can be safely indulged in. New friends, even good & well-beloved ones, are apt to misunderstand. The meeting broke up about half past four. [9 February 1897]

Mrs. Cochrane said to me the other day "I was thinking at our last Council Meeting that of all the women who joined it a little more than a year ago, you have improved the most in appearance." I don't suppose any thanks are due to the Council for that – it wasn't to improve our looks we joined it. I wonder if the change is any more than skin deep!! [23 February 1897]

Miss MacIntyre & I had quite a lively discussion over this new scheme of Lady Aberdeen's to celebrate the Queen's Jubilee.[24] She wants to establish a new order, called "Victorian Order of Home Helpers"[25] to train women to go to the sparsely settled western districts as nurses or general helpers. I can't go quite into all the particulars but it does *not* commend itself to my mind atall. One rule is, no woman under thirty is eligible, & I think that a huge mistake. Quite as many women are capable, unselfish & hard working under – as over – thirty, and they usually have a good deal more energy and enthusiasm to put into their work. Any way I don't believe (even if they establish the order) that it will help atall the class of people they are hoping to help. [26 February 1897]

... I went to a Woman's Council meeting – they were to talk over the hospital business. [10 June 1897]

Despite Alice's misgivings, the committee did get things done, and she was happy to donate many needed items to the hospital:

Vernon seems pretty healthy this fall, perhaps because they have a hospital ready. It is a good thing if that will prove a preventive of diseases. [19 October 1897]

The new hospital has been opened[26] – Mrs. Pratt[27] is in charge as nurse, matron, cook – all combined. I think they just have two patients as yet. [2 November 1897]

There was a meeting at Mrs. Cochrane's to appoint lady visitors for the hospital, & they asked me to go in, so I did. [14 November 1897]

The Aberdeens paid their final visit to Vernon in 1898:

... in the evening we went up to the recreation grounds where the citizens were to assemble to give a farewell address to the Aberdeens. They had erected a platform & hung it round with Chinese lanterns, and the city fathers were assembled in full force – Mr. McGowan to read a very laudatory address, the mayor made a speech and Lord Aberdeen responded expressing himself as greatly delighted with the *"unique"* manner in which the citizens had done him honour. I thought the word most apt as it certainly was an original performance. While Lord & Lady Aberdeen shook hands with, & said good-bye to all the crowd fire works were sent up. [1 August 1898]

The bazaar went off very well and the Woman's Council cleared the $100.00 they hoped to make. I was there all the afternoon ... [15 April 1899]

Another feminist Alice met was Georgiana, wife of a mineral prospector and syndicate manager, Arthur Henry Craven. Intrigued, baffled, resistant to the philosophy of "New Womanhood," Alice nevertheless welcomed the newcomer to her home.

We are so surprised – Mr. Craven[28] is married. Hal saw it in the last Kamloops paper – he is to bring his bride out almost immediately & they will live at Ducks. [7 February 1896]

I think Mr. Craven has pretty well decided to take hold of the Swan Lake claim & begin work. He goes back home today and talks of bringing his wife[29] over next week to visit us, while he goes prospecting for a few days. She is a very clever woman I believe. We feel very curious to meet her. She is a terrible radical, Mr. Craven says, but she really is quite a "swell" – I know from little things he says. She is one of the political women of Lady Henry Somerset's[30] ilk – goes in for women's suffrage etc. She has visited the Aberdeens in Ottawa. She will find quite a different phase of life here. [15 May 1896]

Mr. Craven arrived Tuesday night, *without* his wife. She had a cold, & he had no very suitable vehicle to bring her in. He ... expects to bring her next time he comes. [24 May 1896]

The Parkes' curiosity would soon be satisfied:

... as there was no letter from Mrs. Craven, we concluded that she would not be here before Tuesday, as we were expecting them by train, & they had said they would let us know when. Hal & I both went to lie down. I had not done any sweeping or dusting that day – had not even washed the breakfast dishes, and of course no Sunday dinner was prepared. I fell asleep, & had only wakened up, when we heard wheels stop at the door, & there were the Cravens! Of course I had to get up hurriedly. Hal went down & helped Mrs. Craven out and I was down in time to welcome her in. I have said so much about her in my letters that I won't give any long description of her here – suffice it to say that she is the only real specimen of the "New Woman" that I have ever known intimately, and while I rec- ognize the honesty of her intentions I hardly admire her methods. She is very "advanced" in all her notions, believing in Woman's suffrage as a gen- eral cure for all political & public abuses. I can't see it in that way, because even granting that women are as wise & as good as men in public matters they are certainly not *more* able or more far-seeing, and it will be simply multiplying the number of advisers, without improving the quality of the advice. Mrs. Craven was very nice in many ways. She has travelled a great deal, talks very fluently (indeed she lectures in England on woman suffrage, temperance etc.) and was very thoughtful about trying not to make any extra work – & most anxious to come in the kitchen and help me. Still we had very few thoughts in common. She is not fond of books, cares nothing for flowers and very little for music. I did not really enjoy her companionship and neither did Hal. [20 June 1896]

Mrs. Craven was very nice today – I really liked her better than I ever had done before. She was not quite so dictatorial – not so "new." I wonder if she has taken to wearing petticoats instead of bloomers (under her dress skirt). I believe she must have as she seems so much more womanly. [22 May 1897]

Two years later Alice made the acquaintance of another feminist; her comment on the woman's looks is indicative of the myths she had learned during her upbringing:

[Miss Fleming's] sister, from Portland, Oregon, was with her, just for a few days. Such a very clever attractive looking woman. I was telling Hal when I came home how much out of the common she seemed – gentle, quiet ways, but such strength of mind & intellect in her face – & he says she is Court crier in Portland – the first woman who has ever been elected to that office in Oregon. She isn't a bit masculine looking. [9 October 1898]

Alice had definite ideas on who should be allowed to vote in elections:

I went to Miss MacIntyres and we had a great discussion about woman suffrage.[31] She rather thinks women ought to be allowed to vote, but I don't see that it would make matters any better – and it would certainly be a great trouble to have a vote if one didn't want to use it – for all the politicians would be bothering after us. Instead of increasing the number of votes I'd take the franchise away from a good many who now possess it. I think a man should have or *be* something before he has any voice in settling the affairs of his country – but I suppose I am old fashioned – and non-progressive. [22 March 1899]

CHAPTER 14

I think if I were a man I'd want to go in for [politics]

Political Life at the End of the 1800s

Throughout her life Alice Barrett Parke was intensely interested in politics at all levels. A staunch Conservative, she followed election campaigns, attended political meetings, and commented on candidates and party members. Both the Parkes enjoyed an argument on the subject, though more often than not they were of the same mind.

Hal Parke's first post after his marriage was offered to him by Vernon's first city council:

Hal had to go to a meeting of the new council,[1] & thought he might be late, but he came in about nine. [16 January 1894]

[Hal] is very well satisfied over the result of the municipal election. He has a good many friends on the Council now, & was very glad Mr. Martin[2] was made Mayor instead of Armstrong, who is an obstinate, rather quarrelsome man. [18 January 1894]

I believe there was a very lively meeting of the Council this afternoon over the flour mill. Some man from Fenelon Falls is here asking a bonus, & the Council ill favour his offer. Mr. Martin (the Mayor) however was wanting to favour Mr. Wood, & the discussion was very active. However the other man asks a smaller bonus, & will put in electric light as well, so I think he will be accepted. His name is Ellis[3] & comes from Lindsay [Ontario] originally. [15 March 1894]

... I think it would puzzle a Napoleon to manage this town. Maybe I have used an unfortunate name, for it wouldn't atall puzzle any body to manage to start a fight, but I doubt if even Napoleon could have led the united Vernonites against a common enemy. I think there are so many clashing interests here that unity is almost impossible. [19 September 1895]

We are greatly disgusted over municipal matters.[4] The Mayor and three aldermen were appointed by acclamation, and a poorer selection could scarcely have been made. It seems too bad that the business men here who would make good City fathers will not take the office. The Vernon men remind me strongly of the Lotus eaters[5]

"There is no joy but calm"
"Give us long rest or death, dark death, or dreamful ease"
"Surely, surely slumber is more sweet than toil"

Sooner than exert a little energy they will let things drift along into a most unsatisfactory state. Sometimes one finds it hard to be patient with people who have time & ability to conduct public affairs well, & yet who will not come forward. I am afraid my fault would lie in quite a different direction. I might become a busy body, but I really don't think I ever could be a drone. [14 January 1896]

... the Council and Health Officers have a great deal to say about the impurity of the water[6] we are drinking and are strongly advocating a system of waterworks. [3 September 1896]

Hal Parke included information on the local election when he made the following diary entry:

Armstrong has been elected mayor and with the exception of McGowan all the aldermen[7] are new.[14 January 1897]

They are having rather a lively time in Vernon over municipal matters. Mr. Ireland,[8] the police magistrate, is smarting under a cessation of salary & is writing very bitter & rather foolish letters to the Council. Mr. Henderson of the Vernon News is one of the new Aldermen, & one that Mr. Ireland evidently blames for his losing his pay, & so he says as nasty things as he can about Mr. Henderson and the Vernon News. They published his letter, but answer it very well in an editorial.[9] Mr. Davies has lost the City Clerkship & Mr. McGowan has got it – at a much lower salary. The new Council seem really to mean to keep their promises, to the electors, of retrenchment. [11 February 1897]

[Hal] did not leave town until the result of the election was known. There was quite a lively contest[10] over the civic honours this year. [14 January 1898]

Hal was going to a Water Works[11] meeting ... [14 May 1898]

Provincial politics evoked a slightly more respectful tone:

The town was quite excited yesterday – over politics. Mr. Vernon,[12] the
present member arrived on the morning train and the opposition had a
convention in the evening to nominate opponents. [19 May 1894]

I was up at Mrs. Ellison's yesterday afternoon helping them hull strawberries for the evening. It was quite a pleasant evening. Mr. Vernon was
there, & was the lion, of course. I had the pleasure of having strawberries
& cream with him. I hope he may be elected – but time only will tell. He
is quite confident of success, but on the other hand the opposition men
feel sure they will win. "Who wish are hopeful" – and we can only wait to
see. [22 June 1894]

Mr. Graham[13] (our M.P.P.) came in for a few minutes. He goes down to
Victoria on Saturday – the House opens on Feb. 10th. Hal got an invitation to the opening in the new buildings.[14] Everyone who had seen them
says that they are very beautiful – a credit & ornament to our Province. I
only wish the Members of the Government were as much of a credit, but
some of them are not famous for brilliancy. I rather fancy there will be
important changes in the coming election. Report says that Mr. Ellison is
going to run for our Constituency[15] – on the Conservative ticket – & I
suppose Donald Graham will oppose him. [1 February 1898]

We hear that Mr. Robert Wood means to come out as a candidate in the
approaching election – on the Government side this time. He worked
hard for Opposition last time, but I believe he says he has been down to
Victoria & found that the leaders of the opposition are fools, so he will
support the Government. I think probably Mrs. Wood is a government
sympathizer, and that accounts for his change of views. She seems to
dominate him thoroughly. I'm afraid Mr. Ellison will be beaten if he runs,
& he will be a disappointed man, for I think he cares very much. Mr.
Cameron was asking Hal to come out – I only wish he could afford it. [30
March 1898]

Mr. Ellison came out & we talked politics. He is not quite certain whether
he will come out as a candidate in the next election. He, of course, is a
Government man, & I think he'd have rather an uphill fight in this constituency, especially since the new redistribution measure has been
brought down. It will be most unpopular over all the Mainland, and is

particularly hard on our constituency [of] East Yale – they have cut off the southern portion of the riding & joined it to Rossland, giving Kootenay two extra members. Even Mr. McKelvie, who is a strong party man, has quite a strong editorial[16] condemning the Government for this measure. It looks as if the old saying were true "Whom the Gods wish to destroy they first make mad" and the Government seems to be making itself as unpopular as possible. I'd be sorry to see Mr. Ellison defeated if he runs – I think he'll be bitterly disappointed. [23 April 1898]

Price Ellison aroused Alice's wrath when he attempted to play politics with her husband's career:

Yesterday morning Hal drove in to town, and when he came home he said to me "I'm afraid I've done something you won't approve of." Price Ellison had met him & told him that he – Hal – had got the appointment, & Price asked Hal to give it up in favour of another man, who they think can command a good many votes in the coming election, & makes this appointment the price of turning them for Ellison. Hal has always felt more or less under an obligation to Price Ellison for his exertions in first getting him into the Govt office – so he felt that this was a chance to repay his kindness, & he gave way. He sent a telegram to Mr. Norris saying that he waived his right to the appointment at Price Ellison's request. I feel now that he is more than even with Ellison as far as any favour is concerned as he has done far more than the other would have done for him – far more than he would have asked of any man. I can not help feeling a little hurt at both Price Ellison & Jack McKelvie – they have always professed to be our real friends – & yet they do not hesitate to sacrifice Hal for the sake of what they believe to be their political interest. You see they think Hal will do his best for Ellison any way – while the other man is uncertain. I feel quite convinced that (quite apart from the meanness of their action) they have made a mistake in policy – as Hal is far more popular than the other man. It is hard for me to say nothing. I was very sore and angry yesterday, and yet I oughtn't to be, for it only makes me love and admire Hal all the more. His friendship for a man means something. I always think of him when I think of that text "He that sweareth to his neighbour and disappointeth him not, though it were to his own hurt." He will not do any thing just for self seeking unless he feels it to be just and upright. I know it counts to his credit in the best set of books; but he gets very little thanks here. Twice this Spring he has had the chance to better himself at the expense of Price Ellison's interests & he wouldn't do it because they were *friends*. I believe it is better to have nothing to do with politicians – there is always more or less disappointment. I am sorry for Hal – it is always hard to be disappointed in some one you have thought well of. I really believe that running for Parliament perverts most men's sense of honour. [11 May 1898]

The writs for the election are out – it is to take place on July 9th. I think Mr. Ellison is very much excited. It is reported that Mr. Graham is going to withdraw from the contest – it is rather late to put in another man now. I would be very glad if there was no election – it would save such a lot of trouble if Mr. Ellison were put in by acclamation, but I suppose there is small chance of such a desirable state of affairs. [9 June 1898]

Mr. Ellison wanted to talk politics – Graham is going to run after all, & I think it will be a pretty close election. Mr. Ellison & his friends are very sanguine, but so are the others. Jim Martin is going to run in Rossland on the opposition ticket. I hope he'll get in, for I think he'd make a good member. [10 June 1898]

Mrs. Ellison is greatly excited over the election – she says she can't settle at any thing. I think she will be terribly disappointed if Mr. Ellison is defeated. There is to be a big political meeting[17] here tonight. Mr. Turner[18] the Premier is here – also Mr. Semlin,[19] leader of the Opposition – Mr. Eberts, and I don't know how many other bright particular stars. I wish I could go & hear them but so few ladies go here that one is conspicuous and I believe Hal would rather I didn't go. He has been in for a few minutes. He says Mr. Turner & Mr. Eberts have both been talking to him, & tell him they depend a good deal on him to "keep things straight" in this part. He says he certainly will "keep things straight as far as lies in his power" – that he will do what he honestly believes to be just & fair to all the settlers, & to do good work without fear or favour. Whether that is just what they mean is open to question. Mr. Turner is, I believe, a fine man, respected alike by friend & foe. British Columbia Politics are rather peculiar – there are no party lines, one side being Reform, another Conservative: there is just Government & Opposition and each faction number[s] some Conservatives & some Liberals in their ranks – so that one hardly knows where one belongs. The Government party have a progressive & liberal policy while the Oppositionists cry for retrenchment and economy. Each side feels certain of victory – or says so – in the coming contest. I don't know the last bit which will win. Mr. Ellison is confident in this riding – so is Mr. Graham. Mr. Ellison "knows" that the Government will be sustained – Mr. Graham "knows" that it won't – & there is the situation. [20 June 1898]

I did go to the political meeting after all. I saw Lizzie in the afternoon, and she said all were going from Mrs. Cochrane and we heard of several other ladies who were going – so – as Hal said he didn't mind in the least, I joined Mrs. Cochrane's party & went with them. I did enjoy the excitement and noise of it all – though really when one summed up the merits of the speakers, & the points they had scored for their respective sides, there was very little to speak of. I was disappointed in Mr. Turner – he isn't much of a speaker – neither he nor Eberts seemed to me to come really to the point. Mr. Graham & Mr. Semlin, the Opposition speakers, of course aired the old grievances that the ones out of power always have – extravagance and influence on the part of the leaders – it is so easy to make a point like that. I don't see why some one doesn't ask such grumblers to state clearly just exactly how they would run the country satisfactorily & economically. Altogether, I tried to follow carefully, and it seems to me that there is not, this time, any definite and important charge that can be laid against the Government. Last election the Parliament Buildings at Victoria formed a very popular theme for building a grievance upon – all the mainland was considered "stirred up" over the matter – so many thinking that it was not fair to the Province to anchor the capital at the extreme end instead of in a central part.

I never did know how rude men can be to each other. Each & all of the speakers contradicted the statements of their opponents, & verbally called each other liars – perhaps they each told the truth part of the time!

The funniest thing in the whole performance was the confusion & despair of the poor old chairman – Mr. Simmonds. He couldn't make the audience listen to the speakers he wanted. The majority were bound to have Mr. Eberts speak though the time given to the Gov. side was up, and finally the people carried the day. Lizzie was there too and I think she was very tired before the meeting was over. Mrs. Cochrane and Mrs. Cayley went away before it was over, but I never like to do that – it seems so uncourteous to the speakers yet to come, & always looks conspicuous, and creates a disturbance. It was twelve o'clock when we got home. [21 June 1898]

Hal was telling me on the way down that in Enderby this week he was in George Bell's store and was sitting on the counter listening to a conversation about the coming election. He said he wasn't taking any part in it, was just listening. George Bell said he was going to vote for Graham because he is the nominee of the Liberal party, but that he wasn't going to do any work, but Hal said he turned around & pointed to him and said "Now there's the man who ought to represent this district in Parliament – & if

he ran, I don't care which party he was for, I'd get out and howl for him."
I only wish Hal could afford to run. I do think he'd be the best member
and I think he'd get there too! [30 June 1898]

There is to be a political meeting here [in Kelowna] tonight, but I believe
ladies don't go in Kelowna, so I'll not have a chance to hear Mr. Cotton.[20]
He is said to be the cleverest speaker in the Opposition ranks, but has not
a very good reputation for honesty. Mr. Macdonald, our host, thinks Graham will be elected by a big majority. The opposition party is strong down
here. [1 July 1898]

It is just five o'clock, and I hear a good deal of shouting going on down
town so I suppose the result of the voting here is known – we cannot
know positively, however, which man is elected before the ballot boxes
come up from the lower Country and that won't probably be until next
Tuesday.

I didn't get very much written yesterday, for, before I had been seated
long, Hal came home with the result of the voting here – Mr. Ellison was
87 ahead[21] – this was better than his friends even had hoped for – then
news kept coming in from the other poling places, and I was too excited
really to think of writing. Poor Graham only got 33 of a majority in Armstrong and he had counted on 200! I can't help feeling very sorry for him.
My sympathies always go with the beaten ones, and he felt so sure of the
election. I'm afraid however that Vernon is again going to be represented
by an Opposition man – as the latest reports seem to point to a defeat of
the Government. It is very close, &, of course, we cannot be sure yet, as
all places are not heard from, but it looks as if the Opposition had the best
of it. I don't think Graham can possibly gain now on Mr. Ellison now
[sic], as all the big polling places except Fairview are heard from and Ellison is 94 ahead. I suppose there is great excitement among the men down
town. Mr. Norris was here last night, and (though he tried to be very cool)
one could see that he was really very much excited. Of course he'd like to
see the Government sustained, and so should we. I don't think it will make
any difference in Hal's position – but one never can tell. *He knows* he has
friends in the present Cabinet – & it remains to be seen who would form
the Opposition ministry. If Jim Martin is one he would be a friend at
Court I'm sure. In any case I don't feel uneasy – I suppose because Hal
always has been so fortunate it makes one confident that it will be all right
any way – and I don't see that the Opposition can make much difference
in the expenditures, not for the present, any way. I think I hear Hal's step
and he may have more news. I think we'll go down to Harry's tomorrow
after dinner, & Hal will go on to Enderby on Tuesday. He has been in, &

has gone over to see Mr. Billings. He says he couldn't go to church this morning, as he couldn't get his mind fixed. Elections are rather exciting affairs – beyond a doubt. The returns are not all in, but it looks as if neither side would have enough of a majority to carry on business, & there may have to be another election – I do hope not – I'd like to see it settled one way or the other. Jim Martin is in for Rossland. We are all glad. He is Opposition but he is a good capable man, & there are not many in the ranks of either party. [9-10 July 1898]

I have not heard any more election news today. The wires went down yesterday morning, probably the storm blew a tree on them – I don't know if they are repaired yet. Hal will probably hear some news this morning. [11 July 1898]

... I have almost forgotten [to mention] the election news. It looks very much as if the present Government were defeated – it stands now Opposition 19, Gov. 17 with two constituencies to hear from. Of these one may be Opp – even if both are Government, it leaves the Opp. with one of a majority. I believe many of the members have so small a majority that there are to be recounts – & protests – and all these unsettling & vexatious affairs – so that there may not be a new Cabinet formed for months, & when it is the majority is not enough to work on, so it may mean another election. I wish it had been settled one way or the other. I wish they would draw a definite party line here – Conservative & Reformer. [15 July 1898]

Our political situation remains about the same – however the Government party have a caucus next week, & something may be decided after that. I'm afraid it means another election, and it looks now as if there might be a dominion election soon too. I am sorry, for election times are too exciting. It would be all right if one had nothing to do but attend to politics – then one could just go into it heartily, and I think if I were a man I'd want to go in for it. As it is, I just know enough to be interested but not to really argue. [22 July 1898]

In the evening Mr. McKelvie came in. He seemed so low spirited. The present government has been defeated,[22] and unless some coalition is patched up an election will take place. It is a pity we have such poor men in our provincial Government – Instead of our best & cleverest men. I think we have some very stupid ones. [26 February 1899]

I went to a political meeting last night. The premier – Joe Martin[23] – was here. I have had a great curiosity to see & hear a man who has made himself so much talked about. He is certainly a clever speaker, & gives one the impression of honest purpose and force. I think one thing that made me inclined to listen to him was that I thought he looked a little bit like Hubert – not so good-looking – but something, the same expression and the same twinkle in his eye – occasionally. I can't begin to tell what he said – but he seemed to make some very good hits at his opponents, & to leave a good impression on the crowd. The hall was very full, & it was all most orderly. There were no interruptions or adverse expressions. One old goose of a man kept making remarks but no one paid any attention to him. No one spoke on Mr. Ellison's side atall. [10 May 1900]

Dominion politics were more remote after Alice left Ontario, but she followed developments with keen interest:

Nonah & I . . . have come to a heart-rending part in our history – a story of the terrible persecution of the Netherland Protestants. It makes one's blood run cold to think that such atrocities were committed in the name of Christ – and yet in our own time, in our own land, politicians will, for self interest, pander to the power of Roman Catholicism! [2 February 1892]

Mr. E. Parke's[24] letter was all about the Dominion elections.[25] I suppose there will be quite an excitement even here over them this year. [28 February 1895]

[Hal] says it looks very much as though the Liberals might carry the General Election[26] – they have gained 4 out of the 5 bye-elections and Prior in Victoria (Conservative) had only a very small majority while last time he had a huge majority. It is a long time since we had a Liberal Government. [7 January 1896]

Mr. McKelvie is greatly disgusted over Dominion politics. He thinks now the Liberals are sure to carry the next election, and as he is a thorough Conservative he is very much excited. He had nothing good to say of Montague[27] & Haggart,[28] and indeed I don't think any one ever had much good *to think* about them. However, the Conservative Party worked hard enough to elect Montague, and now must suffer for welcoming such a man to their ranks. [13 January 1896]

The rival political candidates – Mara[29] and Bostock[30] – are in town, so the election excitement is beginning. This promises to be the most interesting election I ever remember in the Dominion. Hal thinks the question of national education is of vital importance. He says he would like to see both parties defeated, & a third – of the clean & clever men on both sides – formed to reform the constitution. We have not much liking for Laurier, and I think it is a disgrace to the country to have the Tuppers[31] at the head of affairs. [15 May 1896]

Tuesday – yesterday – was the eventful election day. The town here was very quiet, though there was a kind of undercurrent of excitement & unrest. I couldn't settle down to much. I went over to the post office in the afternoon – my home letter came yesterday instead of Monday, & there was so much in it to think over, that rather upset me too. I took some roses & pansies down to Mrs. Macdonald. Hal came home rather early, but of course nothing was known then about the elections. He went out soon to hear the news ... Hal came in before tea with word that Mara had the majority here, but Enderby & Armstrong had gone strong against him. After tea Lizzie came over again, & Hal said I'd better keep her all night, & he'd go out and stay till he heard definite news from the eastern constituencies. He came in two or three times to tell us results of latest bulletins. I think nearly everyone is surprised. The Liberals are well ahead, so there will be a change of government – whether for the worse or better remains to be seen. Bostock has, so far, a majority – 177 here – so there is almost no chance of Mara going ahead. I really can hardly believe that there has been such a turn over in the minds of the people. At the last general election the conservatives had 30 years of a majority – this time they are in the minority. All the constituencies have not yet been heard from, but it is certain that the Liberals[32] will have a small majority at least. [24 June 1896]

Mr. McKelvie came in about half past eight & stayed until nearly eleven, talking over the elections. He's a great deal disappointed. [3 July 1896]

CHAPTER 15

People really seem to be getting sanguine over the mining prospects around here

Exploration and Prospecting in the Okanagan

The Okanagan Valley attracted many miners and prospectors during the second half of the nineteenth century. Vernon became a hive of mining activity while Alice lived there, but no large finds were made:

Mr. Rabbit came in as we were sitting down to tea, and wanted to bet me his interest in a quartz mine that I would not go home. I readily took the bet, & when I asked him what stake I was to put up, he said "Your hand." I don't know whether that might be considered a proposal, but I know I'd much sooner have an interest in the mine than in Mr. Rabbit. I am afraid, though, he won't keep his word. [2 January 1892]

I had had a talk with Joe John's man at the gate. He brought back some books and was telling me about himself and that he was coming in for a "visit" some evening before I left. He has been a miner, and says he has been about long enough in a "farming country" and is yearning to get back to the mountains. [21 March 1892]

While out sight-seeing:

We halted near the mines, & took our dinner in the woods, and then began exploring again. First we went to where two men were placer mining. We had a steep climb to get down to them. One was a very tall handsome fellow. He reminded me of Frank. He was more striking than conventional in his dress, but was very polite, doing the honours of his domain very gracefully. We stayed down there quite a long time but did not get any gold – the men are making fair wages, no more. We climbed up the hill, packed ourselves in the traps, & drove on a few miles farther, & then went down the hill (I might almost say precipice) again. This time we struck men who are digging a tunnel hoping to strike something rich. Harry wanted us all to explore this so in we went. It wasn't high enough to walk upright, and unless we kept on the wooden car track, we were apt to step in water, so the entry was slow, & in my case at least "skeary" for I felt all the time as if the roof might cave in. We had to have candles, & went in 700 feet. There we found two little wizened men working away.[1] I asked them what they expected to find, & one said they were hoping if they struck bed rock to find a rich vein of gold – but they don't seem very hopeful. One week lately the earnings (or rather findings) of the three amounted to just fifty cents! I think it seems like gambling with the luck dead against one. I don't think I could work underground like that for any amount of money. I was very thankful to see the sunlight again, though it was a scorching sun indeed – over 90 in the shade. [4 July 1894]

[Mr. Girouard] has an old cronie staying with him – a miner named Mac-Intyre.[2] He is a fine old Scotchman, but painfully deaf. He has lived for eighteen years – by himself – in an out of the way mining cabin, and has sunk a large fortune $30,000.00 in seeking a rich ledge which he vainly hopes to find, but which has proved like the pot at the end of the rainbow. He only comes down to town occasionally for stores. [12 November 1894]

Two of the Martins leave this week for Rossland.[3] It is a new mining town to the south of us which is having a great boom just now. Several of our merchants are taking quite large stocks of goods down there, & some excitement prevails over the fortunes to be made – but Hal says he has been through too many booms to have much faith in this one – the collapse is almost sure to come and few men come out as they expected. [25 July 1895]

[Mr. Craven] has gone now to see Mr. Smith about some of the mines at Camp Hewett.[4] He thinks the mine just near Vernon – Swan Lake Camp[5] – shows about the most promise. I wish it would amount to something I'm sure. [16 September 1895]

Mrs. Thompson had a great tale to tell of a wonderful new gold rush, in which her brother & Mr. Charlie Costerton are interested. I was asking Hal about it, & he says it is just like all the other claims which have caused excitement for a few days, & then nothing more. [30 October 1895]

Hal says Mr. Kirby & Mr. McKelvie may be in tonight. I daresay they may come to talk over the letter Hal had today from Mr. Craven about the

Swan Lake Mine. He hopes to be able to find a purchaser in England and asked Hal to see the Company here, & try & make arrangements with them. It would undoubtedly be a good thing for the Valley if these mines from here should be developed. [8 November 1895]

People really seem to be getting sanguine over the mining prospects[6] around here. [15 November 1895]

If our mines turn out any good, maybe we can all go back to live at home. To be sure it is very doubtful. Hal has an interest in three claims – so far he has only invested a few dollars – for license, recording etc. – and there is the chance of realizing something out of them. But I suppose it wouldn't be wise to build very bright hopes even on this rock foundation. If some of the mines near by don't turn out good, there is rather a dull prospect for Vernon. A good many people are moving away from here & none coming in their places. [8 March 1896]

Mr. Craven arrived Tuesday night ... [and] went up to the Monashee Mine[7] with Mr. Cameron Wednesday morning, & came back to us yesterday afternoon. [24 May 1896]

[Mr. Craven] & Hal went down town after tea to see some of the shareholders in the Mining Co. I think Mr. Craven has pretty well decided to take hold of the Swan Lake claim & begin work ... Hal went out to Swan Lake with Mr. Craven after the office closed so they did not get in till nearly six. I had dinner in the Evening and afterwards Mr. Latimer[8] came over & talked "rock" until bed time. [15 May 1896]

Jack Lawrie is back in the cabin – the mine[9] at Salmon River has closed for the present. [8 August 1896]

The Parkes purchased mining shares. Hal wrote:

Mr. & Mrs. Latimer came in – he wanted to see me about doing the assessment work on some mineral claims that he, Kerby and I hold in partnership. [14 January 1897]

Mrs. Latimer is feeling quite happy and hopeful over some of Mr. Latimer's mining properties. She thinks Mr. Craven will bond one claim for $10,000. He & Mr. Latimer have been in communication about the matter, & it is nearly settled. Every one wants to see these mines[10] go ahead – it means the making of Vernon & the surrounding ranches if they do. [16 February 1897]

... I think really B.C. has a great disadvantage in the unsettling element of chance which the mines introduce. In eastern Canada the first settlers knew that they must wrest their hard earned homes and fortunes from the land – here each man fancies that he might become suddenly very rich if he could "strike it lucky" – & it isn't a healthy feeling. [9 February 1897]

Jack Lawrie was telling me that he had got a situation at the coast in a gun smith's store.[11] He was to leave by yesterday's train, so I suppose he got off. I am glad he has got something settled to do. I don't think he seemed very glad. He said he did want to go prospecting this summer, & was half sorry the situation had been offered to him. He thought "there were fortunes to be made in these hills" this summer. I think the poet must have lived among miners or he never would have been so sure that "hope springs eternal in the human breast." They are the most sanguine with the least encouragement of any class of men I ever saw. Once let a man taste the uncertainty and excitement of a "prospector's life" – & he always contemplates the possibility of a sudden rush of riches – White is only one out of many hundreds who really fulfils the dream. Great hopes are excited near Vernon just now by some rich quartz found in one of the hills. [26 March 1897]

Hal went up to the Bon Diable mine[12] in the morning to get some samples of rock. [13 May 1897]

I suppose mining operations will begin at once now – I do hope with good results. [17 April 1897]

Mr. Ellison says he is really thinking of going to the Klondike[13] in the Spring, and seemed quite disgusted with me because I didn't like the idea of Hal's going as his camp-mate. I asked Mrs. Ellison what she thought of the notion, and she said she didn't consider it atall – she thought it all talk – but Hal says Mr. Ellison is in earnest and if he can get any one to take care of the place, will probably make a start with cattle. Jack McKelvie says the best way to go is through the Cariboo – that is the route he thinks he will take. [24 October 1897]

Mr. Ellison was here to dinner, and for a long visit. He was talking quite seriously about his desire to go to Klondyke, but report says that he is thinking of running for member, & he can hardly do both. I don't know which will prove stronger, the desire for gold or fame. I don't know that either would be reached in the roads mentioned, but hope springs eternal in the human breast, & particularly in Price Ellison's. His sanguine way of looking at every thing is proverbial – even now, when every one else believes that winter has come, he is prophesying a thaw, fine weather, and being able to plough for a month! [20 November 1897]

Hal was tempted to go to the Klondike, and wrote:

... Capt Shorts whom report had hanged in Alaska about two years ago appears to be very much alive in the Klondike and has written to some of his friends here. His talk is of millions. I hope he gets them and comes back here – it would be a liberal education to hear him tell about it. [24 November 1897]

The only possible road I can see leading to Ontario is by way of the Klondike and either leave my old useless bones there, or make enough to live elsewhere. [28 November 1897]

Later, Alice wrote more about the frenzy:

[Mr. Marshall] was telling us a wonderful story – of some woman who is a kind of prophetess. He says not far from his ranche (down near Kelowna) a company of men from Winnipeg have take[n] up a mineral claim and have put a good deal of money & labour on the development of it. They were told to come out here by an ignorant Swedish woman named Anderson. She was living in Winnipeg and had never been in this country, but she had a vision telling her that there was gold to be found in a certain spot of the Osoyoos Division of B.C. How she persuaded any one of the truth of her vision I don't know – but at any rate this Co. was formed & started for B.C. with her as their guide. Her leadings must have been rather vague for she took them first to Rossland, then up to Penticton, & finally she recognized the landmarks of her vision & led them to a spot on the shores of Okanagan Lake where she told them to dig. They have followed her directions closely, & Marshall says they are quite confident that success will attend them. It seems a little hard to believe, but Marshall says although he knows nothing except what they have told him of the woman's vision, he knows for a fact that they are working the mine under her directions, and in full faith in her ability. They say when ever she walks over ground in which there is mineral she becomes perfectly rigid. She foretells a time of depression for Vernon this year, & then great prosperity[14] from the mines round about. [2 February 1898]

Mr. Cuppage talks of going to the Klondike in the Spring. [18 February 1898]

[The road] was first built when the Cherry Creek mining excitement was on, & I confess – unless the mines produce largely, I do not think it is worth while making roads to the out of the way spots, where there is so little farming land. The road gang board at the Stansfields – we came up to them where they were working on our way to the house. Hal introduced me to all of them. Hollingsworth was there – the man who found the bones of poor Mr. Byam a few years ago. He is a typical trapper – gaunt, muscular and grim; Dell Thomas,[15] the man we supplied with books last winter – a happy looking little fellow – he lives up at Cherry Creek, is married to Stansfield's daughter – I'll say more of her bye & bye. Dan Macdonald, Angus' brother, a fellow with a most picturesque moustache, and two others completed the gang. Oh! I forgot young Stansfield who came over to the buggy to meet us & went with us up to the house. [23 June 1898]

Mrs. Macdonald says she thinks they really will leave Vernon soon – her husband is so dissatisfied with the dullness. I then went to the Robinsons – Hal wanted me to call there – Mr. Robinson is one of the owners of the Peachland Mines, & Hal knew Mr. Robinson's brother[16] long ago in Winnipeg. I quite liked them. There were two Mrs. Robinsons there, and some funny little children. [28 February 1899]

Old MacIntyre – from the Monashee mine – told Hal that he believes this year will show the highest water B.C. has known. He says if he owned land on the Lower Frazer he would not put in any crop, so firm is his belief that there will be floods. He says he never saw so much snow at this time of year up at the Monashee, & that it has not begun to go *atall*. I know the snow still lies quite low on the hills about us – I do hope the floods won't be serious. [19 April 1899]

CHAPTER 16

It really is shameful the way I neglect my poor old diary lately

The End of the Diaries

As early as January 1894, a few weeks after Alice had taken up her pen once more at the urging of her brother Harry, entries began to appear concerning her lack of will or energy to keep the diaries truly up to date. By 1896 she was no longer attempting to write daily; and three years later, the competing demands of home, post office work, and friends relegated her writing to the lowest of priorities. It had become an onerous duty.

I quite meant to have begun yesterday, with the New Year, to keep a record of each day's doing – and not let anything interfere with a daily entry – but alas! Before I began even, the good resolve was broken, so I will have to go back now and tell yesterday's events. [2 January 1894]

I think I'll have to call this a "weekly" instead of a diary – & upon my word it wouldn't be inappropriate to spell it "weakly." I don't seem to be in a very good mood for writing lately. [26 April 1895]

I suppose it is not strange that the more there is to write about the less time one has for writing. All of last week I was not able to begin a diary. [3 September 1895]

I am afraid I'll have to call this a "weekly edition" instead of a diary – again I have allowed a long time to go by without writing. Visitors & visiting are again to blame for my neglect. [10 April 1896]

My good resolutions rather fell to the ground. The Evenings are so busy with the garden, and the days are so very hot that I hardly get any writing done. I must, however, make an effort now, as I cannot send any letters home for awhile, so must keep up the diary more faithfully. [2 July 1896]

I won't write more tonight – my ink is thick, my pen is poor, my eyes are tired and my brain feels quite empty. I think I ate too hearty a tea, and all my energies are occupied in my stomach. [29 January 1897]

I don't know why I choose tonight to make up for past omissions for I am positively stupid with a cold in my head. I have been lying down all the afternoon. It was my day at home but I felt too miserable to see any visitors, so I just locked the front door, & went to bed.

It has been rather hard on Hal, for his cold isn't gone either, but he wouldn't let me stay in the office. [10 November 1899]

It is strange that when Spring begins to come, & all vegetable life feels a mighty impulse of new life, humans (as a rule) feel dull & lazy. I don't know that I can honestly blame Spring balminess for my laziness of the past week, as it was hovering around zero until the last two days – but it ought to be Spring weather, & one must find some excuse (besides innate depravity) for one's failings. [17 March 1897]

It is nearly bed time, but I don't want to leave another day unrecorded. I thought I'd start this year on a new plan & be sure to write *every* night – but alas for good intentions! There has been such a rush and bustle today that I don't seem to have had time to think even. [1 January 1898]

I am sadly in arrears and ought to write pages and pages – but I have a sore thumb, sleepy eyes and a lazy mind, so I'm just going to give in to the inclination of all three & do very little. [6 September 1898]

I seem to be getting very lazy about writing, & yet I don't think I am quite to blame – so many things happen to interrupt. I go out so much more than I did at the ranche, & have so many more visitors. [10 September 1898]

After the loss of Hal's job as road superintendent, the Parkes lived on savings for a few months and Hal lent a hand to the hapless Charlie Costerton in the post office:

Hal went down to the post office in the morning, & helped to sort the mail. He felt so sorry for the unfortunate perdicament they were in – Mr. Costerton in the house with measles and Mrs. Macdougal's baby ill with congestion of the lungs. The young boy from the mail car went after the train got in and Hal & he sorted the mail – but it was so cold and draughty in the office that Hal did not dare to go back in the afternoon. [9 February 1899]

Hal told me when he came home in the afternoon that the Inspector was here. Mr. Costerton was not expecting him – he came up from the Southern Country. He was going over the books with Costerton last night, & Hal may know something definite before he leaves town. I think we'll probably be settled before very long now. I am very much afraid Costerton is not going to get the Provincial appointment, and what he will do I cannot imagine. [9 April 1899]

Hal was rather cool to [Mr. Norris] for he is provoked with him. He thinks he has not acted well over the matter of Costerton's appointment. He led Hal to suppose that he would do all he could to further it, & now that he thinks Hal will get the Post Office anyway he doesn't seem to want Costerton[1] in the office here. Hal says it makes him feel so badly, for although the Department had decided to dismiss Costerton anyway, he may think that Hal had worked against him. I don't believe he will, still I heartily wish he would get something else to do. Hal wouldn't ask Mr. Norris in – indeed he told him that he was going down to the Post Office to work for awhile. I went with him to take a lesson. I am sure, if we get it, I'll really enjoy working in there when it is clean – everything is horribly dirty & dusty. We stayed down there until after nine ... [11 April 1899]

Hal was there alone. He knows nothing definite yet ... I think next week will probably settle something. If not Hal says he won't stay any longer in the P.O. I often wonder at him – how he can be so good natured & cheerful – never making me uncomfortable or unhappy by so much as a hint that I am to thank for his being out of employment. I know he'll get a reward sometime. [19 April 1899]

Mr. Costerton had got the Provincial appointment so he sent in his resignation as Post Master, by telegram on Friday, & Hal will likely hear in a week or ten days. He feels sure of the appointment – it is only a matter of time ... [30 April 1899]

Hal heard on Friday from Ottawa, getting the appointment of Post Master. He had to sign a paper and return it to Vancouver and when it comes back the Inspector will probably come too and formally hand the office over to him. I am so glad it is settled. [14 May 1899]

Hal got his appointment last week,[2] but Tuesday the Office was formally handed over. [21 May 1899]

Alice became a working woman acting as unofficial and unpaid assistant postmaster. She was working outside her home for the first time in her life, and helping to operate the post office was enjoyable and challenging for her. She and Hal made a fine team:

All last week was such a hurry and a bustle that Hal and I were both too tired at night to think of any thing. I don't seem to have had time to take in where I am yet. We have the carpets all down now, & the heavy furniture placed, but there are a lot of small things still to do. I have a lounge I want to re-cover and some new cushions to make – then the hall isn't settled atall, or the stair carpet down. [4 June 1899]

Hal says there is one part of the Post Office work I excel him in and that is in remembering the children – such a number of little ones come in, & they must be careful as we never hear any complaints about their losing mail. [15 July 1899]

I am writing in the post office. Hal is tying up the mail for the South … I didn't go out – I sewed a little, but we had a very busy day in the office. [14 June 1899]

I am again trying to write in the post office, but it is something like reading in the dictionary – the subject is changed very often. However it has been very quiet both yesterday and today – no one seems to be doing much business. Of course they all come for their letters but don't do much money order or postal note business.

There has been quite an interval of *wicket* amusement and some of the interviews really are amusing, particularly when the children come. [21 June 1899]

Today news comes that the stage from Greenwood has been held up & the mail stolen. The thieves however missed seven thousand dollars in gold which was coming by express. We have not been used to "hold ups" in this part of the country. Of course Greenwood is scarcely in "this part" but is near enough when such tricks take place. [4 July 1899]

We were very busy in the office all last week but it has been quieter this week. It has been too hot for people to be energetic. [13 July 1899]

I did not write on Sunday – indeed I think I am getting very careless over my entries in this. I often think of it but if the inclination siezes me up stairs, the book is probably down in the office, & when I am down stairs, & am moved to write, very likely the diary is up here, so the opportunity passes. [27 July 1899]

I don't know whether it is handling so much paper & ink, as I do now, that makes me more dilatory about writing – or what it is – but it seems about all I can do to get my letters written. Of course one never manages so much of either reading or writing in the summer; but the days are getting perceptibly shorter now ... Winter seems so much more of a home season than summer ... My ink bottle is nearly empty & I have no more ink upstairs, so I really think I must stop. It is too trying to the nerves to have to dip so constantly. [1 August 1899]

I know a lot of things have happened that I ought to tell about but I am not going to try & tell all I should in this volume. It will be easier to do more in my old way when I begin a new book, & when the winter comes nearer there won't be much temptation to go out in the evenings – so far we have nearly always gone for a walk after tea. [13 September 1899]

This last week was so busy, just a rush from beginning to end. We had visitors every day, & the fair was going on. The inspector was here one day, and I coaxed Hal to go out to the Fair Thursday afternoon & leave me in charge. I got on all right for there really wasn't any business doing, & I only had the mails to manage. Hal ... was very much amused. Old Simpson, a farmer of the Commonage, came up to him on the Fair Grounds, & said he wished to present me with the largest pumpkin in the country – as a recognition of my promptness in the Post Office. Hal wouldn't take it, however, as he said two people could never eat it – but I was greatly surprised. It shows how one never knows who is taking notes – for I am sure I never thought this old fellow ever noticed who gave him the mail. [1 October 1899]

We have to have a drum[3] put in the parlour, so I had to change all the furniture. I haven't got it quite settled yet – nor our room. I had time to cook a nice dinner at noon today. Roast beef, strawberry jam roly poly, vegetable marrow and potatoes – then I was busy in the office till nearly four – then Lizzie came & we went out together, down to see Mrs. Cameron, who isn't any better, and then over to the Johnsons to see poor Mrs. Meighan. [10 October 1899]

In October 1899 Alice began writing about the Boer War. Excitement in the town was high; many of Alice's friends wanted to serve, and her own views were decidedly mixed:

The papers say that war[4] has actually begun in the Transvaal. I am so sorry – I can't help a sympathetic feeling for the Booers though no doubt they have not acted wisely, perhaps not rightly – still they are the weakest, & no doubt will be beaten. [15 October 1899]

The last news from the Transvaal is not very good – if it is authentic. Report says the whole British force has had to surrender,[5] give themselves up as prisoners of war. They will not find the Dutch any easy people to fight – of that I'm sure. [30 October 1899]

News comes today that the Booer leader is killed – Gen Joubert.[6] I wonder if it will hasten the end of the war. How glad we'd be to hear that it was over ... We have been in the Post Office just six months today. It doesn't seem that long in some ways. [16 November 1899]

Alice found great difficulty in continuing the old routine as she approached her first Christmas in the post office; her usual perfectionist self naturally attempted to do everything:

I made my Xmas Cake – or rather cakes – today and got them very nicely baked. It is early, but I had time, so thought I'd better make them. I also cut out my new blouse – but I only got it cut out, nothing more. Tomorrow morning, of course, I'll be busy down stairs, but I may get a little sewing done in the afternoon. [16 November 1899]

... I was very busy until about ten, when I went down to the office for a little while. Of course I had to go back there after dinner until we had got the afternoon mail off, then I came up stairs & cut out some work. ... I don't think I can remember to tell all that I have done each day since I last wrote. I went out two afternoon last week collecting for the hospital – I hated to do it, but I don't suppose any one really enjoys collecting, & it is only fair I should sometimes take my share. I didn't get much money so far. I'll have to go nearly every where over again but I don't know when I'll manage to do so. I want to stay home part of this week any way and do some Xmas sewing. [26 November 1899]

... the muddy roads & mild weather are bad for trade and the merchants grumble but one cannot help thinking how much easier it is for poor people. They do not need much wood, or nearly so much food and clothing as they do in bitterly cold weather and for us, it has been nice, because we have been able so far to use the little back kitchen for all kitchen work. I sometimes, indeed generally, get tea in on the dining room stove, but otherwise use the kitchen as usual. On Monday we had a very busy day – fourteen sacks of mail to distribute, & other business as well. Then Hal had Cryderman here putting in some new boxes in the P.O. When Mr. Dorman was here he told Hal that they were replacing the old boxes in the Victoria post office, and they were selling the old ones cheap – so Hal sent for a nest of thirty-two and had them put in. Boxes freight, & Carpenters charges came to $25.00 and he has already rented eight at $4.00 a year – it is pretty good interest on the money invested. Of course the people only pay one quarter in advance – still allowing for some poor pay I think it was a good move to get them in. We have pretty good hope of renting several more at once. I did not get up stairs on Monday afternoon till after four, but I had been able to sew for a couple of hours in the morning before the train came in – again on Tuesday I sewed. I did not go down that morning, as there wasn't much doing in the office. I did not go out in the afternoon until just before tea. I ran down to Mrs. Cameron's for a few minutes, & in to the store. Yesterday again we had a pretty big mail, but not so large as Monday's. [30 November 1899]

Old friends moved on:

Saturday was a beautifully bright morning. I didn't plan to do much in the house, as I wanted to go up & say good-bye to Miss MacIntyre & Mrs. Martin.[7] I went up about ten & we all felt so badly that I felt used up and tired all the rest of the day. I sewed the rest of the morning and after dinner had to go down to the office, of course, until the train went out – then I came up again & sewed until it got too dark, so then I went over to old Mrs. Godwin's for a few minutes. I took her some apples, & she gave me a nice loaf of bread. I didn't bake yesterday as usual. It was so late when my callers left on Friday that I had no time to go for yeast. [10 December 1899]

Christmas preparations continued:

I don't much believe I'll have this finished to send by Xmas & I really don't think it will be worth sending any way. I write in such a desultory manner, & often so hurriedly. [10 December 1899]

I want to get some little gift for Uncle & for Clare & some thing for Carrie Macdonald's children – then I have quite a lot of letters to write. I want to get something too for Annie & Lizzie Harding. I am hoping the nuts will get here before Xmas, for I want to give some to a few of my children friends here. Xmas is such a lovely time of year I think – one wants to show some kindness to all that one can. [12 December 1899]

The mails are very heavy now, so we are extremely busy in the office. I have my mince meat made and Xmas cake long ago, but still have the pudding to make. [19 December 1899]

I was quite surprised today – there is a young English fellow named Helmer staying with the Copley Thompsons. He got some letters with odd stamps on today, & when Mr. Thompson came in for the mail I asked him if he thought Mr. Helmer would mind giving them to me. He said he was sure not, but would ask. By & by he came over to the other door, & said "Shall I tell you why I think Mr. Helmer wouldn't mind giving you these stamps." Of course I said yes, & he said "Well – when he first came to Vernon he knew no one, & he said he used to come to the Post Office for letters, & none came and he was so homesick and unhappy he just dreaded asking for fear of another disappointment and one day he came in and you gave him a letter and" Mr. Thompson said "he said you looked just as pleased to give it to him as he was to get it and it was like a friendly act – it quite cheered him up." Since then he has got to know Mr. Thompson and asked him who I was, & told the little incident. I do feel awfully sorry for some of the men who come day after day & get nothing – it reminds me of that mournful song Hubert used to sing about the letter that never came. Hal says he's going to put a stop to all these "wicket flirtations" of mine. He says everyone is far too attentive, & they'll be making me conceited but indeed I think I'm about as conceited now as I'll get, & I'm sure acts of kindness are more apt to make us humble than vain. People seem more grateful for a little kindness than the occasion demands … Mrs. Billings has asked us there for Xmas dinner. We had meant to go to the Kalemalka[8] but, of course, it will be nicer to go there. [20 December 1899]

Nearly the end of the week – end of the year – end of the century! All this week the evenings were so taken up that I couldn't get a chance to write. [29 December 1899]

By the new year the Boer War continued, and the demands of work and friends brought even more ambivalence about the diaries:

We are all very eager and anxious for the next war news. One hears all sorts of rumours but the only thing that seems at all certain is that fighting is going on. Tonight there is a report that Buller[9] is getting the best of the engagement, but those poor brave people in Ladysmith[10] are still unrelieved. East Yale is anxious to send fifty men in the next contingent – so many of our young men have put down their names as volunteers – of course they may not be accepted. Mr. McKelvie is wild to go, & Arthur & Maurice Cochrane (Junior)[11] have both volunteered. I had a letter from Mrs. Pelly[12] yesterday, & she says Mr. McMullen, too, has sent in his name. I was sure he'd want to go. He is a trained soldier and was fond of his profession. It is all so terrible – I hate to think of it – the sorrow, suffering & sin that there is in all this warfare. [18 January 1900]

I burned two fingers & the thumb on my left hand tonight – not very badly – but enough to make me rather awkward. I have wrapped them up in soda, & hope they'll be nearly well in the morning, for I had planned quite a lot of work. I was in the office most of today. The train was late, & we had a very big mail ... I ought to go & call on [Mrs. Pemberton] on Thursday but may not be able to get up there – Thursday is generally a busy day here – in the office – & it will be Hal's birthday too, so I don't believe I'll try to go out.

On Friday last we paid a lot of calls – Mrs. Morris, Mrs. Ellison, Mrs. Taylor & Mrs. Cameron. Mrs. Cameron gave is a little jug of cream to bring home. Mrs. Taylor and Mrs. Morris were not in. [22 January 1899]

Rumours that Buller has been defeated[13] – at any rate there surely can't be any thing very good. We have waited so long for word of the relief of Ladysmith. It looks as if those brave & suffering people would not get help in time. [24 January 1900]

I am going to make yet another effort to begin a diary, but I don't even promise myself, this time, to write regularly. Often, when I have time, I don't feel a bit inclined to write, & sometimes when the spirit moves me I have no leisure ... [14 February 1900]

Last week we were all greatly taken up with the coming of a recruiting officer, and the excitement of wondering who would be chosen by him for our share in the "Strathcona Horse,"[14] for South African service. He chose fifteen men all Englishmen but two – one of these a half breed. They went off on Saturday. It made me feel dreadfully – it brings the war so near. I did not know any of the men intimately but knew several of them a little, & Mr. McMullen was one of the chosen ones. I feel so sorry for May Pelly.[15] Mr. McMullen came in on Friday afternoon to say goodbye. It was my day at home, so I had a lot of other people here. I felt really sorry for him, though, of course, he wanted to go. I feel pretty sure that it will be the end of his & May's engagement. Mr. McKelvie, who has been nearly crazy with excitement over the prospect of going, was plucked at the very outset of the exam, not being able to ride well enough.[16] There is no better new[s] about the war. No great advantage seems to be gained by either side. It may yet be long & tedeous. [14 February 1900]

I wish Hal really liked the Post Office, but I don't think he does – though he never grumbles. He has been suffering from indigestion lately, &

it is hard to like any place − I fancy − with a lump in one's chest. [15 February 1900]

I meant to do a lot of writing on Sunday but was too sick all day. I had such back cramps that Hal got the doctor. He said it must have been caused by something I had eaten. It lasted a little all day, but the very bad pain only for about two hours. Hal went down to Mrs. Cameron's & got her hot water bottle, she came over in the evening to see me and brought me some chicken broth. Mr. Norris was in in the afternoon and the doctor came again in the evening. I felt very weak & sore yesterday, but have been all right again today ... The war news seems to be very good now. The tide of fortune has turned entirely, & England is getting the best of it − maybe they'll not need our soldier boys atall. [20 February 1900]

Best friend Lizzie Harding decided to leave Vernon and teach elsewhere:

I am not trying to do anything much upstairs today − am in the office just now while Hal has gone out to do some shopping for me ... We heard from Lizzie. Her vaccinated arm has been very sore. She has accepted a school way up the Cariboo road[17] − said she might drive in here tomorrow. [26 February 1900]

Lizzie had decided to go up to Williams Lake[18] − to take a school there. It is two days stage journey up the Cariboo road from Ashcroft. It is a long way for her go away from us all and I really think she is foolish to try to teach again before Midsummer − but otherwise I daresay she will enjoy the novel experience. [3 March 1900]

The town was crazy on Tuesday with enthusiasm over Crongi[19] defeat. Men & boys paraded the streets all day, waving flags and singing Rule Britannia − etc − and talking about the victory "we" had won. I cannot rejoice over the victories of war − except that this seems to bring the end of the bloodshed nearer. [3 March 1900]

We have been greatly taken up lately with the project of building or buying a new post office − but I think we have just about decided to stay where we are for another year any way. Mr. Jim Martin was in town for a week, and he was most anxious that Hal should buy his building. He offered it at a great bargain − & in some ways it would be nice to own the place − then Mr. Megaw does not want us to move from this part of the town, & offers to put up a new & very convenient building − on the corner next this − & let us pay for it on the instalment plan − however we have pretty thoroughly considered all the pros & cons & have pretty well decided to stay where we are for a while longer any way. Hal hates to move out unless Mrs. Macdougal can rent or sell it to some one else. She has very little besides this building, & I do dread another move.

Last week there was a big slide on the main line, & the mails were thoroughly disorganized. [17 March 1900]

Yesterday the train didn't get in till seven in the evening. It was such a tiresome day – we were waiting all day, & couldn't get at any thing else, & then had to distribute the mail after tea – it was nearly nine when we finished & I was tired. We went early to bed. [5 April 1900]

Alice made one final effort to keep up her writing:

I have brought this down stairs, and am going to try a new plan, to keep my diary down in the office, and see if I can't manage to write a little each day. I have been pretty busy since I made my last entry. I have the house-cleaning all done. I got my big Chinaman for one day, & he did the cleaning of the dining-room & kitchen but I did some extra's this year in the way of varnishing furniture. I believe if I can get up my courage I'll paint the kitchen floor – it would be so much easier to keep clean – & altogether nicer. We have the garden nicely settled, & very soon I think I'll put out my geraniums. My flowers are just beautiful now – every one admires them. [3 May 1900]

I am waiting in the office for the train to come. The mail carrier told us that it would be on time, or I'd have begun at some sewing up stairs. I have been waiting round for half an hour – just doing nothing, which is, after all, pretty hard work. [4 May 1900]

This morning I was very busy. I got up early, & baked bread, made cake, roasted a chicken, and made brioches – & washed my hair – so I was fairly busy. I have been in the office since dinner, but am going up stairs now. [5 May 1900]

On Wednesday morning, 16 May 1900, the first anniversary of Hal's appointment as postmaster, Alice wrote her final entry in the diaries. It was an ordinary account of daily activities and there was no inkling that the end had arrived:

It is just a year today since we took the Post Office over from Mr. Coster-ton. The daily trains began on Monday – so now we'll have a mail every morning. In some ways it is easier, though it doesn't give me as much time up stairs – for after I have been busy in the office for two or three hours I feel too lazy to get at any thing in the way of work. It is afternoon now, we didn't have very much of a mail this morning. I had a nice long letter from Wese. Mrs. Taylor came in the office and was telling me that she was going down on this afternoon's train. She was at Mrs. O'Leary's, & had not meant to go until tomorrow, and meant to send the Youngs word today to meet her, as she was to go out there for a while, but Mrs. O'Leary got word that the O'Keefe's[20] were coming in to stay all night, so Mrs. Taylor thought she'd have to go today, and run the risk of getting out to the Young's. I asked her to come and stay here until tomorrow's train. Of course I'll not be able to spend much time with her, but she will understand that. I have coaxed Hal to go up stairs and lie down – he was so sleepy. When he comes down I'll go out for a little while before it is time for Mrs. Taylor to come. I have the spare-room all ready, and I have some things cooked – but I want to make hot biscuit for tea, and do some steak. She will have the baby and Olive with her, so we'll have quite a houseful. Mrs. Smith was here last night and we arranged to go tonight to the woods for earth – but now I can't go. It rained any way last night, so it might be too wet. I didn't hear from Lizzie today. I thought she'd have written, but I suppose she has so many letters to write ... Mrs. Birnie had sent me a nice little dish of ice cream – all packed in ice – so we had it, & I had cold meat, & boiled eggs. It didn't take long to get tea ready. Mrs. Birnie is so very kind and thoughtful. It rained quite hard last night, but has cleared off nicely now – still I won't be able to go out much, as Mrs. Taylor may come early – and I have some little

The diaries came to a sudden and unexplained end in the middle of a sentence, in the middle of a page. From Barrett family records May 1900 did not coincide with a traumatic event such as the death of either a family member or a close friend. The handwriting on the final half-page took on a steeper slope and was more careless, but that is an insubstantial clue. Since by that time Alice was writing the entries mostly downstairs in the post office, it is not surprising that she should have been interrupted by the arrival of a customer who needed postal services. But she never began again.

However, the final entry in the diaries coincided with a momentous event in her life, for on 16 May 1900 Alice, at the advanced age of thirty-eight (and assuming that she experienced a normal pregnancy), had just conceived her only child, Emily Louisa. Although the diaries had ended, there exists a letter from Alice's mother concerning the happy event:

We conclude that all's well as we have not heard to the contrary . . . Surely some-
one will write and give us all particulars . . . I do hope Annie is with you, and
I think you did quite right to advise Clare to go, I noticed when she was with
us how unhappy she seemed to be at times . . . When you are able to write you
must tell me who baby is like, she will look sweet and pretty I am sure in all the
pretty things she has . . . I am glad they were all ready awaiting her arrival . . .
all your friends seem so pleased; I hope to hear often and that you are getting
stronger and that you will have no trouble with the leg that has been lame for
so long.[21]

Born on 14 February 1901, Emily Louisa Parke died nine months later.

CHAPTER 17

I wonder when I'm a grey haired old woman if I will enjoy reading these papers!

The Final Years

After the death of little Emily Louisa the Parkes remained in Vernon for a further five years, during which there were two deaths in the family. The first was Uncle Henry Barrett, who never returned to British Columbia. After his departure in February 1899 he lived with his brother Joseph at Merced, California, and died there on 30 April 1901 in his seventy-third year. The cough, which he had already suffered for more than a year before he went south, was, together with his severe loss of weight, probably a symptom of lung cancer. Alice also lost her mother. Emily Barrett had suffered for many years from a variety of bronchial ailments and, in her final years, developed emphysema. She died a year after her brother-in-law, on 29 April 1902. She had been married to her dear "Toby" for fifty-two years.

The Parkes, meanwhile, did indeed purchase the post office building from Louise Macdougall in 1902. Hal resigned as postmaster on 30 September 1905, the *Vernon News* of 12 October that year noting that he did so on account of "his eyes not being able to stand the confining duties of the office ... It is understood that Mr. & Mrs. Parke will leave for Dover, Ont., at the end of the month and will spend some months in the east. We are pleased to announce, however, that they expect to return and will continue their residence in the Okanagan." The Parkes' departure for the east at the beginning of November 1905 was covered in two paragraphs by Jack McKelvie, who wrote:

A pleasant surprise awaited them at the station. Just before the train pulled out, G.A. Henderson, W.R. Megaw, S.C. Smith and other gentlemen called the popular postmaster and his wife apart from the group of friends who had assembled to bid them farewell, and, on behalf of the people of Vernon, presented Mr. Parke with a handsome gold chain and diamond ring, and Mrs. Parke with a gold watch and chain. The accompanying address expressed appreciation of the unfailing courtesy, untiring attention and the manner generally in which Mr. Parke had conducted the business of the Vernon post office during the past six and a half years, and also of the way in which Mrs. Parke had seconded his efforts, and of her kindly manner which always made business with the office a positive pleasure.[1]

The Parkes returned to Vernon in the spring of 1906 but not to take up residence again. The *Vernon News* stated: "H.R. Parke has sold his residence on Schubert Street to M.J. O'Brien of Revelstoke ... the many friends of Mr. & Mrs. Parke will be sorry to learn that they expect to leave shortly on their return to Port Dover, Ont., Mr. Parke finding it necessary to be within reach of the eye specialist who is treating him."[2] Alice kept detailed records of the sale of their household contents. Mrs. Cryderman paid ten dollars for the Parkes' bedroom suite, and Mr. Norris purchased bookcases and an encyclopedia set for twenty dollars. Mr. Hull, the fire chief, bought three stoves and Alice's chair for twenty-two dollars, and Mesdames Jacques, French, Birnie, Smith, Costerton, Robson, and Godwin each went home with several items of kitchen ware.

During 1906 the Parkes also sold the post office building to Thomas Ellis. The local newspaper reported their departure once again for Port Dover, stating that "Mr. & Mrs. Parke will take up their residence in Port Dover, Ont., and it is unlikely that they will return to the Okanagan except for short visits."[3]

The Barrett family remained scattered. Alice's elder brother Frank continued to live and work in New York, and died there in 1907, at the age of fifty-three. In 1907, younger brother Clarence had joined an architectural firm in the booming town of Regina. While there he followed family tradition by becoming a Mason and was architect of the new Masonic temple in Regina. He contracted diphtheria, and rather than remain in Saskatchewan, he boarded a train for home and died a few days after his arrival, on 12 October 1907. He was only thirty-eight years old. His death greatly affected the rest of his family and friends.[4] The funeral took place at St. Paul's on 17 October, followed by interment at the Port Dover Cemetery.

The Parkes were still living in Port Dover in 1909; it was clear, though, that Hal's dislike of eastern living was surfacing again, and he set off once more for the west, this time as far as Alberta. By November that year his wife's small memorandum book recorded frequent letters between Edmonton and Port Dover. By spring the following year, she herself had moved to the Alberta capital to join her husband, and by May 1910 plans had been settled to move to Fort Saskatchewan. We know of no prior connection with that town other than the likelihood that Hal already had contacts there from his days in the North-West Mounted Police. The Parkes built a small white clapboard home and barn on the prairie and soon developed and operated a market garden, selling fresh vegetables, eggs, and butter to the townspeople. They did not rely on the market garden as their only source of funds; they received regular income from several mortgages on properties in Edmonton and the Okanagan (the latter account administered by Vernon lawyer and friend, Fred Billings).

Alice's beloved father was eighty-three years old when Alice's diaries ceased, and by the time his daughter left once again for the west in 1910 he was still acting as Port Dover agent for the Norwich Union Insurance Company. Besides his Masonic activities he continued to be a regular churchgoer. On 27 December that year he arrived home from work and asked his grandson Toby to unharness his horse – a most unusual request, since he usually undertook that task himself. Saying that he felt tired, he lay down on the sofa to take a nap. He could not be roused, and died from natural causes at the age of ninety-three.

During the Parkes' Alberta interlude there was continued personal contact with members of the Barrett family. Wese accompanied Toby Barrett (Alice's favourite nephew) on a visit to her sister between May and September 1911 and completed a series of watercolour sketches of wild flowers in the area. Toby later told his own son of sneaking under a fence in Fort Saskatchewan to watch the execution of two men behind the stockade.

Another diary, which covers the years 1912 to 1915 in Fort Saskatchewan, belonged to Hal and was continued by Alice only when, in November 1913, her husband became too ill to carry on with it. Alice's beloved Wese was with her in Fort Saskatchewan during that final year, since both Barrett parents were now dead and Wese was finally free of caregiving commitments. Wese helped Alice to plant the final vegetable crop in 1914, and they were assisted by a local boy who took the produce to market and made other deliveries.

Beginning in January 1914, Alice's entries noted Hal's declining health – "Hal very ill," "Hal worse," "Hal about the same," "Hal no better." He suffered from thrombosis for most of that final year, and, by 12 September, the Parkes were looking for someone to rent their Alberta home; they were successful, and the entry for 17 October 1914 reads: "Leaving tonight for Dover." The three were met at Toronto station by Harry Barrett, who took them all to Port Dover, where Alice and Hal stayed with Hubert and Maude Barrett at their home on Drayton Street. On 22 November Alice wrote that Hal did not get up and the doctor came twice. By Sunday November 24 Hal was worse. The following day's entry reads "no better." A major crisis occurred on Tuesday November 26, when Alice wrote: "Hal was very ill. I thought he was going in the afternoon, Oh, how he has suffered." The next day Hal was "very low but he knows me and wants me with him." Two days later Hal was no longer able to take nourishment, and the following day he died, prompting the poignant entry on 30 November: "Hal is gone – ." His death certificate gave myocarditis as the final cause of death. He was sixty-nine years old and was interred in the Barrett family plot in the Port Dover cemetery. His grief-stricken widow faced his death with Christian forbearance and a strong faith that he had moved on to a higher life.

Alice had no desire to live permanently in the west, and, three months after Hal's death, Wese accompanied her to Fort Saskatchewan to settle her affairs and sell the house. Once there, Alice wrote, on 7 March 1915: "Everyone is kind, but oh! how lonely it is!" Alice realized $4,000 on the sale of the Alberta property, and a month later left the west, never to return. She would spend the remainder of her days living with Wese in Riverbank Cottage. The two elderly women were greatly loved and respected by members of their family; whenever young family visitors called, Wese took care of the welcome at the front door, while Alice headed immediately for the cookie jar.

The Barrett family continued to be centred in Port Dover. After finally deciding not to return to the Okanagan, Harry Barrett had enrolled in the veterinary program at the University of Toronto and graduated in 1906. He remarried that year, his new wife being the nineteen-year-old Hattie Mabel James, who was organist at St. Paul's. A shared love of music had brought the couple together, and they had grown close as they planned for a Gilbert and Sullivan production. Hattie welcomed and showered with loving care Harry's two sons; his third son Frank returned to the family fold upon the death of grandmother Pelly in the Spallumcheen in 1909. In 1912 the Barretts had their own child, Hubert James Harold; Harry's second marriage proved to be lasting and happy.

In 1928 Harry's luck changed unexpectedly when, as the eldest surviving Barrett son, he inherited a considerable estate from the Dick family in Ireland; the total legacy in cash and real estate was valued at more than two million dollars, and it had lain unclaimed for almost seventy years after the death of bachelor Quintin Dick, former head of the Bank of Ireland. Some neighbours had pointed out to Harry an advertisement in the *Canadian National Farm Magazine,* where, in a section entitled "Unclaimed Estates," there appeared the following: "BARRETT – Any male descendant of the sons, grandsons or more remote male issue of Mary Dick, who married William Barrett, and any male issue of Hugh Massey Barrett, who was believed to be living in Montreal in 1846, are requested to communicate with Messrs. Arnold and Henry White, 12 Great Marlborough Street, London, W.1." Harry wrote to the English and Irish lawyers and had little trouble proving his claim. Later that year Alice and Wese accompanied him, his wife Hattie, and son Dick on a journey to London and Ireland to inspect the valuable English real estate and to settle matters with Mr. Dick's lawyer. With the inheritance he built a large and impressive brick home on Prospect Hill in Port Dover, which he named "Clonmel," after property belonging to his Irish ancestors. Harry ensured that other members of his family shared in his good fortune.

Harry developed a prize-winning flock of Shropshire sheep that won many awards through the years. He never learned to drive an automobile, saying he had no use for them; on the farm he continued to use horses where necessary, and Hattie drove the family vehicle. During the 1930s Harry would gather the family together for outings to the movie theatre in Hagerville. His wife drove, and Alice and Wese went along with the group.

Wese Barrett taught Sunday school at St. Paul's Anglican Church for over forty years. After Hal Parke's death, she helped Alice grow a beautiful garden of fruits, flowers, and vegetables for as long as she was physically able; in 1920 she and Alice harvested over 136 bushels of potatoes. Apart from one trip to England and Ireland in 1928, Wese remained with her sister until her death on 26 March 1931, at the age of seventy-four; her heart had become weakened over the years by the unstinting care she gave to members of her family.[5]

Alice's great-nephew, Harry Bemister Barrett, wrote: "While I attended high school in Port Dover & Simcoe from 1936 to 1941 I stayed with my Auntie Alice as it was felt that she should not live alone in the old house after Wese's death. In the summers I looked after a large potato crop to the north of the house, and enjoyed Auntie's rich apple pies and oatmeal cookies. She was a marvellous cook and when I joined the Navy in 1942 Auntie lived on alone quite happily with regular visits from her beloved Harry & my father, Toby." Harry B. also told of an incident during which Alice came up from the cellar, calling out "Oh Harry B. can you help me – I seem to have a rat up the back of my dress." She did indeed;

Harry B. clubbed it between her shoulder blades with a piece of two by four, stunned the animal, and it fell to the floor, where he finished it off.

Ten years after inheriting the Dick millions, Harry Barrett developed cancer of the throat, and family members remember him, at the end, willing himself to die. The disease killed him at the age of seventy-eight in 1942. Hattie lived on at Clonmel until her death in 1970 at the age of eighty-seven.

Alice remained a strong individualist, and after returning to live in Port Dover she chose not to join organizations other than the Women's Auxiliary of St. Paul's Church. Riverbank Cottage was fitted with a supply of natural gas that was used to fuel the cooking stove and gas mantles and was also hooked up to running water and sewer systems. While Alice had a radio and telephone, she made do without many of the modern appliances that were being produced in the 1930s and 1940s. To the end of her life she did all her washing by hand, using large sinks and a scrubbing board in the cellar. She did not have a refrigerator but stored baked items in a wire mesh cupboard outside on the porch. Regularly once a week in later years she would make her way to Hubert's house with an apple pie she had baked for him.

Apart from a serious bout of pleurisy in 1935 and a broken collarbone five years later, Alice's health remained good. To the end of her life her mind was sharp and clear, and she never suffered fools gladly. Her nephew Toby would read Shakespeare to her while she baked apple pies. One day her little great-niece Emily asked her which was her favourite animal; without a moment's hesitation, Alice replied "Men!" She continued to nurture her friendships with great care. She played bridge regularly with Mrs. Battersby, Mrs. Dempster, and a Miss Watson at the Battersby home close by. She was punctilious over correspondence with all her friends, especially those in the west. She kept a little memorandum book and carefully noted all the letters she wrote and received; the well known names in the diaries, including Mrs. McKelvie, Mrs. Costerton, Mrs. Cochrane, Mrs. Jacques, Mrs. Billings, and Miss Byam, all appear here year after year. Jessie and Jack McKelvie visited Alice in June 1923, after his election to the federal Parliament, and received a warm welcome. Harry B. also remembers her receiving a package of preserved ginger every Christmas from Mrs. Ng Shu Kwong; he developed a lifelong taste for the confectionery.

Religion remained of central importance in Alice's life, and to the end she maintained her standards of polite behaviour, the observance of good manners, and the conventions that had shaped her life. Her nephew Toby, who was devoted to his Aunty Alice, wrote in his own diary one Sunday: "Shocked [stooked] oats, and Auntie Alice too!" (She continued to believe that on the seventh day one should rest.) She retained her little vanities, dressing always in either black or purple, with touches of white about the face. Her hair, too, retained its jet-black colour, while her face and eyes showed the age and the wisdom of a life lived. That life remained independent and active to the very end.

Alice celebrated her ninety-first birthday on 5 November 1952, and one month later suffered a mild stroke; afterwards she received home nursing care for three days. Her nephew Toby had been in the habit of calling in every morning for coffee to check up on her, but on that particular day, 8 December 1952, he had an appointment elsewhere, so he asked Jock Noble, the groundskeeper and handyman at Clonmel, to call and deliver milk and the mail to Riverbank Cottage. Noble knocked on the door but received no reply, and he noticed that the blinds were still down. He went in and called out Alice's name, but still there was no reply. He then went upstairs and found her in her bedroom, dead from a massive stroke.

A few days later Alice was buried next to Hal and close to her loved ones in the Port Dover cemetery. Her headstone is small – about eighteen inches high – and simply states: "Alice Butler Barrett, wife of H.R. Parke, 1861-1952." The stone is worn by the weather, and the writing is now faded and difficult to read.

Alice's estate totalled almost $10,000 in cash and real estate. In her will, she bequeathed Riverbank Cottage and its outbuildings to Toby, but since he was already living in his own fine home his wife took charge of the Bridge Street property and made an unsuccessful attempt to turn the old home into apartments. Alice also made several cash bequests – to her brother Hubert and assorted nephews and nieces – and left all her books to Toby. A detailed list of smaller bequests exists, which concludes: "I have not much to leave, only my undying love to all."

Epilogue

Alice's younger brother Hubert survived Alice by a year, dying of natural causes in Port Dover in 1953 at the age of eighty-three.

Nephew Toby had gone into farming with his father, Harry, and on 16 October 1920 he married Marjorie Hazel Clarke at St. George's Church in Haliburton, Ontario. Of British descent, Marjorie was a schoolteacher for five years in Port Dover. She taught Sunday school there and ran the girls' branch of the Women's Auxiliary. She was also admired as a gardener and rug maker. During the Second World War she spearheaded a drive to produce jam from all the windfall fruit lying on the ground and send it to Great Britain under the sponsorship of the Red Cross. One year over twelve tons of jam were shipped. The couple built a large and impressive home, Crabapple Creek, just outside Port Dover, and, during the Second World War, Toby served in the militia in Manitoba and British Columbia. Upon his return at the end of the war, he became a Progressive Conservative member of Parliament but, in 1949, was unsuccessful in retaining his seat. He and Marjorie had five children, the eldest of whom, Harry Bemister Barrett, is the donor of the diaries. Toby died in 1969, a few days after suffering a stroke. His wife survived him by five years, dying in March 1974. They are both buried in the Port Dover cemetery. After Toby's death Riverbank Cottage was willed to his children, and it is now the home of his son Harry B.

Little Dick Barrett did not seem to show a great interest in agriculture. He joined the bank in Port Dover and spent a great many evenings and week-ends in town at plays, hockey, or ball games or skating and swimming in the creek or lake Erie. He rarely seems to have missed a dance. Before the end of the First World War, Dick served overseas with a machine gun unit and was sent to Russia; it was some time after the end of hostilities before he came home. He returned to the bank, and, on 22 November 1934, he wed Alice Roberts of Rockport, Indiana. They had one daughter, Alice Elaine, two years later. Dick obtained a seat on the Toronto Stock Exchange, in partnership with George McCullough (who later became publisher of the *Globe and Mail*). He gradually became blind and died at his home in Rosedale in 1981 at the age of eighty-four.

Once resettled in Port Dover with his father and brothers, Frank Barrett spent many happy hours fishing and hunting, but he never displayed the love of farming or learning that his elder brother Toby displayed. He lived at the Barrett farm until his marriage to neighbour Irene Grace Pickford in May 1928. The couple moved to a large home on Prospect Hill in Port Dover; from there they travelled extensively and led a life of leisure. Frank was physically active until the end, though he did develop problems with his vision. He died in 1981; Irene survived him by eighteen years.

The population of Port Dover today hovers around 5,000 and swells to almost double that number during July and August as the town fills with visitors. For reasons of economy and convenience it has been incorporated into the community of Nanticoke. The village of Port Dover remains a holiday destination and a haven for summer cottagers whose small (and not-so-small) homes line the shores of Lake Erie. The perch and pickerel fishery remains an industry of tremendous importance and is celebrated each July with an annual FishFest. The agricultural character of the surrounding area has been retained, and tobacco growing is widespread. Also grown are corn, grain, fruit, and vegetables.

Heavy industry came to stay during the 1960s, and an oil refinery and coal-burning Ontario Hydro plant are concentrated about eight miles east of the town. (Proximity to heavy industry in the United States causes increasing numbers of air quality alerts during periods of high temperature and weather inversions, and a large area in southwestern Ontario, including Port Dover, is blanketed with a brown haze for several days at a time.) Prospect Hill and Main Street still display many of the impressive brick homes that Alice visited regularly.

The Barretts kept in touch with their western-based Pelly relatives. Nonah's father survived his wife by several years and, after his retirement, went to live with his two daughters on Vancouver Island. He died in Victoria in February 1928 at the age of eighty-two.

The eldest son, Henry Conway Dobbs Pelly, married his cousin Brenda Horsley, who lived on a ranch near Whiteman's Creek. He and his family of six children operated a farm at Knob Hill in Armstrong, which stayed in the family until it was sold in 1938.

Second son, George Stuart Pelly, worked on the farm and on survey work until 1914, when he went overseas with the army. While abroad he was the recipient of a scarf knitted for the troops by Ada Sovereign, who lived in Port Dover. After the war he visited the town with his nephew, Frank Barrett, and he met, fell in love with, and married Ada Sovereign, subsequently making Port Dover his home.

The third daughter, Frances Kathleen (Leena), married Ralph Stanley Worsley, who had emigrated from England in 1908 and articled to Frank Tupper, BCLS, in Vancouver. In 1912 he transferred his articles to R.S. Pelly in Armstrong, where he lived until 1914, when he joined the 2nd Canadian Mounted Rifles in Victoria. The marriage took place in 1915 in a service conducted by Leena's uncle, Charles Pelly, in the old cathedral in Victoria. After the war the couple and their four children lived on a small farm on Noble Road in Armstrong and moved to Victoria in 1927.

May Pelly married her sweetheart Hugh McMullin and raised three children with him. McMullin had served with distinction during the Boer War and was awarded medals for his service in the Transvaal. On his return he joined the British Columbia Provincial Police (BCPP). By 1904 he had been promoted to chief constable in Fernie, and by 1911 he was inspector for the Vancouver Island District, a member of a force of 186 men and officers that policed a population of 392,000. During the First World War he fought overseas and was again decorated for gallantry. He rejoined the BCPP and, in 1923, was appointed superintendent. He was an impressive organizer and introduced a number of reforms and new policies, including the new Police and Prisons Regulation Act, the reorganization of the force into divisions, the use of short-wave radio, the BCPP *Constable's Manual*, and the new uniform of khaki and dark green. In failing health, and after an illustrious career spanning thirty-five years, Hugh McMullin retired from the force in 1939.

The people Alice had met in the Okanagan remained close to her heart. Her dear friend Clara Cameron grew increasingly depressed about her deteriorating health during 1900 and, on 17 December that year, committed suicide by drinking carbolic acid. Her death was a devastating blow to all her friends. After Clara's death, William Fraser Cameron continued to operate his store. In failing health, he closed it in 1911, and the site was eventually incorporated into the parking lot of Eaton's department store. W.F. suffered from Alzheimer's disease and died in Guelph, Ontario, in 1912.

Five months after Alice's diaries came to an end, William Maurice Cochrane died suddenly on 16 October 1900, aged fifty-six. His widow Addie continued to do good works in Vernon. She died in 1920, and her funeral was one of the largest ever seen in the city.

Frederick and Maude Billings continued to live in Vernon. Freddie's condition did not improve, and he continued to lead a secluded life. Twins, a son and daughter, were born on 12 September 1901, but the girl, Muriel, died five months later. After the death of his partner, Pa Cochrane, Billings entered into partnership with Cochrane's son Arthur, and the firm continued to act on the Parkes' behalf for several years. Billings himself died in Montreal (where he had gone for surgery) at the age of forty-eight on 11 June 1915.

Price Ellison held portfolios in the McBride provincial government. He was commissioner of lands in 1909, commissioner of finance in 1910, and commissioner of agriculture in 1913. He continued to live in the Okanagan, purchasing more land (including the Postill Ranch in 1903) and died in 1932. Sophie Ellison lived on in Vernon and died there in 1954 at the advanced age of ninety-seven.

Lord and Lady Aberdeen left Canada in November 1898. In May 1906 Lord Aberdeen sold the Coldstream Ranch to the Coldstream Estate Company, in which he was a partner. Privately the family acknowledged that none of the money spent on developing the property as rich orchard land ever came back, and, once in Great Britain, they found themselves forced to live in somewhat more straitened circumstances than they would have liked. From 1906 to 1915 the Aberdeens served another vice-regal term, this time in Ireland. Once more Ishbel threw herself into good causes, supporting the home craft of lace making and establishing the Women's National Health Association to fight tuberculosis; she oversaw the opening of the Peamount Sanitarium in October 1912. She fought for the protection of handloom weavers and for urban renewal. The Aberdeens were both known sympathizers with the movement for self-rule in Ireland, and they left their posts after the Easter Uprising of 1916.

The couple made a farewell visit to the Coldstream while travelling through North America in the winter of 1915-6, and the ranch finally passed into the hands of Lord Woolavington in 1921. Lord Aberdeen left public life in 1920, when he was seventy-three and the countess sixty-three. They settled down at Cromar, a retirement villa not far from the royal family retreat at Balmoral. There they wrote their memoirs, *We Twa*, and kept up a prodigious correspondence with people and organizations on both sides of the Atlantic. They celebrated their golden wedding in 1927, and Lord Aberdeen died seven years later. Lady Aberdeen moved from Cromar to a house in Aberdeen and suffered a fatal heart attack on 18 April 1939. She was eighty-two years old.

In November 1897 Edgar Dewdney retired from his position as lieutenant-governor of British Columbia and continued to supervise his varied business interests. Jane Dewdney died from cancer in January 1906 and was buried in Victoria. Dewdney visited England three years later and married Blanche Tynte, of Halswell, Somerset, who was probably the girl he left behind when he immigrated to Canada. Blanche inherited his entire estate when he died in August 1916.

Young Walter Robert Dewdney was able to make good use of his family connection to the lieutenant-governor; between 1901 and 1912 he was a member of the government office staff in Grand Forks and was government agent in Greenwood. He married Kathleen Stuart Ferguson in 1912 and, with her, raised a family of one daughter and three sons. On 1 April 1922 he opened the first government office in Penticton and worked there as government agent until his retirement on 1 January 1947. In September two years earlier he had been acclaimed "Dean of the Government Agents" by a gathering of his peers in Victoria. He died in Penticton at the age of seventy-nine on 26 February 1956.

To Alice's great dismay Lizzie Harding decided to marry Billy Holliday in 1905 (Alice and Hal did not stay in town long enough to attend the wedding). The couple had three children and made their home in the Okanagan for over thirty years before moving to Victoria in 1937. In 1948 Holliday published his own book of recollections of life in the Okanagan Valley; it was entitled *Valley of Youth*. In old age he suffered from atherosclerosis and hypertension, and he died in the provincial capital after a heart attack on 18 July 1955, aged eighty-five. Lizzie died there three years later at the age of eighty-seven.

After he left Vernon, Alice's dear friend Forbes Kerby moved first to Midway and then opened an office in Greenwood. Between 1899 and 1901 he surveyed the townsites of Deadwood, Rendell, and Carmi, and he developed a wide knowledge of the Boundary area. After his marriage to Ida Birnie he established an office in Grand Forks in 1902 and was in practice there until his death in 1938. The Kerbys had three children: a daughter born in 1904, a son born in July 1908 who died three months later, and a second daughter born in October 1909. He was active in his adopted community in political, educational, fraternal, civic, church, and social circles and was remembered for his many kindnesses to others. Kerby died on 10 March 1938; Ida and their two daughters survived him, and Ida died at the age of seventy-one in March 1952.

Jack McKelvie married Jessie Stuart MacIntyre in 1902 and continued to manage his beloved *Vernon News* until he entered federal politics. He was known as the "Encyclopedia Okanagansis" because he had such a vast knowledge of the valley's history and people. Elected as a member of Parliament in 1920, he was renowned as a public speaker, and his maiden speech in the House was said to be the best in many years. He died after a heart attack in Ottawa on 24 June 1924, aged fifty-nine. So many people wished to pay their respects that his civic funeral in Vernon had to be held in Polson Park. His body lay in state in the courthouse, and pallbearers included many of the most illustrious names in Vernon's history. Jessie survived her husband by three years and died in Vernon in February 1927, aged seventy. There were no children.

In 1907 Osborne Morris was appointed public health officer to the growing community of Coldstream, which had been incorporated in December 1906. In this capacity he had to deal with the frequent outbreaks of typhoid in the area, and he pushed for a water system that was developed within a few years. Dr. Morris enjoyed a forty-eight-year medical career in the Vernon area. He served as CPR surgeon, city medical officer, district coroner, and health officer. He also became a member of the board of the BC Medical Association. He died in 1944.

Leonard Norris continued as government agent for thirty-three years until 1926. He remained an active Mason and was co-founder of the Okanagan Historical Society, which had its inaugural meeting on 4 September 1925. Norris never married and, after his retirement, he spent the winters in Victoria. He died on 18 April 1945, shortly after his final return to the Okanagan.

Almira McCluskey's experiences as a widow made her determined to change the inheritance laws of the province. After her marriage to William Furniss in 1898, she followed Sophie Ellison as president of the Women's Institute and lobbied doggedly as far as the provincial Parliament to have changes made in the law so that widows and orphans would not be rendered destitute after the death of their bread-winner. Furniss died in 1912, and Almira survived him by almost thirty years. She died in Vernon in October 1941, aged eighty-seven.

By 1900 Cornelius O'Keefe had married his third wife, Elizabeth Tierney, and owned over a thousand head of cattle and a large acreage. The third O'Keefe marriage produced six children. In 1907 he sold 5,700 acres to the Land and Agricultural Company of Canada for $184,193. He died at the age of eighty-two on 29 May 1919.

Catherine Schubert lived on in the Okanagan Valley until her death in 1918, and her funeral in Armstrong was one of the biggest ever held there. In 1926 a monument was unveiled to her memory in Armstrong, and its inscription reads: "In honour of Catherine Schubert who in company with her husband and three small children was a member of the hazardous overland expedition of 1862 across the Canadian Rockies from Fort Garry to Kamloops. A brave and notable pioneer. Erected by her friends and admirers throughout British Columbia."

For most of its life the *Vernon News* was a weekly, then in 1954 it moved to two editions a week. By 1970 the paper had been bought by the Thompson newspaper chain and had moved to a location on 31st Avenue. In 1973 it became a daily newspaper. For twenty more years it struggled to make the profits that its new owners demanded, but, with the debut of the *Morning Star,* a free publication, the struggle ended, and the *Vernon News* ceased publication in 1996.[6]

The first decade of the twentieth century brought rapid growth to Vernon's population as well as many amenities. By 1902 gas streetlights were replaced with electric ones, and the first high school class accepted twenty-four students. The first city hall (which also served as a fire station and public reading room) followed a year later. By 1904, Vernon had grown to be the biggest town in the valley. Commercial fruit farming was going from strength to strength, thanks to an influx of mainly British immigrants who settled in the Coldstream area to the southeast of the town. By 1908 one million fruit trees had been planted, and the Grey Canal irrigation system, stretching for twenty-nine miles from Lavington to Okanagan Landing, delivered water to them.

Automobiles had become a common sight in the streets, a school of nursing had been opened, telephone service arrived, and the Royal (now

National) Hotel opened. Cattle ranching on a huge scale was drawing to a close, and ranches were being subdivided into smaller lots. Steamboats now made daily trips south from Okanagan Landing.

A large sewage system was installed and cement replaced wood in the sidewalks on Barnard Avenue. Central School on Mara opened in 1909 – an impressive three-storey red brick building with a large cupola on top; it still stands today and is home to Beairsto Elementary French Immersion School. A new Jubilee Hospital was built on Mission Hill, and the shores of Okanagan Lake were the site of the first cavalry training camp in British Columbia. For leisure there was a new rink on Langille Avenue; Price Ellison converted an old freight shed into a rough and ready "opera house," and, in 1908, Vernon saw its first moving pictures.

After the First World War, Vernon's importance gradually diminished, while Kelowna, with the advent of the railway, a connecting highway, and a floating bridge across the lake, eventually became the Okanagan Valley's major centre. Today the population of Greater Vernon stands at almost 44,000.

Introduction

1   An alternative version of the Barrett family lineage showed them to be of Latin descent, with the name "Barretti"; indeed, all of Alice's surviving siblings had black hair, dark eyes, and swarthy features.

2   Alice was named "Butler" after the minister who had performed her grandparents' wedding ceremony.

3   "British Columbia's aboriginal peoples were among the world's most distinctive. Linguistic divisions were complex, economies self-sufficient, and cultures more developed, in many respects, than in any part of the continent north of Mexico." See Jean Barman, Neil Sutherland, and J. Donald Wilson, eds., *Children, Teachers and Schools in the History of British Columbia* (Calgary: Detselig Enterprises, 1995), 59.

4   Susan Moir Allison wrote down as many aboriginal myths and stories as she could, and she always held aboriginal people in high regard. The wife of pioneer cattleman John Fall Allison, in 1868 she was the first white woman to arrive in the Similkameen Valley; she later came to be known as the Mother of the Similkameen. For several years she remained isolated and coped with tremendous loneliness as she raised a family of fourteen children. For her, writing became a substitute for companionship. Alice, on the other hand, regarded her aboriginal neighbours with humorous disdain. Both women were complicated, multifaceted personalities who showed tremendous strength of character in adversity and who shared a deep faith in a protective God. Both were middle-class white women proud of developing skills they had never needed before; they were resourceful, practical, devoted to husband and family, and, indeed, they proved to be invaluable helpmeets to their husbands. The two shared a deep love of the natural landscape and natural history, and everyone they met aroused their curiosity. Susan and Alice wrote about many of the same people – ranchers, government officials, merchants, and pioneer women – and each described the destructive floods that wrought such havoc in their valleys in 1894. Both women later worked in their respective local post offices, and Susan also served in the local store and kept accounts for her husband. Susan had adjusted quickly to her new surroundings and attained a deep sense of contentment with life in the Similkameen; Alice, on the other hand, never looked upon the Okanagan as her home, always feeling herself to be an exile and longing to return to her family in Port Dover. Both women lived into their nineties and survived their husbands by many years. For further reading, see Margaret Ormsby, ed. *A Pioneer Gentlewoman in British Columbia* (Vancouver: UBC Press, 1976).

5   Writer Agnes Maule Machar (1837-1927) was born in Kingston, Ontario, to parents who both came from religious and scholarly backgrounds. A committed social crusader, she examined many issues largely overlooked by her peers, such as the negative effects of industrialization, women's rights, compulsory education, and workplace conditions. She was respected as a compassionate social critic.

6   Indeed, we have to wait until Volume 25 before we see her emotions expressed with unfettered candour.

7   Emily Louisa Parke died on 13 November 1901. There is no record showing the cause of her death, although we do know that it occurred after an illness of several weeks.

8   Harry Bemister Barrett to Jo Fraser Jones, 25 February 1997.

Chapter 1: *Quite away from all my people*

1   William Henry Barrett, born in Port Dover, Ontario, in 1864, was the second son of Theobald
    Butler Barrett and Emily Langs. He had worked in Chicago for a time in 1886, and in 1887
    he accepted his Uncle Henry's invitation to go out to Spallumcheen in British Columbia to
    help him work the Mountain Meadow Ranch. Over the years, Harry had grown close to
    his uncle: "I think a lot of him. He is outspoken, but you can bet on just what he says; darn
    if he doesn't write me quite affectionate letters." See WHB to TBB, 7-9 February 1888. Harry
    had been farming for more than three years before his sister arrived. Well educated and ever
    keen to improve himself, he learned by heart Scott's *The Lady of the Lake* while walking
    behind his plough.
2   Henry Harding (1867-1943) was originally a friend of the Barrett family in Port Dover,
    Ontario. He was the only son of Hugh B. Harding (1812-1902), a farmer there, and Louisa
    Mencke (1827-1915); he had seven sisters, three of whom had come west to train as teach-
    ers in Vancouver. Harding had pre-empted land in the Pleasant Valley area, east of Otter
    Lake, in October 1885.
3   Port Dover native Elizabeth Harding (1871-1958) was Harry Harding's sister, the youngest
    child and seventh daughter of Hugh B. Harding and his wife Louisa Mencke. Although she
    was ten years younger than Alice, she was to become one of her greatest friends and her
    closest confidante.
4   Alice's mother, born Emily Langs on 10 October 1827, was the daughter of Phoebe Sovereign
    and Joseph Langs, a prosperous farmer of Pennsylvania Dutch stock who owned land in
    Windham Township north of Simcoe, Ontario. She married Theobald Butler Barrett on 28
    March 1850 and gave birth to eight children, of whom Alice was the fourth daughter.
5   Sicamous was a small railway station about forty-two miles north of Vernon, located at the
    junction of the CPR main line and the Shuswap and Okanagan (S&O) branch line that
    went to Vernon.
6   English immigrant Richard Noble Taylor (1865-1897) was a druggist at that time. He had
    trained at the Manchester College of Pharmacy and was also a graduate of Edinburgh Uni-
    versity. Taylor had arrived in the Okanagan Valley in 1889, ready to do anything, and Alice
    considered him an engaging, friendly, and handsome young man.
7   Colonel Forrester had served under General Gordon in China and now operated the Lake
    View Hotel in Sicamous.
8   Mountain Meadow Ranch, near Otter Lake, was about nine miles northwest of Vernon.
    Uncle owned 320 acres, the northern half of Section 36 Township 7 ODYD. Henry Barrett
    had written: "None of it is clear, but a good deal of it could be got ready for the plow for
    less than five dollars an acre. There are no buildings on it. Now, if Harry chooses to come
    out here I will give him a SHOW – take him in as a partner, and do what I can for him
    ... If Harry comes out and does not like the country I will pay his way back ... I am not
    able to work it myself, still at times I could lend a helping hand, if I had someone to take
    hold of it." See HB to TBB, 2 April 1886.
9   Henry Barrett was the eleventh child of Hugh Massey Barrett and Caroline Butler Barrett
    and the younger brother of Alice's father, Theobald Butler Barrett. Born in Ireland on 6
    August 1828, Henry was not yet two years old when the family immigrated to Sorel in Lower
    Canada. In 1849 he had gone to California with his older brother, Joseph, and together they
    filed a number of gold claims near the Merced River. He did not have great success with
    his gold-seeking ventures, but he did become an accomplished builder and finishing car-
    penter. In January 1879 he was already at Cherry Creek, assessing mining opportunities there,
    and in the early 1880s he had pre-empted land in the Spallumcheen area of British Columbia
    and built the cabin to which Alice would come in 1891. "I pitched my tent here because I
    was weary of roaming about the world, and not because I thought this an exceptionally good
    locality." See HB to TBB, 12 March 1882. He recognized that he was no farmer, and prob-
    ably never would be. A life-long bachelor, he was a crusty individual known for his waspish
    tongue and critical attitudes.
10 Emily Louisa "Wese" Barrett was Alice's devoted and cherished elder sister. Born in

Port Dover in 1857 she would never marry, remaining in Port Dover to look after her aging parents and others. She was selfless in the love and care she lavished on her less fortunate relatives. After the death in 1884 of the oldest Barrett child, Carrie, she helped care for her two nephews, Walter and Roy Scott. She was a self-taught artist, creating beautiful paintings and collages for the members of her family and her friends. She wrote voluminous letters and cards and taught Sunday school regularly.

11   At the time Alice arrived in the Okanagan there was no organized Anglican parish with regularly scheduled services. Ministers were itinerant and services were held in barns, meeting rooms, and people's homes. The little church was St. James, in Lansdowne.

12   Born in Port Rowan, Ontario, Robert Wood (1841-1921) originally intended to go into engineering, but that was frowned on by his parents, so after farming at home for three years he had first joined in the gold rush in the Cariboo and later farmed in Washington State; after farming on the North Arm of the Fraser River for ten years, he moved, for health reasons, to the Spallumcheen, where he and Daniel Rabbitt (a new arrival from Nova Scotia) became partners in a trading store in Lansdowne. The store was destroyed by a disastrous fire in 1886, and Wood lost between $7,000 and $8,000 worth of goods. But he was a man of diverse interests and dreams. He set about purchasing tracts of land, including the swampy "Island" on which Armstrong now stands, and laid out the townsite. He wanted to develop the Vernon-Midway Railway to open up the southern section of the valley, and later he envisioned a continuous waterway through the Okanagan – a waterway that would connect the Fraser and Thompson water systems. He was unable to secure federal funding for the latter and so it came to nothing. He turned his sights to the southern end of the valley, where he bought two sections of land in the Boundary Creek area; this would subsequently become the community of Greenwood.

13   Alice was deeply affected by the beauty of the Okanagan landscape. "Looking out of the [kitchen] door you see immense mountains about 5 miles off; & today there have been such lovely clouds hovering around them; there will be a cloud and then higher up you see the trees or the mountain side, then more clouds and then the top – it is lovely, but I can't half enjoy anything alone." See ABB to WB, 16 March 1891.

14   Arthur Clarence Barrett was the youngest of the Barrett children, the fourth son. Born in 1869, Clarence had considerable artistic talent; many examples of his art work still exist, including beautiful pen-and-ink drawings of Riverbank Cottage and its outbuildings. Clarence graduated from the University of Toronto with a degree in architecture. With his brother Hubert he was known in the family as a great joker and raconteur.

15   Born in 1830, Englishman James Crozier, his Ontario-born wife Lucinda, and five of their six children had arrived in the north Okanagan in 1867 and were among the first settlers in the area. Crozier was a flour miller and had been joined by his son, Charlie, after the latter's graduation from the Agricultural College in Guelph, Ontario. Seventeen-year-old Lucy Marshal Crozier was born in Lillooet.

16   Gulliver was Harry Barrett's dog.

17   Of Scottish descent, widower Henry Swanson (1850-1928) was a close neighbour. He owned land due north of Mountain Meadow Ranch, which he worked with the help of two farmhands.

18   Of Scottish descent and born in Prince Edward Island, Myles Macdonald (1864-1930) had walked to Spallumcheen from Vancouver with Leonard Norris in 1884. He farmed land to the west of Mountain Meadow Ranch and was the Barretts' nearest neighbour.

19   Augustus Schubert Jr. was the eldest child of Francis Augustus and Catherine Schubert, pioneers in the valley, who in 1862 had been members of the group of Overlanders who made their way on horseback and in ox-carts from Manitoba to the interior of British Columbia. He would acquire the deed to the Gum Boot Ranch, immediately south of the Barrett place, from his brother James in October 1891. Gus and his wife, Elizabeth, had three daughters and were expecting a fourth when Alice first knew them.

20   Carrie Macdonald was the daughter of Louisa Maria Barrett and Frederick R. Wyld, a merchant in Toronto, Ontario. She was a cousin and close friend of Alice, but their relationship did not always run smoothly.

21   Hugh Jacob Francis Barrett was the eldest son and second child of Theobald and Emily Barrett. Born on 4 January 1854 in Port Dover, he had married Hattie Sayles in 1884. He operated dry goods stores in Chicago and, later, in New York.

22   Catherine Honora Schubert was the youngest child of pioneers Francis Augustus and Catherine Schubert and was born in Lillooet on 18 January 1872; she was called "Nora" to avoid confusion with her mother.

23   Church activities were a part of most women's lives. Besides teaching Sunday school, they belonged to special organizations through which they could make a practical contribution to the church. Church attendance was an important social occasion and offered a welcome change from the labour and drudgery of daily life.

24   Forty-year-old Welsh-born widow Bessie Waters was Daniel Rabbitt's housekeeper and had previously held the same position at the Vernon Hotel.

25   John Knox Wright was the Presbyterian minister for Spallumcheen and Vernon, and he was an outstanding ecclesiastical authority of the Presbyterian Synod. He and his family had lived in Trinidad for over four years and came to western Canada for the sake of Mrs. Wright's health; the rest of his family came out from Ontario in 1890. Wright had succeeded the Reverend Jaffray in 1889 and covered the same wide territory until the following year, when the field was divided and the Reverend Langill took charge of the Vernon area.

26   Enderby was a small town, with an area of 1.02 square miles, located twenty-three miles north of Vernon. It had previously been known as Steamboat Landing, Fortune's Landing, Lambly's Landing, and Belvidere. The town was the terminus for the riverboat service from Sicamous and had thriving ranching, farming, and logging operations.

27   A go-devil was a type of heavy sled used to move logs and other bulky materials.

28   The children were Alice's nephews. Born on 11 August 1876, Walter Barrett Scott was the elder son of her late sister Carrie and James Scott. Since their mother's death in 1884 Walter and his younger brother Roy, born on 22 August 1879, had been cared for by their aunts Wese and Alice. Walter would eventually go on to study at the University of Toronto and become a lawyer. Roy Scott would also attend the University of Toronto and would train as an architect.

29   Minnie Shickluna (1874-1902) was a young Roman Catholic woman of Maltese heritage living at the Riley residence in Enderby in 1891; Mrs. Riley was her aunt. Minnie was the granddaughter of the well known Maltese ship builder, Louis Shickluna, who had died in eastern Canada in 1880.

30   The first stagecoach service in the Okanagan had been established in August 1872 by Francis Jones Barnard and ran as far south as the O'Keefe Ranch. His Barnard Express offered weekly services for passengers, freight, and mail. From small beginnings, using two-horse coaches, the BX progressed to the impressive and colourful Concord stagecoach, with red body-work and yellow running gear.

31   Fifty-year-old Irish-born Senator George Riley was secretary-treasurer of the Shuswap and Okanagan Railway (this was the "road" referred to). Railroad House had previously been a hotel built by the Lambly brothers; the Shuswap and Okanagan Railway bought the building and used it as headquarters for the railway and as a temporary home for railway supervisory personnel and their families. Thirty-four-year-old Roman Catholic Emma Riley was Minnie Shickluna's aunt, and she was exceedingly protective of her young niece. Upon completion of the railway, the Rileys would move to the Nicola area.

32   Born in Scotland in 1856, Thomas Patterson and his Ontario-born twenty-five-year-old wife, Emma, were temporary residents in the Okanagan Valley and lived in Enderby during the construction of the Shuswap and Okanagan Railway, on which Patterson worked as one of those in charge of construction.

33   Forty-year-old Scotsman William Smith and his twenty-seven-year-old Ontario-born wife Ida lived in the former Lambly Hotel in Enderby during the construction of the Shuswap and Okanagan Railway. Smith was a supervisor on the project.

34   The earliest recorded Chinese immigrants in western Canada came as labourers, carpenters, and shipwrights with Captain John Meares in 1788. He arrived in search of otter pelts to sell in China, where they were used in the making of mandarins' robes. Within thirty or

forty years these Chinese men no longer existed as a recognizable group. Some accounts say they were taken by marauding Spaniards; others say they were assimilated into the aboriginal population. By 1849, to escape over-population and oppression in their own country, Chinese workers were flocking to the goldfields of California, later working their way north into British Columbia to pursue mining opportunities there. By the final decade of the nineteenth century the Chinese had become a large and important component of the life of western Canada. They were heavily involved in mining, canneries, and railroad building; in towns they could be found working as merchants, servants, cooks, launderers, and general handymen.

35 Born in England in 1819, seventy-three-year-old Elizabeth P. Lambly was the widow of Jonathan R. Lambly, who had been registrar of titles for the Province of Quebec; she was the mother of leading citizen Thomas McKie Lambly and a resident of Enderby.

36 A native of Holland born in 1850, physician Edo Johannes Offerhaus had arrived in Lansdowne in 1883 and owned property northeast of Mountain Meadow Ranch. Before his coming, settlers either had to manage as best they could or go to the coast for treatment. Offerhaus's practice covered the Armstrong/Enderby area.

37 In 1887 the forty-one-year-old Englishman George Richard Lawes, a rancher in the Enderby area, had gone into partnership with George Rashdale to construct a five-storey roller mill there. Lawes was an experienced miller, but the partners found themselves in financial difficulties soon after the mill was completed, and by August 1888 the property had been conveyed to their creditors.

38 Named after an earlier governor general of Canada, Lord Lansdowne, a hotel had been opened on 1 July 1885 by E.M. Furstineau at a convenient stopping place for visitors about two miles north of Otter Lake. A small village of 100 residents had grown up around it; Lansdowne was the nearest community to Mountain Meadow Ranch.

39 Doing the wash was a physically wearing and time-consuming operation. Whites had to be boiled in a big pot on the stove and coloureds were scrubbed on the washboard. Hand-made lye-based soaps were used, and everything had to be rinsed thoroughly by hand afterwards. After wringing (and if you were lucky, mangling, the items) everything was hung to dry, either on lines outdoors (in favourable weather) or festooning rooms indoors (in unfavourable weather). Alice heated heavy flatirons on the stove, using each one until it cooled, then replacing it with another. "I often think of the fuss I used to make at home if I couldn't have room on the stove for all the irons – and here I have only two little ones – but I manage – one never knows how little one can do with." See ABB to TBB, 29 April 1892.

40 Born at Leeds, Megantic County, Quebec, in 1851, bachelor Thomas McKie Lambly had sold his bookstore in New Westminster in order to follow his brother, Robert, to the Okanagan. The brothers had settled in the Spallumcheen in 1877, ranching on the present site of Enderby. In 1878 Thomas had been appointed assistant commissioner of lands in the area, and before his appointment as government agent he served a term as chief licence inspector for Yale District.

41 Alice did not know it, but it was during her visit to Enderby on 19 April that she was first seen and admired by the man who would become her husband – Harold Randolph Parke.

42 The twenty-year-old Maud Scofield, Alice's friend in Port Dover, was the youngest daughter of the late Norman B. and Calista Scofield, who had operated a dry goods, hardware, and ship's chandler's store for several years in the business block they owned on Main Street in Port Dover. Maud was already being courted by Hubert Barrett.

43 Ontario friend Nellie Workman was about to immigrate to New Zealand.

44 Irish-born Charles Warburton Ireland (1852-1928) had come to the Okanagan Valley from New Zealand and would use his legal training when he became police magistrate in Vernon.

45 Frances Ann Finch Bales was the seventh daughter of old Mrs. J.R. Lambly and lived in Enderby with her mother, two-year-old daughter Olive, and brother Thomas.

46 George H. Rashdale was a young Englishman from Suffolk who, in partnership with George Lawes, built a large grist mill in Enderby in 1885. This operation would prove to be unsuccessful, and he moved to Nelson to become mining recorder.

47 Born in Nova Scotia in 1854, Daniel Rabbitt was a partner with Robert Wood in a trading

store in Lansdowne, the first in the area. He would become the first postmaster in Armstrong, holding the position from 1892 to 1897.

48 Rabbitt's two sisters were Mary, born in Nova Scotia in 1856, and twenty-two-year-old Hanna.

49 Cornelius O'Keefe (1837-1919) was born in Ottawa and went to the Cariboo in 1862 to help build the Cariboo Road between Clinton and Bridge Creek. In 1867, with Thomas Greenhow (later his partner) and Thomas Wood, he headed a cattle drive from Oregon to Big Bend. All three saw the Okanagan Valley as a good prospect for cattle ranching and pre-empted land there. Between 1868 and 1871 O'Keefe acquired 640 acres at the head of the lake, and in 1883 he bought 715 acres from Colonel C.F. Houghton. By 1891 O'Keefe owned a herd of 1,000 cattle and extensive lands. In 1877 he had returned to Ottawa to marry Ontario-born Mary Ann McKenna (1849-1899), with whom he had nine children.

50 Henry Schneider (1859-1922) was born in the United States of German Lutheran descent and had come from Kamloops to Lansdowne in 1887 to set up in business as a blacksmith; in March 1892 he would move his building and operation to Armstrong, where he also acted as community policeman. Schneider also operated the Black Hawk livery stable.

51 The Pleasant Valley area was east of Otter Lake. Pleasant Valley Road followed an old aboriginal trail that connected the Spallumcheen Valley and Vernon.

52 Edward "Ned" Thorne was a close neighbour at Otter Lake and was one of the acknowledged "characters" of the area. "He had started life as a London 'bobby,' but that disciplined life was not for him, and he had drifted out to Spallumcheen, where he pre-empted land – certainly Ned did not lack 'guts,' for he had cleared some forty acres and put up log buildings, a cabin, stable and chicken house." See C.W. Holliday, *Valley of Youth* (Caldwell, ID: Caxton Printers, 1948), 265.

53 Alice did not write about Harry's business affairs in the diaries. However, she did confide the following to Wese: "I asked him if he really knew what he owned here & he said yes – a half interest in the ranch – which he considers well worth ten thousand dollars." See ABB to WB, 16 March 1891. Later she wrote home that "Harry had a talk with Uncle and they are going to have some settled arrangement made about the partnership before I go home. Harry said he told Uncle he thought it would be only right, and Uncle agreed with him." See ABB to EB, c. April 1892.

54 George Birkett Taylor (1861-1945) was an English immigrant who owned property in the Upper Deep Creek/Gardom Lake area, close to Mount Ida.

55 Born in Scotland in 1859, William Berry Paton was a general merchant and would become Spallumcheen postmaster in 1894, holding the position for eighteen months. He would marry Annie Carter Wright in September 1893 at Lansdowne.

56 Railway worker Patrick Joseph Mulraney (1844-1923) and his wife Mary, born in 1852, were immigrants from Ireland and were known throughout the valley for their colourful characters and flamboyant language. They boarded a gang of railway workers during the construction of the Shuswap and Okanagan Railway; Mary was an excellent cook and took great pride in showing people what spectacular meals she could produce.

57 Hubert Baldwin Barrett, Alice's brother, was born in 1867 in Port Dover. He enjoyed fishing and hunting, and, with his younger brother Clarence, played many tricks at the expense of family and friends. In February 1896 he would marry Maud Scofield and open a haberdashery shop.

58 The Shuswap and Okanagan Railway Company was building the railway spur line from Sicamous to Okanagan Landing (west of Vernon) at that time.

59 Oliver Harvey operated a general store and post office in Enderby.

60 English native Samuel Gibbs (1849-1925) had succeeded George Lawes as manager of the Columbia Flouring Company in Enderby but would lose that position within two years. He was also a local magistrate and the father of eight children.

61 Charles E. Perry was in charge of the construction teams then building the Shuswap and Okanagan Railway. He was living in Enderby while the task was under way, and upon its completion he would move on to more railway work in the Kootenays.

62 This could have been either Charles Ernest Costerton or his brother Clement Fisher; each would later make his home in Vernon.

63   The 1891 census shows that Oliver Harvey shared lodgings with Dick Taylor, George Rashdale, and Clement Costerton.

64   In October 1875 Toronto native James Scott had married Carrie Barrett, Alice's eldest sister. The couple lived in Chatham, Ontario, for several years, where James operated a dry goods store. Born in 1851, Carrie died on 24 March 1884, two weeks after giving birth to her second daughter, Caroline Louise, and was brought home to be buried in Port Dover cemetery. (Besides their two sons, Walter and Roy, another daughter, Mildred Bell, had been born in September 1881 and had died, aged two, in June 1883, ten months before her mother.) After his wife's death, the distraught James left his two young sons with the Barretts in Port Dover; Alice and Wese looked after them with great devotion. His baby daughter was raised during her early years by the Scott family in Toronto, and James himself soon moved there to explore business opportunities. By 1894 he was operating an agency representing the Cornwall Manufacturing Company and the Richelieu Woollen Company of Chambly Canton, Quebec.

65   The Pellys were among the closest neighbours to Mountain Meadow Ranch and owned property bordering the road between Vernon and Enderby, south of Mountain Meadow and just west of Otter Lake. Born in Madras, India, surveyor Richard Stuart Pelly was the grandson of Sir John Henry Pelly, Baronet (for many years the governor of the Hudson's Bay Company). Pelly had first come to Canada in 1870 to work as a surveyor at Fort Garry and had returned to marry Frances Anna Robinson in County Mayo, Ireland, in May 1875. After spending several years in Winnipeg, they and their children had arrived in the Spallumcheen Valley in 1886 and built the Otter Lake Lodge, which became a way station for travellers at a time when such facilities were very scarce. When Alice made their acquaintance in 1891 there were five Pelly children – fifteen-year-old Rebecca Julia (Nonah), Henry Conway Dobbs (thirteen), Ella May (twelve), four-year-old Frances Kathleen (Leena), and George Stewart (three). The family would play an important role in Alice's life.

66   The Sandwich Islands are better known today as the state of Hawaii.

67   "Siwash" is Chinook jargon for "aboriginal" and is a corrupted form of the French "sauvage."

68   Born in Brantford, Ontario, author and journalist Sara Jeanette Duncan (1861-1922) was extremely popular for her vivid, personal style. An early feminist, she became the first woman to be employed full-time by the *Toronto Globe* (1887-88), and she also worked for the *Montreal Star* the following year. During a world tour in 1888 she met Everard Cotes in Calcutta, married him, and lived in India for the next twenty-five years, subsequently moving to England.

69   Louisa "Lulie" Skey, born in 1866, was a longtime friend of Alice's and the only daughter of a prominent Port Dover family. Lulie married Harry D. Williams of Buffalo, New York, at St. Paul's Church on 29 April 1891.

70   Born in Anson, Maine, Elizabeth Mary Fulton (1866-1931) was the daughter of Thomas Bailey Fulton (and allegedly the granddaughter of Robert Fulton, the famous American steamboat engineer). She had married Gus Schubert on 4 July 1883 and, by 1891, was the mother of several daughters.

71   Rose Anna LeDuc, née Schubert, had been the first white child born in the interior of British Columbia when her mother, Catherine Schubert, gave birth on 14 October 1862, the day following the Overlanders' arrival at Kamloops.

72   This is the first reference to the Island, a large, swampy area between Otter Lake and Lansdowne. The land was drained, and, after the station house was built, this area became the centre of the town of Armstrong.

73   D.V. is the abbreviated form of the Latin "deo volente," meaning "God willing."

74   Bread-making in those days was a slow process. Fast-rising yeasts were unknown; usually the ingredients – flour, weak yeast, and water – were combined, left to rise overnight, and the loaves formed and baked early the following morning. Store-bought bread was both appreciated as a great luxury and frowned upon as an inferior product.

75   "Dinner" was the noon-hour meal, "tea" the evening one.

76   Nkamaplix, or Head of the Lake, is located at the northern end of the west arm of Okanagan Lake; it is part of the Okanagan Indian Reserve, which had been marked out by 1861.

The original reserve had covered almost 54,000 acres but was gradually whittled away both the by white settlers' disregard for aboriginal land and by the attitude of the government, which did not rush to defend aboriginal boundaries but, indeed, supported European settlement. William Smithe, premier and land commissioner, had written of "the almost criminal wrong [which] had been done in withdrawing from settlement so large a tract of fertile land." See William Smithe to Israel Wood Powell, 5 December 1884. The Head of the Lake Reserve encompassed 24,742 acres, including the Commonage outside Vernon, and 29,392 acres on the range west of Vernon. By the time Alice first visited the reserve it had become much smaller, but the remaining area was considered an excellent one, with good bottomland. In this recently reduced permanent village, and under the influence of Roman Catholic priests, councils were established based on European Roman Catholic tradition, which, in a rigidly authoritarian way, directed the social, economic, and religious activities of the residents. The Okanagan Band was agriculturally progressive and produced enough food for subsistence as well as a small surplus to sell. Band members also grew sufficient grain and hay for their livestock. However, aboriginal attempts to integrate with white society were continually thwarted by pro-settler government discrimination, competition for land and water resources with European settlers, and racially biased legislation governing education and alcohol use.

77   The Roman Catholic Church had sent priests to convert the local tribes, and a small church still stands at Head of the Lake. Uncle's sour outlook on the Roman Catholic religion was conveyed to his brother several years earlier, when he wrote: "So much for white civilization: it exterminates, it debauches, but it never improves the native." See HB to TBB, 28 February 1886.

78   There was some one-upmanship between the O'Keefes and Greenhows when it came to house building. The latter had constructed a large, impressive home about 100 yards behind the O'Keefe house; Cornelius would soon decide upon a large extension to his own home in order not to be outdone.

79   Born in Quebec in 1856 Elizabeth Coughlan had married Thomas Greenhow in Ottawa in 1877; he was at that time the business partner of Cornelius O'Keefe. Elizabeth was the niece of Cornelius O'Keefe's wife, Mary Ann, and had met and married Greenhow during the trip he made to Ottawa to accompany O'Keefe to his wedding. The two newly wed couples returned to the Okanagan together and set about building neighbouring homes on the O'Keefe Ranch. By 1885 Greenhow owned thousands of acres and 800 head of cattle. Left a widow with two young children after his death in September 1889, Mrs. Greenhow sold 8,906 acres to the Land and Agricultural Company of Canada for $315,000, making her a very wealthy woman. The impressive twenty-one-roomed Greenhow house would be completed under Elizabeth's direction in 1894.

80   Cornelius O'Keefe was the first postmaster in the North Okanagan and built a small post office, which he operated from 1872 to 1884, on his ranch at the head of the lake.

81   Set in an ancient trough-like glacial valley 1,130 feet above sea level, Okanagan Lake is sixty-nine miles long, with an average width of just over a mile. Its two arms lead north to Head of the Lake and east to Okanagan Landing. The lake terminates at Penticton and drains southward to flow into the Columbia River.

82   The Spallumcheen Valley's name derives from the Chinook jargon meaning "flat rim or edge" (of a river). Spallumcheen municipality would be incorporated on 1 May 1892; its boundaries extended to the Shuswap River, giving it a total area of 65,000 acres.

83   Rebecca Julia Pelly was the eldest daughter of the Pelly family; her nickname "Winonah" (Chinook for "eldest daughter") had become shortened to "Nonah" by the time Alice met her. Within a few weeks of her arrival, Alice was taking some young girls under her wing for "readings" and general discussion to improve their minds.

84   Born in Durham, England, of British yeoman stock, Robert Storey Hall (1862-1935) was the driver of the stagecoach that passed regularly by Mountain Meadow Ranch. "One young fellow I saw in the store – Mr. Hall – spoke very nicely – Harry says he is a gentleman, but he looked so rough and uncouth ... And that is about the style they all dress in." See ABB to WB, 16 March 1891. Price Ellison offered him work as a driver on his stage line from

Vernon to Sicamous and Vernon to Okanagan Mission. "This made a drive of about 280 miles a week, sometimes over roads so bad that it taxed the strength and courage of the best horses, tugging long hours through mud and slush in the winter months; in the summer there was the heat and dust." See Robert S. Hall, "Pioneering," *OHSR* 19 (1955): 108. Alice was strongly attracted to the handsome young driver.

85 Named in November 1887 after Forbes George Vernon, the town was the largest and most important community in the Okanagan Valley when Alice arrived. (Earlier, the community had enjoyed several different names; for example, after the establishment of Okanagan Mission in 1857, the priests had built a cabin near Luc Girouard's property to use occasionally as they travelled through the area; this led to the valley between Vernon and Okanagan Lake being called "Priest's Valley." Later on, in the late 1870s, there was a prominent blacksmith's shop by the road, which gave rise to the name "Forge Valley." It also enjoyed the name "Centreville" for a time.) Upon incorporation, the City of Vernon contained but few streets, with some scattered homes on Pleasant Valley Road. Beyond the streets were bush and some land that had been cleared to grow wheat. The city had a population of only 400 in 1891. Most of the building and business activity took place at the west end of town, and it was only with the coming of the railway that the town began to expand towards the east.

86 In 1891 Harold Randolph Parke was in partnership with Robert Macdougall in Vernon and lodged in his home. He first caught sight of Alice in Enderby a month after her arrival and almost immediately began a determined, and eventually successful, courtship.

87 John Thompson (1827-1915) was born in Edinburgh, Scotland, and had immigrated first to Whitby, Ontario, where he married Brooklyn resident Elizabeth Dow Lamont in May 1869. They had two children, Jack and Katie. In 1877 the Thompsons were well known for their conviction that the area was well suited to fruit growing, and John was successful in developing a flourishing orchard.

88 Harold Parke.

89 Alexander Leslie Fortune (1831-1915) was born in Huntingdon, Lower Canada, and had been the first white settler in the north Okanagan. A leader of the Acton group of the Overlanders who crossed Canada in 1862, he was one of the governing committee on the journey, and, since he had studied for the Presbyterian ministry, he conducted many of the Overlanders' Sunday services. He settled first in Kamloops and arrived at Enderby in June 1866. He married Bathia Ross in 1862, just before the Overlanders set out, and she joined him in British Columbia in 1874. Once settled north of Enderby, he operated a ranch and a freighting business and was active in missionary work among the aboriginal people.

90 The former Sarah Jessie Day was the wife of Maurice Scollard Baldwin, bishop of Huron. The bishop had earlier been rector of St. Paul's Church in Port Dover, and the Barrett family knew the Baldwins well.

91 Simcoe is located at the headwaters of the Lynn River about eight miles northwest of Port Dover. The village grew steadily with the development of foundries, grist mills, distilleries, carriage works, and retail stores. By the time Alice knew the community it had 2,000 inhabitants and was connected to Port Dover by the Grand Trunk Railway. The Barrett family had many friends and acquaintances in the town.

92 By the time Alice left for the west from Union Station on Front Street, Toronto's population was over 150,000. From the beginning, the city had a markedly British population, and by the 1850s large numbers of Irish Protestants and Roman Catholics had arrived. The city was renowned for church life, Sunday observance, and moral conservatism. The city was also a lake port and the focus of industry and the railway. Alice knew Toronto well, having spent weeks at a time there with various members of her family.

93 London is located in southwestern Ontario, about sixty-five miles northwest of Port Dover. The Parke name belonged to a well known and highly respected family there.

94 James Chadwick Grinton owned land in Pleasant Valley bordering Harry Harding's ranch.

95 Norris would become a faithful and devoted friend to Alice throughout the years she lived in Vernon.

96 The former Henrietta MacInnes had married Joseph Barrett, Uncle's elder brother, in Vittoria, Upper Canada, in 1857. The Joe Barretts had subsequently settled in Merced, California,

and Joe became an American citizen in July 1878. The California branch of the family always welcomed Uncle to their home, and he enjoyed wintering there.

97 English-born physician John Chipp (1833-93) had arrived in British Columbia in 1862 and practised medicine first at the Royal Cariboo Hospital in Barkerville between 1864 and 1880 and later in the Nicola area. He came to Vernon in 1891 to be near his daughter, Clara Dewdney, and became the town's first resident doctor that year. The English-born Clara Matilda Chipp (1866-1900) had married Walter Dewdney in Kamloops on 19 September 1888 and became step-mother to his three children by Matilda Leigh – Rose (twelve), Walter Robert (fourteen), and Edgar "Teddy" Dewdney (ten). Walter Sr. was the brother of the famous Edgar Dewdney, who had earlier broken trail from the coast to the interior and had subsequently become lieutenant-governor of the Province of British Columbia.

98 Uncle Henry was helping to construct the station house and other buildings in Armstrong. It was easier for him to live close to the job than to make the lengthy walk from and to the ranch every day.

99 The Reverend Alfred J. Shildrick had come from Kamloops in 1883 to minister in Lansdowne and Armstrong. He held services in his own home until a small church, Saint James, was erected in Lansdowne in 1885. Saint James's Church was moved to its present site in Armstrong in 1891, and Shildrick remained minister there for a further four years.

100 Effie Lawes was the daughter of George Lawes of Enderby.

101 Donald Graham (1848-1944), a neighbour of the Barretts, had been one of the earliest settlers in the Spallumcheen. Born in Scotland, Graham had immigrated to Ontario as a young man in his twenties and made his way west to pre-empt land in Pleasant Valley in 1876. He married Adelaide Christian and raised a family there. In July 1892 he would become the first reeve of Spallumcheen municipality and serve for just over two years He enjoyed a reputation as a man of unimpeachable integrity.

102 A democrat was a square, box-like American buggy, with two or more cross-wise seats on the same level as the driver's seat. Pulled by two horses, the name derived from the practice of jamming large numbers of people together, all in much the same state of discomfort.

103 The former Bridget O'Brien had been born in Ireland and was married to Isle of Man native Duncan Gordon Cumming. In his youth he had taken part in the defence against the Fenian Raid in March 1866, when he was a member of No. 7 Company, 11th Battalion, at Grenville, Quebec. He graduated from military school in 1868 and had captained a boat on the Mississippi River. The family had pre-empted land in the Pleasant Valley area in June 1883, and Captain Cumming soon became captain of the *Red Star*, a steamer that plied the river from Sicamous to Enderby. The couple had three children – Maria, Hugh, and Margaret.

104 A native of Peoria, Illinois, the diminutive Sophia Christine Johnson (1857-1954) and her cousin had come to Vernon to visit their uncle, Peter Anderson, who had pre-empted land in what is now the City of Vernon. Sophie remained and became the first school teacher in Vernon in 1883 (although she had no formal teacher training). She married local businessman Price Ellison on 1 December 1884. In June 1891 she was already the mother of three daughters and was to become one of Alice's closest friends.

105 Born in Exeter, Devonshire, in 1837, Walter Dewdney had served with distinction in the British Army in the Crimea and India. After immigrating to Canada he tried his hand at mining but had to sell his claim in the Cariboo for lack of capital to develop it. He married Matilda Leigh, daughter of a former city clerk in Victoria, in 1874 and had three children with her. He then became a provincial constable and was appointed government agent in Yale in 1881. He moved to Spallumcheen (Enderby) in 1884 and to Vernon the following year; his wife died that same year in Victoria. This conscientious man worked extremely long hours and developed a painful kidney disorder; overworked and under great stress, he became convinced that he was losing his mind and took his own life on 24 January 1892. He was succeeded as government agent by Moses Lumby.

106 Edgar Dewdney (1835-1916) was born in Bideford, England, the son of Charles Dewdney and Fanny Hollingshead. The member of a well-to-do and well connected family, he had been trained in Wales as a civil engineer, and, spurred on by stories of the fortunes to be made in the goldfields of the Fraser Valley, he arrived in Victoria on 13 May 1859. He

immediately found work with Colonel Moody and his Royal Engineers, who were surveying the site of New Westminster, recently chosen to be capital of the mainland colony of British Columbia. By 1860 he was making his name as a maker of trails and builder of roads. He married Jane Shaw Moir in Hope on 28 March 1864 and, four years later, made his first foray into the world of colonial politics. In 1872 he ran for Yale in the general election and was elected a member of the Conservative government of Sir John A. Macdonald. Not long after re-election in 1878, he was appointed Indian commissioner for Manitoba and the North-West territories; in 1881 he was appointed lieutenant-governor of the North-West Territories. During the North-West Rebellion he played a pivotal role in pacifying aboriginal peoples but must share some of the blame for the repressive policies that followed. Later, as a member of the federal Cabinet, he served as minister of the interior and superintendent-general of Indian affairs. He resigned from the dominion government in 1892 in order to take up the long-coveted appointment as lieutenant-governor of British Columbia. The position involved few responsibilities and frequent social events, which Dewdney enjoyed immensely. He had no children of his own but was known and respected for his kindness and generosity to his own and his wife's nieces and nephews.

107   A native of Elden, Ontario, Robert Macdougall (1860-94) had lived for a time in Lindsay, where his father was sheriff of Victoria County. He had come west in 1882, working on the construction of the CPR. By 1886 he was managing Megaw's store in Vernon, then he became associated with James Schubert in the express and stage business. He had an interest in the Vernon Hotel, and by 1891 he was also Harold Parke's partner in the freighting business and in running a brick kiln in the city. His other business and community activities included being an agent for several companies, a member of the fire brigade, and a member of the building committee for the Presbyterian church. That same year he built a new store on Barnard Avenue and used it to house the post office, of which he became postmaster in 1891.

Chapter 2: *The real, the useful, the necessary*

1   Alice did not expect Wese "to like the idea of my coming here to live – I know that isn't possible – but dear you must never think that I am hurt or disappointed by anything you say – I would not have you ever one bit different to what you are – my own darling sister – Wait till we can talk about it." See ABB to WB, 18 April 1892.

2   It is apparent that Mr. Parke was exerting a very strong appeal.

3   This letter was evidently from Mr. Parke.

4   We do not know if Alice was formally engaged to Parke at this time; it is certain, however, that she had an understanding with him.

5   Samuel Cameron Smith (1849-1933), with his wife Elizabeth Jessie (née Brand), was resident in Vernon. Of English heritage and born at Acton, Ontario, in 1849, Smith had gone into the lumber business in Turtle Mountain, Manitoba, in 1881 and had been elected mayor there. His first wife, Katherine Thompson, died fifteen months after their wedding, leaving him with a young daughter. He remarried, and after a disastrous fire that wiped out his lumber business, came to British Columbia and, in 1891, set up a sawmill in Vernon near Okanagan Landing, where logs floated in from the lake were rough-cut before being transported to the finishing mill in town. Smith owned a sawmill in Enderby as well as branch plants in Deep Creek, Naramata, and Kalamalka Lake. "Sawmill" Smith was a highly respected member of Vernon society; he and Lizzie raised six children and were to become close friends of the Parkes. (In the end Harold Parke and Robert MacDougall did not go into partnership with Smith; had they done so their fortunes would have been made, for the terms for purchasing and leasing timber lands were extremely generous. Operators paid a rent of five cents per acre on a thirty-year lease, and a fixed royalty of fifty cents per thousand feet.)

6   William Maurice Cochrane was the leading lawyer in Vernon.

7   Okanagan Mission had been established in 1859 by Father Charles Pandosy, Brother Surel, and Father Pierre Richard of the order of the Oblates of Mary the Immaculate. The Mission's first site was at the southern end of Duck Lake, but in 1860 it was moved to Rivière de l'Anse aux Sables (Mission Creek) on the east side of Okanagan Lake. The first church was built in 1861. Father Charles Jean-Baptiste Félix Adolph Pandosy (1824-91) was responsible for the first plantings of grape vines and apple trees in the Okanagan Valley. He also

performed the roles of doctor, teacher, lawyer, orator, botanist, agriculturist, musician, and peacemaker. Father Pandosy's death in 1891 coincided with the coming of the railway to the Okanagan Valley, an event that sparked a land rush in the valley and resulted in the founding of the City of Kelowna a mile to the north.

8   January 1892 saw the final run of the stagecoach between Vernon and Sicamous.

9   Minnie had left the Okanagan on 15 October. "We saw Minnie [at the railway station] and said goodbye to her as she really thinks she is going today – poor girl – she is so anxious to go home – and has been so undecided." See ABB to TBB, 15 October 1891. "Harry heard from Minnie – she hopes to go to St. Catherine [sic] ... & says she looks forward then to visiting [Port] Dover." See ABB to WB, 18 April 1892. Minnie Shickluna did not return, and Harry soon went on to romance another young woman.

10 Famous French soldier and politician Georges Ernest Jean-Marie Boulanger and Chilean statesman José Manuel Balmaceda both committed suicide in 1891.

11 The availability of fresh meat throughout the year was sporadic. "Mr. Campbell brought me the heart this morning & some liver for the dog ... It will make a pleasant change, we get so much salt meat with only roast beef as a variation – I wish we could have some wild duck, but Uncle doesn't seem inclined to hunt & Harry hasn't time." See ABB to EB, c. 1891.

12 The Dominion census of 1891 showed Vancouver with a population of just over 13,000, when the city was already the Pacific terminus of the Canadian Pacific Railway. Until May 1886 its site had been covered with a dense forest. "Within two years of its founding, Vancouver had 36 miles of graded streets and miles of wooden paving; waterworks and sewerage; warehouses, foundries and factories; and the wharves, round-houses, office buildings and four-storey hotel built by the Canadian Pacific Railway." See Margaret Ormsby, *British Columbia: A History* (Toronto: Macmillan, 1958), 300.

13 Over 850 miles long, the Fraser River rises in the western slopes of the Rocky Mountains and flows northwest through Prince George before turning southward. The Fraser River Canyon section of the railway journey offered the traveller truly spectacular scenery for over 100 miles.

14 The sisters were attending teacher training classes at Vancouver High School to obtain their third-class teaching certificates.

15 False Creek, the stretch of water narrowing eastwards from English Bay, had already been designated Vancouver's industrial zone. A noisome atmosphere pervaded the whole area.

16 Born in 1866, Mary Harding was Lizzie's sister.

17 Margaret Maria Harding (1864-1948), another sibling, was also in Vancouver training to become a teacher.

18 The Harding girls had taken rooms in the new subdivision of Mount Pleasant, which was south of False Creek and the city of Vancouver. From their home it was just a short walk to Vancouver High School.

19 The gulf was Georgia Strait, which separates the city of Vancouver from Vancouver Island.

20 English Bay.

21 The Vancouver Electric Railway and Light Company Ltd. had been established on 15 November 1889, with an authorized capital of $500,000. It bought the track, plant, and franchises of the Vancouver Railway Company and the Vancouver Electric Illuminating Company, thus consolidating the three companies. It was the recently built powerhouse on Barnard Street at False Creek that produced the polluting fumes.

22 Colonel Richard Moody had originally set aside the 950-acre peninsula as a military reserve, and by the 1870s the best trees had been selectively logged. Many of the skid roads used for logging during the 1870s survived as the system of trails that is still in place. Grounds were also built for lacrosse, cricket, and bicycle racing.

23 Thomas Kains, DLS (1850-1901), and his wife were long-time friends of the Barrett family. Born in Grenville, Quebec, Kains was a qualified land surveyor and, after moving to British Columbia, worked as a clerk in the office of the surveyor-general, W.S. Gore. He did very well indeed and, shortly before Alice's visit, had been appointed surveyor-general for the province.

24 Marion was the young daughter of the Kainses.

25   The celebrated physician and politician Israel Wood Powell Jr. (1836-1915) was a friend of the
      Barrett family and had been born in Port Colborne, Ontario. He entered McGill University
      in Montreal, graduating as a physician in 1860, at the age of twenty-four. After two years
      practising in Simcoe, the young doctor decided to see the world and set off for New Zealand
      via the Straits of Magellan. When he arrived in Victoria, he found the colony a beehive of
      activity associated with the Cariboo gold rush. He decided to stay in the young colony and
      rapidly established a thriving practice. Following family tradition Powell ran for a seat in
      the Island House of Assembly. He worked for responsible government and entry into the
      Canadian Confederation, but such ideas were not popular at the time, and he was defeated
      in the election of 1868. Sir John A. Macdonald, however, considered him a hero and, after
      British Columbia's entry into Confederation in 1871, offered him the lieutenant-governorship
      of the province. Powell declined, but the following year accepted the position of superin-
      tendent of Indian affairs for British Columbia, which he held for seventeen years. He worked
      hard to improve conditions for the aboriginal tribes, and the city of Powell River was named
      after him. He was instrumental in establishing a university; in 1890 the Legisature passed
      an act creating the University of British Columbia, and Powell became its first chancellor.
      The home in Victoria, to which he welcomed Alice, was close to the Inner Harbour.
26   Beacon Hill was a large public park situated quite close to the new government buildings.
      Its name derived from the two beacons erected by the Hudson's Bay Company to illumi-
      nate Brotchie Ledge, a considerable hazard to shipping.
27   Victoria's Chinatown was the first in Canada and grew to be, at one time, the largest in the
      country. It was established in 1858, when the Chinese left California to move north in search
      of gold. They bought property in the community, and by the 1880s Chinatown had its cen-
      tre on Fisgard Street. The buildings there were designed and built by local builders and
      then rendered more Oriental in appearance by the addition of ornate balconies, decorative
      corner roof tiles, and lanterns.
28   By the 1870s the area to the north and south of the north arm of the Fraser River was well
      established as productive farming country, having been developed through Crown grants of
      land.
29   Mount Tolmie had been named after Scottish surgeon, fur trader, and politician William
      Fraser Tolmie (1812-86). (In June of 1998 I climbed to the top of Mount Tolmie with Nor-
      man Worsley, the son of Lena Pelly, and was treated to an astounding 360-degree panorama
      of the City of Victoria, the Strait of Juan de Fuca and Olympic Mountain range, the Gulf
      Islands, and Mount Baker in the distance. The peak of Mount Tolmie shows heavy scarring
      from glacial scouring during the last ice age.)
30   Emma Cecilia Thursby (1845-1931), at forty-six years old, was already beyond her best vocally.
      The famous American singer toured extensively throughout North America. The *Victoria
      Daily Colonist* declared, on 10 September 1891, that "Her voice is in its decline and any num-
      ber of apologies cannot explain away the fact ... it is so evidently hard work for Miss Thursby
      to sing the music that her audience suffers in listening to her ... she is still possessed of the
      remains of a magnificent voice, but the remains alone are left."
31   Both originally from the United States, thirty-five-year-old William J. Meighan and his
      twenty-five-year-old wife Mary were near neighbours at Mountain Meadow Ranch, own-
      ing land in Pleasant Valley. When Harry first arrived at Otter Lake in 1887 he had worked
      for pay at the Meighan Ranch during seeding and harvesting.
32   Clare Langs (1850-1922) was one of four children of Ezekiel Foster Langs, elder brother of
      Alice's mother. Although her cousin was eleven years her senior, Alice was deeply attached
      to Clare. During the period of the diaries Clare worked as a children's nurse in Seattle.
33   Barrett raised merry hell about his superannuation. He had written a vitriolic letter to his
      superior in Ottawa, demanding to know what he had done to bring about his dismissal from
      Her Majesty's service. He was already long past retirement age and finally accepted the
      inevitable; he refused, however, to hand over the keys to his office until formally advised by
      Ottawa of the appointment of his successor. He refused to retire and became an agent for
      the Norwich insurance company.
34   The Enderby Cliffs are a famous landmark in the area, a huge monolith rising vertically
      from the valley floor east of the town.

35 Alec Scott was the brother of the Barretts' brother-in-law, James Scott, and was visiting from Ontario.
36 Sophie Ellison and Alice Barrett found much in common. Each was hospitable, well educated, and domesticated and enjoyed paying and receiving visits.
37 The three Ellison children at that time were six-year-old Anna Johnson, four-year-old Ellen Fearnaught, and toddler Myra King; Sophie was pregnant with her fourth daughter.
38 The new post office building had just been built by Robert Macdougall at the west end of Barnard Avenue. It still stands today.
39 Dr. Osborne Morris delivered Sophie Ellison's fourth daughter, Elizabeth McIlvaine, on 21 April 1892. Sophie was thirty-five and Price forty-one years old at the time.
40 Founded on 14 May 1891 by Angus Stuart and W.J. Harber, the weekly *Vernon News* was the pioneer newspaper in the Okanagan Valley.
41 Price Ellison (1852-1932), one of Vernon's leading citizens, was born at Lymm, Cheshire, and as a young man had been apprenticed as a metal worker. He crossed the Atlantic to Boston and made his way from there to California. He arrived in the Okanagan Valley in 1876 and began acquiring land, eventually gaining ownership of the Postill Ranch and the Simpson Ranch, near Okanagan Mission. He also owned property near Lumby and Swan Lake, and he leased Winfield Ranch from Thomas Wood. In 1893 he would become a major shareholder in the company that owned the *Vernon News*. He would be elected to the provincial Legislature in 1898. He was a jolly, good-hearted, welcoming man, an inveterate matchmaker, and he and his wife Sophie became very close friends of Alice and Harold Parke.
42 This account by Catherine Schubert of the Overlanders' travails during their crossing in 1862 was not published. It filled nearly six pages of Alice's diary and remained hidden there until now. (We know of nine first-hand accounts of the trek — four are narratives and five are diaries, and only two of these accounts have been published [in abridged form].) Most miners in search of gold travelled from the east by ship either round Cape Horn, or to Panama, then overland to the Pacific coast, and north to British Columbia.
43 Born in Rathfriland, Ireland, Catherine O'Hare (1835-1918) had emigrated to the United States with her brother from Ireland shortly after the Irish potato famine years of 1847-49. She had married German emigrant Francis Augustus Schubert, who was a year older than she, and, with him, kept a beer hall in St. Paul, Minnesota, before moving north to Canada. Catherine was the only woman among nearly 200 men who, in 1862, set off on the trail from the Red River Settlement in Manitoba to the Cariboo in search of gold. The mother of three young children, (Augustus Junior, born in 1857; Mary Jane, born in 1858; James, born in 1860), the twenty-seven-year-old woman was pregnant with her fourth child, but told no one, fearing expulsion from the train. Catherine gave birth to Rose Anna the day after the Overlanders arrived at Kamloops, on 14 October 1862. After finally settling in the Armstrong area in June 1883 she became well loved for the help she offered to newcomers.
44 Rose Anna Schubert.
45 Lillooet is located about 200 miles northeast of Vancouver and stands at the foot of the Cascade Mountains and above the Fraser River; its name means "wild onion." Thousands of miners had come to the settlement during the 1850s gold rush, and the new community quickly gained importance as Mile Zero on the Cariboo Road, the route to the Cariboo and Fraser River goldfields.

Chapter 3: *A very cosy, happy home*

1 *Vernon News*, 22 December 1892.
2 Clare Langs, Alice's cousin, was visiting from Seattle.
3 The former Nora Bessie Manley (1862-97) was the wife of William Ward Spinks (1851-1937). He was born in England in the Aintree area near Liverpool and had articled in that city. He and his brother had married sisters in England, and the two couples came to Canada in March 1884. He practised law at Kamloops from 1884 to 1889, when he was appointed to the judiciary; he also pre-empted large tracts of land throughout the valley. In 1891 Judge and Mrs. Spinks came to live in Vernon, from where he supervised the County Court circuit of Yale and Kootenay, travelling many hundreds of miles every year. He later took over the Nicola circuit.

4   William Maurice "Pa" Cochrane (1844-1900) and his wife, the former Adaline A. Gallagher, were leading citizens of Vernon. Raised in Whitby, Ontario, Cochrane moved to Minnesota in 1880; six years later he arrived in New Westminster. The parents, three daughters, and four sons moved from there to Kamloops and finally to Vernon. By 1892 he was operating a successful law practice and acted for the City of Vernon during the town's incorporation in 1893. Cochrane "was a portly man with long side whiskers ... [which] did a lot to set off the famous [court] costume: a long, immaculately fresh black frock coat, low cut waistcoat which exposed a large acreage of white shirt front bisected vertically by a thin black tie ... a pair of trousers of a surprisingly startling black-and-white shepherds plaid check; rather short in the leg, they allowed a good view of bright red socks; a red handkerchief carried out the color scheme, and always there was a red rose or some other red flower in his buttonhole." See C.W. Holliday, *Valley of Youth* (Caldwell, ID: Caxton Printers, 1948), 287-8. Addie was a dynamic woman who worked for many worthy causes, and she and Pa would figure prominently in the diaries.

5   Dr. and Mrs. D.L. Beckingsale arrived in Vernon in 1892, and the doctor set up a practice there. Before he moved on to California two years later he put forward, anonymously, a detailed plan for the establishment of a cottage hospital in Vernon. Dr. Beckingsale and his wife Amy had three children: Winifred, Jack, and Minna.

6   Osborne Morris was born on 20 January 1869. A graduate of McGill, the young physician arrived in Vernon in 1893 and soon earned the respect of the community and a reputation for kindness, particularly in dealings with children. This genial and cordial young man, a first cousin of the Martin brothers, became a very good friend to Alice, enjoying a medical career spanning forty-eight years.

7   The former Elizabeth Campbell (1804-99) was born at Mount Alexander, Forthingale, Scotland. In 1827 she married Donald MacIntyre and lived with him in Clunes, Inverness-shire, until his death in 1873. Mrs. MacIntyre's father had been a captain in the Scots Guards, and her grandfather was Colonel Donald Robertson of Woodshiel, who commanded the Clan Robertson at the battle of Culloden. After coming to Canada, Alice's dear "old lady" lived at Milton and, later, Waterdown, Ontario. Although she had three daughters, this marvellous old woman made her home with her granddaughter Kate and loved to regale all her visitors with stirring tales of her ancestors.

8   A native of Arbroath, Scotland, the former Kate MacIntyre had married English-born William C. Martin in 1882; he was one of three brothers working in Vernon (the other two were James and John). Bill Martin had preceded his family to the Okanagan and, by May 1891, had built a fine new hardware store in partnership with his brother Jim at the junction of Seventh Street and Barnard Avenue. The Martins soon developed an active social life and welcomed the Parkes into their circle.

9   Mrs. Wood was the wife of the Reverend James Alexander Wood, Methodist minister in Vernon from 1893 to 1895.

10 Margaret E. Coryell was a widow living in Ontario when her sons came west to seek their fortune. She followed them and made her home in Vernon for a few years. At the time Alice knew her, the Coryells owned a home to the west of the Parkes on Schubert Street.

11 Charles Ernest Costerton (1850-1926) married Gertrude Anna Perry (1869-1935) in the new Anglican church in Vernon on 10 May 1893 – the first wedding to be held there. Gertie was the daughter of Charles Perry, who had been in charge of construction on the Shuswap and Okanagan Railway and whom Alice had met in 1891 when she visited Enderby. Alice soon regarded Gertie as her best friend in Vernon, and the two women remained faithful visitors and confidantes. Charlie Costerton was a financial agent at that time and later held a series of government posts.

12 Allan McDonald and his wife had arrived in Vernon in 1893 from Wingham, Ontario; McDonald set up a law office on Barnard Avenue, and the couple quickly became close friends of the Parkes. McDonald would become a member of the bar in April 1896.

13 Born on 12 April 1862 at Flamboro Mills, near Hamilton, Ontario, Forbes Murray Kerby had entered the Royal Military College in Kingston in 1879. After his graduation in 1883 as a surveyor/engineer he was employed by the CPR and worked in the mechanical department at Montreal for some years. He arrived in Vernon in 1891 and went to work for the

firm of Coryell and Burnyeat. He became a member of the Canadian Society of Civil Engineers in 1893 and was in the process of qualifying to become a provincial land surveyor when
Alice first knew him. He was to become one of Alice's firmest friends and was always ready
with offers of help whenever Hal had to leave town. He was one of Alice's four devoted
"cavaliers," the others being Jack McKelvie, Leonard Norris, and Osborne Morris.

14   Clement Fisher Costerton (1859-1930) was the younger brother of Charlie Costerton and
had arrived in British Columbia in 1878. He came to the Okanagan in 1886 and went into
partnership in a general store in Lansdowne, which was sold to Wood and Rabbittt before
1887. He then went north to Enderby and partnered Mr. Rashdale until 1892, when he settled in Vernon. He became the town's first real estate agent and was also an insurance and
financial agent. As a notary public he did much of the conveyancing in Vernon in the early
years.

15   Born on a farm in Brampton, Ontario, in 1865 Leonard Norris (1862-1945) had moved to
Langley, British Columbia, with his family when he was nine years old. He arrived in the
Okanagan at the age of seventeen and worked for a time on various ranches in the Lumby
area. In 1887 he pre-empted land near Round Lake and the following year was invited to
become a temporary provincial police constable at Lansdowne. He succeeded Moses Lumby
as government agent in Vernon in 1893. His duties as agent included registering births, mar-
riages, deaths, and deeds; he was also gold commissioner, magistrate, and administrator of
all the roads in the district and overseer of the jail. His office was used as a police court,
and he lived in the official government cottage, located near the western edge of Vernon.
Young Norris and Alice frequently lent each other books, and he never forgot her birthday.
A quiet, reserved man, he was a dedicated Mason and would remain in public service for
the rest of his working life.

16   Ainsley Megraw (1858-1923) was returning to Wiarton to take a position at the *Canadian*
newspaper. He would return, however, during the mining boom in the Okanagan and, by
November 1899, owned the Minnehaha claim at Camp McKinney.

17   The former Helen "Nellie" Oliver Scott was born in Scotland and had married Hal's nephew
Thomas Edward Parke in Port Arthur, Ontario, in June 1885. Alice had met Nellie during
her honeymoon, and the pair corresponded frequently.

18   Englishman C.W. Holliday (1870-1955) was born in London and educated in private schools.
"In 1887, at the age of sixteen, Charles William Holliday was sent to sea ... Holliday sailed
around Cape Horn to San Francisco, thrived physically and mentally, and developed a taste
for adventure and wide open spaces." See Mark Zuehlke, *Scoundrels, Dreamers and Second
Sons: British Remittance Men in the Canadian West* (Vancouver, Whitecap Books, 1994), 14.
Billie had arrived in the North Okanagan in 1889 to work on the railway line between Sicamous and Vernon and quickly settled into life on the frontier. Only twenty years old when
Alice met him, Billie was also a talented painter and a skilful photographer; he was able to
earn extra money by photographing settlers and their homes. Holliday opened a photographic studio in Vernon in October 1893 but did not remain in that business very long.
When visiting, he never seemed to know when to leave. He later wrote: "I am afraid we did
not realize at the time what a lot of extra work this meant for [the women] ... But they
really were awfully good to us ... I daresay that after having seen no one but their husband
all the week, it was a pleasant change to talk to someone else and well worth a little extra
cooking." See C.W. Holliday, *Valley of Youth* (Caldwell, ID: Caxton Printers, 1948), 311. Even
by the time he wrote his own book, his awareness and sensitivity concerning this issue were
not exactly profound. Holliday had long since been given the nickname that would stick to
him during his stay in the Okanagan – "Coyote." The locals called him that because he
always turned up where he was not wanted.

19   Born in Springfield, Nova Scotia, William Fraser Cameron had come to British Columbia
with a CPR construction crew. By the 1880s he was operating a general store in Vernon,
located at the western edge of town near Government House; in 1884 it had become the
first building used exclusively for business purposes. In 1892 he moved this small store to
the back of its site and built a new two-storey building, whose upper floor he allowed to
be used for city council meetings, dances, and public gatherings. He was acclaimed the first
mayor of Vernon in 1893. Alice was a frequent visitor to his store, and he became a

good friend. (Cameron's was one of forty businesses that opened in Vernon between 1891 and 1895.)

20 The former Emily J. Pittendrigh was born in England in 1852 and was the widow of Judge John Carmichael Haynes, one of the most celebrated settlers in the southern Okanagan.

21 In 1860 Governor Douglas had established Osoyoos at the north end of Osoyoos Lake as a trading and customs post in order to prevent American penetration of British Columbia's goldfields. The name was an aboriginal one, meaning "the narrows." Osoyoos and Oliver were in a desert-like region, covered with bunch grass, cacti, and sagebrush. At that time this area was used solely as range land for cattle.

22 John Carmichael Haynes was an Irishman born in County Cork in 1831. He had arrived in British Columbia in 1859 and spent some time in Yale before moving to Osoyoos. He became a stipendiary magistrate, Crown receiver of customs, and gold commissioner for Osoyoos. Like many men in the early days, Haynes married an aboriginal woman; her name was Julia, and she came from Colville, Washington. Haynes fathered three children by her before marrying a white woman who was much younger than he. Charlotte Moresby, born in 1851, was the daughter of an English barrister, and their wedding took place at Hope on 26 September 1868. Haynes provided a house for his aboriginal family at a little distance from the home he shared with Charlotte, and his aboriginal children acted as waiters and housemaids when visitors appeared. The sweet-natured Charlotte died in childbirth after giving birth to a son, Fairfax Moresby; the widower married Emily Pittendrigh in New Westminster on 14 January 1875 and had seven more children with her. Besides his twenty-five-year career as a government representative, during which he was highly respected for his courtesy, integrity, and fairness, Haynes amassed over 21,000 acres of land, on which he ran 3,000 head of cattle. He died very suddenly in July 1888 while on his way home from the coast; he had drunk large quantities of snow water on the journey, which caused severe inflammation of the bowels. His ranch operation was purchased after his death by Thomas Ellis.

23 Born at Grantley, Quebec, in 1821, Luc Girouard had lived an exciting and varied life. He left home at twenty-four to spend two years whaling out of Boston; later he mined and prospected at Lake Superior and captained a boat on the lake. In 1853 he had joined the United States Army and, afterwards, prospected for gold in California. Girouard had been prospecting at Cherry Creek, thirty miles east of Vernon, before finally, in 1867, preempting 160 acres in what later became Vernon; later that year he built the first pioneer cabin in the area and planted the first fruit trees and the vegetables for which he became known throughout the Valley. His second home, at the foot of what is today called Community Hill, served as a local post office over which he presided as Vernon's first postmaster from 1887 to 1891; after sorting the mail he placed letters in the cracks between his floorboards – a different position for each recipient! He was also a justice of the peace. Girouard's only known descendant was a part-aboriginal daughter, Ashnasia. Alice was intrigued by the old man, writing: "I was introduced to old Girouard on the way out, a queer old Frenchman, with a beard he braids up and tucks under, a queer, wild-looking old fellow with just one front tooth in his upper jaw, which hangs down so far and makes him look like Red Riding Hood's wolf – but he is very kind, & has a lovely orchard." See ABB to WB, 29 April 1892. Everyone in town called him "the old man," and he enjoyed the respect and admiration of the community.

24 This was druggist Dick Taylor, one of the first people Alice met after her arrival from Ontario. In 1892 he moved his business to the larger town of Vernon, where he became as popular as he had been in Armstrong and where he offered a wide selection of drugs and chemicals. He also took part in many community activities, sang and played the piano at concerts, and joined the operatic society and the Masonic lodge.

25 Born in London, England, Thomas Godwin (1869-96) was the son of Alice's elderly friend Mrs. Godwin. He worked as a teamster for the firm of McDougall and Parke. After McDougall's death and the dissolution of the company, Tom would go into the livery business and purchase two teams of horses, one for heavy draying and the other for express delivery. He had established a comfortable home for his mother, and he was always most helpful and obliging to the Parkes.

26 Hal was still helping his friend and partner, Robert McDougall, in the post office.

27 Jack Lawrie, a resident of the Otter Lake area, and a good friend of Harry Barrett.

28 Born on 14 September 1865 at Saint John, New Brunswick, John Armstrong McKelvie had come west in 1883 and served with the Alberta Rifles during the Northwest Rebellion of 1885. After his arrival in the Okanagan in 1889 he worked at the BX Ranch and in a local store until he became editor of the *Vernon News* in 1893. (The *Vernon News* had opened for business as a weekly newspaper in 1891 and followed the *Kamloops Inland Sentinel* to become the second newspaper in the British Columbia interior. McKelvie succeeded Ainsley Megraw as its editor.) McKelvie had known Harold Parke for several years, and they were good friends. He took to Alice immediately and became one of her staunchest allies; as for Alice, from now on her pages would be dotted with references to Mr. McKelvie – coming to tea, playing whist, accompanying the Parkes to church, or supervising the Sunday school where Alice would soon teach. They never had a falling out, and over the years the pages of the *Vernon News* recorded faithfully the Parkes' doings.

29 Born in India in 1861, Angus Kilbee Stuart was the son of Reverend J. Kilbee Stuart of Castle Gresley, Burton-on-Trent, England, and had been the first editor of the *Vernon News*. Stuart would not remain long at the helm of the newspaper, and he moved south to the Boundary District.

30 Born in Somerset, England, Mary Godwin (1833-1909) was the widow of Sydney Godwin. She and her family had come from Ontario and settled in Vernon in 1892. Alice visited her frequently and lent a sympathetic ear to her troubles.

31 Angeline Birnie was the wife of Vernon blacksmith Alexander Birnie (1857-1943).

32 Born in Petrolia, Ontario, in February 1889, Rose was the eldest child of Lottie and Edwin Weddell, of Kelowna.

33 The Presbyterian church, Saint Andrew's, had been dedicated in February 1892.

34 John "Jack" Martin was one of the three Martin brothers who had come to Vernon. His elder brother, James, was senior partner in Martin's store, and his other brother, William, was the husband of Alice's close friend Kate Martin.

35 Clement Smith was one of the six children of the "Sawmill" Smiths.

36 Canada's Parliament had decreed in 1879 that 6 November should be observed as Thanksgiving Day, to be celebrated as a national rather than a religious holiday. Later and earlier dates were also observed for many years, and in the Okanagan at that time the date of the American holiday was observed.

37 The young Saul Layton Smith (1871-1963) had arrived in Vernon in November 1891 from Saint John, New Brunswick. With his younger brother Frank he operated Smith Bros. stationery and bookstore in Vernon for more than twenty years. (Many of the scribblers Alice used for her diary have the Smith Bros. stamp on them.)

38 Fraternal Orders in North America were voluntary non-profit associations established for the mutual aid and sociability of their members. They used a lodge system of organization and democratic form of self-government; they practised doing business in confidential meetings and developed elaborate rituals. Hal was a member of the local Oddfellows Lodge 18, which met every Tuesday at 8:00 PM in the Odd Fellows' Hall on Barnard Avenue. The name signifies "something different, out of the ordinary and unmatched" and was originally given to those who believed in helping others. To qualify as a member Hal was required to believe in a supreme being and to be of good moral character; he could later progress through several degrees of membership. The commands of Odd Fellowship were (and are) to visit the sick, relieve the distressed, bury the dead, and educate the orphan; its covenants were (and are) friendship, love, and truth.

39 This, the first Methodist church in Vernon, had held its inaugural service in January 1893. At that time a ministerial incumbency lasted three years.

40 In 1891 the Okanagan Land and Development Company built the Kalamalka Hotel for $20,000. It was an attractive building and, for many years, one of the major social centres in Vernon. The hotel featured a spacious billiard room; the foyer contained a large open freestone fireplace, and the ceilings were finished in the style of an English baronial hall. Bedrooms were furnished in English oak and walnut, and the very best Brussels carpets covered the floor. Rates were seven dollars per week for board only, ten dollars and up for board with room, and $1.50 for "transients."

41   Harry and Mountain Meadow Ranch still exerted a huge influence upon Alice. Hal was an
      understanding husband, allowing his wife go off at regular intervals and for days at a time.

42   Born in Ontario in 1849, Annie Donogh Megaw (1858-1940) was the wife of Vernon mer-
      chant William Riggs Megaw (1848-1939). They settled first in Kamloops, and in 1891 Megaw
      put up a new building in Vernon. The imposing fifty-foot-long structure was faced with
      brick and contained a saddle emporium, pianos, organs, sewing machines, and fancy goods.
      Megaw also sold groceries, dry goods, hardware, footwear, and paints. The upper floor was
      divided into seven rooms that could be used for public meetings and concerts. Annie Megaw
      was a member of several local community organizations and delighted in doing good works.

43   German-trained ear, eye, and nose specialist William Reinhard had arrived in Vernon with
      his family in 1892 (one month before Dr. Beckingsale). He left his wife and children in the
      town while he went north to practise briefly in Barkerville, returning the following year to
      open an office. In 1895 he built a combined office/residence on Railway (now 29th) Street
      opposite the present railway station and worked as a general practitioner.

44   Larkin was located about eight miles north of Vernon, between the O'Keefe Ranch and the
      communities of Otter Lake and Pleasant Valley.

45   The name of Cornelius O'Keefe appeared more than once in police records of the time.
      (He was well known for his fiery temperament; on 2 July 1897, for example, he would be
      charged with assault; however, after he pleaded not guilty, the case was dismissed.)

46   Headcheese was the flesh from a pig's head chopped, moulded, and boiled.

47   Mary Manley "Maisie" Spinks, the niece of Judge Spinks, had lived with her uncle and aunt
      since the death of her mother. She and Mrs. Spinks did not have an easy relationship, and
      Maisie was sent to Toronto for schooling.

48   Walter Cochrane was training in his father's firm to become a lawyer.

49   Vernon's population at this time was just over 400.

50   Harold Randolph Parke had served with the North-West Mounted Police from 1878 to 1880.
      His training in the Force prepared him well for all the positions he held thereafter. He is
      known to have written an account of only one incident during his time in the police, and
      this detailed a tense, yet hilarious, encounter between himself, Major Walsh, and Sitting
      Bull.

51   Born in Manitoba, Catherine Nina Smith (1880-1957) was the daughter of Samuel Cameron
      Smith and his first wife, Catherine Thompson.

52   A.C. Cann and his wife (the daughter of Canadian nationalist poet and Kelowna resident
      Charles Mair) came to Vernon from Kelowna to open a book and stationery store; he also
      sold pianos, organs, sewing machines, wall paper, and croquet equipment. He later sold his
      business to the Smith brothers.

53   Kate Wright was the sister of the Reverend John Knox Wright in Armstrong. Her attempt
      to become Mrs. Jack McKelvie came to naught; she would marry J.E. Matheson of Vernon.

Chapter 4: *How many people I have got to know!*

1   After the suicide of her first husband, Walter Dewdney, Clara had moved into a new home
      next door to her father, Dr. Chipp. It was located close to Cameron's store at the west end
      of town. She married W.F. Cameron eight months later at Gleichen, Alberta, in August
      1894.

2   Born in Lanark, Ontario, on 21 September 1838, Charles Mair – Canadian poet, patriot, and
      land promoter – was working on a land development in the Benvoulin area outside Kelowna.
      In 1868 in Ottawa he had been a founding member of the Canada First movement, which
      believed that annexation of the west was necessary for the preservation of Canada as a nation.
      Resolutely anti-American, Mair had for many years been influential in the expansionist
      movement. By the time Alice met him, he was half way through his four-year stay in the
      Okanagan and was becoming somewhat disillusioned about economic prospects for the
      west, though he retained his faith in the land; he had also come to believe that the east was
      jealous of the west's early success. Mair left Kelowna in May 1896 for Prince Albert,
      Saskatchewan.

3   Born in Brampton, Ontario, Donald M. McIntyre was the first head miller of the Enderby

grist mill, which had been built in 1887. McIntyre had courted Effie Gibbs assiduously but was sadly deceived in her.

4   Mrs. Edgar Dewdney (née Jane Shaw Moir in 1843 in Ceylon) had arrived in Canada with her family in 1860. Jeanie, as she was known affectionately in the family, lived for many years in Ottawa and Regina but returned to British Columbia in 1892 as the wife of the new lieutenant-governor of the province. Childless herself, she was remembered for the kindness and generosity she showed to her many nieces and nephews.

5   After their wedding, the Keatings moved to Seattle.

6   Albert Johnson Ellison was born on 7 August 1897.

7   Quebec-born Laura Mallette had married C.E. Poulin in San Francisco on 11 December 1894; she was only eighteen years old and was described as having a winning and graceful appearance.

8   The S.C. Smiths had six children – Nina, Oliver, Clement, Addie, Charles, and Alfred.

9   Designed by R.B. Bell and built high on a hill, the new two-storey Smith house would become the most outstanding home in Vernon. It featured a classical portico at the entrance, with simulated marble pillars and a ballroom on the upper floor beneath a gambrel roof. It still stands today.

10 Irishman James "Dasher" Donegan was a well known character in the area; his erratic habits and alcohol dependency were responsible for his death in the snow in mid-December 1897.

11 Cornelius Finn had married Mary Hayes in Vernon in July 1895; the couple lived in a home on the south side of Schubert Street and so were close neighbours of the Parkes. Conn was the son of Elizabeth Pulsifer and would later become railway section foreman based at Enderby.

12 William L. Germaine was the accountant at the Bank of Montreal in Vernon.

13 This was Leanora Cochrane, daughter of Alice's good friend Addie Cochrane.

14 Alice Moss and Jane Parnell were members of the Victorian Order of Nurses.

15 Born in 1842, Arthur Gore Pemberton was sheriff for the County of Yale, a vast area, and the Pemberton Range is named after him. By April 1900 he would retire to the ranch he owned at Ducks.

16 By 1900 there were complaints that Robert Sparling's teaching methods were haphazard, that he was lazy, and that he read the newspaper when he should have been teaching.

17 Mrs. Stevenson was the widow of lawyer Ralph A. Stevenson, who died at their home on Long Lake on 21 May 1895.

18 Henry Watson, the brother of assayer Arthur Watson, was a mining engineer from Australia who had been engaged by the Camp Hewitt Mining Company to investigate and report on claims near Peachland.

19 Mrs. Watson was the wife of the second Watson brother, Henry.

20 Fred the Dutchman, a veteran of the Battle of Waterloo, lived in Port Dover and worked for a time as school caretaker. His wife was severely cross-eyed and one time fell down the stairs, breaking her arm. Fred explained at the time that he had "put her aside mit force."

21 The CPR steamer on the lake stopped at the little village by the wharf called Kelowna; it now began to supersede the Mission as the major settlement in the central Okanagan Valley. The community of Kelowna, two square miles in area, flourished and, in 1892, became widely known under that name, which means "grizzly bear."

22 Irishman Daniel Pulsifer was a railway section boss who worked out of Sicamous. His Irish-born wife, Elizabeth, was fifty-one years old when she died.

23 Rattlesnake Point jutted out into the west side of Long Lake about seven miles south of Vernon. It overlooked Cosens Bay and Turtle Point, and was home to a colony of rattlesnakes.

24 The land on which Guisachan stood had been staked out in 1861 near Kelowna by Johnny MacDougal, a "mixed blood" who worked for twenty years as a packer with the Hudson's Bay Company. The property later became the Guisachan Ranch, owned by Lord Aberdeen and named after Lady Aberdeen's childhood home. Coutts Marjoribanks was appointed manager.

25 A native of Aberdeenshire, Arthur Booth Knox claimed descent from John Knox, the Scottish reformer. Born in 1851, he had arrived in the Okanagan Valley in 1874. Within ten years

he had established a large ranch on Okanagan Lake just north of what would become the City of Kelowna. In 1891 Knox had had a serious dispute with Tom Ellis as a result of which he was sentenced to three years' hard labour for setting fire to Ellis's hay stacks. Knox served some time in the New Westminster penitentiary but appealed the sentence, and, by February 1894, he was back in the valley managing his ranch once more.

26 Of Irish descent, the former Margaret Dowling had married Bernard Lequime in San Francisco in September 1892.

27 A dynamic businessman, Lequime was the scion of one of the earliest settler families in the Okanagan. Born in California in 1857, the gold rush brought him and his family to Rock Creek three years later. The family soon moved north to the Mission, and his father, Eli Lequime, was appointed postmaster for the Okanagan area in 1872 and built a flour mill near his general store in 1885. Three years later the senior Lequimes sold their business interests to their sons Bernard and Léon and retired to California. In addition to the already existing businesses, the brothers established a large and soon-thriving sawmill operation on the lakeshore near the Mission. They also owned the largest herd of cattle and the most extensive tract of land in the central Okanagan; other interests were a hotel and a small orchard. By 1892 the Lequime brothers bought the SS *Penticton* and arranged to meet the Shuswap and Okanagan trains at Okanagan Landing and convey passengers south. After moving their sawmill further north on the lake, the brothers built a boarding house for the workers, a large freight shed, a new wharf, and another general store. By 1892 Lequime had purchased Neil Hardy's blacksmith shop and, that same year, acquired the steamer *Okanagan* to tow log booms for his sawmill. Also in 1892 he had purchased 300 acres of flat land and had it surveyed by Vernon resident Jack Coryell for the townsite of Kelowna; he and his family moved north to the new city three years later.

28 Georges Léger had come to Lumby in 1890 from Saint John, New Brunswick. Nine years later he purchased a lot on the main road between Vernon and Lumby and built a large home there. In 1895 he married Emma Bessette and they had four children. He cultivated a huge crop of hay and freighted hay, wood, and lumber into Vernon. He was known as a great raconteur and devout churchgoer.

29 Mr. Verdun was one of the early pioneers in the Lumby area and had pre-empted land in Creighton Valley, east of the village.

30 Harry Barrett, throughout his second diary, referred to Hal Parke as "Frank." It is not known where this nickname originated.

31 The young Eveline Stanfield had married Delphas Thomas in Kamloops in July 1895.

Chapter 5: *I do hope I'll be able to do something useful and good*

1 Luc Girouard died on 22 January 1895; the cause of death listed by Dr. Morris on the death certificate was amyloid disease, a non-specific condition that caused enlargement of some organs and was associated with chronic illnesses such as lung disease and tuberculosis. His funeral was the largest that had ever taken place in Vernon, the procession being over a quarter of a mile in length.

2 Born in 1876, Selbourne Aylesford Shatford was one of four Nova Scotian brothers who were all known in Vernon by their initials. They neither arrived together nor stayed together; S.A. was the only one to remain in Vernon, and he operated his own millinery and women's wear store for a time.

3 The Shatford baby was three months old when it died on 11 April 1896.

Chapter 6: *A great many people have ailments here*

1 Hudson Bay was a brand of rum popular at the time.

2 Coutts Marjoribanks (1861-1924) was the Earl of Aberdeen's brother-in-law, the younger brother of Ishbel. A remittance man and heavy drinker, his father had cut off his allowance, and for many years he had been supported by his sister, who sent him £400 a year. Coutts spent some years at the Horse-shoe Ranch in North Dakota, and Ishbel was instrumental in his being employed as manager of the Guisachan Ranch and, later, the Coldstream Ranch, though his regime there would prove disastrous for the Aberdeens' purse. In 1894 he would

receive his inheritance from the estate of his father, Lord Tweedmouth, and return to England for awhile. He married Agnes Nicholls and returned to Vernon to build his lovely home "Invercraig" on Lake Kalamalka. Coutts was a familiar figure in Vernon and Kelowna, and he was nicknamed "the Major."

3   After Macnamara's visit, Alice wrote: "It makes me feel so sad, the rough, wild ways so many men fall into here. I cannot laugh as so many people do. Life is real, life ought to be earnest here particularly – one seems so near the vital springs of life – and yet I think I never saw so many good qualities going to waste as I have here." See ABB to EB, c. 1891.

4   The former Addie Elliot was the wife of Sydney Wentworth Lobb, and early in June 1894 she had been shot through the heart at her home in Nanaimo. The preliminary hearing took place on 12 June 1894. Lobb denied shooting his wife; he later claimed that Addie had committed suicide. However, there was strong evidence pointing to murder, and experts were brought in to assess the powder burns on her clothing; they covered an area at least nine inches in diameter, and it was hardly likely that Addie could have held a pistol far enough from her chest to cause such a large burn mark. After Lobb's arrest, evidence was heard from doctors that, during the previous three months, they had been called in at least twice to deal with Lobb's problems with alcohol. His lawyer brother arrived from Toronto to take up his defence, and by late July the prisoner was released on $5,000 bail. There were several delays in bringing the case to trial, and Lobb finally appeared at the fall assizes of the Supreme Court at New Westminster. The jury returned with a verdict of not guilty, and Lobb was discharged.

5   Richard Noble Taylor died in Greenwood on 30 December 1896; he was thirty-one years old. A genuinely shocked Jack McKelvie wrote: "His gentle and courteous manner, his business integrity, his manly beauty and kindly good fellowship all contributed to make him one of the most popular of men." See *Vernon News*, 7 January 1897, 4

6   Isaac Hann had married the seventeen-year-old Elizabeth Nelson in August 1895. He had operated the Brookside Garden at B.X. Ranch for some time and, by December 1895, was reported to be in Victoria.

7   In 1859 Francis Jones Barnard had arrived in Yale from Quebec, and he began delivering mail on foot, charging two dollars per letter and selling newspapers for a dollar each. From these small beginnings grew the Barnard Express and Stage Line. The horses for the business came from Southern California and New Mexico and were reared at the 6,300-acre BX Ranch, north of Vernon.

8   Born in Quebec in 1873, Eleanor Schultz was the recipient of much physical abuse from her brawny husband. Her husband Henry was a 40-year-old Prussian-born martinet. On 8 April 1896 this local blacksmith and repairer of tools and vehicles was charged with assaulting his wife. "[T]he defendant, who had been grumbling all day, swore at her. She cooked some meat and he threw it out: he struck her with his fists: she locked herself in a room: he broke open the door and struck her again ... She admitted throwing a lamp out of the window and said that she had no marks to show. She denied that the house was in a filthy state or that she neglected the home." See *Vernon News*, 16 April 1896, 1. After pleading not guilty Schultz was acquitted.

9   The Billings toddler was exhibiting early signs of the continuum of neurological conditions that includes autism, bi-polar disorder, and schizophrenia. His condition was characterized by an abnormal withdrawal from the world of reality and severely limited responsiveness to other people. At the end of the nineteenth century such a condition was not understood, and there was no treatment. Because of the shame felt by their families, sufferers were usually shut away from the public gaze, and such would eventually prove to be the case with this child.

10   Local residents were generous in donating books and magazine subscriptions, and, by the spring of 1896, the collection numbered 249 volumes, including an encyclopaedia. Born in West Ham, England, in 1867, Henry Ward Base died on 29 October 1896 and was buried two days later.

11   Typhoid fever is a generalized infection caused by salmonella typhosa; it is caused mainly by contaminated water or milk or by other carriers. Tom Godwin's symptoms would not

have appeared until ten to fourteen days after infection, and they would have included a high fever, red spots on the chest and abdomen, diarrhea or constipation, and enlargement of the spleen.

12 Louisa Middleton was seventeen years old when she died.

13 A distressing irony concerning Tom's death was that, in late August 1896, he had been cited by the health inspector for creating a nuisance by allowing the pile of horse manure to accumulate on his property, and he was warned to get rid of it. A letter from him to city council countered: "I have not and cannot comply with this request, owing to the fact that you have not provided us with a dumping ground for such so-called nuisances." See *Vernon News*, 20 August 1896, 1. T.S. Godwin died at the age of twenty-seven and was deeply mourned by most of the town.

14 Ivy Frances Schubert died at the age of ten months, on 7 September 1896.

15 Stanfield Gabriel Tunstall died at the age of eight months on 25 September 1896.

16 Leonard Vernon Crowell was only thirteen months old when he died.

17 Lottie Weddell was well known for her sweet singing voice and was well loved in the community.

18 Diphtheria was a highly contagious disease caused by the Corynebacterium diphtheriae bacillus. Bacteria attacked the membranes of the throat, destroying the tissue and forming a tough grey membrane, which, if it spread to the larynx, caused suffocation. With this outbreak of the disease it was acknowledged that there was an urgent need for a place to nurse the sick. Two cottages were acquired for that purpose, and two nurses belonging to the Victorian Order of Nurses (VON) arrived to provide care.

19 Between 1892 and 1906, Fairview, two miles southwest of the modern community of Oliver 100 miles south of Vernon, boasted a population of 500 people and some substantial buildings.

20 The Thompsons' seven-year-old daughter, Clover Gray, had died en route to Vernon on 16 November 1894, and the parents had brought her body with them to Vernon. Neither parent attended the little girl's funeral; Mrs. Thompson was too ill with the disease, and her husband remained by her side. Mrs. Thompson would survive the disease, but her brother, Robert "Bertie" Armstrong, succumbed on 23 November.

21 Formerly a physician at St. Thomas's Hospital in London, England, Dr. Gerald Williams opened an office at the corner of Schubert and 8th Streets in 1894, and he treated several of the Fairview diphtheria patients. He later sued the city for non-payment of the resultant fees. This litigious man engaged in a long and bitter feud with Dr. Morris and, at one point, caused the resignation of the entire nursing staff at the Vernon Jubilee Hospital.

22 Diphtheria precautions were rudimentary and primitive at the time. Inoculation against the disease was unknown, and the best way to escape infection was to avoid any known contacts.

23 Scarlet fever is an acute infection caused by contaminated food, milk, and articles, and it may be spread by droplet spray from carriers. Typical symptoms are a severe sore throat, fever, headache, flushed face, and charateristic red spots on the body. The incubation period was three to five days, and the infectivity lasted about two weeks. In the 1890s there was no treatment other than bed rest.

24 Gertrude Loewen was a sister of Mrs. Barnard and a daughter of Joseph Loewen, partner in the large Victoria brewing firm of Loewen and Erb.

25 Nora Spinks died of scarlet fever on 10 November 1897.

26 Vaccination against smallpox had been introduced into North America in 1798 by the Reverend John Clinch, a classmate of Edward Jenner, who had been the first to prove that vaccination (the rubbing or scraping of cowpox virus into the human skin) produced only a small lesion and prevented the development of the full-blown disease.

27 William and Salome Hawksby had come to Vernon a few weeks earlier from Victoria in the hope that a change of climate might help alleviate her illness. Forty-nine-year-old Salome Hawksby died a few days later, on 20 November 1895, and was buried in the old cemetery. The following week, her husband placed a notice in the *Vernon News*, both thanking the people of Vernon for their sympathy and asking for employment as a carpenter.

28 Fanny Schubert had travelled to Victoria in the hope of improving her health but had recently

returned to the Okanagan. It was while staying at Gus Schubert's home that she succumbed to tuberculosis.

29   Laura Poulin was only twenty years old when she drank the carbolic acid.

30   Mary Ann O'Keefe succumbed after a fatal stroke on 30 January 1899. She was forty-nine years old.

31   The cause of Clara Cameron's distress is not known. Theron T. Ponds had introduced his Pond's Extract in 1846 in New York City; it was the forerunner of Pond's Cold Cream, which was used as a skin cleanser and moisturiser.

32   Ned Meighan was the son of W.J. and Mary Meighan, who operated a ranch near Mountain Meadow.

33   Celery compounds were commonly used as tonics. Ingredients were ground celery seed (25 parts); coca leaves (25 parts); black haw, ground (25 parts); hyosyamus leaves, ground (12 and one-half parts); powdered podophyllum (10 parts); finely grated orange peel (6 parts); granulated sugar (100 parts); alcohol (150 parts); and water (400 parts). The alcohol was mixed with 150 parts of the water, and the drugs were then steeped in the mixture for at least twenty-four hours, after which a further hundred parts of water were added and the whole was strained and sugar added. Paine's Celery Component was widely advertised at the time. "No product of medical science has ever attained such a reputation and popularity as Paine's Celery Component; no other agency in medicine has ever saved so many people that were given up to die." See *Victoria Daily Colonist*, 7 July 1894. It is not surprising that this particular combination of ingredients (the first two of which are a poison and a narcotic, respectively) should produce a change in spirits.

34   Herbert McCluskey had gone camping with two friends, and near Oyama the group faced a steep descent. McCluskey unloaded one of his guns but stumbled and the other went off, shattering his arm between elbow and shoulder. The loss of blood was fatal.

35   The Parkes were comfortably off. Alice kept a separate account into which she deposited her monthly spending money and the balance of which was usually over $200; Hal's account contained over $2,000 by the time he became postmaster.

36   Mrs. Perkins was being cared for by her son; she moved around with him and the two would settle later in Grand Forks.

Chapter 7: *How I love them all*

1   Alice was pleased that Harry had found a bride at last; he was, after all, thirty years old. Two years earlier she had written: "I think his prospects are good – and if only he is happily married his future looks very hopeful." See ABB to TBB, 29 April 1892.

2   Harry Barrett and eighteen-year-old Nonah Pelly were married on 23 October 1894. After a two-week honeymoon at the ranch Nonah, as a matter of course, was expected to care for Uncle as well as her husband.

3   Harry wrote to the home ones: "I know how you all wish to see Nonah, and I am just as anxious to show her to you. I have just been wondering if a fellow would be as happy with a lazy wife as with an energetic one. I have never lived in a house yet where they were not always on the go. You know what Mother, Wese, Alice and Clare are like, and here is Nonah right after them. Why – I have to keep busy for the very shame of being idle." See WHB to TBB, 9 November 1894.

4   Darby and Joan were a "devoted old married couple, characters in a poem published in the Gentleman's Magazine in 1735." Lesley Brown, ed., *The New Shorter Oxford English Dictionary* (Oxford: Clarendon Press, 1993).

5   Theobald Butler Barrett was born 24 July 1895. Throughout his life he would be known as "Toby," after his grandfather. "I believe little 'Toby' is going to be like his old Grandfather. He has a splendid chest on him now, just as round as a little barrel ... If he turns out half as good as the only Toby I ever knew, he'll do." See ABP to the Barrett family, 18 August 1895.

6   In July 1896 Nonah was pregnant with her second child.

7   "If only you could see [little Toby], he is such a bright, happy little man, but a terror for mischief, he is all over ... I just laugh till I am sore watching him play with the cat, she is just splendid to him." See WHB to TBB, 19 October 1896.

8 Richard Pelly Barrett was born on 8 January 1897.

9 Alice seemed to ignore totally the fact that Frances Pelly not only had a large family and a home of her own to care for, but that she she also operated a lodging place for travellers on the road between Vernon and Enderby.

10 Quintin Barrett, born in October 1896, was the son of Alice's younger brother Hubert.

11 Frank Barrett was born on 18 October 1898.

12 "Pinnie" is short for "pinafore," an apron.

13 Scottish-born George Brown (1818-80) had launched the *Globe* newspaper in 1844 with the help of a group of Reform Liberals in order to promote responsible government.

14 Henry Barrett had acknowledged his perverse character for many years. "[Living off my friends is] what I'll have to do some of these days, and God help my friends, when that time comes ... The seven plagues would be as nothing in comparison to such an one as I..." See HB to TBB, 12 March 1882. In his early years in Norfolk county he had been unlucky in love when Mrs. McInnes, the mother of his beloved Elizabeth, interfered to prevent a match with her daughter, and the experience had soured an already volatile character. Several years later he wrote: "Are all the McInis [sic] girls married? Where is *Bessie* now? Eh man, It's almost a lifetime since then. And then the Old Woman! What a two-faced old rip! Bless her old Soul I don't know to-day but what she did me more good than harm – small thanks to her – you say. I may forgive, but I never forget – and I may live to thank her great unintentional kindness." See HB to TBB, 11 December 1883.

15 Uncle was seventy years old in 1898.

Chapter 8: *I wish I could hear someone who would stir me up*

1 By December 1891, T. Williams Outerbridge, formerly of Mitford, Ontario, and Banff, had been appointed the first rector of the parish of Vernon and was given charge of an area covering Vernon, Enderby, and Lansdowne. (He would remain until 1900, when he returned to England.) Services in 1891 were held in places such as the old schoolhouse in Vernon and, later, the courthouse. By April 1893, when a new church opened its doors, the congregation ceased its itinerant lifestyle. Reverend Outerbridge, who usually wore mauve gloves with black trim, lived alone with two cats.

2 Alice was horrified that an Anglican minister would even reflect on transubstantiation – the Roman Catholic belief in the literal transformation of the host and wine into the body and blood of Christ during Holy Communion. For Anglicans, communion wine and wafers are symbolic – an acknowledgment of the presence of Christ during the Eucharist and a memorial of His sacrifice on the Cross.

3 Born in 1854, Reverend John R. Newell had been minister at St. Paul's Church in Port Dover for several years. Mr. Newell was a good friend to the Barrett family and was an earnest and sincere preacher, but he found it hard to overcome the parsimony of his Port Dover flock. Later he would write: "Dover has got a hard name. It is reported that I was starved out, and I declare it was true. Then again some of the people there are always wanting 'a cheap man' ... a young man alone can be supported in Dover ... I am told, the Bishop would have great difficulty in filling the vacancy ... so fearful are the clergy of having anything to do with the parish. That cry for 'a cheap man' must cease." See Reverend J.R. Newell to WB, 13 October 1899 (Barrett Family Collection).

4 Frank McGowen was a Yorkshireman who had a established a law office in Vernon in January 1893.

5 Reverend J. Hilary Lambert, born in Durham, England, came to Vernon in 1900 from Prince Albert, Saskatchewan, and conducted his first service on 29 April 1900.

6 At an altitude of 2,530 feet, Donald was "a charmingly situated town in the shadow of the Selkirks, the head-quarters for the mountain section of the railway, with repair shops, etc. It is an important supply point for the mining country about it and at the great bend of the Columbia below. Here the time goes back one hour, to conform with the Pacific standard." See *Canadian Pacific Railway: Annotated Time Table* (Montreal: CPR, 1892), 41.

7 The Reverend George "Billy" Butler was a portly man with a long black beard. In July 1896 the Okanagan missionary district was divided, creating a separate charge for the area embracing Mara, Enderby, Grand Prairie, and Armstrong. The Reverend Butler arrived in

December 1895 and became the first full-time Anglican parson in Armstrong. He supervised the moving of the St. James church building from Lansdowne to Armstrong, using volunteer labour.

8   Ebenezer Robson (1835-1911) was born at Perth, Upper Canada, and educated at Sarnia and at Victoria College, Coburg. He was the younger brother of John Robson, who had become premier of British Columbia in 1889. In 1859 Ebenezer Robson had been one of the first Methodist missionaries to come to British Columbia. After fulfilling several missions, he and his wife returned to Ontario in 1866 because of her poor health. Robson returned to British Columbia in 1880, and, for the next twenty years, he took his Methodist ministry to New Westminster, Vancouver, Nanaimo, Victoria, and Vernon. He was the first president of British Columbia Methodism (1887-8).

9   The Venerable Edwyn Pentreath was the Anglican archdeacon of Columbia.

10 The object of Alice's scorn was the Reverend R. Williams, Methodist missionary for the area around Vernon. He came to live in Vernon and also had charge of the Mission and White Valley.

11 This visit was astonishing in light of Alice's previous statements condemning Roman Catholicism.

12 Maurice Scollard Baldwin was born in Toronto on 21 June 1836 in Toronto and was related to two prominent Ontario families. He was educated at Upper Canada College and Trinity College, where his Methodist-style meetings and evangelical attitudes caused strong concern. Baldwin began his professional ministry in southwest Ontario, and the Barrett family came to know him well while he ministered at St. Paul's Church in Port Dover and in Port Stanley from 1862 to 1865. He was then called to Montreal, where he developed a reputation as the city's greatest anglophone preacher. His next call was to Christ Church Cathedral, where he was curate, rector, and, by 1882, dean. The following year he succeeded Isaac Hellmuth as the first Canadian-born bishop of Huron and decided to devote his efforts chiefly to the spiritual life of the diocese. He did not forget his friends from the early days. Baldwin was noted for his earnest demeanour and personal humility, and he was admired as an outstanding evangelical preacher.

13 John Dart M.A. (Oxon) had been consecrated Bishop of New Westminster in June 1895 and succeeded Bishop Sillitoe, who had recently died; the Okanagan formed part of Dart's diocese. He had been president of King's College in Windsor, Nova Scotia, and organizing secretary of the Society for the Propagation of the Gospel in the diocese of Manchester. He arrived in New Westminster with his wife and four sons in August 1895 and found financial matters in the diocese in a critical state. His nineteen clergymen were dispirited and despairing, and Episcopal income was almost non-existent because its endowment fund had been invested in New Westminster real estate, which, because of the depression, had failed to yield any income. He formed the New Westminster Missionary Association in England to help ease the situation.

Chapter 9: *A man of Mr. Parke's ability*

1   Alice is referring here to the assessment roll for the City of Vernon. She was of great help to Hal in completing the roll accurately and on time.

2   The new government building had been built in 1892 and was located on Coldstream Avenue at the western end of town, next door to the cottage where the provincial government agent lived.

3   The use of alcohol by aboriginal people was exacerbated by the gradual breakdown of the authority once exercised by village councils as well as by the inability of those councils to remain isolated in the face of the flood of immigrants entering the valley. Increasingly, aboriginal people turned to alcohol and lawlessness out of frustration with their poverty and their marginalization. Many aboriginal people also regarded alcohol as a status symbol and drinking as a display of behaviour acceptable to their white neighbours.

4   R.J. Baker had gone on trial in November 1894 for possession of an illegal still and was acquitted. He was re-arrested on the same charge and, at the end of that month, was found guilty. Baker continued operating a still and was subsequently charged with selling liquor to aboriginal people.

5   Vernon's Trilby Minstrels performed songs and music, ostensibly of black origin, that cari-
    catured black peoples.
6   The ten-volume *The Wandering Jew*, the book in which Alice had become so totally en-
    grossed, was published in 1844-5 by the French Romantic writer and political activist Eugène
    Sue (1804-57). The original Christian legend of the wandering Jew depicted a character
    doomed to live until the end of the world because he taunted Jesus on the way to His
    crucifixion.
7   Jack McKinnon was charged by Cornelius O'Keefe with stealing four cattle. He was also
    accused by Patsy Mulraney of the same offence.
8   Alexander Macauley, proprietor of the hotel at Okanagan Landing, would later stand trial,
    accused of aiding and abetting the escape, but the case against him was dismissed. The
    McKinnon saga continued for months; he escaped south of the border and, for a time,
    worked in a mine near Wallace, Idaho. Constable Simmons was sent in pursuit and finally
    traced him to Spokane, where he was arrested and put in jail while extradition proceedings
    were undertaken. By March 1897 he would be released and allowed to remain in the United
    States.
9   Born in 1834, George Anthony Boomer Walkem was a lawyer trained in western Canada.
    After entering politics, he served two terms as premier of British Columbia, from 1874 to
    1876, and from 1878 to 1882. While premier, Walkem, an astute, principled man, had been
    prominent in the struggle to force the federal government to keep its quite reckless promise
    to build a trans-continental railway, despite pleas that there was no longer sufficient fund-
    ing to do so. Walkem would brook no alteration to the original plan, although attempts
    were made to modify the scheme considerably, and he threatened to take British Columbia
    out of Confederation if the Conservatives in Ottawa reneged. On 14 May 1880, almost nine
    years after the province had entered Confederation, a dynamite blast at Yale finally marked
    the beginning of construction. At the time the Parkes knew him, Walkem was a justice of
    the Court of British Columbia.
10 Born in Quebec in 1845, Pierre Bessette was the founding settler in White Valley, which is
    located east of Vernon. He pre-empted 320 acres in the upper Coldstream Valley. He was
    part-owner of a sawmill, and his home served as post office, store, and church. The Bes-
    settes were highly respected throughout the whole area for their kindness and generosity,
    and both died relatively young – Pierre at fifty and his widow five months later at forty.
11 A magic lantern was a simple optical device that used glass slides to display a magnified
    image on a white screen or wall in a darkened room.
12 P.A. Ball and his brother George toured Canada from Toronto and presented an entertain-
    ment consisting of a slide show of exhibits on slavery in the United States, followed by anec-
    dotes of plantation life, humour, black songs, and readings from *Uncle Tom's Cabin*.
13 The Vernon Hotel was the oldest in town.

Chapter 10: *I have been as busy as I could be*

1   Francis Stillman Barnard had come to British Columbia in 1860 to join his father, who was
    already establishing an express service throughout the province. He had begun work as a
    clerk with the company and worked his way up to become manager of the Barnard Express
    in 1881, becoming its president from 1885 to 1889.
2   Hal Parke succeeded Angus McDonald as manager of the BX Ranch. McDonald had died
    suddenly from heart disease at the age of twenty-eight.
3   Barnard was active in many businesses, including the BC Electric Railway, the Victoria
    Transfer Company, and the Hastings Sawmilling Company in Vancouver. A member of the
    Conservative party, he was elected a Victoria alderman in 1886 and 1887, and as member of
    Parliament for the Yale-Cariboo District in 1888. Re-elected in 1891, he served until 1896.
4   Miss Dunsmuir was one of the eight daughters of the controversial Scottish industrialist
    and British Columbia politician Robert Dunsmuir (1825-89). Since 1890 she had lived qui-
    etly with her mother and five unmarried sisters at Craigdarroch Castle in Victoria, a mag-
    nificent Scottish baronial building furnished with the finest of stained glass, oak panelling,
    Persian rugs, silk and tapestry upholstery, and a Steinway grand piano.

5   The Chinatowns in the New World helped to maintain the identity of the Chinese and became the centre of their culture. They could buy goods similar to those in China and practise their culture without having to go beyond the borders of their own area. Vernon's Chinatown was located in the area of Coldstream Avenue, east of the initial settlement. Jack McKelvie would write that celebrations were heralded by "the customary fusilade [sic] of fire crackers which are exploded to frighten off all evil spirits and malign influences ... The entertainment proffered consisted of cake, oriental sweets, wine, cigars etc., and it is a point of honor among all Chinamen to vie with each other on such occasions in profuse demonstrations of good will." See *Vernon News,* 13 February 1896, 5

6   Gambling rooms were set up by merchants in their stores as a form of business. Besides formal gambling, there were different kinds of lotteries, and both the Chinese and white communities in Vernon spent large sums on this activity.

7   Opium was the drug of choice for the Chinese, the equivalent of the alcohol and caffeine used by Caucasians. Opium-smoking also took place in the back rooms of Chinese stores. The drug was manufactured at centres on the west coast and sold openly throughout the province. Vernon City bylaws required a fifty-dollar annual licence fee for anyone, except chemists and druggists, who sold the drug.

8   "Tyee" is Chinook jargon for "chief," or "elder."

9   An excellent cook, Lou-Ee prepared all the food at the ranch and produced huge delicious meals for everyone. A typical breakfast included "two kinds of porridge, hot cakes and syrup, eggs and bacon, beefsteaks, toast, bread, hot biscuits, two kinds of stewed fruits, tea or coffee, lots of canned milk, and butter." See C.W. Holliday, *Valley of Youth* (Caldwell, ID: Caxton Printers, 1948), 280.

10 Alice was typical of her time. The prejudice that Chinese immigrants had experienced in California during the gold rush followed them north to Canada. The Workingmen's Protective Association had been formed on the west coast, and one of its objectives was the "mutual protection of working classes of British Columbia against the great influx of Chinese." The Chinese were called "chink, chinees, slanteyes, rat-eaters, orangutans, Mongolians, pig-tails, almond-eyed heathens and worse." See Richard Thomas Wright, *In a Strange Land: A Pictorial Record of the Chinese in Canada, 1788-1923* (Saskatoon: Western Producer Prairie Books, 1988), 4.

11 Under the Dominion Chinese Immigration Act, 1885, Chinese immigrants had to pay fifty dollars in order to enter Canada. Such a high tax was a deterrent to men hoping to bring in their wives and children. There was ongoing agitation on the part of white Canadians to raise the tax, and their efforts bore fruit; in 1900 it would be raised to $100, and three years later it skyrocketed to $500.

12 A bill to exclude Chinese from Canada would be passed in 1923. For a time it caused a serious decline in the numbers of Chinese immigrants.

13 The population of most Chinatowns in British Columbia originated in the same village, or clan, in China. Like the Scots in Ontario and the English in Victoria, the Chinese tended to settle in areas where they found their own people. In the 1880s Canada was home to Chinese from 129 clans, with ten large clans dominating.

14 Many Chinese were educated by Presbyterian and Methodist missionaries, who supported and taught them when they entered Canada. The Methodist and Presbyterian Churches were able to banish the west coast traffic in slave girls and were able to provide them with an education. According to Frank Burnett, president of the United Canners Company in Vancouver: "Their profession of conversion in nearly every case is hypocrisy. They become tremendous rascals, when they pretend to become Christians. An unconverted Chinaman is generally honest, and can always be relied upon to keep a contract. The more converted a Chinaman becomes the worse he becomes." See "Report of the Royal Commission on Oriental Immigration," Ottawa, 1902, p. 149. Racism was, indeed, alive and well.

15 At the time, most Chinese immigrants in Canada were illiterate. Vernon's Chinatown boasted a "letter writer," an educated man who made his living writing letters for others.

16 Victoria resident A.B. Winchester made regular tours of the interior of the province to talk about his missionary work among the Chinese.

17 Chinese immigrants did not limit themselves to being laundrymen, gardeners, and cooks. They soon became general merchants, some of whom established chains of stores and became importers and wholesalers as well. Ng Shu Kwong had come to Canada in 1882 and mined for gold at Cherry Creek; he later worked at S.C. Smith Lumber Company. A member of the Chinese Masonic Lodge, he owned two businesses in Vernon's Chinatown: one was a prosperous general store, the other housed a placement agency for cooks and farm labourers. It was the store that led to his name change; he named it Kwong Hing Lung and painted these three Chinese characters (which meant good fortune and good business) on his sign. As a Chinese woman, Mrs. Ng was a rarity in British Columbia at the time, and she was diligently sheltered from the public eye. However, she was very ready to befriend Alice, and, indeed, the pair struck up an enduring friendship. They would correspond and exchange gifts regularly after Alice returned to live in the east.

Chapter 11: *There is much of the untamed animal nature in me*

1   English writer, critic and artist John Ruskin (1819-1900) championed the Gothic Revival movement in architecture and exercised a wide influence upon public taste in Victorian England.
2   Tableaux vivants consisted of a group of people re-enacting a picturesque scene, frequently of a historical event or from a well known book, in which the participants remained silent and held their pose for some minutes.
3   Abraham Cowley (1618-67) was one of England's metaphysical poets, and he published his first volume of verse at the age of fifteen.
4   The identity of Iniw is unclear. He is possibly a figure in Ojibwa mythology.
5   The self-deprecating Alice was respected throughout her life for the orderliness and cosiness of her home.
6   The First Church of Christ, Scientist, was founded by American Mary Baker Eddy, (1821-1911). It was based on the life and teachings of Jesus, in particular the healings attributed to him in the New Testament. Christian Scientists turned to prayer rather than conventional medicine to heal the sick.
7   Spain and the United States did indeed go to war in 1898. It was a short-lived conflict that arose out of Spanish policies in Cuba. Alice knew that the battleship *Maine* had been sunk in Havana harbour in February 1898, with the loss of 260 men, and President McKinley declared war on Spain not only in Cuba, but also throughout Spain's colonies. Peace would be declared on 10 December 1898, and, under the terms of the treaty, Spain was required to yield almost all its empire.

Chapter 12: *The women work much harder than the men*

1   Edward John Tronson (1842-1909) was one of the earliest settlers in the valley, and, in 1865, he pre-empted land between Vernon and the north arm of Okanagan Lake. He was also a justice of the peace in 1891 and owner of the Victoria Hotel. When Alice first knew him, he bore a strong resemblance to George Bernard Shaw and was a pillar of the church. Tronson was one of those who had laid out the townsite of Centreville in 1885.
2   Tronson married his aboriginal wife at Okanagan Mission in July 1873. Nancy Louis was the daughter of the Salish chief Louis and sister of Chief Gaston Louis. "On his ranch he [Tronson] maintained an Indian wife and a large half-breed family; a quite separate establishment, none of them ever appeared in public with him." See C.W. Holliday, *Valley of Youth* (Caldwell, ID: Caxton Printers, 1948), 176. Edward and Nancy Tronson raised seven children, and, unlike many settlers who abandoned their aboriginal wives for white women, Tronson remained married only to her.
3   "Papoose" was the term used to describe an aboriginal baby and its cradle. "Some of the klootchmen would have a baby fastened up in a sort of case, with just its head sticking out ... [it] made the baby look somewhat like a mummy; the case had a loop at the top and the baby could be hung over the mother's back, on the horn of the saddle, on a fence ... I have seen a klootchman riding with one slung on each side of the saddle ... and the babies never seemed to object." See C.W. Holliday, *Valley of Youth* (Caldwell, ID: Caxton Printers, 1948), 148.

4 Henry Millar had been appointed night constable and pound keeper in Vernon after the first municipal election in January 1893. He was now working for the provincial government.

5 "Black-town" was the name given by white settlers to part of the Head of the Lake Reserve, and it indicated that this was the home of dark-skinned people.

6 Isaac Harris was married to Christina, the half-aboriginal daughter of Cornelius O'Keefe. Harris was a highly controversial figure. An impressively handsome man of mixed blood, with black hair, piercing dark eyes, and a wide moustache, he was fully accepted neither by the Okanagan Band nor by the white community. The Okanagan insisted that he was the son of a white father and a Lillooet mother and, therefore, not a member of their band. He was trusted by the white community, which used him as an interpreter and later supported him has a candidate for chief; however, he was denigrated by the local aboriginal people as a man who interpreted falsely and worked hand in glove with the white man.

7 City police records show that Big Bazille (Basil Moses) had been arrested several times for offences that included drunkenness and assaulting his wife. In 1891 he had been sentenced to eighteen months in prison. Unfortunately, this behaviour continued; in January 1898 he would again be charged with spousal abuse and found guilty. He was fined five dollars, with $3.50 costs, and discharged.

8 "The chief did not rule so much as guide; his status and knowledge were important in maintaining community relations and ensuring that certain tasks, economic and ceremonial, were carried out for the benefit of the whole community. A council of elders, drawn from the community at large, advised the chief on relevant matters and helped choose a successor." See Douglas R. Hudson, "The Okanagan Indians of British Columbia," *Okanagan Sources* (Penticton, BC: Theytus Books, 1990), 71.

9 Long Edward "was an arresting figure when he rode into town on his lovely grey – straight as an arrow and with his proud hawklike face." See Jean Kidston, "Old Memories of Pleasant Valley Road," *OHSR* 52 (1988): 14. Long Edward had several run-ins with the law; in October 1897 he would be brought before stipendiary magistrate Price Ellison on charges of being drunk and disorderly on an Indian reserve. He was sentenced to a fine of twenty-five dollars or, in default of that, six weeks in jail with hard labour. He paid the fine.

10 Chinook was the language through which Hal and the chief communicated. Chinook developed as a convenient trade language and was used by over 100 different aboriginal tribes. Many settlers quickly became bilingual, and, at its zenith, Chinook was spoken by perhaps 100,000 people. "Chinook" was the name of an aboriginal tribe that lived south of the mouth of the Columbia River. The vocabulary and sentence structure of Chinook followed patterns similar to those found in English, so it was fairly easy to learn. It consisted of over 250 words. "Of these 18 were Nootkan, 40 English, 34 French and 111 from Tsinuk (Chinook), the language used along both sides of the Columbia." See Janette Anderson, "Some Indian Tribes of North America and their Communication," *OHSR* 43 (1979): 48. (Chinook began to fade after 1862, when a devastating epidemic of smallpox ruptured many of the traditional trading relationships; the decrease in the fur trade and the development of resource extraction industries also meant that there was no longer so great a need to communicate with aboriginal communities. There are now thought to be fewer than 100 fluent speakers of Chinook.)

11 "Klootchmen" was the name given to aboriginal women.

12 Johnny Pierre's name appeared regularly in police records. In September the previous year he had been charged with bring drunk and having intoxicants in his possession at the Coldstream hop yard. That offence netted him three months in jail with hard labour, but he escaped from jail and was not recaptured until 27 November. He was serving this sentence when Alice wrote about him.

13 Born in March 1861 on the Six Nations Reserve near Brantford, Ontario, poet Emily Pauline Johnson was the daughter of Chief George Johnson and his white wife Emily. By the time Pauline was born, her father had built a mansion called *Chiefswood* for his family on the reserve, and the poet grew up isolated from other reserve children. She composed poems before she could write and would later use the aboriginal name Tekahionwake. After the death of her father in 1884, Pauline made her living by writing poems, which she published

in newspapers and in an anthology called *Songs of the Great Dominion;* she also made an income by reciting her work. By 1891 she had begun to appear in professional recitals and was so successful that she toured all over the country, attired in a ball gown during the first half of her program and switching to aboriginal costume for the second. She knew exactly how to "play" an audience and could arouse many different emotions during her presentation. "Her manner was full of unseen audacities which kept her hearers on the strain of eager expectancy, both in her tragedy numbers and her pieces in lighter vein, she held easily under control the attention of her audience." See J.A. McKelvie, *Vernon News,* 20 April 1899, 8. Johnson would move to Vancouver in 1907 and, once there, worked on *The Legends of Vancouver* with Squamish chief John Capilano. She loved to paddle her canoe in the stretch of water she named "Lost Lagoon." After her death in 1913 she was buried near Siwash Rock; hers is still the only marked grave in Stanley Park.

Chapter 13: *Hob-nobbing with a Countess*

1   Born on 3 August 1847, John Campbell Hamilton Gordon, seventh Earl of Aberdeen, held one of the oldest titles in the Scottish peerage. (He was the scion of a highly politicized family; the fourth earl had been prime minister of England from 1852 to 1855.) He had married the remarkable young Ishbel Marjoribanks in November 1877, and their stay in Canada would prove highly controversial. A Gladstonian Liberal, Aberdeen had been appointed governor general of Canada and arrived at Quebec City on 17 September 1893 to take up the appointment. He was of medium height, rather delicate looking, with a black moustache and beard.

2   For a history of Coldstream, see Margaret A. Ormsby, *Coldstream Nulli Secundus: A History of the Corporation of the District of Coldstream* (Alton, MB: Friesen, 1990).

3   In 1890, when travelling as tourists across Canada, the Aberdeens had commissioned George Grant Mackay to purchase land for them in the Okanagan Valley. The first purchase of 480 acres at the Mission would form the nucleus of Guisachan, their ranch there. In 1891 Lord Aberdeen paid £50,000 for Forbes Vernon's ranch just outside the town of Vernon, which he renamed "Coldstream." It was a general purpose operation, running cattle and playing an important role in the development of fruit-growing on a commercial scale in the North Okanagan.

4   An activist and dedicated Liberal, Lady Aberdeen used the office of governor general as an instrument for social reform. In 1894 she established the National Council of Women in Canada and, in 1897, the Victorian Order of Nurses, which continues to flourish today. She hoped to reform society by ensuring that women played a more important role. During her association with the people of the Okanagan Valley, she pushed for social reform, and her dynamic leadership brought about many changes. Her passion for reform was wide-ranging, and the problems of working women and children, the elderly, the sick, domestic servants, health, and education all received her close attention. "This remarkable woman, attractive, ardent, intelligent, loyal to a fault ... dominated, energized, antagonized, battled and won over whole battalions of Canadians who remember her today in some awe as 'Canada's Governess-General.'" See Doris French, *Ishbel and the Empire: A Biography of Lady Aberdeen* (Toronto: Dundurn Press, 1988), 7. Jack McKelvie was, as usual, fulsome in his praise, writing that "Lady Aberdeen has shown a wonderful capacity for grappling with the serious problems of our complex modern civilization, and her earnest efforts among the women of the Dominion have done much to advance a motto which we believe is a favourite of hers 'Upward and Onward' [sic]." See *Vernon News,* 28 July 1898, 4. The Aberdeens were in residence in the Okanagan for a total of only four months during their six visits, but they helped publicize the attractions of the valley throughout Canada, England, and Scotland.

5   By 1896 this establishment had "become quite popular. Two years ago when it was started there were great doubts about it being able to exist and the first year they only kept it open during the winter ... Before this reading room was opened the many young bachelors about had no place of [refuge] save the saloons." See Lady Aberdeen, *Journal,* 4 December 1896. This and all subsequent citations from Lady Aberdeen's journal are taken from R.M. Middleton, ed., *The Journal of Lady Aberdeen: The Okanagan Valley in the Nineties* (Victoria: Morriss, 1986).

6   The brainchild of Elizabeth Cady Stanton and Susan B. Anthony, the International Council of Women held its inaugural meeting in Washington DC in 1888. After the Congress of Women at the Chicago World's Fair in 1893, the council was looking to Great Britain for a new president, and it appointed Lady Aberdeen. Lady Aberdeen made a point of approaching the most influential women in a community to form a local council – thus was Alice co-opted. It was hoped that the opinions of council women would be heard and respected by the city fathers. Lady Aberdeen "was an 'autocrat-democrat' ... she had incredible energy, uncommon powers of organization, and enough experience to give her poise and self-confidence. Whatever the occasion, she seemed to dominate it ... She was at times too zealous, too overbearing, too frankly critical. But the work got done." See J.T. Saywell, *Canadian Journal of Lady Aberdeen* (Toronto, Champlain Society, 1960), xvi et seq. On 5 October 1895 Lord and Lady Aberdeen held a public informational meeting in Vernon that was reported in great detail in the *Vernon News* the following week. In typical fashion, at the end of the meeting, Lord Aberdeen invited the men present to express their opinions about the formation of such a council, and all were in favour. Judge Spinks asserted that "in every respect the average woman was superior to the average man. He would be glad to see women on the board of school trustees, and thought the movement would meet with certain success." See *Vernon News*, 10 October 1985, 8.
    Reverend Wilson wished "God speed to the National Council because it will enable the women of Canada to impress the boys of our land with elevating sentiments about themselves, about others and about their country." Ibid.

7   By the late nineteenth century an awareness of the absence of rights for women had taken firm hold in Canada, particularly among female university graduates. They were already using their numbers to push for such reforms as increased enrollment of women at universities, female suffrage, the right of a widow to her husband's estate, and the right of a woman to have custody of children in cases of divorce. Women wanted to be accepted as full-fledged members of society.

8   Lady Aberdeen was a brilliant example of this emancipated creature. The "new woman" was a well educated, able, original thinker who dared to cast aside the bonds of conventionality and assume the role of leader in social and political affairs; she would also be willing to fight for women's suffrage. As was to be expected, the inevitable backlash followed. "The male establishment, at first amused by women's aspirations, reacted to the threat to the old order by emphasizing the destructive nature of reform. For the sake of society, women must remain 'true women.'" See Sylvie McClean, *A Woman of Influence: Evelyn Fenwick Farris* (Victoria: Sono Nis Press, 1997), 37-8. Alice's conventionally strict religious upbringing had scarcely prepared her to question the exhortation in *Ephesians* 5: 22: "Wives submit yourselves unto your own husbands, as unto the Lord. For the husband is head of the wife, even as Christ is the head of the Church." She would have felt disloyal to her father, her husband, and her faith had she deviated from those long-internalized teachings.

9   Mrs. Jellyby was a character in Charles Dickens's *Bleak House*. She was an enthusiastic, unthinking do-gooder who forgot that charity should begin at home. While willing to do anything for the workers in distant Borrioboola-Gha, she neglected her own children and sent beggars away from her door. Alice had no intention of tolerating anything that interfered with the priorities she had set for herself, and she felt some guilt at the way she was allowing herself to be distracted.

10 Alice's pessimism was unwarranted. By the following year, Lady Aberdeen would write: "It was their failure to get a Hospital started last year which disheartened them, but they were somewhat ambitious in their ideas and the local doctors being all at daggers drawn and refusing to meet one another made it difficult." See R.M. Middleton, ed., *The Journal of Lady Aberdeen*, 4 December 1896. "Mrs. Parke was decidedly in favour of dropping the scheme at once, and she urged that as far as the council was concerned they should give up responsibility of such a movement." See *Vernon News*, 23 January 1896, 1. However, under the able and indefatigable leadership of Clara Cameron, Vernon Jubilee Hospital would be established and go on to celebrate its centenary in 1997. It took less than two years from the time of Alice's diary entry to bring the idea to fruition.

11 The Countess of Aberdeen was as tall as the Earl, but she was decidedly heavy. She had

weighed close to 129 pounds by the age of thirteen and, upon her marriage, had been called "a great fat girl" by General Gordon, governor of Sudan.

12   American man of letters James Russell Lowell (1819-91) had written *The Vision of Sir Launfal* in 1848. It was an enormously popular long poem that extolled the brotherhood of man.

13   The Aberdeens' sons were George, Lord Haddo (born in January 1879 and a lifelong sufferer from epilepsy), Dudley Gladstone (born in May 1883), and Ian Archibald (born in October 1884, a year after the beginning of Lady Aberdeen's liaison with Henry Drummond, he was probably Drummond's child).

14   Lady Marjorie Gordon, born in December 1880, was the only daughter of the Aberdeens.

15   Dr. Gibson was the Aberdeens' family physician, an accomplished musician who played piano and organ.

16   Of Scottish heritage, George Arthur Henderson was born in Quebec City. In 1874 he joined the staff of the Bank of Montreal in Quebec at a salary of $200 per year and decided to make banking his career. Henderson had arrived on the west coast in 1891 and, the following year, began a reconnaissance in the Okanagan Valley to assess its suitability as a place of business for the bank. (He arrived in Vernon in October 1892 on the same train as George Alers Hankey, who established a branch of the private bankers Wulffson and Bewicke one month before the Bank of Montreal opened.) Henderson frequently took part in musical entertainments and courted his future wife while performing duets with her.

17   Sophie Ellison recited the satirical monologue *Miss Maloney and the Chinese Question* with an exaggerated Irish accent. The piece "fairly convulsed the audience with laughter, and formed one of the most enjoyable items on the programme." See *Vernon News,* 7 November 1895, 8.

18   The two Japanese men were Nasu and Hoshee. They sang the hymn to the tune of *Bringing in the Sheaves.*

19   Jack McKelvie was also doing his job as a journalist. Alice was one of his prime sources for information on what was happening in town.

20   Mary Postill was one of the well known characters in the valley. She was "one of the pioneers of the district and a great character, who loves to tell of the early days when she was the only white woman and made her own candles and her own soap." R.M. Middleton, ed., *The Journal Lady Aberdeen,* 22 October 1895.

21   The Aberdeens had begun to plant hops in the spring of 1892. The early hop plantings covered forty acres and produced about forty tons; in the beginning prices on the British market were good, and the ranch expanded its kilns and machinery; however, by 1898 the price had fallen to seven cents per pound. aboriginal peoples who came to harvest the hops included groups from the Nicola and Thompson tribes as well as, later, the Nez Percé, who rode in all the way from Nespelem in Washington State. Their route took them from the border along the west side of Okanagan Lake: "They moved their wives and families, hundreds of them, hundreds of packhorses. It was a real show. We'd stand and watch these people riding by and it took a long time for them to go through ... they wore the buckskins and moccasins and cowboy hats." R.J. Sugars, quoted in "Bright Sunshine and a Brand New Country: Recollections of the Okanagan Valley, 1890-1914," *Sound Heritage* 8, 3 (1979): 13.

22   In 1892, at the urging of the Countess of Aberdeen (who called him "the Boy"), Captain John Sinclair had stood as a Liberal in the British general election and had won a seat in Forfarshire. He was a great favourite of Ishbel's, and, when in need of someone with political acumen to help her husband, she urged him to become "special secretary" to the governor general. He agreed to do so. This caused great consternation in Liberal circles in England, and Sinclair's position in the party was jeopardized.

23   Riding was one of Lady Aberdeen's favourite recreations while in the Okanagan: "Before the snow came, we had done a good deal of riding – I have indeed ridden more than I have done for years & we all went out en famille for a couple of hours most days." R.M. Middleton, ed., *The Journal Lady Aberdeen,* 4 December 1896.

24   In 1897, the Diamond Jubilee of Queen Victoria celebrated sixty years of her reign.

25   This organization developed into the Victorian Order of Nurses, which was organized by Lady Aberdeen to celebrate Queen Victoria's Diamond Jubilee. The order's aims were to provide in-home services and to establish cottage hospitals in isolated areas. Today the order has seventy-two local and nine provincial branches.

26 By June 1897 the Women's Council in Vernon had raised $1,765, and a large house was pur-
chased as a home for the hospital at what is now the corner of 28th Avenue and 35th Street.
The president of the first board of directors was George Henderson, and forty-nine patients
were treated during the hospital's first year of operation. Rates for patients were established
at $1.50 per day in the public ward, and two dollars per day in the private ward, exclusive
of medication and attendance by a physician. Admission took place by order of a physician,
countersigned by a director.

27 Mrs. Pratt received ten dollars per week as well as board in payment for all the duties she
performed. Little is known about her credentials; several complaints were received about her
methods and ability, and soon her husband, who had been a medical assistant at a hospital
in England, began to interfere in daily activities. By January 1898 Mrs. Pratt was informed
that the hospital would provide accommodation only for herself and her children – not for
her husband.

28 On 14 January 1896 Arthur Henry Craven and Georgiana Emily Conybeare, of Ingatestone,
Essex, exchanged vows at St. Andrew's Church, Westminster.

29 The Cravens stayed at the Kalamalka Hotel during their lengthy visits to Vernon. An energetic feminist, suffragette, and friend of Lady Henry Somerset, Mrs. Craven threw herself
into local social causes. She "had promised aid to the [hospital] Institution on condition
that women were included on the Board." See *Vernon News*, 17 June 1897, 1. As a result, three
women were appointed to that first hospital board. Then she took up the causes of education and temperance. At a meeting of the Women's Council "she strongly advocated that
women should go on the board of school trustees, and urged the Council to take up the
matter of temperance work, especially among the children, who should be systematically
instructed upon the evil effects of alcohol. They should not fear to be called 'cranks' ... they
should strive to be 'womanly' but not 'womanish.'" Ibid., 20 January 1898, 1. A local chapter of the Woman's Christian Temperance Union (WCTU) was formed, with Mrs. Clark
as president. At that time, the WCTU was the largest organization of women in the world,
and its motto was "For God and Home and Native Land." Its educational aims were preventive, educational, evangelistic, social, legal, and organizational.

30 The English aristocrat Lady Henry Somerset was an early feminist, a suffragette, a leading
member of the WCTU in Great Britain, and a world honorary vice-president of the international WCTU.

31 A vote to allow women's suffrage had been introduced in the provincial Legislature and, at
the end of February 1899, had been narrowly defeated.

Chapter 14: *If I were a man I'd want to go in for [politics]*

1 Newly elected members of council were Mayor James Martin and Aldermen William Riggs
Megaw, E. Goulet, F.A. Meyer, Thomas Crowell, and W.F. Shatford.

2 Born in Ontario in 1849, of Scottish heritage, wealthy bachelor Mayor James Morris Martin was Kate Martin's brother-in-law. He was then at the height of his powers, a caring,
dynamic community activist with a finger in many pies. Besides his civic duties, he found
time to be an active Mason, an avid hunter, chairman of the curling club, and promoter of
the need for a local hospital. He would soon establish a hardware store in Rossland, which
prospered during the mining boom in the Boundary Country.

3 The Vernon roller mill was built by W.E. Ellis in 1894, with the help of a Vernon City bylaw
that enabled him to borrow $5,000. Ellis came from his home in Ontario to oversee con-
struction; in exchange for the donation of building lots he was required to agree to produce
fifty barrels of flour a day and to have the facility up and running by 1 October 1894. He
was also required to operate the mill for at least ten hours per day and for ten months per
year. The mill had several buildings; the main one was 36 feet by 24 feet and was one and
one-half stories high. The final structure would have four stories. At that time, the price
paid to farmers for their wheat rarely rose above twenty dollars per ton. The facility was
named the Vernon Flouring Mills, and, by 1896, the company would be sold to the large
Victoria-based Rithet and Company, with the same financial advantages devolving upon the
new owners.

4 In January 1896 F.A. Meyer had been elected mayor. His aldermen were William Courtice

Pound, C.E. Mohr, Charles Costerton, Frank McGowen, A.C. Carew, and George Alers Hankey.

5   The lotus-eaters (λοτοφαγοι) were a mythological tribe encountered on the coast of Libya by the Greek hero Odysseus. Local inhabitants gave the mysterious plant known as "lotos" to the Greeks, who, upon tasting it, were so overcome by a sense of bliss and forgetfulness that they had to be dragged back to the ship and chained to their rowing-benches.

6   Establishing a system to supply clean water would prove a lengthy and contentious business; city council would not approve its first water supply bylaw until 1897.

7   Elected to serve as aldermen on Vernon City Council in January 1897 were Frank McGowen, W.H. Lawrence, E. Goulet, G. Henderson, H.C. Cooper, and S.C. Smith.

8   Charles Warburton Ireland had been appointed police magistrate after the first city council election in January 1893.

9   The highly principled, righteous Charles Ireland was critical of the cozy relationship and financial arrangement between city council and the *Vernon News*, since it was the latter that published civic announcements and council minutes and not the *British Columbia Gazette*. Ireland saw a conflict of interest, and Jack McKelvie replied to him in an icily sarcastic editorial on 28 January 1897. The newspaper had urged the abolition of his office, saying that very few crimes were being committed – thus war had been declared. This quarrel had been going on for more than a year and had reached a venomous level. The locals enjoyed the joke going around at the time – "What is it that the British Parliament has in common with City Council? Problems with Ireland." Ireland would eventually resign in 1899 and move to Vancouver to practise law.

10 The city council elected in January 1898 was led by Mayor Walter Tyrrell Shatford, with Aldermen S.C. Smith, E. Goulet, G. Henderson, A.C. Carew, and W.C. Pound. Shatford received a thirty-five-vote majority.

11 As early as July 1897 city council had adopted a bylaw to raise $53,000 for water delivery from Long (Kalamalka) Lake, and on 18 October that year it entered into an agreement with Price Ellison to take 750 miner's inches from the two records, totalling 1,700 inches upon which he had a ninety-nine-year lease. (A miner's inch "was defined as that quantity of water measured at the sluice head in a trough which would go through an opening two inches high and one inch wide with constant head of seven inches above it." See Robert Cail, *Land, Man and the Law* [Vancouver: UBC Press, 1974], 115.) Thus Ellison had sole access to huge volumes of water. His first record, for 200 inches, was granted in August 1886; the second, for 1,500 inches, was granted in May 1890. (He had never used more than 300 inches to irrigate his land.) Half the debentures authorized by this bylaw had already been sold when the provincial government refused to approve it, saying that others already had a record on the water. Ellison remained uncharacteristically silent on the issue; nor, despite his political connections, did he lobby the government to review its decision. The *Vernon News* was filled with reports and comments on the issue; poor Jack McKelvie had to tread a very delicate line between providing information, allowing disgruntled citizens their say, and defending his employer, Price Ellison. City council then approached Francis Stillman Barnard to ask him to cede some of his record on Deep Creek, above the BX Ranch. Waterworks bylaw no. 47 was introduced on 12 June 1899: "It provided for the installation of a waterworks system with gravity feed from B.X. Creek and a small reservoir at the upper end of Pine Street. This system went into operation in the spring of 1900. It served the needs of the people for a time." See Burt R. Campbell, "Vernon's Diamond Jubilee," *OHSR* 16 (1952): 58. An agreement between the city and Barnard was signed on 28 September 1898, allowing the city to draw ten miner's inches from that source and, thus, to permit a flow of 140,000 gallons per day for Vernon's 800 citizens. Despite forceful opposition from Price Ellison, who said that the supply of water from Deep Creek would not be consistent because it would freeze in the winter and dry up in the summer, the electorate voted overwhelmingly in favour of the $40,000 bylaw (there were only two dissenting votes). This time the provincial government offered no opposition and the project went ahead. By 1900 the city would have its first working water system; hook-up rates would be set at one dollar for the first tap in the house, twenty-five cents for subsequent ones, and fifty cents for a lawn tap. "It was shown on Monday night evening that a strong stream [of water] could be thrown to a height of eighty feet

on Barnard Avenue, and there is now not a shadow of doubt that the system will do all that was expected of it in the way of fire protection." See *Vernon News,* 1 February 1900, 5.

12   Forbes Vernon was campaigning for a seat in the provincial Parliament.

13   Donald Graham, the Barretts' Otter Lake neighbour, farmer, and first reeve of Spallumcheen, defeated Forbes George Vernon in the provincial election of 1894 and would run against Price Ellison in 1898. The *Vernon News,* although it claimed impartiality in the campaign, supported Ellison, its owner. Just before voting day, it published, in the middle of the front page, a replica of a ballot paper with a large X against Ellison's name.

14   The recently completed legislature building in Victoria had been designed by the twenty-five-year-old English architect Francis Mawson Rattenbury (1867-1935). He won other government contracts and also designed hotels, banks, and homes for many wealthy clients; his designs were characterized by classical grandeur and Victorian flamboyance.

15   The constituency to be contested was East Yale.

16   As early as 1896 local residents were distressed by the inequities they saw in the weighting of votes: "[H]ow unfairly parts of the Province are treated as regards proportional representation in the Provincial House of Parliament ... the single member [for] East Yale has at his back nearly the same number of electors as all the constituencies of Cassiar, East and West Lilloet, south Nanaimo and North Victoria put together, these constituencies carrying no less than five seats." See F.A.M Warren, *Vernon News,* 20 February 1896, 8. In April 1898 four new seats were established on the mainland. The Kettle Valley and Boundary Creek Districts were taken from East Yale and added to Rossland, which received a second member. Vancouver received a fourth representative, Cassiar its first, and East Kootenay was divided into two. East Yale (which included Vernon) was the most populous of all the rural constituencies, with 1,600 registered voters. Jack McKelvie called for either an extra MPP or a division of the present boundary at Penticton, and there was much dissatisfaction among citizens with the continuing inequity.

17   "In those days we took our politics ... hilariously ... we had a good time over them as we did with everything else. In provincial politics there was no party, liberal or conservative, just the government and the opposition – the ins and the outs ... electioneering was great fun; a pre-election meeting was looked on as a sporting event ... and provided an excellent opportunity 'for making whoopee' of which we took full advantage." See C.W. Holliday, *Valley of Youth* (Caldwell, ID: Caxton Press, 1948), 306.

18   English-born John Herbert Turner (1834-1923) had moved from eastern Canada to British Columbia in 1862. He was elected alderman and, later, mayor of Victoria and was first elected to the Legislature in 1886, becoming premier in 1895. He served in that capacity for three years: "Turner epitomized the role of Victoria in late 19th century BC; his firm was typically engaged in a wide variety of operations – salmon canning, importing, wholesaling, finance and insurance. Turner's premiership marked the final flowering of the Victoria class in BC politics." See H. Keith Ralston and Mairi Donaldson, "Turner, John Herbert," in *The 1998 Canadian and World Electronic Encyclopedia,* CD-ROM (Toronto: McClelland and Stewart, 1997). Turner was most indignant when, after the election, whose results proved inconclusive, Lieutenant-Governor Thomas R. McInnes dismissed him.

19   Prospector and rancher Charles Augustus Semlin (1836-1927) had come to British Columbia from Ontario in 1862. A Conservative, he had first been elected MLA for Yale in 1871 and became leader of the opposition in 1894. He did become premier of the province in August 1898, during the chaos that resulted from the inconclusive results of the election, but his government would be defeated in 1900.

20   English-born Francis Lovett Carter-Cotton was a newspaper editor in Vancouver, a steady, deliberate, thorough man and a staunch supporter of the Conservative party. He was anxious to introduce party lines into British Columbia politics in order to do away with the factionalism and in-fighting that characterized the political situation in 1898. Charles Semlin appointed Cotton finance minister, with Joseph Martin as attorney general, but the smouldering enmity between these two men soon degenerated into open hostility.

21   Price Ellison was elected with a majority of seventy-four. The election, however, ended in chaos, accompanied by cries of serious election day irregularities. Lieutenant-Governor Charles McInnes called upon Semlin to form the government; the latter needed support

from both Martin and Carter-Cotton, and both accepted Cabinet positions in the new administration. Thus began a series of crises exacerbated by the personalities involved.

22 After the election in 1898, Lieutenant-Governor James McInnes had invited Charles Semlin to form a government, which was able to struggle on until 23 February 1900, when it was defeated by one vote on its redistribution bill. Semlin asked for time to try to form a coalition, but his resignation was demanded by McInnes four days later. Then began a struggle between the Legislature and the lieutenant-governor, and Joseph Martin attempted to form a cabinet.

23 Born in Milton, Ontario, in September 1852, Joseph "Fighting Joe" Martin was a recent newcomer to the province. A Liberal, and one of the most colourful and querulous politicians in Canadian history, he identified strongly with working-class causes and had represented Winnipeg in the provincial and federal parliaments, after which he came to Vancouver to practise law. He made a fortune there, selling lots in his Hastings Manor subdivision. Martin was brilliant but egocentric and headstrong, with a hair-trigger temper. He was elected to the British Columbia Legislature and became attorney general; however, after a near-riot, during which he fought with the guest of honour at a banquet for mining magnates, he was dismissed from the provincial government. Incredibly, he was invited to form a government in February 1900; however, unable to attract sufficient support, he resigned after three months. After this setback he would move to England, where he sat in the British Parliament from 1910 to 1918.

24 Hal's eldest half-brother Ephraim Jones Parke (1823-99) was born in York, Upper Canada; the Parke family came to London in 1832, and he was educated at the London District Grammar School. He became a highly respected, busy, and wealthy corporate lawyer in London, and he was also a director of several large Ontario companies. He was twenty-three years older than Hal and had begun to practise law the year his youngest brother was born, having spent the first three years of his law studies in the Kingston office of Sir John A. Macdonald. At the age of forty-six he married Mary Helen Southwick in St. Thomas, Ontario, and the couple had a son and two daughters. E. Jones Parke was described as having a splendid legal intellect; he represented a number of commercial interests in London and southwestern Ontario and was solicitor for the county of Middlesex. He was also a police magistrate for the city of London from 1882 to 1899, having been appointed a Queen's Council in 1885. Despite his exceedingly heavy work schedule, he kept in regular touch by mail with his stepbrother out west.

25 Sir Wilfrid Laurier (1841-1919) would win the coming election and serve as Canada's prime minister until 1911.

26 The federal Liberal party had not held power in Canada since 17 September 1878, when Sir John A. Macdonald defeated the Liberal government of Alexander Mackenzie. The general election of 1896 set the pattern for all future elections. The Tory grip on Quebec, which had been engineered so successfully by Sir John A. MacDonald, was loosened. Wilfrid Laurier was able to assemble a broad coalition of interests that turned into an efficient political machine, and, against the ineffectual Tories, the Liberals swept to power with a majority of thirty-five. Thus arrived the beginning of the "Liberal Century."

27 Jack McKelvie was incensed over the "nest of traitors" opposed to Sir Mackenzie Bowell. One of these traitors was Walter Humphries Montague (1858-1915), born in Adelaide, Middlesex County, Ontario, the son of a farmer. He had trained as a physician and practised medicine at Dunnville. In 1890 he had been elected to represent Haldimand in the federal parliament. In 1895, for a few months, he became secretary of state in the Bowell administration and, at the end of that year, was appointed minister of agriculture. In 1896 Bowell charged the MP with conspiring against him, and Montague became a member of the Tupper administration that same year. He would retire from office after the defeat of the Tupper government in July 1896, and he was defeated in the general election in 1900.

28 John Graham Haggart (1836-1913) was regarded as a co-conspirator against Sir Mackenzie Bowell. Born in Perth, Upper Canada, he was educated there and entered his father's milling business. In 1872 he was elected as Conservative member of Parliament for South Lanark, and he served in several portfolios under Sir John A. Macdonald, including those of postmaster general (1888-92) and minister of railways and canals (1892-6), holding the latter until

the resignation of the Tupper government in July 1896. That year he was one of the "bolters" who resigned from the Bowell Cabinet. Throughout the Laurier administration he was a prominent member of the Conservative opposition, and he held his seat until his death in Ottawa on 13 March 1913.

29   John Andrew Mara of Overlanders fame.

30   Hewitt S. Bostock, a graduate of Trinity College, Cambridge, was called to the bar at Lincoln's Inn. He and his wife, Lizzie, came to British Columbia in 1888 and settled in Victoria; they also bought a 3,380-acre ranch at Monte Creek from Jacob Duck. Bostock then established a lumber company and a printing business. He worked first for the *Victoria Colonist* and founded the *Vancouver Province* newspaper in 1894. A Liberal, he defeated John Mara in the 1896 federal election and represented the Yale, Cariboo/Kootenay District for four years. He chose not to stand for re-election in 1900, but four years later he was appointed to the senate, where he eventually became speaker.

31   Trained as a physician, Conservative politician Sir Charles Tupper (1821-1915) was the last surviving Father of Confederation. As Sir John A. Macdonald's lieutenant he served in numerous federal portfolios and finally became prime minister on 1 May 1896; he served only ten weeks, the shortest tenure in Canadian history, and was routed by Laurier in the 1896 election.

32   The Liberals took over the government with a thirty-seat majority.

Chapter 15: *The mining prospects around here*

1   Such men "lived their lives alone in the mountains, their sole possessions often nothing but their old clothes and blankets, a rifle for shooting the game on which they subsisted; and the tools of their trade, a pick and shovel ... I never did know one who struck it rich, or indeed who struck anything at all really worth much." See C.W. Holliday, *Valley of Youth* (Caldwell, ID: Caxton Printers, 1948), 229.

2   Born in 1834, Scotsman Donald MacIntyre had been working in the Monashee Mine area since the 1870s. It was he who, in the early 1880s, christened the site with the Gaelic name "Monadh Sid," meaning "Mountain of Peace." He claimed to have discovered a rich silver-bearing ledge and, with his partner L.W. Riske, built a quartz mill and cut a ditch two miles long from the Kettle River, but the volume of water they achieved was not sufficient to operate their mill. By 1897 MacIntyre left for the Klondike.

3   James and William Martin were leaving to set up a new branch of the family hardware business. Rossland, in the Kootenays, was a mining town enjoying a boom in 1895. "A year ago there were but two houses there – since then an American found a mine, tested the value of the ore (gold) with the result that it proved to be all that could be desired. Now there is a population of 2000 mostly from the other side of the line." See R.M. Middleton, ed., *The Journal of Lady Aberdeen*, 15 October 95. The following year she would write that it was "growing by leaps and bounds. Last year it had a population of 2,000 – now it has 6,000 – and they talk of 15,000 next year." See ibid., 4 December 96. "Lots that last year could have been purchased for from $25 to $50 are now held at $1000 to $1200." Report by S.A. Shatford in the *Vernon News*, 8 August 1895, 5. Rossland would be incorporated in November 1896.

4   The ten claims at Camp Hewitt were in the Trepanier Creek area, in the Boundary country south of Vernon. The mining and development company was headquartered in Vernon and was attempting to raise a million dollars in capital by selling shares at fifteen cents each.

5   The Swan Lake Mine was located in the north BX area and was owned by William Armstrong. Great hopes were expressed for a wealth-generating operation: "Assay made under the new cyanide process gives $5.60 per ton in gold ... it must be remembered that very frequently it is just such low grade ore that returns the best profit. Should it prove to be as valuable as anticipated it will afford employment for at least 500 men." See *Vernon News*, 22 August 1895, 8. Mining fever was at its height; during the month of October 1895, thirty-four miner's licences were issued for claims with names such as Little Dorrit, Wanderer, Black Horse, White Horse, Smiling Tom, and Wee Willie Winkie. Armstrong, however, would not find the mining wealth he expected; the bubble burst and by August 1899 he would leave Midway and make his way to Kelowna, where once again he established a hardware and tinsmithing store.

6   Between 20,000 and 30,000 men had surged north from the United States during the spring
     and summer of 1858 on rumours that the Fraser River strikes would prove even larger than
     those in California. The biggest claims, however, were not staked until 1862 in the Cariboo
     placer lode. Gold fever lasted until well after the turn of the century: "We all dreamed gold,
     and mining was almost the only topic of conversation; we formed mining companies and
     gambled ridiculously in their shares ... We all carried around chunks of rock in our pockets
     which we would fish out to show anyone who would look at them and talk learnedly of
     geology and petrology of which we really knew nothing." See C.W. Holliday, *Valley of Youth*
     (Caldwell, ID: Caxton Printers, 1948), 192. Despite the many share issues and ubiquitous
     digging the mines failed to produce commercial quantities of precious metals and closed
     very quickly. Only the Cherry Creek placer mine near Lumby was found to have larger
     deposits of gold, and it was mined successfully.
7   Monashee camp was situated at an elevation of 4,000 feet on Monashee Mountain, between
     the headwaters of Cherry Creek and the Kettle River, about forty miles east of Vernon.
     Although hopes were high that its yield of precious metals would be as great as that at
     Cherry Creek, Monashee Mine, too, would prove to be a disappointment.
8   In 1892, thirty-six-year-old surveyor and engineer Frank Herbert Latimer, a native of Kin-
     cardine, Ontario, had been engaged by Lord and Lady Aberdeen to lay out the Coldstream
     Ranch's small internal irrigation system. He was already an experienced railway surveyor and
     had worked for railway companies in Michigan, Manitoba, and the Vancouver area.
9   Unlike most of the mines in the Okanagan, the Salmon Valley Mine was not being worked
     for precious metals but for gypsum. It had first been staked in 1894 and had aroused great
     interest among the settlers.
10   On 25 February 1897 Alice purchased ten shares in the Camp Hewitt Mining and Devel-
     opment Company for a dollar each.
11   Jack Lawrie was on his way to Vancouver to work at the gunsmith's store belonging to C.E.
     Tisdall (later a mayor of Vancouver).
12   The Bon Diable Mine was located three and one-half miles north of Vernon at the back of
     the BX Ranch and was owned by Captain Carew, Clem Costerton, and Leopold Simmons.
     It was capitalized at $75,000 held in one-dollar shares.
13   The Klondike gold rush had been touched off by the August 1896 discovery of placer gold
     on Rabbit (later Bonanza) Creek. It was not until 1897 that the rest of the world heard of
     the discovery, which immediately caused a stampede of over 100,000 gold-seekers, many of
     whom made their way overland from Skagway, Alaska, along the White and Chilkoot Passes
     to Dawson, at the mouth of the Klondike. With a fluctuating population of about 30,000,
     Dawson became for a while the largest town north of Seattle. We will never know how seri-
     ous was Price Ellison's intention to set out for the Klondike River, but by 1898 the human
     stampede was over and Ellison remained at home.
14   Mrs. Anderson did not foresee the situation that really developed. Although there was intense
     mining activity in the hills surrounding Vernon, very few of the shafts dug produced profitable
     quantities of precious metal-bearing ores. Vernon would continue to experience a period of
     recession until the end of the century.
15   Delphas Thomas lived at the head of the Kettle River and was well known as a fur trapper
     in the area.
16   Born in Wellington County, Ontario, in December 1855, and of Irish descent, John Moore
     Robinson had founded the *Brandon Times* in 1886 and had been a member of the Manitoba
     Legislature. He and his wife had come to the lower country in 1890, and, seeing the poten-
     tial of the area, he settled south of Vernon, introduced the irrigation that enabled the pro-
     duction of soft fruits, and used his capital and promotional skills to develop the communities
     of Peachland, Summerland, and Naramata: "John Moore Robinson was a super real estate
     agent. He brought more settlers to the valley than anyone else. He stimulated interest in
     the soft fruit industry and saw it develop from practically nothing to one of the leading
     industries of British Columbia, even of Canada." See F.W. Andrew, "Peachland, Summer-
     land and Naramata," *OHSR* 19 (1955): 72.

Chapter 16: *It really is shameful the way I neglect my poor old diary lately*

1   Charlie Costerton was postmaster for one year, from 1 April 1898 to 28 April 1899, and had applied for the position of government clerk vacated by Willie Lawes. Leonard Norris was not keen to have him as a colleague.

2   The approval given to Hal's appointment was universal. Jack McKelvie wrote that he had "already effected a material and commendable alteration to the interior arrangements of the post office ... [other changes were also made which] permit of the mails being handled in a more expeditious manner than was formerly possible." See *Vernon News*, 25 May 1899, 5.

3   The drum was the wood-burning part of a stove.

4   The South African (Boer) War would last from 1899 to 1902. Anti-British sentiment had been high in the Boer Transvaal since its annexation by Great Britain (1877-81), and when British businessmen poured into the country to exploit its gold and take over most of the commercial enterprises, the Boer government retaliated by refusing them citizenship and imposing upon them punitive levels of taxation. The British therefore decided to preserve their commercial rights by dispatching troops; war was declared by Transvaal and the Orange Free State on 12 October 1899. This was not a "white man's war," since all the population groups were involved at various levels. As the war escalated Great Britain brought in reinforcements from Australia, New Zealand, and Canada as well as some volunteers from other British colonies. The casualty rate was extremely high on both sides. The Boer forces had a potential of 54,000 men but never used more than 45,000 at once, while the British forces grew to 450,000 at the height of hostilities. Great Britain lost 7,792 men in battle and 13,250 from disease. The Boers lost 6,000 fighting men, and the number of Boer women and children who died in concentration camps numbered 26,370. Over 20,000 blacks also died in the camps. During the final phase of the war, the Boer forces resorted to guerrilla warfare, and the British responded with a scorched earth policy and removal of civilian women and children to concentration camps. Peace was finally achieved by the Treaty of Vereeniging, signed on 31 May 1902, whereby the Orange Free State and the Transvaal became a part of British South Africa.

5   The Boer forces had been well equipped by Germany and were larger than those immediately available to Britain. During the first phase of the war, Boer armies were able to take the offensive and, in December 1899, defeated British forces at Colenso, Spion Kop, and Magersfontein.

6   Petrus Joubert (1831-1900) was commander-in-chief of the Boer forces. South Africa's most famous soldier had defeated British troops at Majuba Hill on 27 February 1881, and he commanded the ultimately unsuccessful siege of Ladysmith. His death caused great consternation among the Boer high command. (Alice recorded the death of a Boer general, yet omitted to mention the passing, in November 1899, of Hal's oldest brother Ephraim, who suffered a fatal heart attack while working in his office in London. Ephraim Jones Parke was seventy-six.)

7   The death of old Mrs. MacIntyre had dissolved Kate Martin's ties to Vernon, and she and Jessie Macintyre departed for Rossland, where the Martin brothers had already established a business.

8   The Parkes missed a culinary treat. The menu for Christmas dinner at the Kalemalka Hotel offered: "Oysters; Mock Turtle soup à la Quenelle or Consommé Royal; Boiled Salmon with Genoase [sic] Sauce or Fried Soles à la Tartare; Fried Chicken and Mushrooms, Lamb Chops en Papillote or Shrimp Patties à la Americanie [sic]; Sirloin Beef and Horseradish, Leg of Mutton and Onion Sauce, Roast Goose and Apple Sauce or Roast Turkey and Cranberry Sauce; Ham and Champagne Sauce; Roast Mallard and Jelly or Willow Grouse and Bread Sauce; French peas and mashed potatoes; Boned Turkey, jellied; Lobster salad; Plum Pudding & Brandy Sauce, Mince Pie, Lemon Cheese Tarts, Fruit Cake, Jelly cake, Orange Cake à la Savoy, Cocoanut Meringals [sic], Charlotte Russe, Fruit Jelly, Wine Jelly, Strawberry Jelly, Curacoa Jelly [sic], Almonds and Raisins, Figs, Walnuts and Oranges." See *Vernon News*, 28 December 1899, 5.

9   British General Sir Redvers Henry Buller (1839-1908), an experienced campaigner in Africa, had been made commander-in-chief of troops there in 1899 but was out-gunned and out-manned by the well equipped Boers. His failure to relieve Ladysmith led to his replacement by Lord Roberts of Kandahar.

10 The siege of Ladysmith lasted 119 days, from November 1899 to February 1900, when newly arrived British reinforcements under General Lord Roberts and his chief of staff, Lord Kitchener, arrived and succeeded in dealing crushing blows to Boer forces under General Joubert.

11 Born in Port Perry, Ontario, in 1876, Maurice Bothwell Cochrane was the son of Pa and Addie Cochrane. He would be the only one of the Cochrane boys not to practise law.

12 Alice also relied on letters from Frances Pelly to learn about the baby Frank Barrett's development. Her apparent indifference to her brother's third son is puzzling; between his birth in October 1898 and this date she recorded only one visit.

13 Under General Buller, British reinforcements had been unable to dislodge the Boers from Mafeking, Natal, and Ladysmith.

14 Scottish-born Donald Smith, later Lord Strathcona and Mount Royal, had been appointed a junior clerk at the Hudson's Bay Company in Labrador at the age of eighteen. He rose to become the chief factor and, during the Riel Rebellion of 1868, had been sent to Fort Garry with wide powers from the federal government to quell the uprising. In December 1870 he became a member of the Manitoba legislative assembly and, in 1889, the governor of the Hudson's Bay Company. It was he who, at Craigellachie, drove in the last spike of the first transcontinental railway. "Lord Strathcona had offered to recruit, arm and equip, mount and transport to South Africa a complete cavalry regiment. This generous offer was promptly accepted by the British Government ... The men were recruited in the four western provinces and North West Territory ... Embarkation took place at Halifax ... and on 17 February the S.S. *Monterey* sailed with 548 all ranks and 600 horses." See "Okanagan Reaps Rich Harvest from Patriotic Deed of Noted Canadian," *OHSR* 24 (1960): 73-4. North-West Mounted Police Inspector Wilson visited Vernon and, after tests in riding and shooting, selected fifteen men from the ninety-eight who volunteered. In Vernon the group received a stirring send-off, with large crowds at the railway station, patriotic speeches, a cannon firing, the singing of the national anthem and "Auld Lang Syne."

15 Hugh McMullin was May's fiancé by then.

16 "Mr. John McKelvie, editor of the Vernon News, tried but was rejected because he started to mount from the wrong side! They rightly judged that no first rate horseman would do that!" See Myra DeBeck, "A Pioneer Childhood," Greater Vernon Museum and Archives (unpublished manuscript, n.d.). Jack McKelvie put up a brave front, writing that "There are many amongst us who are suffering from a feeling of bitter disappointment because they were unable to secure enlistment in Strathcona's Horse, but nothing can in fairness be said against the manner in which Inspector Wilson made his selection." See *Vernon News,* 15 February 1900, 2.

17 In 1862 the construction of the Cariboo Wagon Road had been begun over what had previously been the Douglas Trail. Contractors employed a thousand Chinese labourers during the construction period, which ended in 1864. The wagon road was 543 miles long and cost $1,339,915 to construct.

18 Williams Lake was located 340 miles northeast of Vancouver. The town's economy was based mainly on agriculture, and it was the centre for the huge cattle ranches on the Cariboo and Chilcotin plateaux.

19 General Pieter Arnoldus Cronje (1836-1911) commanded Boer forces at the siege of Mafeking; he was forced to surrender after the relief of Ladysmith and Kimberley by Roberts and Kitchener.

20 Born in 1877, Elizabeth Tierney had married landowner Cornelius O'Keefe earlier in 1900; this marriage would produce six children.

21 EB to ABP, 22 February 1901.

Chapter 17: *Reading these papers!*

1   *Vernon News,* 9 November 1905.

2   Ibid., 29 March 1906.

3 Ibid., 12 April 1906.

4 The former rector of St. Paul's in Port Dover wrote to T.B. Barrett: "I just cried like a child. I could not help it ... Dear Clarence was a member of my first or second confirmation class. Never have I had such gentlemanly boys to deal with as I had at Dover, and Clarence was one of the best. I can remember nothing but good of him." See Reverend J.R. Newell to TBB, 15 October 1907 (Barrett Family Collection).

5 In 1961 her sister-in-law Hattie donated vestry furnishings to St. Paul's Church in Wese's memory, with the moving inscription: "She lived so close to heaven, the transition was not very great."

6 A complete set of issues of the *Vernon News*, from 1891 to 1996, is located in the Greater Vernon Museum and Archives.

Chronology of the Diary Volumes

VOLUME		Location	Words
VOLUME 1:	22 March 1891 – 16 June 1891	Spallumcheen	13,915
VOLUME 2:	22 June 1891 – 15 August 1891	Spallumcheen	11,924
VOLUME 3:	18 August 1891 – 16 November 1891	Spallumcheen	15,022
VOLUME 4:	18 November 1891 – 22 March 1892	Spallumcheen	30,088
VOLUME 5:	23 March 1892 – 9 June 1892	Spallumcheen	16,536
VOLUME 6:	27 January 1893 – 6 February 1893	CPR Train	4,325
VOLUME 7:	3 November 1893 – 14 December 1893	Vernon	12,389
VOLUME 8:	2 January 1894 – 6 February 1894	Vernon	8,769
VOLUME 9:	6 February 1894 – 17 March 1894	Vernon	11,564
VOLUME 10:	1 April 1894 – 13 June 1894	Vernon	15,055
VOLUME 11:	16 June 1894 – 15 December 1894	Vernon	18,846
VOLUME 12:	19 December 1894 – 8 March 1895	Vernon	20,166
VOLUME 13:	12 March 1895 – 24 June 1895	Vernon	22,478
VOLUME 14:	18 July 1895 – 27 August 1895	Vernon	9,088
VOLUME 15:	3 September 1895 – 8 November 1895	Vernon	19,678
VOLUME 16:	9 November 1895 – 25 December 1895	Vernon	14,338
VOLUME 17:	1 January 1896 – 28 March 1896	Vernon	23,365
VOLUME 18:	31 March 1896 – 13 July 1896	Vernon	14,523
VOLUME 19:	22 July 1896 – 2 October 1896	Vernon	16,485
VOLUME 20:	22 October 1896 – 25 December 1896	BX Ranch	17,934
VOLUME 21:	1 January 1897 – 9 March 1897	BX Ranch	18,391
VOLUME 22:	17 March 1897 – 30 June 1897	BX Ranch	16,368
VOLUME 23:	24 September 1897 – 21 December 1897	BX Ranch	21,982
VOLUME 24:	1 January 1898 – 30 March 1898	BX Ranch	16,084
VOLUME 25:	12 April 1898 – 10 June 1898	BX Ranch	14,320
VOLUME 26:	13 June 1898 – 16 July 1898	Vernon	11,415
VOLUME 27:	21 July 1898 – 19 October 1898	Vernon	14,503
VOLUME 28:	21 January 1899 – 25 March 1899	Vernon	11,485
VOLUME 29:	30 March 1899 – 19 September 1899	Vernon	13,105
VOLUME 30:	1 October 1899 – 24 January 1900	Vernon	8,470
VOLUME 31:	14 February 1900 – 16 May 1900	Vernon	6,464
TOTAL			469,075

Family Tree of Hugh Massey Barrett and Caroline Butler

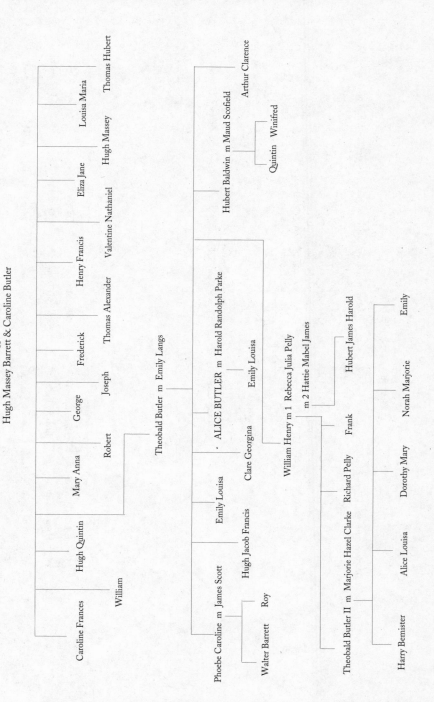

Family Tree of Charles Pelly and John Dobbs

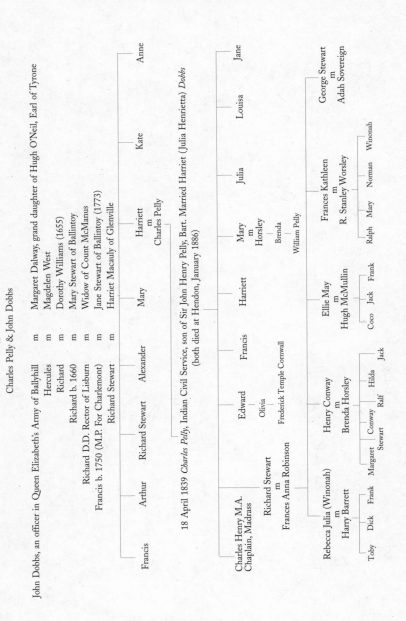

Family Tree
of
Charles Pelly & John Dobbs

John Dobbs, an officer in Queen Elizabeth's Army of Ballyhill   m   Margaret Dalway, grand daughter of Hugh O'Neil, Earl of Tyrone

Hercules   m   Magdelen West

Richard   m   Dorothy Williams (1655)

Richard b. 1660   m   Mary Stewart of Ballintoy

Richard D.D. Rector of Lisburn   m   Widow of Count McManus

Francis b. 1750 (M.P. For Charlemont)   m   Jane Stewart of Ballintoy (1773)

Richard Stewart   m   Harriet Macauly of Glenville

Francis   Arthur   Richard Stewart   Alexander   Mary   Harriett   Kate   Anne
                                                            m
                                                      Charles Pelly

18 April 1839 *Charles Pelly*, Indian Civil Service, son of Sir John Henry Pelly, Bart. Married Harriet (Julia Henrietta) *Dobbs*
(both died at Hendon, January 1886)

Edward   Francis   Harriett   Mary   Julia   Louisa   Jane
                                           m
                                        Horsley

Olivia   Brenda

Frederick Temple Cornwall   William Pelly

Charles Henry M.A.   Richard Stewart   Henry Conway   Ellie May   Frances Kathleen   George Stewart
Chaplain, Madrass   m   m   m   m   m
                      Frances Anna Robinson   Brenda Horsley   Hugh McMullin   R. Stanley Worsley   Adah Sovereign

Rebecca Julia (Winonah)   Coco Jack Frank   Ralph Mary Norman Winonah
         m
    Harry Barrett

Toby Dick Frank Margaret Conway Ralf Hilda Jack
                   Stewart

Bibliography

Published Works

_____. *Bunch Grass to Barbed Wire*. Knutsford, BC: Rosehill Farmers' Institute, 1984.

_____. *Canadian Pacific Railway – Annotated Time Table*. Montreal: CPR, 1892.

_____. *Dictionary of Canadian Biography*. Toronto: University of Toronto Press.

_____. *Grassroots of Lumby, 1877-1927*. Lumby, BC: Lumby Historians, 1979.

_____. *Historical Souvenir of Penticton, B.C., 1908-1958*. Penticton, BC: Penticton Branch, Okanagan Historical Society, 1958.

_____. *In the Shadow of the Cliff: A History of North Enderby*. Enderby, BC: North Enderby Historical Society, 1976.

_____. *Merritt and the Nicola Valley: An Illustrated History*. Merritt, BC: Nicola Valley Archives Association, 1989.

_____. *Valley of Dreams: A Pictorial History of Vernon and District*. Vernon, BC: Greater Vernon Museum and Archives, 1992.

Aberdeen, Countess of. *Through Canada with a Kodak*. Toronto: University of Toronto Press, 1994.

Akrigg, G.P.V., and Helen B. Akrigg. *British Columbia Place Names*. 3rd ed. Vancouver: UBC Press, 1997.

Altick, Richard D. *Victorian People and Ideas*. New York: W.W. Norton, 1973.

Balf, Mary. *Why that Name?: Place Names of Kamloops District*. Kamloops, BC: Kamloops Museum and Archives, 1978.

Barman, Jean. *The West beyond the West: A History of British Columbia*. Toronto: University of Toronto Press, 1991.

Barman, Jean, Neil Sutherland, and J. Donald Wilson, eds. *Children, Teachers and Schools in the History of British Columbia*. Calgary: Detselig Enterprises, 1995.

Belyea, Barbara, ed. *Columbia Journals: David Thompson*. Montreal: McGill-Queen's University Press, 1994.

Berton, Pierre. *The Promised Land: Settling the West, 1896-1914*. Toronto: McClelland and Stewart, 1984.

Boyko, John. *Last Steps to Freedom: The Evolution of Canadian Racism*. Winnipeg: Watson and Dwyer, 1995.

Bridge, Kathryn. *By Snowshoe, Buckboard and Steamer: Women of the Frontier*. Victoria, BC: Sono Nis Press, 1998.

_____. *Henry and Self: The Private Life of Sarah Crease, 1826-1922*. Victoria, BC: Sono Nis Press, 1996.

Buss, Helen M. *Mapping Our Selves: Canadian Women's Autobiography in English*. Montreal: McGill-Queen's University Press, 1993.

Cail, Robert. *Land, Man and the Law: The Disposal of Crown Lands in British Columbia, 1871-1913*. Vancouver: UBC Press, 1974.

Calam, John, ed. *Alex Lord's British Columbia: Recollections of a Rural School Inspector, 1915-36*. Vancouver: UBC Press, 1991.

Caley, Hugh, ed. *Vernon's Centennial Celebration, 1892-1992*. Vernon, BC: Arla Publications, 1992.

Canadian Pacific Railway. *Annotated Time Table*. Montreal: CPR, 1892.

Cancela, Julie. *The Ditch: Lifeline of a Community*. Oliver, BC: Oliver Heritage Society Museum and Archives, 1986.

Chenevix Trench, Charles. *Charley Gordon*. London: Allan Lane, 1978.

Cole, Douglas, and Bradley Lockner, eds. *The Journals of George M. Dawson: British Columbia, 1875-1878*. Vancouver: UBC Press, 1989.

Crease, Gillian, and Veronica Strong-Boag. "Taking Gender into Account in British Columbia: More than Just Women's Studies." *BC Studies* 105/106 (Spring/Summer 1995).

Fisher, Robin. *Contact and Conflict: Indian-European Relations in British Columbia, 1774-1890.* Vancouver: UBC Press, 1992.

French, Doris. *Ishbel and the Empire: A Biography of Lady Aberdeen.* Toronto: Dundurn Press, 1988.

Gellatly, Dorothy Hewson. *A Bit of Okanagan History.* Kelowna, BC: Kelowna Printing Company, 1932.

Gray, Charlotte. *Mrs. King: The Life and Times of Isabel Mackenzie King.* Toronto: Viking Press, 1997.

_____. *Sisters in the Wilderness: The Lives of Susanna Moodie and Catharine Parr Traill.* Toronto: Viking Press, 1999.

Gwyn, Sandra. *Tapestry of War: A Private View of Canadians in the Great War.* Toronto: HarperCollins, 1992.

Harris, R. Cole, and Elizabeth Phillips, eds. *Letters from Windermere, 1912-1914.* Vancouver: UBC Press, 1984.

Hayman, John, ed. *Robert Brown and the Vancouver Island Exploring Expedition.* Vancouver: UBC Press, 1989.

Hinchman, Hannah. *A Trail through Leaves: The Journal as a Path to Place.* New York: Norton, 1997.

Hiscox, Gardner D., ed. *Henley's Formulas for Home and Workshop.* New York, Avenel Books, 1979.

Hobson, Robert. *This Is Our Heritage.* Vernon, BC: Wayside Press, 1987.

Holliday, C.W. *The Valley of Youth.* Caldwell, ID: Caxton Printers, 1948.

Hurst, Theresia. *Vernon and District Pioneer Routes: The Stories behind Our Street Names.* Vernon: Okanagan Historical Society, 1997.

Innis, Mary Quayle, ed. *Mrs. Simcoe's Diary.* Toronto: Macmillan, 1965.

Latham, Barbara, and Cathy Kess, eds. *In Her Own Right: Selected Essays on Women's History in B.C.* Victoria, BC: Camosun College, 1980.

Lax, Roger, and Frederick Smith. *The Great Song Thesaurus,* 2nd ed. New York: Oxford University Press, 1989.

Leduc, Joanne, ed. *Overland from Canada to British Columbia: By Mr. Thomas McMicking of Queenston, Canada West.* Vancouver: UBC Press, 1981.

Light, Beth, and Alison Prentice, eds. *Pioneer and Gentlewomen of British North America.* Toronto: New Hogtown Press, 1980.

Macdonald, Bruce. *Vancouver – A Visual History.* Vancouver: Talonbooks, 1992.

MacDonald, Cheryl. *Port Dover, A Place in the Sun.* Vol. 1: *1669-1914.* Port Dover, Ontario: Port Dover Board of Trade, 1998.

MacDonald, David A., ed. *75 Penticton Years to Remember.* Penticton, BC: City of Penticton, 1983.

Malik, Kenan. *The Meaning of Race: Race, History and Culture in Western Society.* New York: New York University Press, 1996.

Mallon, Thomas. *A Book of One's Own: People and Their Diaries.* New York: Ticknor and Fields, 1984.

Manheim, Ralph, trans. *Grimm's Tales for Young and Old.* New York: Doubleday, 1977.

McClean, Sylvie. *A Woman of Influence: Evelyn Fenwick Farris.* Victoria, BC: Sono Nis Press, 1997.

Melvin, George H. *The Post Offices of British Columbia, 1858-1970.* Vernon, BC: Wayside Press, 1972.

Metcalf, Vicky. *Journey Fantastic: With the Overlanders to the Cariboo.* Toronto: McGraw-Hill Ryerson, 1870.

Middleton, R.M. *The Journal of Lady Aberdeen: The Okanagan Valley in the Nineties.* Victoria, BC: Morris Publishing, 1986.

Mika, Nick, and Helen Mika. *Place Names in Ontario.* Belleville, Ontario: Mika Publishing, 1977.

Miller, W.C., ed. *Vignettes of Early St. Thomas: An Anthology of the Life and Times of Its First Century.* St. Thomas, Ontario: City of St. Thomas, 1967.

Mitchell, David, and Dennis Duffy, eds. "Bright Sunshine and a Brand New Country: Recollections of the Okanagan Valley, 1890-1914." *Sound Heritage Series,* no. 8. Victoria: Provincial Archives of British Columbia, 1979.

Morton, James. *In the Sea of Sterile Mountains: The Chinese in British Columbia.* Vancouver: J.J. Douglas, 1974.

Morton, W.L., ed. *God's Galloping Girl: The Peace River Diaries of Monica Storrs, 1929-1931.* Vancouver: UBC Press, 1979.

Norton, Wayne, and Wilf Schmidt, eds. *Kamloops: One Hundred Years of Community, 1893-1993*. Merritt, BC: Sonotek Publishing, 1992.

Ontario. *Census Records* (1871, 1881, and 1891). Ottawa: Government of Canada.

Oram, Edna. *Ninety Years of Vernon*. Vernon, BC: Great Vernon Board of Museum and Art Gallery, 1982.

Ormsby, Margaret, A. *Coldstream Nulli Secundus: A History of the Corporation of the District of Coldstream*. Alton, MB: Friesen, 1990.

――――. *British Columbia: A History*. Toronto: Macmillan, 1958.

Ormsby, Margaret, ed. *A Pioneer Gentlewoman in British Columbia*. Vancouver: UBC Press, 1976.

Owram, Doug. *Promise of Eden: The Canadian Expansionist Movement and the Idea of the West, 1856-1900*. Toronto: University of Toronto Press, 1980.

Parker, Haidee, et al. *Historic Armstrong and Its Street Names*. Armstrong, BC: Armstrong-Spallumcheen Museum and Archives Society, 1982.

Paterson, T.W. *Okanagan-Similkameen*. British Columbia Ghost Town Series, no. 4. Langley, BC: Sunfire Publications, 1983.

Peake, Frank A. *The Anglican Church in British Columbia*. Vancouver: Mitchell Press, 1959.

Perry, Adele. "Oh I'm Just Sick of the Faces of Men: Gender Imbalance, Race, Sexuality, and Sociability in Nineteenth-Century British Columbia." *BC Studies* 105/106 (Spring/Summer 1995).

Powell, Barbara. "The Diaries of the Crease Family Women." *BC Studies* 105/106 (Spring/Summer 1995).

Pritchard, Allan, ed. *Vancouver Island Letters of Edmund Hope Verney, 1862-65*. Vancouver: UBC Press, 1996.

Rayburn, Alan. *Place Names of Ontario*. Toronto: University of Toronto Press, 1997.

Roy, Patricia E. *Vancouver: An Illustrated History*. The History of Canadian Cities Series. Toronto: James Lorimer, 1980.

Rubio, Mary, and Elizabeth Waterston, eds. *The Selected Journals of L.M. Montgomery*. Vol. 1: *1889-1910*. Toronto: Oxford University Press, 1985.

Ryerse, Phyllis A., and Thomas A. Ryerson. *The Ryerson Family, 1574-1994*. Ingersoll, Ontario: Ryerse-Ryerson Family Association, 1994.

Schneir, Miriam, ed. *Feminism: The Essential Historical Writings*. New York: Vintage Books, 1972.

Selody, Marjorie M. *Meeting of the Winds: A History of Falkland*. Vernon, BC: Wayside Press, 1990.

Shannon, Richard Thomas. *Gladstone*. London: H. Hamilton, 1982.

Shaw, Rosa L. *Proud Heritage: A History of the National Council of Women of Canada*. Toronto: Ryerson Press, 1957.

Smith, William H. *Smith's Canadian Gazetteer 1846*. Toronto: H. and W. Rosell, 1846.

Sovereign, Right Reverend A.H.A. *A Tree Grows in Vernon: The History of All Saints Parish Vernon, B.C*. Vernon, BC: Wayside Press, 1953.

Spinks, William Ward. *Tales of the British Columbia Frontier*. Toronto: Ryerson Press, 1933.

Stonier-Newman, Lynne. *Policing a Pioneer Province: The B.C. Provincial Police, 1858-1950*. Madeira Park, BC: Harbour Publishing, 1991.

Strong-Boag, Veronica, and Anita Clair Fellman, eds. *Rethinking Canada: The Promise of Women's History*. Toronto: Copp Clark Pitman, 1991.

Surtees, Ursula, ed. *Kelowna, British Columbia, Canada: A Pictorial History*. Kelowna, BC: Kelowna Centennial Museum, 1975.

Tausky, Nancy Z., and Lynne D. DiStefano. *Victorian Architecture in London and Southwestern Ontario: Symbols of Aspiration*. Toronto: University of Toronto Press, 1986.

Thirkell, Fred, and Bob Scullion. *Postcards from the Past: Edwardian Images of Greater Vancouver and the Fraser Valley*. Surrey, BC: Heritage House, 1996.

Thomas, Edward Harper. *Chinook: A History and Dictionary*. Portland, OR: Binfords and Mort, 1935.

Traill, Catharine Parr. *The Canadian Settler's Guide*. Toronto: McClelland and Stewart, 1969.

Thuillier, Daphne. *A Century Of Caring: The Story of Vernon Jubilee Hospital and of Men and Women Who Have Made Its History*. Vernon, BC: Vernon Jubilee Hospital, 1997.

Turner, John Peter. *The North-West Mounted Police, 1873-1893*. Ottawa: King's Printer, 1950.

Turner, Robert D. *Sternwheelers and Steam Tugs: An Illustrated History of the Canadian Pacific Railway's British Columbia Lake and River Service*. Victoria, BC: Sono Nis Press, 1984.

Webber, Jean, and En'owkin Centre, eds. *Okanagan Sources*. Penticton, BC: Theytus Books, 1990.

Whitehead, Margaret, ed. *They Call Me Father: Memoirs of Father Nicolas Coccola*. Vancouver: UBC Press, 1988.

Whittaker, John A., ed. *Early Land Surveyors of British Columbia (P.L.S. Group)*. Victoria, BC: The Corporation of Land Surveyors of the Province of British Columbia, 1990.

Woodland, Alan. *New Westminster: The Early Years, 1858-1898*. New Westminster, BC: Nunaga Publishing Company, 1973.

Wright, Richard Thomas. *In a Strange Land: A Pictorial Record of the Chinese in Canada, 1788-1923*. Saskatoon: Western Producer Prairie Books, 1988.

Zuehlke, Mark. *Scoundrels, Dreamers and Second Sons: British Remittance Men in the Canadian West*. Vancouver: Whitecap Books, 1994.

Electronic Sources

Encarta 98 Encyclopedia. CD-ROM. Microsoft, 1993-7.

Encyclopedia Britannica 98 CD. CD-ROM. Chicago: Encyclopedia Britannica Inc., 1997.

The 1998 Canadian and World Electronic Encyclopedia. CD-ROM. Toronto: McClelland and Stewart, 1997.

<lcweb.loc.gov/library/> Library of Congress, Washington, DC (search for records on the Civil War service of Harold Parke).

<www.geocities.com/Heartland/Meadows/8636/Parke/indooo8.htm> (information on the Parke family).

<www.library.ubc.ca/cgi-bin/ubc-cat.cgi> University of British Columbia Library (search for publishing records).

<vpl.vancouver.bc.ca/general/catalog.html> Vancouver Public Library (search for publishing records).

<www.bcarchives.gov.bc.ca> British Columbia Archives (vital statistics records).

<www.infed.org/walking/wa-ward.htm> (information on Mary Augusta Arnold).

<www.pythias.org/pythstry.html> (information on the Knights of Pythias).

<www.royal.okanagan.bc.ca> Okanagan University College, *Living Landscapes* (census records and index to Okanagan Historical Society reports).

Periodicals

BC Sessional Papers, 1891-9

Kamloops Sentinel, 1889-93

Okanagan Historical Society Annual Reports, 1925-98

Port Dover Maple Leaf

Seattle Street Directory, 1898.

Vernon News, 1892-1906

Victoria Daily Colonist, 1894

Unpublished Works

Bank of Montreal. *Transaction Record Book, 1893-7*.

Barrett Family. *Letters, 1870-1905*.

Barrett, Harry Bemister. *The Barrett Family*.

Barrett, William Henry. *Journal: 1886-7*.

Barrett, William Henry. *Journal: 1896-8*.

Bonson, Anita. "A Tale of Two Susans: The Construction of Gender on the British Columbia Frontier." PhD diss., University of British Columbia, 1997.

DeBeck, Myra. *A Pioneer Childhood*.

Eva Brook Donly Museum and Archives, Simcoe, Ontario. Newspaper records, people files, business files, vital statistics files, death registers, land records, obituaries, cemetery records for Haldimand and Norfolk Counties.

Fortune, A.L. Records of pioneer Alexander Leslie Fortune.

Greater Vernon Museum and Archives. People files, business files, cemetery records, maps, land records, city directories, police records, photograph files, mining records, hospital minutes, and patient records.

National Archives of Canada. Information on Harold Randolph Parke's NWMP service.
Parke, Alice Barrett. *Ministers I Remember at St. Paul's*.
Schubert, Trevor. *The Schubert Family*.
Vancouver Museum and Archives. People files, business files, maps, cemetery records, land records, city directories, photograph files.
Vernon Family History Society. Vital statistics files.

Index

THE PIONEERS OF BRITISH COLUMBIA

Visit the UBC Press web site at www.ubcpress.ca for information and
detailed descriptions of other UBC Press books

Ask for UBC Press books in your bookstore or contact us at info@ubcpress.ca

You can order UBC Press books directly from Raincoast,
TELEPHONE: 1-800-663-5714, FAX: 1-800-565-3770